D0849724

CATHOLIC EMANCIPATION

Daniel O'Connell
and the Birth of Irish Democracy
1820-30

FERGUS O'FERRALL

CATHOLIC EMANCIPATION

Daniel O'Connell
and the
Birth of Irish Democracy
1820-30

GILL AND MACMILLAN
HUMANITIES PRESS INTERNATIONAL, INC.

Published in Ireland by
Gill and Macmillan Ltd
Goldenbridge
Dublin 8
with associated companies in
Auckland, Dallas, Delhi, Hong Kong,
Johannesburg, Lagos, London, Manzini,
Melbourne, Nairobi, New York, Singapore,
Toyko, Washington
© Fergus O'Ferrall, 1985
7171 1218 7
Published 1985 in the USA and Canada by
Humanities Press International, Inc.
Atlantic Highlands, NJ 07716
ISBN 0-391-03353-0
Print origination in Ireland by
Galaxy Reproductions Ltd, Dublin
Printed and bound in Great Britain by
Biddles Ltd, Guildford and Kings Lynn

British Library Cataloguing in Publication Data
O'Ferrall, Fergus
   Catholic emancipation: Daniel O'Connell and
   the birth of Irish democracy.
     1. Political parties — Ireland — History —
     19th century   2. Catholics — Ireland — Political
     activity — History — 19th century
     I. Title
     322'.1'09415   JN1571

   ISBN 0-7171-1218-7

Library of Congress Cataloging in Publication Data
O'Ferrall, Fergus.
   Catholic emancipation.
   Bibliography: p.
   Includes index.
     1. Catholic emancipation.   2. O'Connell, Daniel,
     1775-1847.   3. Ireland — History — 1800-1837.   I. Title.
     DA950.3.036   1985   941.5081   85-14178
     ISBN 0-391-03353-0

To the
'New Irelanders'
North and South
Protestant and Catholic

We will plant in our Native Land the Constitutional Tree of Liberty. That noble tree will prosper and flourish in our Green and Fertile Country. It will extend its protecting branches all over this lovely island. Beneath its sweet and sacred shade, the universal People of Ireland, Catholics and Protestants, and Presbyterians, and Dissenters of every Class, will sit in peace and unison and tranquillity. Commerce and Trade will flourish; Industry will be rewarded; and the People, contented and happy, will see Old Ireland what she ought to be,
Great, Glorious and FREE,
First flower of the Earth, first gem of the Sea.

'Address To the Honest and Worthy People of the County Tipperary', by Daniel O'Connell, 30 September 1828.

Contents

List of Maps

Preface

In 1856 Walter Bagehot, in an essay on 'The Character of Sir Robert Peel', optimistically enquired 'Who now doubts on the Catholic Question? It is no longer a "question". A younger generation has come into vigorous, perhaps into insolent life, who regard the doubts that were formerly entertained as absurd, pernicious, delusive . . . The difficulty is to comprehend "the difficulty"' (5, 1). Today in Ireland we are acutely aware of 'the difficulty'. According to Rev. Ian Paisley 'traditional Unionists' are loyal above all else to

> the Williamite Revolution Settlement Constitution and the Queen, being Protestant. It's as simple as that. My loyalty is to the Williamite Revolution Settlement Act, which guarantees civil and religious liberties for all men, and to the Protestant monarchy because it has been seen, as the Act says, it has been seen that it is not good for a nation to be controlled by a Roman prince, whose first loyalty is to a foreign monarch, that is, the King of the Vatican, that is, the Pope.[1]

Northern Protestants continue to express fears about what they perceive as the power and the nature of the Roman Catholic Church in terms very similar to those who opposed Catholic Emancipation in the long struggle before 1829.

There is, therefore, still a very serious 'Catholic Question' for many Protestants in Ireland. There can be no question of condescension by us in the 1980s towards participants in the struggle in the 1820s: a perusal of the Report of the New Ireland Forum, published in May 1984, will reveal statements which directly reflect cardinal points made in the 1820s:

> The Protestant tradition, which unionism seeks to embody, is seen as representing a particular set of moral and cultural values epitomised by the concept of liberty of conscience. This is often accompanied by a Protestant view of the Roman Catholic ethos as being authoritarian and as less respectful of individual judgment. There is a widespread perception among unionists that the Roman Catholic Church exerts or seeks to exert undue influence in regard to aspects of the civil and legal organisation of society which Protestants consider to be a matter for private conscience.

The Report recognised that what unionists seek to prevent

> varies to some degree but includes: an all-Irish state in which they consider that the Roman Catholic Church would have undue influence on moral issues; the breaking of the link with Britain; and loss of their dominant position consequent upon giving effective recognition to the nationalist identity and aspirations.[2]

How was the 'Catholic Question' resolved in the 1820s? The purpose of this book is to tell the story of the struggle for Catholic Emancipation. It has been said for a long time – Thomas Moore quoted it in 1824 – that 'You may trace Ireland through the statute-book of England, as a wounded man in a crowd is tracked by his blood'.[3] Irish historians have, indeed, very often to write of violence, conspiracy and failure. This book is different: it tells the story of the mass struggle for Catholic Emancipation which was peaceful, public and triumphant.

The story is a novel one in Irish history and an exceptional episode in European history. The first half of the nineteenth century was an age of plot, conspiracy, riot and revolt on the one hand; and repression, censorship and military rule on the other; varying only in degree from country to country. Daniel O'Connell, who led the Irish struggle, avoided the politics of plot and revolt: instead he created the first modern political party and became, for Europeans, the pioneer of political democracy. This striking political innovation can hardly be over estimated. According to *The Economist*, in the modern world of 160-odd states there are only thirty truly open democracies where 'the government stands a chance of being peacefully booted out by the ballot box. About half the states on earth allow their citizens practically no say at all in who should rule them or why'.[4] A major achievement of the struggle in the 1820s was the harnessing of the people as a major force in constitutional politics. O'Connell greatly enlarged parliamentary politics, and thus the world's political repertoire, by creating and foreshadowing modern democratic parties in almost every respect.

The impact of the struggle on British and Irish history was profound. The Epilogue treats of the immediate and the long-term significance of the epic struggle. In tracing these events I have become deeply indebted to many people and I cannot hope to express adequately my sense of gratitude by a brief acknowledgment. I should, however, like to record my thanks to the following: Professor J. V. Rice, Miss S. M. Parkes, Professor M. R. O'Connell, Rev. Dr K. Kennedy and the then Archbishop of Dublin, Most Rev. Dr D. Ryan, the Auxiliary Bishop of Dublin, Most Rev. Dr J. A. Carroll, Mr David C. Sheehy, Dr W. E. Vaughan, Dr Francis Griffith, Dr Eoin McKiernan, Professor J. A. Murphy, Dr W. E. White, Dr J. R. Hill, Miss Marian Keaney, Miss Ann Barry, Mrs M. Connolly, Miss Phoebe Lefroy, Mr D. Griffith, Most Rev. Dr C. Daly, Father

Owen Devaney, Mr Jude Flynn, Father F. J. Gilfillan, Mr Gerald Lyne and Mr George Birmingham, T.D. I owe an outstanding debt to Mr Fergal Tobin of Gill and Macmillan for his professional advice.

To all who helped me in the Public Record Office and State Paper Office, Dublin; in the National Library of Ireland; the Royal Irish Academy; the Public Record Office, London; the Newspaper Library, Colindale; University College, Dublin; St Patrick's College, Maynooth; and in my *alma mater*, Trinity College, Dublin; I record my deep appreciation. I have, of course, trespassed on both the time and patience of my family while writing this book. To my mother, especially, I am indebted, and to Rory, Dorothy and little Caitlín.

Finally, and most important, to my wife Iris without whose help as my partner this book would not have been written, and baby Eilís, for not tearing up any parts of the typescript, I offer my love and thanks.

Fergus O'Ferrall

December 1984   Cabinteely, Co. Dublin

Abbreviations

Add. Mss	Additional Manuscripts, British Library
C.A.C.	Cork Archive Council
C.M.C.	*Cork Mercantile Chronicle*
DDA, CP	Dublin Diocesan Archives, Catholic Proceedings
D.E.M.	*Dublin Evening Mail*
D.E.P.	*Dublin Evening Post*
F.J.	*Freeman's Journal*
G.O.	Genealogical Office
H.L.	House of Lords
I.H.S.	*Irish Historical Studies*
ISPO CAP	Irish State Paper Office, Catholic Association Papers
M.R.	*Morning Register*
N.L.I.	National Library of Ireland
Parl. Deb. N.S.	Parliamentary Debates, New Series
PRO HO	Public Record Office, London, Home Office
SPO CSO RP	Irish State Paper Office, Chief Secretary's Office, Registered Papers
TAB	Tithe Applotment Book, Public Record Office, Dublin
UCD	University College, Dublin

Notes on References

Citations from works listed in the Bibliography are referenced in parentheses by bibliography number (indicated in italic), volume number (where appropriate) and page number. Thus a reference to pages 202-3 from the first volume of *The Croker Papers: the Correspondence and Diaries of Rt. Hon. John Wilson Croker*, ed. L. J. Jennings, 2nd edition revised, 3 vols., London, 1885 – which is listed as item number 56 in the Bibliography – will appear as (*56*, I, 202-3). Citations of letters from *The Correspondence of Daniel O'Connell*, ed. M. R. O'Connell, Vols I-VIII, are referenced in parentheses by volume number and number of letter. Thus, O'Connell to the Knight of Kerry, 8 April 1821, letter 895 in Volume II, is cited as (II, 895).

All other sources are listed in the References, arranged by chapter heading, and are indicated in the text by superior numbers. These include newspapers, parliamentary papers, manuscript collections and contemporary pamphlets and works. It should be noted that, where possible, the printed and published sources are cited rather than the manuscript sources for ease of reference.

Prologue:
'The State of Things in Ireland'

'How was it . . . that a population so numerous, inhabiting a
country unexampled in fertility, composed of men who had
distinguished themselves in every quarter of the globe by their
activity, intrepidity and intelligence, should appear degraded
only in the island which gave them birth? The question cannot
be answered, but by reference to the system under which they
are governed'.
Sir John Newport, opening a debate on the state of Ireland,
House of Commons, 22 April 1822.

On his fifty-ninth birthday, 12 August 1821, less than a month after his
coronation, King George IV crossed the Irish Sea in the royal yacht. He
landed at Howth before driving to the Viceregal Lodge in the Phoenix
Park. It was the first visit by a sovereign to the Kingdom of Ireland
since William III's decisive victory at the Boyne against James II in 1690.

Shortly before the visit Catholics and Protestants in Dublin had
joined together to celebrate the king's coronation: over four hundred
Dubliners paid two guineas each for a public dinner in Morrison's Hotel
at which the Lord Mayor, Abraham Bradley King, as representative of
Protestants, joined with Lord Fingall, representing Catholics, to demonstrate publicly an unprecedented unity and their resolve to make the
king's visit a triumph. 'A strange madness', Lord Cloncurry later recalled,
'seemed at that conjuncture to seize people of all ranks in Ireland'
(*109*, 277).

George IV, proclaiming his 'Irish heart' and gesturing pointedly to
the national emblem, entered Dublin with glorious pageantry and enormous popular enthusiasm. He met the Catholic bishops in their full
episcopal robes, and gave ample indication of his friendliness, approach-
ability, and generosity. It was a triumphant visit. On his departure on
3 September the king issued a public letter indicating his wish for
reconciliation and his hope 'that every cause of irritation may be avoided and discountenanced'; as he embarked at Dunleary (renamed
Kingstown in his honour) he declared, 'Whenever an opportunity offers,
wherein I can serve Ireland, I shall seize on it with eagerness'.[1] Had a
new era as well as a new reign opened for a troubled Ireland? A per-
ceptive Irish Tory, John Wilson Croker, noted in his diary on the king's
arrival: 'The people *shouted*. The Irish, it seems do not know how to

hurrah or *cheer*; they have not had much practice in the expression of public joy' (*56*, I, 202-3).

King George IV was a most unlikely figure for their adulation. He could not escape the consequences of his past behaviour: the record of his boon companions; the mistresses; the secret marriage to Mrs Fitzherbert, a Catholic; the debts; all revealed a reprehensible character capable of both vicious and selfish behaviour quite reckless of the happiness or welfare of others. He had consorted with Whigs during his youth but had dropped them upon becoming Regent in 1811, and the Whigs could not forget this 'betrayal'. As he was setting out for Ireland news arrived of the death of Caroline, his separated and adulterous wife, whom he had tried to prevent from claiming her rights as Queen at the start of his reign. Lord Liverpool's Tory government became embroiled in the ensuing political storm; the Whigs, with Henry Brougham to the fore, took up Caroline's less than savoury cause.

When the Irish crowd greeted George with 'Cead Mille Fealtach' [*sic*] on the massive arch on his public entry into Dublin on that sun-drenched August day they could hardly have suspected that ahead lay ten years of bitter sectarian struggle, rather than an historic reconciliation between Ireland's divided people. The reign of George IV from 1820 to 1830 was dominated by the struggle for Catholic Emancipation in Ireland. Both the real character of the king and the crude and brutal realities of Irish life had been hidden from view during the carnival atmosphere of the royal visit. Byron rebuked the footlicking Irish for their reception in his scornful 'Irish Avatar' but other contemporaries were equally appalled. The Countess of Glengall wrote on 27 August:

> Bedlam broke loose would be tame and rational to the madness of this whole nation . . . He was dead DRUNK when he landed on the 12th of August – his own birthday . . . Alas! poor degraded country! I cannot but blush for you . . . It is a melancholy farce from beginning to end, and they have voted him a palace! . . . Nothing is so indecent as the total neglect of mourning (*85*, II, 29-31).

Why were the Catholics prepared to demonstrate so readily and publicly their loyalty to such a monarch? In the spring of 1821 William Conyngham Plunket, an Irish lawyer of first rate ability, successfully carried a bill granting a qualified Emancipation for Catholics but it was rejected in the Lords. This was the first time a bill incorporating Emancipation had been successful in the Commons. The autumn session of 1821 would be a test of the politics of the new reign. The appropriate policy for Irish Catholics was to proclaim their loyalty as ostentatiously as possible during the royal visit in order to counter the frequent Protestant accusations of Catholic disloyalty to the Protestant monarch of Great

Britain and Ireland. Besides, it was still believed that George IV was more favourable to Catholic relief than his father had been. George III had been inflexible on the Catholic question: he felt bound by his coronation oath to maintain to the utmost of his power 'the laws of God, the true profession of the Gospel and the Protestant Reformed religion established by law'. George IV's calculated theatrical behaviour during the royal visit encouraged the misplaced hopes of Irish Catholics.

The Catholic question had an epic parliamentary history reaching back to the 1790s. Since the end of the eighteenth century every ministry had been divided on the question: it had cost Pitt, the Prime Minister who had carried the Union, his office and it had put out of office the Grenville-Fox ministry of 'all the talents' in 1807. In 1812, at the start of Lord Liverpool's long premiership, it was settled that the question of Emancipation should be an 'open' one in government. This policy of official neutrality, representing as it did in-built division within the government, was in fact a full admission of the inability of the existing political system in Westminster to resolve the question: each minister was left free to take his own course in parliament regarding Catholic Emancipation.

What was at stake which made the question so fraught with difficulty? In simple terms Emancipation would restore to the Roman Catholics of Britain and Ireland the right to sit in parliament and to be eligible for the highest offices in the state. Catholics were rendered ineligible by the oaths of allegiance which involved a declaration against transubstantiation and an admission that the sacrifice of the mass was idolatrous. Such oaths had been designed to preserve intact the Protestant Constitution established by the Glorious Revolution of 1688. Though there existed a powerful anti-Catholic tradition in Britain, one which was a potent factor in the struggle for Emancipation, the heart of the matter lay in the constitutional problem. The Church of England was a branch of the state and was subject to regulation by the state: this union of church and state meant that parliament was accepted as the proper legislature for the spiritual as well as the temporal estate. This Protestant Constitution became entrenched in both theory and practice during the eighteenth century and it remained a powerful concept long into the nineteenth century.

If Catholics were to participate in public life, safeguards and securities were generally agreed by parliamentary advocates of Emancipation to be necessary to preserve the Protestant Constitution in its essential aspects. A number of suggestions had been made: the crown might have a 'veto' on appointments to the Catholic hierarchy or the Catholic Church in England and Ireland might have 'domestic nomination', by which they would elect their own hierarchy without reference to Rome. In 1813 it was suggested that an oath-bound commission of Catholic laity would exercise the veto on behalf of the crown and another oath-bound commission composed of Catholic laity and hierarchy with some Protestant members of the government would inspect all bulls and rescripts from Rome for their political implications.

Such state control of all churches was common enough in the Europe of the early nineteenth century as, for example, in Prussia and Russia. In 1814 Monsignor Quarantotti, acting for the Pope who was held captive by Napoleon, issued a rescript in favour of a limited veto and of a commission to inspect all bulls and rescripts not of a spiritual or ecclesiastical nature. This was repudiated by the Irish bishops, ironically demonstrating their independence from the 'foreign jurisdiction' of Rome. In 1815, after the Pope's return, the support for the commission was dropped but the crown's right to a limited veto was reaffirmed and in February 1816 the Pope in a letter to the Irish bishops confirmed this as Rome's approach in order to facilitate Catholic Emancipation.

Throughout the long repetitive debates in Westminster on the Catholic question it became increasingly clear that the conduct of the Irish Catholics had become the decisive factor in the outcome of the struggle. From 1810 onwards, when Grattan mooted the 'domestic nomination' idea in parliament, to the time when Plunket's bill failed in the Lords in 1821, Irish Catholics were quarrelling bitterly amongst themselves over the 'veto' and with their parliamentary advocates over possible securities which might be given for the loyalty of the Catholic Church to the Protestant Constitution.

The central figure in Irish Catholic politics was Daniel O'Connell. John Banim, with a novelist's eye, saw O'Connell in the streets of Dublin as a

> tall, lusty gentleman, with the Oxford-grey surtout, buttoned below, but wide open at the breast, and with the quaker-like hat, and the healthy, good-humoured face, and his eyes cast down, thinking, and the umbrella lying along his arm: he that walks so firm and stout . . . See how all the people turn to look after him . . . they like to see him walking so bravely along, with his broad shoulders and his full breast; and 'tis thought he likes to be seen by them, stepping out over the flags of Dublin, through thick and thin, friends and foe . . .[2]

In the early 1820s O'Connell, in his mid-forties, was already a legendary figure because of his exploits in law and politics. Almost single-handed he had, since 1808, prevented Irish Catholic opinion accepting a qualified form of Emancipation — such as the Veto — and he had divided Catholic organisations in bitter debates as he sought an unqualified Catholic Emancipation and no state interference with the Catholic

Church in Ireland. O'Connell then had plenty of friends and many foes: the big, handsome man, with the head of copper curls and the bright blue eyes, was charged with enormous energy and his cocky swagger inspired lowly Catholics with a confidence previously outside their experience. Political activity amongst Catholics had hitherto centred upon the country houses of aristocrats like Lord Fingall, or the drawing rooms of landed gentlemen or wealthy merchants or lawyers in Dublin. These Catholics wished to obtain full equality and the right to participate fully in the civil and judicial life of the state but they were as a rule cautious, conservative, deferential men. This was hardly surprising as they were the first generation of Catholics to have benefited by partial relief from the Penal Laws.

O'Connell, as the 'Man of the People', was conscious of the vast numbers of Irish Catholics and of his ability to make their numbers count in politics. His assertive tone received support from a small band of Catholic lawyers and journalists involved in successive Catholic committees and boards. Throughout the towns of Munster also, where he had an extensive legal practice as the ablest member of the Irish Bar, he was greatly admired. O'Connell was not a man to be crossed: his popular oratory was capable both of bitter sarcasm as well as sublime declamation. He could be unsparing in coarse scurrility and his dictatorial and self-assured manner was frequently resented in Catholic circles. To ordinary Catholics, however, who faced armed Orangemen swaggering at local fairs, who were burdened with rents, rates and tithes as well as county cess, who went in fear of magistrates and the law and who often faced despair and famine O'Connell loomed as a great hero, the Counsellor, who could stand up against the Ascendancy and win against the odds. His swaggering, loud-mouthed, abusive and boastful behaviour in public controversy gave him a mass audience and the potential to bridge the gulf between the play of high politics and the popular political feelings of the people.

Henry Grattan, the hero of Irish parliamentary independence, died in 1820; by then it was clear that his moderate pro-Catholic politics had led only to frustration and futility. W. C. Plunket now assumed Grattan's mantle in the Commons. Plunket had associated with the Grenville group which had left the Whigs and he gravitated towards the government. He was a supporter of the Veto, a fact that troubled O'Connell, despite his respect for Plunket's ability. Plunket, for his part, disliked what he saw as O'Connell's extremism. He worried that O'Connell would take up radical issues such as parliamentary reform, thereby alienating pro-Catholic Tories (*110*, I, 394-406). The new Catholic spokesman in the Commons was therefore distrusted both by the Whigs and by O'Connell: the first essential to a Commons majority and the latter to Irish acceptance of Emancipation proposals.

Plunket's speech in favour of Catholic claims in the Commons on 28 February 1821 equalled in argument and eloquence that which he had made in 1813 and which had made his parliamentary reputation. Examining the religious, constitutional and political issues he claimed, in the name of every man 'who possessed buoyancy enough to float down the stream of time', in each case that concession was irresistible. He proposed two securities: one that the state should have knowledge of all correspondence between Catholics in the United Kingdom and Catholics abroad; the other the Veto.

Robert Peel led the opposition to Plunket's motion. Peel, who had served as Chief Secretary in Ireland for six years and who had clashed to the point of duelling with O'Connell, was the prime example of a member of an industrial family making his way into the exclusive elite of the Tory Party by wealth and ability. Peel had, however, both a first-rate knowledge of Ireland and a political mind increasingly alive to the changes being wrought by economic and social forces. Peel thought the Catholic question posed 'a choice of evils': he would not accept the case for 'such innovation upon the British Constitution' as 'it was only reasonable that persons who were to be intrusted with high office, or with legislation, should give security for their attachment to the doctrines of the reformed religion'. However, and significantly in the light of events during the 1820s, he declared that if he thought Emancipation would act 'as an operative' to restore concord to Ireland 'all his fears of danger to the church would give way'; he did not think 'that the repeal of the laws affecting Roman Catholics' would harmonise the Catholics and Protestants of Ireland because their divisions sprang from a 'struggle for mastery' stretching over centuries and involving perpetual transfers of power and repeated confiscations rather than from the penal laws.[3]

Plunket's motion passed by a majority of six, the first pro-Catholic majority on such a motion since 1813. After the victory Lord Grenville wrote a long letter to the king trying to win his support for the Catholic cause: delay would lose all the advantages of concession which would ultimately have to be made (*3*, II, 419-21). The royal reply was brief and non-committal. Early in March two bills were proposed: the first a general relief measure, seeking to modify the Oath of Supremacy by including an 'explanation' of its terms in order that Catholics might take it with an easy conscience; the object was to minimise the denial of the Pope's spiritual authority which was demanded in the original Elizabethan oath. The second bill comprised the two proposed securities, each to be enforced by a commission: one was to certify the loyalty of all newly appointed Catholic bishops and deans, and the other to examine all communications from Rome. O'Connell opposed these measures in a public letter to the Catholics of Ireland in the *Dublin Evening Post* on 22 March 1821. He told the Knight of Kerry on 8 April that if the bill (the original two had been consolidated into a single measure on 26 March) was passed 'in its present shape' it would 'tend to exasperate and render matters worse in point of popular tranquility than they are at present' (II, 895). Later to his wife he was more frank, wishing with all his heart 'that the present rascally Catholic Bill was flung out' (II, 898). English lay Catholics, more amenable, were ready to accept all the proposals, but the ultamontane Dr Milner, Vicar-Apostolic of the Midland District, led the opposition to the securities. Irish clerics like James Doyle, Bishop of Kildare and Leighlin, took a moderate line such as that expressed in resolutions of the Dublin clergy on 26 March which welcomed the Relief Bill and its modified Supremacy Oath but disapproved mildly of the securities. However, provincial clerical reaction was very much more hostile. Doyle believed that if the cause was lost in the present session it would 'probably make no progress for several years to come' (*36*, I, 158-9).

Richard Lalor Sheil, a young prominent Catholic barrister and writer, praised Plunket's efforts and as a Vetoist found no fault with the securities. Sheil, now aged thirty, was the son of an Irish merchant who had bought an estate in Waterford. He was representative of the well-to-do commercial and professional Irish Catholic middle class which increasingly had gained a landed interest either through purchase or leasing. Educated at Stonyhurst and Trinity College, Dublin, he was called to the Bar in 1814 and had become well known as a dramatist and a writer. He was a different figure entirely from O'Connell and a leading public opponent of O'Connell on the critical question of the Veto. Banim observed him as a '. . . low, slight, little gentleman, who walks so rapidly, jerking his arms, and pushing out his under-lip so often, and whose complexion is so bilious, and whose nose is rather short and cocked, and . . . whose eyes are so dark, and fine, and expressive'.[4]

The bill passed the Commons on the third reading by nineteen votes on 2 April. The ultras, the staunchly Protestant element of the British establishment, now focussed on having it defeated in the Lords, where Lords Liverpool and Eldon did their utmost to sink it. The king appears to have vacillated for a time but he was kept on anti-Catholic lines by the strong ultra influence of his brother the Duke of York. When the debate began in the Lords, Lord Donoughmore (Richard Hely Hutchinson) with whom O'Connell had correspondence (the Hely Hutchinson family, through Christopher Hely Hutchinson, MP for Cork City, had championed the O'Connellite view in the Commons) opened with a speech condemning all the proposed securities as an insult to the Catholic clergy; and Lord Grenville, who had previously advocated securities, now supported Donoughmore's line. Lord Chancellor Eldon, however, gave a classic exposition of the anti-Catholic case:

> He had always felt that it was one of his first duties to maintain the established religion of the country. Fortunately for the country, it had adopted the purest system of Christian faith in its established religion; by connecting with the laws, which established its Church, laws securing a liberal and enlightened toleration as to those who dissented from its Church, it had probably placed upon the best and surest foundations, the civil and religious liberties of all who lived in the kingdom . . . that the object of such an establishment was not to make the Church political, but to make the state religious.

Eldon went on to combat Plunket's argument that the times had changed and politicians must be buoyant to float down the stream of time:

> The times, it is said, are changed and the Catholics, it is said, are changed; be it so; but such change does not affect the soundness of the principles, upon which this kingdom has established itself as a 'Protestant kingdom' with the powers of the state in Protestant hands, and with a Protestant church establishment, and toleration, — toleration from time to time enlarged to the utmost extent the public welfare will admit; but toleration only, for those who dissent from it.[5]

The Lords threw out the bill by thirty-nine votes. The Duke of York, who was expected to succeed George IV, effectively sealed the Bill's fate with his anti-Catholic speech.

The Catholic cause had failed again. O'Connell wrote to O'Conor Don on 23 April:

> What is to be done now? That is the question. Everyone agrees that we should meet. Some are for addressing the king, some for declaring against any further petition, some for proclaiming reform. But I think *all* agree to meet. It would be desirable to heal the miserable little schism which has arisen amongst ourselves. It can be done only by coming together. Even the Vetoists must admit that *securities* do no good because we are kicked out as unceremoniously with them as without them . . . We are cast down by our enemies, and we may make ourselves despicable by either a stupid acquiescence or by absurd dissension (II, 901).

O'Connell was astute enough to recognise the defeat that had been incurred by the Vetoists: 1821 was the last occasion when quarrels over the Veto played a prominent part in the struggle; 'unqualified Emancipation' now became the slogan. The basic pattern for the struggle ahead was now set, with a small pro-Catholic majority in the Commons whose wishes were to be rejected by an anti-Catholic majority in the Lords. Royal opposition to reform was stiffened by the Duke of York, whose influence continued to be felt until his death in 1827. Other lessons were drawn by O'Connell: until Irish Catholics, who had revealed deep divisions over the Veto, could present a unanimous and forceful front, it was clear that the cause could not succeed in any shape or form. Part-measures confined to the English, class-measures in the interests of the peers, whole-measures, invested with securities no matter how cleverly conceived, were all similarly defeated by Lords and crown. The relentless logic of this drove O'Connell to meditate on how the Irish Catholic masses could extort Emancipation from the Protestant establishment.

The strength of the Catholic cause had, however, impressed Liverpool and the government. The king's conciliatory visit to Ireland was a blow to the Orange faction in Ireland because of its official recognition of Catholicism, in the form of the bishops and O'Connell. Supporters of Emancipation were careful to foster the view that the king's personal desire was equality for all his Irish subjects. Liverpool accordingly made up his mind to remove the Irish Attorney-General, William Saurin, a noted anti-Catholic lawyer and a mainstay of the Ascendancy. His office went to Plunket, the Catholic champion. Saurin had succeeded Plunket as Attorney-General in 1807 after the fall of the Whigs and for fifteen years was said to have governed Ireland from the powerful Attorney-General's office (*114*, I, 51-5). For the government this had the advantage of securing Grenvillite support in the Commons, dented by the 'Queen's business' and a coercive domestic policy.

The Irish executive was headed by Lord Talbot, Lord Lieutenant since 1817. He was strongly anti-Catholic but O'Connell regarded him as impartial; Mary O'Connell sent the O'Connell carriage to the funeral of Lady Talbot in January 1820 as Talbot was 'not a bad man' (II, 807). Nevertheless Talbot opposed any further pro-Catholic infiltration into the Irish administration. The major disturbances in the south and west which accompanied the serious famine in the winter of 1821 led to divisions within the Irish government. Talbot wished to enforce the Insurrection Act against the rioters but this was opposed by Charles Grant, the pro-Catholic Chief Secretary, who was anxious not to antagonise Catholic opinion. Liverpool dismissed Talbot and Grant and in a series of changes the men who were to govern Ireland for most of the 1820s assumed their posts.

The Marquess of Wellesley, a pro-Catholic and brother of the Duke of Wellington, was appointed Lord Lieutenant and Henry Goulburn, an anti-Catholic, was appointed Chief Secretary. In January 1822 Peel returned to the government as Home Secretary and Plunket was appointed Attorney-General for Ireland. Wellesley was the first Irishman to be appointed Lord Lieutenant since the seventeenth century and the first Emancipationist. He had an autocratic manner: Walter Scott described him as 'talking politics like a Roman Emperor'; he had been Governor-General of India and he came to Ireland 'boasting of his past victories over Indian cabals and anticipating his future ones over Irish'. Wellesley was notoriously flamboyant and self-important — characteristics highlighted by his small stature and which accorded ill with his embarrassed personal finances. He made a state entry into Dublin in December 1821 with his horses' heads wreathed in shamrock and soon was heard to say: 'The Irish government, Sir! I am the Irish government' (*42*, 184). Wellesley's defects as an administrator were quickly apparent to Peel but the political aspect of his appointment had more significance than his incompetence. Goulburn was a descendant of a Jamaica family and his career and opinions were almost inseparable from those of his intimate friend Robert Peel; he was quiet, solid, honest and loyal.

This major reshuffle was of real consequence. The Catholic cause was now championed from the government benches where Plunket, lulled by his office, would have to be content, under the 'open' system to let the stalemate continue. However, as compensation, the Wellesley-Plunket combination could try to ensure impartial administration in Ireland: 'Does the Marquis not . . . carry the olive branch with him and, if he does, should not the Catholics address him as a conciliator and peacemaker without delay?' O'Conor Don asked O'Connell on 30 December 1821 (II, 929). O'Connell on 5 January 1822 told 'Hunting-Cap', his uncle in Derrynane:

> I trust we have lived to see something done for the Catholics. Mr Plunket and I have had many meetings. I have got him to give up much of his obnoxious securities and I strongly hope that he will completely accede to our wishes and allow us to be emancipated without any of those on our religion for which no civil rights could afford any compensation. He is to be Attorney-General immediately. Saurin, our mortal foe, is I trust extinguished for ever. He *has* refused the Chief Justiceship with a peerage. He thinks that the liberal system will not last six months . . . Mr. Blake, the Catholic barrister who came over with Lord Wellesley, is a very particular friend of mine and is to introduce me on Tuesday to his Excellency. I mean to attend his levées as it will cost me nothing and will afford me perhaps some advantages. Lord Wellesley is, I conceive, the harbinger of Emancipation and is determined to put down the Orange faction (II, 930).

On 7 January 1822 at a meeting of Catholics at D'Arcy's Tavern a congratulatory address to the new Lord Lieutenant was adopted on O'Connell's motion.[6] It appeared now that O'Connell's investment in loyalty during the king's visit had paid some immediate dividends. William Gregory, the anti-Catholic Under-Secretary since 1812 who was married to a sister of Dr Trench, the very evangelical Archbishop of Tuam, observed to Peel in February that he still had not had a private conversation with Wellesley but he had resolved not to be provoked into making an offer of resignation (*74*, 69). The Orange party in Ireland was shocked by the changes and mortified by Saurin's abrupt dismissal. They interpreted Wellesley's policy of administering the existing laws in a spirit of impartiality as a defeat for their interest. However, given that Goulburn, with his decided Protestant sympathies, was Chief Secretary and that all the other partisans of the Ascendancy such as Gregory and Thomas Manners, the Lord Chancellor, were left at their posts, Protestants should not have been unduly alarmed.

Lord Sidmouth privately informed Manners that 'conciliation, not concession' was the principle to be adopted by the Irish government and that Wellesley was sent to administer the laws, not to alter them (*116*, 52). In fact, Wellesley proceeded to deal with the Irish disturbances in the usual coercive way; furthermore Plunket did not wish to bring forward a Catholic motion in the 1822 session. O'Connell urged a 'speedy' revival of the issue in parliament in a letter to Plunket on 4 April:

> ... I solemnly assure you that out of every 100 Catholics of the upper classes 99 are for a speedy discussion. The Catholic clergy of the second order are unanimous in wishing for it because they are convinced that at this moment every man in the House must admit the zeal and energy the Catholic clergy have evinced during the present disturbances. This testimony you will cheerfully bear. This testimony Mr Goulburn, our mortal enemy, and even Mr Peel *must* now admit to be true ... These will at all events be precious advantages — to have admitted in Parliament *the innocence* of the Catholic religion as any part of *the immediate* cause of the troubles now raging and also to have praised and *admired* by all parties the exertions and loyalty of the Catholic clergy (II, 949).

On 10 April Plunket replied giving his strong opinion against bringing forward the question:

> I agree with you that the conduct of the Roman Catholic gentry and clergy has been such during the late disturbances as to give them strong additional claims on the justice and good feeling of parliament ... but all this can be done and will be done again and again in the various occasions which must arise during the session on the discussion on Irish affairs ... You will probably give me credit for being able

to form some rational conjecture as to the probability of carrying the measure at present; my opinion is that it certainly will not pass the Lords and my strong apprehension is that it will not reach that House . . . The question never has been considered an annual one . . . With respect to the measure itself, if it be brought forward, it cannot be offered to the House by me, or with the most distant hope of success by anybody, in a shape substantially different from that in which it was last year offered to the House of Lords . . . I should hope that in the interval between this and the next session the opinion of the See of Rome might be notified in such a way as to secure an acquiescence in the proposed regulations (II, 954a).

Plunket's reply was most disappointing to O'Connell and indeed his attitude was condemned by the Whigs. Henry Fox wrote in June: 'Plunket has quite fallen this year, and has behaved most shabbily in a true *Hibernian* manner' (*53*, 126).

George Canning brought forward a Catholic Peers' Bill on 30 April 1822 which would have allowed Catholic peers to sit again in the House of Lords. Canning, whose father died early and whose mother was an actress, was one whose ability alone had brought him to the fore in the intensely aristocratic social and political world of Westminster. He was the most able liberal Tory in the Commons. He was feared for his ability but distrusted; aristocrats disdained his antecedents – a genius, perhaps, but hardly a gentleman. He had throughout his career championed Catholic Emancipation. Canning's Bill passed the Commons with a majority of five votes but was defeated in the Lords by forty-two votes. After Castlereagh's suicide in August 1822, Canning's appointment as Foreign Secretary and Leader of the House of Commons looked like another pro-Catholic was sacrificing Emancipation for office.

In June 1822 O'Connell made use of a letter by William Saurin to Lord Norbury to expose the manner in which the Orange faction ruled Ireland; the letter was found on the quay near the Four Courts by a young Catholic attorney. It had been discovered in an old chair of Lord Norbury's sold on the quay. Norbury was Chief Justice of the Common Pleas and was a notorious example of corrupt justice under the Ascendancy. The letter revealed an Attorney-General exhorting a Chief Justice to employ his judicial influence in the promotion of a political faction. It seemed to O'Connell to be a 'roving commission to a judge to create every kind of ill blood by every species of calumny'. As he told Thomas Spring Rice:

It would in my humble judgment afford strong evidence of a conspiracy between Lord Rosse, Mr Saurin and Lord Norbury to pervert the judicial office into a political engine of calumny and bigotry. It opens views upon us of the secret management of the anti-liberal part of the Irish administration which will be quite frightful when you recollect that the writer of it has been the efficient organ of the Irish government for about sixteen years and is still the confidential adviser of our Chancellor [Lord Manners] as well as his bosom friend (II, 973).

Plunket refused to take any action against Saurin and O'Connell reacted bitterly in a letter to him:

> In the case of an offending Catholic I should hope that his crime would be . . . sifted, detected, and punished. I am not so foolish or so uncandid as to assert that the case of a Protestant who conspires to injure the Catholics' case can in the present temper of Society in these countries, and under the present system, with at least one half of the administration in both decided enemies of Catholic rights and liberties . . . be weighed in the same scales of gold . . . But yet this is so . . . enormous an offence . . . it furnishes so . . . striking a feature in the causes of Irish misery that I cannot bring myself to believe but on reflection you will see the necessity, or at least the propriety, of not allowing these offenders to escape (II, 974).

Plunket did not wish to instigate an attack on the Orange leader Saurin. Wellesley's policy was to renew the truce which existed during the king's visit by inviting Orange grand masters and Catholic bishops to mingle at viceregal levées. The Ascendancy faction considered Saurin's dismissal a challenge to their power. In July 1822 the government attempted to prevent the 12 July demonstrations and the traditional dressing of King William's statue in College Green, which had been banned in 1821 for the king's visit. This was the first signal for Orange resistance. The Dublin Orangemen defied the Lord Mayor and Lord Lieutenant by dressing the statue and this led to a clash with Catholics on the street. The Orangemen felt threatened not only by the new Irish administration but also by the new constabulary force which was organised to make the police duties of the yeomanry superfluous. The new force was to be divided equally between Protestants and Catholics. Orange influence was to be further weakened by the introduction of stipendiary magistrates who were to be independent of local politics.

On 29 October 1822 an order was issued against decorating King William's statue for the coming Orange holiday of 4 November. The order was defied but Orangemen dressing the statue were stopped by soldiers and police. The Orangemen were furious. On the evening of 14 December when Wellesley was attending a performance of Oliver Goldsmith's *She Stoops to Conquer* at the New Theatre Royal in Dublin — a gala occasion with most of Dublin society present — Wellesley was hissed by Orangemen and during the first act shouts were raised for the singing of 'God Save the King'. The cast complied but while the singing was in progress shouts of 'no popery' and 'a groan for the Lord Mayor' came from the gallery. The Lord Mayor was a liberal Protestant, John Smyth Fleming and he had issued the proclamation forbidding the decoration of King William's statue in November. An attempt was made to resume the play but it was interrupted a second time by cries of 'a groan for the Lord Lieutenant', the 'glorious, pious and immortal memory' and 'no popish government'. An orange labelled 'no popery' was hurled at the Viceroy and landed on the stage. An apple, the blade of a watchman's rattle and finally, an empty bottle were thrown at the Viceregal party in their box where Wellesley stood calmly, receiving the applause of some of the audience until the demonstration was over. Party feeling was now at the highest pitch for many years in Dublin. Wellesley, however, took the incident much too seriously and allowed his self-importance to cloud his judgment. He even believed that a systematic plan to murder him was in progress, believing it to be part of a deep-laid conspiracy. The Irish government, led by Plunket, attempted to have the offenders convicted on a conspiracy charge, which the Orange Grand Jury of Dublin refused to endorse. A charge relating to riot would have been more appropriate and would have avoided further embarrassment for the government.

On Thursday 19 December O'Connell wrote jubilantly to his wife, who was now in France: 'I do not think there ever was the least opportunity of putting down the Orange faction till now, but now, unless we throw away the game we have in our hands, it will reduce the matter to this. Either the government must put down the Orangemen or be put down by them. There is no other alternative'. O'Connell united the Catholics with the general public protests against the rioters; he told Mary on Friday: 'I think it is the commencement of better days and more cheering scenes.' Again, on Saturday he wrote:

> You can imagine what a curious revolution it is in Dublin when the Catholics are admitted to be the only genuine loyalists. For the first time has this truth reached the Castle. Everyone of the Orange rascals is now disavowing his tenets and, if things continue in the present temper, there will be no finding out or discovering an Orangeman for love or money (II, 982).

The insult to the viceroy proved a turning-point and effectively marked the end of public celebrations of Williamite anniversaries in Dublin. O'Connell certainly increased his popularity by the way he handled the aftermath of the 'bottle riot': the favourable editorial he received in the *Dublin Evening Post* on 21 December 1822 was an augury of new developments: 'as no man possesses more influence when he exerts himself in the right way, we are convinced that no man can speak to the public with greater effect'.

How had a political situation developed in Ireland in the early 1820s whereby even the profession by the government of an impartial administration of the existing laws could provoke a public riot by loyalists against the king's representative? How could the new Irish government satisfy both Orangeman and Catholic while at the same time dealing with the extensive and devastating Rockite disturbances throughout the south and west of Ireland? Such questions must have been uppermost in the minds of Wellesley and Goulburn as they grappled, under Peel's guidance, with Irish policy in 1822.

The 1821 census recorded 6,801,827 people in Ireland. The vast majority of these were Catholic with a thinly spread Ascendancy of squires and middlemen in most of rural Ireland. The only places where Protestants predominated was in the north east, especially in Antrim and Down. Irish society had been shaped fundamentally by the consequences of the Williamite victory in 1691: it was this final Protestant triumph which established the Protestant Ascendancy and the Penal Laws against Catholics for most of the eighteenth century. In 1689, as Eldon put it, it was resolved to have 'a Protestant King, a Protestant Parliament, and a Protestant Government' (*124*, II, 330).

In 1792, in response to the Catholic Convention, the first representative gathering of Irish Catholics since the 'Patriot Parliament' of 1689, the Corporation of Dublin spelled out clearly that for Catholics 'the pursuit of political power' was 'a vain pursuit' and the Corporation formally resolved that it considered the Protestant ascendancy to consist of:

A Protestant King of Ireland
A Protestant Parliament,
A Protestant Hierarchy,
Protestant Electors and Government,
The Benches of Justice,
The Army and the Revenue,
Through all their branches and details, Protestant;
And this system supported by a connection with the Protestant
Realm of Britain. (*127*, 62)

However moderate Wellesley's policies were, as a close observer noted,

they could not be acted upon without indirectly limiting the influence of a party in Ireland who were jealous of a monopoly they had long enjoyed, not only of a principal part of the patronage, but also of the *ear* of the Irish government. Their long possession of the exclusive confidence of government had enabled them to keep all other parties aloof from the Castle, and to represent themselves and their friends as the only persons who could safely be employed in places of trust and emolument, or who could be relied upon for correct information regarding the state of the country. Every avenue to the Castle and every office immediately connected with government was filled with their friends and adherents, and it was scarcely possible for the voice of any other party to reach the Lord Lieutenant for the time being or his Secretary (*3*, III, 298).

The total exclusion of Catholics from political power from the 1690s was designed by the Protestant ruling class to protect their settlement on Irish landed estates confiscated at various stages in the seventeenth century. During the first half of the eighteenth century a series of 'popery laws' operated to destroy the Catholic estate owners as a class and to deprive Catholics of social and political rights. No attempt was made by the Protestant Established Church, imbued as it was by a spirit of monopoly and exclusiveness, to enforce Catholic attendance at Protestant churches or to convert the mass of the people. The Penal Laws centred essentially on property in order to secure it in hands loyal to the Protestant supremacy. That the Pope continued to recognise the Stuarts until 1766 when the Old Pretender died and that Catholics were bound to take time before coming to terms with the Protestant succession under the Hanoverian kings made it easier to justify the Protestant Ascendancy. Catholics were subject to constant accusations in press and parliament to the effect that the tenets of their religion precluded them from being good subjects of a Protestant king. The gulf between Protestants and Catholics was enormous: between them lay the conflicting memories of conquest and confiscation, massacre and pillage, conspiracy and persecution. The victors were ever on their guard, the vanquished ever resentful.

During the second half of the eighteenth century a gradual thaw began for Catholics who had been totally frozen out of the political nation. A series of Catholic committees, boards and associations seeking relief from the Penal Laws punctuated a series of measures admitting Catholics to the lesser grades of the army, allowing them to take leases and purchase land, to be educated, and to have bishops and priests resident legally in Ireland. Due to external dangers during the American and French Revolutions further advances were made in relation to marriages between Catholics and Protestants, legal practice by Catholics and the holding of the franchise by Irish Catholics.

Despite these advances Catholics had not secured political, judicial or administrative power. By 1793 Roman Catholics had not been admitted into the constitution but they had been brought within reach of admission. An important distinction emerged between 'formal' and 'virtual' exclusion: there were numerous offices for which Catholics were eligible, particularly under the Catholic Relief Act of 1793, but to which none of them had ever been appointed. An obvious example was the offices and privileges of the corporations which remained almost exclusively Protestant: such 'virtual' exclusion was even more galling than legal exclusion. Another example occurred on 14 January 1822 with the refusal of membership of the Guild of Merchants to Hugh O'Connor of Mountjoy Square, a very wealthy Catholic West India merchant; this piece of anti-Catholicism was applauded at a Dublin Corporation dinner.[7] Hugh O'Connor and his two brothers, Valentine and Malachy, became strong supporters of O'Connell. In 1825 Hugh O'Connor told a Select Committee on the State of Ireland that he was considering leaving Ireland because of the exclusionist policies which made social life so distasteful for Catholic merchants. The extensive local patronage in towns and cities was reserved by Protestant local government for their supporters.

Why were Irish Protestants so determined to resist Catholic claims tooth and nail? Lord Clare had given the answer in a brutally frank speech in the Irish House of Lords during the Union debates:

> What was the situation of Ireland at the Revolution and what is it at this day? The whole power and property of the country has been conferred by successive monarchs of England upon an English colony, composed of three sets of English adventurers who poured into this country at the termination of three successive rebellions. Confiscation is their common title; and from their first settlement they had been hemmed in on every side by the old inhabitants of the island, brooding over their discontents in sullen indignation.

After the Union the Protestant Ascendancy continued to hold sway in Ireland. The Union was an incomplete measure: Ireland continued to be governed by a separate executive. Dublin Castle, with all its traditions of Ascendancy rule, was the centre of an Irish government directed by a Lord Lieutenant and Chief Secretary both of whom were responsible for the execution of the British cabinet's Irish policy. The very idea of an 'Irish policy' or question arose from the fact that Ireland could not be governed on the same basis as Great Britain. The Irish administration was virtually distinct from the British: in many branches of government the Irish departments were independent of the corresponding departments in Britain. The Irish executive, consisting of the Lord Lieutenant, Lord Chancellor, Chief Secretary and Under-Secretary, had never been responsible to the Irish parliament. This administration was both a symbol and the instrument of the Protestant ascendancy. It was exclusively Protestant and was carried on in the interests of the 'English colony' — to use Lord Clare's phrase — or the 'English garrison', which was the description more accurately applied to the old 'Protestant nation' now that their power of independent action in a separate parliament was gone. It is difficult to realise the sense of exclusion felt by Catholics in early nineteenth-century Irish society:

> all the appointments, from the judges down to the very lowest officials, were made from the ranks of this party [i.e. Protestants]. The magistrates were exclusively appointed from it. The municipalities throughout the country were still in the hands of the same class, and were the monopoly of a most intolerant faction. No Catholic could rise to the higher posts in the law. Almost all colleges and schools were still entirely in the hands of members of the Established Church — Catholics were habitually excluded from juries (*116*, 9).

In 1829 Thomas Wyse, with the overwhelmingly predominant Catholic population in mind, itimised 748 offices connected with the administration of justice from which Catholics were legally excluded; of a further 1,314 offices to which Catholics had legal eligibility only 39 were filled by Catholics and of these 20 were police chief constables. Wyse noted that to these offices there 'should be added the long and most important list of Justices of the Peace, and Grand and Petit Jurors, and the army of constables, in which, could they be procured, the same proportions would be found to exist'. When Wyse listed the offices of civil rank, or of honour, from which Catholics were excluded by law they amounted to 780 though some of these, sheriffs for example, overlapped with those involved in the administration of justice; of over 3,000 offices of civil rank, military rank, or of honour or connected with trade, manufactures, education, charitable institutions and so on to which Catholics were legally eligible such as the Bank of Ireland, Royal Irish Academy, and many others less than 140 were held by Catholics (*132*, II, cclxxxii-ccxc). Wellesley's very tentative approach to appointments of Catholics showed how difficult it was going to be to break down Protestant privilege. He used his discretionary power only sparingly and with great caution in respect of some chief constables under the Police Act and appointed three Catholic assistant barristers of counties out of ten possible appointments. He was nearly three years in Ireland before he made a Catholic appointment beyond that of a chief constable (*3*, III, 297-300). The local administration of counties through the Grand Juries was dominated by Protestant proprietors and celebrated for abuses, inefficiency and local patronage (*21*, 169).

The importance of patronage in Irish society at this time lends enormous force to Catholic feelings of exclusion; it would be hard to exaggerate the place occupied by patronage in the day-to-day political life of Ireland during the early nineteenth century, for about half of a Chief Secretary's correspondence related to personal interests. 'I found in Ireland', recalled Robert Peel of his own term as Chief Secretary, 'that every official man . . . thought he had a right to quarter his family on the patronage of government' (*107*, I, 60). As late as 1844 Peel wrote to the newly appointed Lord Lieutenant, Lord Heytesbury:

> The cry . . . has been for a century past, and I doubt not now is 'the Protestants are the friends of the British Connexion; reliance can be placed on them' . . . All this means 'continue to us the monopoly of favour and confidence which before 1829 the Law secured to us. Consider the members of the Church as the garrison of Ireland and govern Ireland on the garrison principle'. The answer is that the system is unjust, is dangerous but above all it is utterly impracticable (*61*, 128).

The struggle for Catholic Emancipation was not simply about the repeal of archaic laws which excluded a minority of Catholics from parliament and the higher offices of state and the bench: it was about a complete change in the system of Irish administration at all levels and the taking of this administration out of the exclusive hands of the Protestant ascendancy. The Protestants, as Lecky put it, had grown up 'generation after generation, regarding ascendancy as their inalienable birthright; ostentatiously and arrogantly indifferent to the interests of the great masses of their nation, resisting every attempt at equality as a kind of infringement of the laws of nature' (*64*, 80).

Looked at from Protestant eyes the 'Glorious Revolution' of 1689 had created a Protestant Constitution which stood the test of time unlike those of other European countries which had succumbed to revolution and Napoleon. This constitution allowed for a measure of religious toleration but it could not survive political and civil equality: to grant Catholic Emancipation was to abandon the constitution which had brought good fortune to Britain and its supporters in Ireland. Obviously since the Battle of the Boyne the Anglo-Irish connection had rested upon a Protestant foundation which should be strengthened, not weakened, to ensure that the links with Britain survived.

Most politicians found it difficult to conceive of a state which did not profess a single well-defined religious conscience — the Protestant Constitution was thought to depend upon the notion of the organic union of Church and State. The fifth article of the Act of Union united the

Church of England and the Church of Ireland and the maintenance of this united Church as the Established Church of England and Ireland was to be 'deemed and taken to be an essential and fundamental part of the union'. Thus recent fundamental law lent credence to the Protestant stance. In the view of Perceval, Prime Minister of a 'Protestant' government between 1809 and 1812: 'England had already done everything which toleration required, and which the Catholics had a right to demand. It was time to make a stand against the principle of innovation. If not, there would ultimately be extorted from its weakness that which its wisdom would desire to withhold' (*116*, 26).

Irish Protestants resisted Emancipation because they felt passionately that numbers alone would turn Catholic equality into Catholic superiority and that a new Catholic ascendancy would, as a matter of course, mean a reversal of the land settlement and ultimately separation from Britain. They deeply distrusted Catholicism, as is evident from the oaths which served to exclude Catholics, because it represented, in their minds, authoritarianism, a foreign power and superstitious and erroneous forms of Christianity. Catholic dogma was held to be medieval and to enslave the intellect: to recognise it as equal was to betray the Reformation heritage of personal liberty in matters of belief. Besides was not the Catholic Church a great *imperium in imperio* with its first allegiance to the international Church of Rome? Moreover, Protestantism became in the early years of the new century deeply imbued by a new spirit of evangelicalism which came to the surface during the 1820s and exacerbated political relationships.

William Magee, the vain, brilliant and arrogant Archbishop of Dublin, effectively began this 'Second Reformation' or 'New Reformation' with a sermon in St Patrick's Cathedral on 24 October 1822. He attacked both Catholicism and non-conformism by saying that Anglicans were 'hemmed in by two opposite descriptions of professing Christians; the one, possessing a church without what *we* can properly call a religion; and the other, possessing a religion without what *we* can properly call a church . . .' A furious pamphlet warfare resulted; Patrick Curtis, the Archbishop of Armagh, J.K.L. (Bishop Doyle), and Rev. John MacHale of Maynooth were amongst those who replied for the Catholics.

During the 1820s public controversial preaching and local confrontations between Catholic and Protestant clerics, such as Father Tom Maguire and the improbably named Protestant cleric Rev. Richard Pope, typified the new sectarianism. As far as people like Archbishop Magee were concerned the Church of Ireland, with its spiritual authority derived from the Scriptures, its apostolic descent from St Patrick, and its civilising mission authorised by the State, was at war with the errors of Catholicism and non-conformity. In fact, however, the state of the unreformed Established Church in Ireland was quite scandalous with aristocratic prelates, politically appointed, drawing large incomes from the tithes of the majority of the people who were Catholic and who received no services in return for their reluctant contributions. In 1822 the Church of Ireland was shocked by a public scandal involving the Bishop of Clogher, the Hon. Percy Jocelyn, son of the Earl of Roden: the Bishop was caught *in flagrante* in a homosexual encounter with a guardsman in a public house in Westminster. But the permanent scandal of the Church of Ireland was the way it had become a symbol for the ascendancy and thus the focus for attack by the majority. Its organisation and structure, loaded with abuses, bolstered an oppressive social structure and provided an avenue of employment for exploitation by Protestant landed and professional families. Peel was conscious of the need to do something to enforce clerical residence and to get the Church of Ireland to provide for the education of the poor in every parish. He wrote to Goulburn: 'such men as Mr Henry Maxwell, drawing enormous sums from Irish livings, and leading a profligate life at Boulogne, are the real enemies of the Establishment' (*40, 375*).

In 1822 Lord John George Beresford became Primate, the first Irishman appointed in over a hundred years. A representative of the family interest which was the very symbol of Protestant patronage, he was hardly likely, no matter how pious, to appeal to Catholic opinion. Apologists found it difficult to convince many that the Established Church was – as it claimed to be – the true Catholic church of the Irish people.

Those Protestants who favoured Catholic Emancipation were influenced by the slow growth of secular liberalism, sceptical or indifferent in matters of religion, and affected by rationalism and a more 'scientific' attitude to the problems of society. Some, like Grattan and the Whigs, favoured Emancipation precisely because they believed that concessions to Catholics would preserve the constitution by giving Catholics a stake in its operation. Rev. Sydney Smith, the only English Protestant cleric who tried to swing public opinion behind Emancipation, believed it would strengthen the Established Church and national security:

> My cry is, *No Popery*; therefore emancipate the Catholics, that they may not join with foreign papists in time of war. *Church for ever*; therefore emancipate the Catholics, that they may not help to pull it down. *King for ever*, therefore emancipate the Catholics, that they may become his loyal subjects. *Great Britain for ever*; therefore emancipate the Catholics, that they may not put an end to its perpetuity.[8]

The Catholic question was linked inextricably with the state of Ireland. Sydney Smith in 1826, pointing out that the majority of Irish Protestant MPs had voted for Emancipation, was able to say that the question 'should be left to those Irish Protestants whose shutters are bullet proof; whose dinner-table is spread with knife, fork, and cocked pistol ... The Irish Protestant members see and know the state of their own country. Let their votes decide the case'.[9] Plunket argued in his speech, on 21 February 1821 in the Commons, that Emancipation would remove the 'serpent of division' between the people of Ireland. To oppose Emancipation was to say in effect:

> ... Catholics and Protestants are in a state of interminable hostility: we are bound to support our establishment to our last gasp, and they to their latest breath are bound to attempt its destruction. Thus are we lashed together, for ever struggling and never in security ... To have the great majority of the people bound by every law of nature to aim at the subversion of the state ... that Ireland should remain as it were a moral jungle only fit for the abode of beasts, and men like beasts.

In a debate on the state of Ireland on 22 April 1822 Sir John Newport argued in the Commons that granting equal rights and privileges to all Irish people would not be an instant or sufficient cure for the evils afflicting Ireland but it was a necessary remedy. Both Charles Grant, the former Chief Secretary, and Goulburn pointed out that the mentality of the lower orders had been created by conquest and the behaviour of the conquerer; Grant favoured Catholic Emancipation but Goulburn maintained that the disturbances raging in Ireland did not originate or depend upon the settlement of the Catholic question. Grant asked pointedly: 'How does it happen that a local commotion becomes so rapidly a general disturbance?' It was because of the rooted distrust among the people 'of the intentions of the British government and legislature – the fatal legacy of six hundred years of injustice and oppression'.

By the end of 1821 the entire province of Munster was in a state of agrarian rebellion. The character of these disturbances consisted of 'sending threatening notices, administering illegal oaths, houghing cattle, seizing arms, burning houses, and committing murders'.[10]

On the night of the 19 November 1821 a party of men burned to death seventeen people including a pregnant woman at the Shea home at Tubber on the slopes of Slievenamon, Co. Tipperary. The possession of an evicted tenant's farm was the cause. The 'burning of the Sheas' was only one of the more horrific outrages during these disturbances. Sheil has left a graphic account of this atrocity which seared in the imagination a brutal image of disturbed Ireland (*114*, I, 253-74). Communal peasant responses to actions which transgressed the peasant code were savage; the legal system was perceived as hostile and inimical by those seeking redress and justice. Since 1760 rural Ireland had been periodically subject to organised peasant resistance. Those favouring Catholic Emancipation argued that an exclusively Protestant domin- ated legal system was bound to alienate the Catholic peasantry: religious separation nurtured their violent passions. Arthur Young as far back as the late 1770s in his celebrated *Tour in Ireland* had condemned 'the abominable distinction of religion' which united with 'the oppressive conduct of the little country gentleman' to produce agrarian outrage: the 'proper distinction in all the discontents of the people is into Pro- testant and Catholic' and he had advised Ireland to 'put an end to that system of religious persecution, which for seventy years has divided the kingdom against itself'. Was it now too late in the 1820s to take this advice? Open engagements occurred between large armed groups and soldiers and police as for example when on 21 January 1822 Lord Bantry and fifty-five soldiers and police were attacked by about four hundred on the way from Bantry to Macroom.

A general insurrection prevailed in the South of Ireland where the civil power had ceased to have any authority, and was incapable of affording protection: the movements of the insurgents had assumed so serious an aspect that it was deemed prudent to con- centrate the troops, to call in small detachments, and to withdraw safeguards from the houses of the gentry, and most persons who could afford to quit their homes had fled to the towns for safety. It is proper to remark that these disturbances had no connexion with political or religious causes. The acts of violence then committed were confined to a lawless resistence to the payment of rents or tithes, to attacks upon the houses of the gentry for the purpose of seizing arms, and sometimes of robbery and also to vindictive out- rages against any person who ventured to occupy a farm from which a tenant had been ejected for non-payment of rent. The insurgents consisted of the peasantry and lower class of farmers who were re- duced to great distress by the fall of prices after the war (*3*, III, 300).

In O'Connell's own barony in Kerry, his brother James told Daniel how he had to combat 'Captain Rock' in February 1822:

Most of your tenants in this parish were not only affected with the wicked spirit of insubordination now unfortunately so general in the South of Ireland but were actually leaders and principals among the infatuated wretches who composed *Captain Rock's Corps* . . . seven of those deluded wretches are now in Tralee jail . . . All the landed proprietors are determined by making such abatements as the state of the times absolutely require not to drive the people to despair . . . (II, 937).

This was O'Connell's own approach to his tenants (II, 985). To deal with this grave situation, described to the Commons as 'nothing short of absolute rebellion', the government passed an Act suspending habeas corpus (for the first time in Ireland since the Union) and the Insurrection Act in February 1822. These draconian measures helped to deal with the crisis of authority in the countryside and the 1822 County Constabulary Act gave greater police powers to the government in Dublin.

During 1822 a serious famine developed due to the failure of the potato crop. There was, however, no actual shortage of food, as a Parliamentary Report stated in 1823:

> The export of grain from ports within the distressed districts of Ireland, was considerable, during the entire period from May to August, infinitely exceeding the imports during that period . . . The meritorious patience of the peasantry under the pressure of want, is here not undeserving of attention and of praise. The calamity of 1822 may therefore be said to have proceeded less from the want of food itself, than from the want of adequate means of purchasing it; or in other words from the want of profitable employment.[11]

In Clare alone 160,000 were forced to rely on relief and 76 per cent of the population in that county had not the resources to carry them through one summer of temporary shortage (*101*, 8). The outbreak of fever quickly followed famine. O'Connell noted to his daughter on 30 May 1822: '. . . There is nothing but grief and woe in Kerry. The people are starving and the gentry in bitter want. No rents, no money, the fever and famine raging. May the great God be merciful to them all' (II, 964). The memory of wretched figures tearing up weeds for their children to eat, crawling in the ditches, dying abandoned in fever huts by the side of the road, of desperate mobs attacking provision carts on the way to the ports or to market, gobbling raw flour or oatmeal which they had stolen, bleeding cows and heifers so they could drink the blood and of the silence as mobs were unable to shout and dogs too weak to bark haunted those who lived through 1822: William Carleton's *The Black Prophet: A Tale of Irish Famine* records the calamity:

> The features of the people were gaunt, their eyes wild and hollow, and their gait feeble and tottering. Pass through the fields, and you were met by little groups bearing home on their shoulders, and that with difficulty, a coffin, or perhaps two of them. The roads were literally black with funerals . . . The people had an alarmed and unsettled aspect . . . The number of those who were reduced to mendicancy was incredible, and if it had not been for the extraordinary and unparalleled exertions of the clergy of all creeds, medical men, and local committees, thousands upon thousands would have perished of disease or hunger on the very highways. Many, indeed, did so perish.

Even a Select Committee composed of politicians who normally recoiled from government interference concluded in 1823 that 'a government must find employment for the people, or else must keep the people alive, or they will rob and murder to keep themselves alive'.[12]

Wellesley and the government were worried lest the grave economic and social discontent in Ireland in 1822 might be directed into political channels. When he arrived in Dublin, Wellesley found the capital city in a great state of alarm.

> The several entrances of the city of Dublin were fortified with palli- sades of cannon. The gates of the Castle were shut, and the guards doubled, stones were carried to the roofs of the house of the Com- mander of the Forces, and of other public buildings in order to be rolled down upon the assailants, and Dublin appeared in a state of siege. The cause of alarm proceeded from exaggerated reports of the objects and hostile intentions of illegal and nightly meetings held in Dublin and the neighbouring Counties as well by Ribbon as by Orange Societies; and it was confidently believed that an attack upon the capital was meditated by the Ribbon men (*3*, III, 301).

While a good deal of the alarm was based on false rumour spread by Orangemen anxious to counteract a favourable policy by Wellesley to Catholics the Irish government could not afford to ignore the dangers or be caught napping while rebellion might be hatched. Indeed a Ribbon conspiracy was exposed in a major trial in November 1822. In early February 1822 Wellesley wrote to Peel about treasonable com- mittees in Dublin: '. . . these Committees proceed on a principle of religious zeal; . . . their object is to inflame the Catholics to massacre & war against the Protestants, & to subvert the establishment in Church & State . . . it is evident that materials are prepared for any Leader of a more distinguished character & of greater Ascendancy'.[13] The Ribbon- men were Catholics generally drawn from social groups below the middle class such as journeymen, carpenters, porters and mechanics. They formed oath-bound lodges and were opposed to Orange lodges. They had vague political aims of a Catholic restoration. They had evolved an underground, embryonic, national network based on the old, violent, sectarian and conspirational tradition going back through Defenders of the late eighteenth century to the rapparees of the seven- teenth century. As Charles Grant pointed out in April 1822, among the Irish people there were 'vivid recollections of past history' and it was 'astonishing indeed to observe the force and intensity of those mental associations'.[14]

Could Irish Catholics combine to present the government with united demands backed by the threat or actuality of physical force? There were great social divisions amongst the Catholic population which made this possibility seem remote. At the top of the scale were a small number of Catholic landowning nobility and gentry such as the Earls of Fingall and Kenmare, Lords Gormanston, Ffrench, Southwell and Trimleston. These had a most conservative aristocratic and cautious outlook and identified themselves socially with the vastly more numerous Protestant nobility. Below these ranged the Catholic gentry: families such as the Bellews of Louth, the Butlers of Kilkenny, the Wyses of Waterford, the Blakes, Kirwans and Brownes of Galway and Mayo. Roman Catholic gentry families were noted for pride of birth; according to Sheil, 'Having no field for the exercise of their talents, and without any prospect of obtaining an ascent in society through their own merits, they looked back to the achievements of their ancestors, and consoled themselves with the brilliant retrospect' (*114*, I, 146). In general such families had the same reason to fear the peasantry as had Protestant landlords. Next in rank came the growing class of Catholic leaseholders, graziers and substantial farmers such as the Lalors, Cullens, Brennans and Morans of Carlow, Queen's Co. and Kilkenny. From the Catholic Relief Acts of 1778 and 1782 which allowed Catholics to lease and purchase land the Catholic landed interest developed considerably and this gave many Catholics a vested interest in the stability of the land settlements of the seventeenth century. Because they had been allowed to trade, there had developed in the towns during the eighteenth century a very considerable class of Catholic commercial and professional families. Some of these became extremely wealthy and began to extend into the landed interest. The family of Richard Lalor Sheil is a good example. Catholics owned a highly significant proportion of the country's middle-class wealth and such Catholics, in law or trade, felt their way impeded by the Protestant monopoly of power in the cities and towns. Below these upper- and middle-class Catholics ranged the lower classes composed of tenant farmers, occupiers, artisans, shopkeepers, the landless labourers and the Catholic poor of the countryside and the towns.

Each of these groups had different economic and social experiences and consequently had different political outlooks. Leaders of the middle and upper classes, both clerical and lay, had developed a political ideology which can be loosely described as liberal Catholicism. Catholic political thought in post-Union Ireland was moulded by historical experience, especially the sense of historical injustice which centred principally on the 'broken' Treaty of Limerick (1691). Catholic demands were, however, put forward as expressions of liberal political theory rooted in the British Whig and constitutional tradition. Interesting attempts were advanced to reconcile the Jacobite Irish and the Whig positions in the 'Glorious Revolution' of 1689. Irish Catholics sought full access to the 'free institutions' which had been inherited from the Williamite victory and they argued with force and conviction for major liberal reforms without violent revolution. In essence the Irish Catholic leadership adopted the constitutional terms of their oppressors and wielded and expanded them in a novel way to evolve a distinctive political ideology unique in terms of contemporary European Catholicism, which was highly reactionary in the wake of the French Revolution. In the era of Papal conservatism and Metternichian reaction Catholics in Ireland increasingly became committed to a great popular and social movement. Catholicism was linked to the cause of liberty.

The supreme purveyor of these views was Thomas Moore whose *Irish Melodies* were playing a key part in the evolution of an Irish political consciousness: Moore provided images – the harp, shamrock and round tower – round which a sense of nationhood could focus in an English-speaking and literate culture. He provided balm for injured national pride and for historical defeats as well as the illusion of a golden age before the intrusion of the Saxon invader. In a series of public letters in the *Dublin Evening Post* between 1820 and 1824 Rev. John MacHale of Maynooth, writing pseudonymously as 'Hierophilos', set out the demands of liberal Catholicism convincingly and pugnaciously. He argued for British liberties for Irish Catholics: he utilised the British Whig constitutional tradition stemming from Locke and Blackstone to show that there was no basis to exclude Catholics from the constitution; like Moore, he emphasised that Catholicism was consistent with the principles of political liberty; in fact, he maintained it was just as favourable to a 'sound and rational freedom' as Protestantism. Gradually Irish Catholic leaders had learned to define political values, goals and means of achievement, which were appropriate to their position and yet which were sufficiently packed with emotional and practical appeal to gain popular support. In the absence of a viable native political tradition, Catholic politics became fixed within terms of reference which assumed the virtues of British constitutionalism and which spoke the same political language as Westminster. Central to their argument was that the Treaty of Limerick of 1691 had been broken and this violation gave rise to the injustices suffered by Catholics. There was a political and moral obligation on Britain to restore Catholics to their rightful position which would have been theirs if the Treaty had been honoured. In April 1822, when writing to Plunket to argue for a discussion in parliament on Catholic Emancipation, O'Connell was careful to distinguish for whom he spoke: 'We have been as humble and courteous in our petitions as we are really submissive in our inclinations. We are sincerely attached to constitutional connection with England. When I say we I mean the Catholic clergy and Catholic gentry including the upper class of farmers . . .' O'Connell was impressing on Plunket the dangers of the misery and discontent amongst the people:

> Was there ever misery equal to that of the Irish? And I ask with confidence was there ever more exemplary conduct than that of the educated portion of the Catholics and of the entire Catholic clergy? What would the state of this country be if our clergy were neutral? What if they fanned the flame? Who then could reckon on extinguishing the conflagration otherwise than with blood, and blood is just the very worst cement of civil society?

The people would support a physical force movement: 'Let them have but an occasion or give them officers and they will soon find an occasion' (II, 949).

The political views of the lower orders were a constant worry to both Dublin Castle and the upper classes. Maxwell Blacker who was appointed to administer the Insurrection Act in 1822 in Cork and Tipperary told the House of Lords Committee of Inquiry in 1824 that the ultimate causes of disturbances lay in history: 'I conceive that the long course of confiscations of property and of Penal Laws had very bad effects at the time (whether they were necessary or not) upon the minds and upon the dispositions of the great body of the people of Ireland'. Thomas Crofton Croker, observing that Ireland in the early 1820s was 'comparatively a *terra incognita* to the English in general' discovered 'that in political feeling, in language, in manners and almost every particular which stamps a national character, the two islands differ essentially'.[15] The Gaelic oral culture was slowly being transformed into a predominantly English and literate culture and the vast majority of the people still lived outside the established structures of politics, government and the administration; indeed they had a general and settled hatred of the law. The mass of the people might be mobilised on the basis of economic grievances, as the Rockite insurrection showed in Munster, or possibly on the basis of sectarian feelings as in the Ribbon lodges uncovered in 1822. The horrors of the 1798 rebellion were still fresh in living memory. There was a popular awareness of great historical injustice and a vague desire to recover lost rights and privileges stemming from events in the seventeenth and eighteenth centuries. The Defender and Ribbon movements indicated the potential in the popular political culture for a violent conspiratorial underground movement should it get the necessary leadership (*38*, 133-4).

The early years of the 1820s set the scene for a struggle of decisive importance for Anglo-Irish relationships, for the political system in the British Isles, for the development of democratic politics and for the

emerging character of Irish nationalism. At the heart of the struggle lay
a fundamental clash over the nature of the British state, the role of
religion in the state, the national identity of Irish people of different
origins, the basis of property and the political privileges conferred by
religion and property. Ireland became the battleground for competing
ideas and forces with ultimate significance for the unity and security of
the United Kingdom established in 1800. Ireland was in effect divided
into two warring camps: the one, Protestant, claiming perpetual ascendancy; the other, Catholic, determined to achieve equality. On 22 January
1823 Grey, the Whig leader, summarised the immediate probable rami-
fications of the situation in a letter to Lord Holland:

> The state of things in Ireland appears to me . . . [a] probable cause
> of division. Peel & his friends . . . talk without reserve against both
> Wellesley & Plunket . . . The Duke of Wellington, tho' not a friend
> to the Catholick Question, would probably wish to support his
> Brother's [Wellesley's] 'Person & Government', & in this matter he,
> Canning & the Grenvilles would naturally be placed in opposition to
> the ultra Tory & High Church part of the government. This too
> would lead to a state of things in which Canning might look to the
> means of strengthening those interests by new connections, & ulti-
> mately of forming a new government, if he can carry the King with
> him (*80*, 39).

The 'state of things in Ireland' was now becoming central and decisive
in British politics. T. Crofton Croker purchased a selection of popular
songs in 1821 and he found more than a third of them of a rebellious
tendency, especially a song entitled 'Cathaleen Thrail' which had a per-
ceptive prophetic strain:

> You, Sons of poor Erin, therefore don't fail
> From Cork to Kinsale, and off to Cape Clear
> Come excite your parties, it's no time to bewail,
> Tho' bad alterations we've plenty this year;
> Now the year 21 is drawing in by degrees
> In the year 22 the Locusts will weep;
> But in the year 23 we'll begin to reap
> And divorce the Black-weed from Cathaleen Thrail.[16]

1
1823-4:
'Beginning a General Rally'

'The times are big, with events of the deepest magnitude'.
Daniel O'Connell to his wife,
12 March 1823 (II, 1002)

Winter weather in January and February 1823 was more severe than anything O'Connell could remember; he felt it much colder than 'the Russian year', 1813 (II, 991). The political outlook for Catholics seemed less bleak. On 11 January O'Connell dined at the Viceregal Lodge in the Phoenix Park but Wellesley was unable to join the party because of illness: 'It was, on the whole, a new scene to me and one a good deal gratifying', he told his wife, '. . . I never abused the Orangemen in my days . . . with half the violence with which they are now abused at the Castle' (II, 988). On 1 February, O'Connell spent an hour, 'tête à tête', with the Lord Lieutenant and was 'exceedingly well received'. He enjoyed the novelty of being 'a great Castle man' not least for the discomfort it caused the Orangemen. He was careful to add, however: 'I am as true to Ireland and to reform and to Liberty as ever I was' (II, 996). As long as Liverpool maintained his 'neutrality' on the Catholic question and as long as Wellesley could only administer the laws but not alter them Catholics could not gain political and administrative power.

In February two events occurred, one public and one private, which fundamentally altered Catholic prospects: through these events the disastrous split over the veto which had divided Irish Catholics since 1815 was ended. Both events were closely connected and were put in train by the death of Sir Hans Hamilton, the long serving MP for Co. Dublin, in 1822. In the election in February 1823 to fill the vacancy Co. Dublin became sharply divided between Sir Compton Domville, representing the 'no popery' and Orange interest, and Colonel Henry White, son of the famously rich Luke White. The Whites, as a *nouveau riche* family of great wealth and a liberal and reforming temper, were anxious to establish themselves in a social position consonant with their means. In pursuit of this goal they were anxious to enter the House of Commons. O'Connell and others formed a committee to organise the Dublin freeholders behind White.[1] O'Connell, using techniques for the first time which were to become synonymous with the Catholic struggle, went to 'the towns of Rush and Skerries and harangued in the streets of each' as he recounted to his wife: 'It was amusing; a kind of wild day, very cold, half snowy. I was then quite fresh for the ensuing day on which the election began. I spoke for an hour and a quarter, I believe, at the least. I never was in my life so well satisfied with myself' (II, 996).

This public engagement with parliamentary politics led directly to the second, private, event which was to have such profound consequences for the future. During the election campaign a private dinner party took place on Saturday 8 February at Glencullen, in the Dublin mountains, the home of Thomas O'Mara, O'Connell's close friend. Among the guests were O'Connell, Sheil and Lord Killeen, a son of the Earl of Fingall. The topic of conversation was the state of Catholic politics. Views were exchanged on the 'utter want of system and organisation' among Catholics, and O'Connell and Sheil, in a historic reconciliation, agreed to forget their differences over the veto. Sheil was now convinced that O'Connell's leadership was necessary in a totally new democratic organisation. They both agreed to contact leading Catholics to lay plans for a new body which would fight for Emancipation and end 'the total stagnation' which had made the political monopoly of Protestants and the abuses of the Ascendancy so secure (*114*, II, 182). It was agreed that the comprehensive and democratic nature of the new initiative, which O'Connell had in mind, should not at the outset be made clear; if the attempt was to be successful, in Sheil's words:

> it must invite and secure the co-operation of persons of every degree; to win the confidence of the wealthier classes it must avoid every semblance of illegality or enmity to the established order of things; and yet it must, to kindle the smouldering passions of an infuriated and oppressed people, deal fearlessly with those many-sided questions about which the opulent and the poor, the well-born and the humble, can seldom, if ever, be expected cordially to agree (*71*, I, 185-7).

The new alliance of Sheil and O'Connell was absolutely crucial to the evolution of the advanced political organisation now contemplated. They would seek to build a mass popular demand for Emancipation. Quickly after this dinner party came the very encouraging result in the Co. Dublin election: White narrowly defeated Domville by 994 votes to 849. O'Connell exulted that it was 'really a great triumph and shows what Catholics can do' (II, 996). He and his supporters savoured this victory over the Orangemen; they mounted a procession to chair White from the hustings at Kilmainham into the city centre. This infuriated the staunch Protestant students in Trinity College, as O'Connell related to his wife:

> I never saw such a crowd. I was in the first carriage next to White's chair . . . We passed through the Liberty, etc., stopped to give four

cheers for the King at the Castle gate and so went on to College Green. The College lads attacked the people with stones, etc. but they were soon put to the rout. I had a great view of part of the battle. In short, no popular triumph was ever half so great . . . (II, 999).

In his enthusiasm O'Connell dreamt of a quick passage of an Emancipation Bill, of his becoming a King's Counsel and not having to slog as a junior on circuit; he even dreamt of becoming an MP. But sober reflection soon dispelled these fantasies. White's victory had been a close-run thing, greatly dependent on lavish expenditure. Its outstanding lesson had been the value of Catholic unity and organisation. O'Connell now concentrated on establishing a new, vigorous organisation with Sheil's help to achieve Catholic unity.

That Catholic leaders faced an unrelenting Protestant Ascendancy in Ireland and a heedless parliament in London was soon made clear as hopes for rapid advance in the House of Commons were quickly dashed. When the Catholic question was debated in the House on 17 April it merely provided an opportunity for the pro-Catholics out of office, the Whigs, to accuse the pro-Catholics in office, especially Canning and Plunket, of treachery to the cause for the sake of places in government. Grey, the Whig leader, had withdrawn temporarily from active politics and decisive leadership was absent in the opposition ranks (*87*, 171). Brougham's famous attack on Canning's alleged sell-out embittered and divided those who favoured Emancipation, whether in or out of office; Canning had become Foreign Secretary and Leader of the Commons in 1822 on the suicide of Castlereagh. Plunket had to abandon his motion for a committee of the whole House to consider the Catholic claims. The debate merely underlined the extent to which the Catholic cause had lost ground in the House since 1821. It was apparent now that the only way to break the parliamentary deadlock was through extra-parliamentary popular clamour and that the only place where this was feasible was in Ireland.

On 25 April, on foot of O'Connell's and Sheil's invitation, a preliminary meeting of Catholics took place at Dempsey's Tavern in Sackville Street. Sheil remembered this preparatory gathering as 'a very thin meeting, which did not consist of more than about twenty individuals'. Lord Killeen, who took the chair, was more assertive in politics than was usual amongst the Catholic peerage. His example was important in winning the support or at least the passive endorsement of other Catholic aristocrats. Lord Gormanston, a wealthy Catholic peer, who had remained aloof from previous agitations, supported the new initiative. The Earl of Kenmare, while unwilling or unable to appear personally, contributed the weight of his name (*132*, I, 203-4). In

Sheil's words, 'the aristocracy was consolidated with the Catholic democracy' (*114*, II, 183-4). The attendance included Sir Thomas Esmonde, Sir John Burke, Nicholas Mahon, Hugh O'Connor and other representatives of the Catholic gentry and wealthy merchant class of Dublin.

It was determined that something should be done to organise Irish Catholics and it was resolved to call an aggregate meeting of Catholics on 10 May to revive the Catholic Board. Nicholas Purcell O'Gorman acted as 'Secretary to the Roman Catholics of Ireland'.[2] O'Gorman was a lawyer and a native of Clare; he had accompanied O'Connell in his famous duel with D'Esterre in 1815 and was a known 'character' about Dublin for his quirkiness and sense of self-importance. John Banim observed him in the Dublin streets as '. . . a very large person, who carries his head very high, and wears his clothes very loose, and has great whiskers, and a profusion of shirt collar, and bears a huge stick or club on his shoulder . . .'[3] On 28 April, O'Connell wrote to his wife 'We are . . . beginning a general rally in Dublin. We are to get up the Catholic Board again and to take the strongest measures the law will allow to enforce our cause on the attention of parliament' (II, 1013). A further meeting, to consider resolutions for the aggregate meeting, was held at Dempsey's Tavern with a 'very numerous' attendance; 145 people signed the requisition for the meeting on 10 May. This preparatory meeting was chaired by Sir Edward Bellew, of Louth, and a committee of eleven was appointed to prepare the aggregate meeting.[4] This committee reported to another preparatory meeting at Dempsey's Tavern where O'Connell declared that 'his first and last recommendation to his afflicted countrymen should be to take the management of *their* own affairs — and to proceed in that management with firmness and unanimity — [*cheers*]'.[5]

O'Connell and Sheil now had continuous Catholic meetings in train; the new concept of a wider agitation began to be mooted. On the day of the aggregate meeting in Townsend Street Chapel the *Freeman's Journal* noted that there 'is no idea of reviving the Catholic Board' but that a new body to manage Catholic affairs would be discussed at the meeting.[6] At the crowded meeting O'Connell spoke strongly in favour of a Catholic Association and his resolution to form one was carried unanimously. The distinction between 'Board' and 'Association' is revealing. In 1816 the pro-veto moderates had been opposed by O'Connell who had promptly formed a Catholic Association. It had failed, but by now choosing to call the new body an 'Association' O'Connell signalled the end of vetoist politics and a more determined and advanced stance. A 'Board', such as that favoured by the wealthy conservative Nicholas Mahon at the aggregate meeting, would have functioned merely as a small group supplying their parliamentary advocates with information on the effects of their disabilities: O'Connell had something far more novel and revolutionary in mind.

A meeting on the Monday, following the Townsend Secret Chapel meeting, was in effect the inaugural of the 'Irish Catholic Association'; it was held in Dempsey's Tavern with Lord Killeen in the chair. It resolved 'that an Association of Catholic Gentlemen should be formed and that an Annual Subscription of One Guinea should constitute a Member'. Over fifty joined by paying the subscription immediately.[7] Within a fortnight a committee had produced the Rules and Regulations governing the new Association (132, II, xxxvii-xxxviii). O'Connell's guiding hand may be seen in the wide scope allowed for in the aims of the Association and in some novel features introduced in the regulations. The broad aim of the new body was 'to adopt all such legal and constitutional measures as may be most useful to obtain Catholic Emancipation'. The Rules specifically set out that the Association was 'not a representative or delegated body' and that it would not 'assume any representative or delegated authority or quality'. This secured protection from prosecution under the Convention Act of 1793 which made illegal any assembly which purported to be representative or which was made up of elected delegates: such prerogatives were then held to reside solely in parliament. O'Connell turned the dangers of illegality to novel ends: the Rules provided for the admission of newspaper reporters to all meetings and ensured that the books of the Association would be 'always open for inspection'. Legal safeguards and the need for publicity were thus made mutually reinforcing. As Wyse later remarked, the Catholic Association was founded upon 'a new principle, that of an open club without canvass or ballot, the members admissible on the *viva voce* proposition of a friend . . .' (*132*, I, 200). Having no secrets in politics was one of O'Connell's cardinal principles which was vital to the legal immunity of the fledgling body.

The government were instantly on the alert: on 12 May Wellesley sent Peel the newspaper reports of the new organisation and discussed the legal situation with the Solicitor-General. He sought Peel's instructions as to how to handle the Catholic organisation. Peel told Wellesley on 16 May that they should keep 'a strict watch' upon the new body but as yet there was no evidence which would warrant legal interference.[8] Later in 1823 the government adopted the policy of having its own representatives attend the Association as press reporters to take verbatim accounts so that the proceedings of the Association could be authenticated if necessary in a prosecution.

Immediately the newly-founded Protestant *Dublin Evening Mail* dubbed the Association 'the Roman Catholic Parliament of Ireland' or the 'Popish Parliament', in order to show the illegality and 'downright sedition' it involved: the *Mail* asked the government if it meant to put down 'the factious crew who call themselves the Catholic Association'.[9] Outright opposition was expected from Orangemen but O'Connell was intent on having liberal Protestants in the Association, as he told his wife on 24 May after a Catholic Association meeting where he had enjoyed 'great debating':

> The principal question was whether we would allow Protestants to be members of the Association by paying a subscription just as Catholics might. You will easily imagine that I was of *this* way of thinking and carried it by a triumphant majority. I wish we may find Protestants liberal enough to join us, that is all; we have done our part. The next motion was that we should allow no visitors but Protestants, that is, that no Catholic should come into the Board without paying one guinea a year. This we also carried, so that you see we have in our little parliament set the Protestants a good example . . . (II, 1023).

The Catholic Association was now a small body led by O'Connell, meeting frequently over Richard Coyne's bookshop in Capel Street. Coyne was more than a mere bookseller. As the leading Catholic publisher and printer he was an important force in Catholic intellectual life. He dined regularly with the bishops at Maynooth and was a frequent visitor at Old Derrig and later at Breganza, the residences of Bishop James Doyle of Kildare and Leighlin. Coyne was a close associate of O'Connell, who now used the two large rooms over Coyne's bookshop as the centre of activity in Catholic politics. Coyne published works by Bishop Doyle and other tracts and pamphlets, thus lending powerful aid to the Catholic protagonists such as Father Tom Maguire for public controversies with Protestant evangelicals. Coyne, the Catholic traditionalist, was later recalled '. . . standing at his shop door, with his silvery hair, his frilled shirt, knee breeches, and silvery shoe buckles, a living memorial of an age whose customs, costumes, and manners were almost of the long past' (*127*, 68).

Prior to 1823 Catholic meetings took place in public houses such as D'Arcy's Globe Tavern, Essex Street, 'a second- or third-rate tavern' which had two small rooms joined by folding doors approached by way of a narrow staircase.[10] Coyne's rooms were larger, more respectable and nearer the Four Courts, where the barristers and lawyers, who were to be the key members, worked. A liberal Protestant member has described the early Catholic Association meetings:

> An oblong table is extended through the centre of the rooms on either side of which, secretaries, reporters, clerks, etc. are seated. The Chairman's position is at the head of the table. The members are

sometimes obliged to stand during three or four hours' discussion of a topic. There are no 'Ministerial or oppositional benches' — no elbow cushions for the most respected auditor! In fact the *tout ensemble* of this 'Irish Parliament' is characterized by anything but arrogant assumption. The members are of a very mixed character: noblemen and hierarchs — professional gentry; divines, barristers, attornies, physicians, commercial folk; merchants, traders, etc. . . . Some members are in no wise influential either by rank or fortune . . .[11]

The social composition of the early Association is revealing: it included one viscount, the younger son of a baron, two baronets, a knight, a Carmelite friar, nineteen barristers, twelve attorneys, three newspaper editors, one surgeon, eleven merchants, and ten landed gentlemen; in total sixty-two members. The thirty-one legal men formed the core of the movement (*113*, 31). The fact that the Association met in the afternoons, after work at the Courts was over, rather than in the evenings, is an indication of its professional middle-class nature — working men would only be free in the evening. It is noteworthy that the Catholic Association had a number of journalists and newspaper editors amongst its leaders. Sheil, while a barrister, was also a writer and journalist who could produce articles for British and French papers. John Lawless had played a prominent part in Belfast politics as editor of *The Irishman*, a weekly radical and Catholic paper. He now joined the Association and brought into its debates his impetuosity, volubility and exhibitionism. Lawless had courage and radical views and he was not afraid to heckle and oppose O'Connell. He was, however, too frequently on his feet speaking amusingly but to little effect: he was too erratic and extreme to provide real and effective opposition to O'Connell.

There were two outstanding newspaper editors in membership of the Association, Frederick William Conway and Michael Staunton. Both were to play key roles in publicising the Association and in the revival of an independent press in Dublin. In the early 1820s, with a more conciliatory government attitude and less government money to support the 'Castle' newspapers, the possibility of a successful 'Catholic' and independent press existed despite the high taxes on newspapers. The opportunity was seized by Conway and Staunton. Conway, a highly literate Protestant, had a long background in journalism; he had become editor of the *Dublin Evening Post* as far back as 1814. Like many newspapermen, he drew a state pension and had co-operated with the government from time to time. As the Association was very open, Conway could not tell the government much that was not already known to the Castle. Conway did, however, retain some independence of both O'Connell and the government and he was to play a central role in the leadership of the Association. Michael Staunton had edited the *Freeman's*

Journal at the very early age of twenty. He had kept some degree of independence throughout Sir Robert Peel's period as Chief Secretary at the price of extreme editorial caution. He was attempting with little success in the early 1820s to run a daily newspaper. He had new ideas on reporting home news in greater detail and on employing a corps of reporters. The Catholic Association was to provide the right context and Staunton's *Morning Register* and *Weekly Register* began to flourish within a year of the Association's foundation.

From May 1823 to April 1824 O'Connell developed his more strident and advanced approach to Irish agitation. At the same time he attempted to retain sufficient support for the new policy amongst the cautious conservative Catholic gentry and wealthy middle class to make the Association credible. Sheil later remembered that the Association 'in its origin was treated with contempt, not only by its open adversaries, but Catholics themselves spoke of it with derision . . .' (*114*, II, 183). The Association was, in effect, a tiny body which barely survived: it was often necessary to adjourn the meetings because the quorum of ten did not turn up: O'Gorman, the secretary, was a stickler for the rules.

In late May, O'Connell set out the new purpose of the Association and contrasted it with the old pattern of Catholic agitation. The aim was not

> to force on Parliament the annual farce or properly a triennial inter-
> lude of a debate on the Catholic claims. Their purpose was practical
> and not abstract questions . . . There were many grievances under
> which the poor and unprotected Catholic peasant smarted, that
> would not admit of waiting for redress until the day of Emanci-
> pation arrived, and which might be made the subject of separate
> applications to Parliament and the laws – such were the objects of
> the Association . . .

He went on to illustrate how 'practical' grievances such as Church Rates 'would come within the objects of the Association' and 'the poor and illiterate man' could not be expected to resist them unhelped 'however well grounded their objections . . . as in the case of a parish in the County of Westmeath where £700 was granted for building a church and afterwards £200 levied upon the parish for the same purpose and no church yet built although another levy of £200 is about to be made'.[12]

O'Connell had realised that the effective way to communicate with the great mass of Catholic Irishmen was to deal with 'practical' questions. An editorial in the *Dublin Evening Post*, shortly before this speech, on the disturbances in the south of Ireland, echoed his own sentiments: 'The truth is – a truth which seems to be forgotten in most of the discussions on Irish affairs – that it is of local grievances, of peculiar hardships the peasantry have to complain, and that it is these, and not any general principle which have produced the present disturbances.' The *Post* also pointed out that the Whiteboys 'have never dreamed of a revolution which would separate the two countries', but they had sought the redress of local grievances.[13] In early June O'Connell was pressing the handful of members at the Association to concentrate on 'peculiar grievances' which afflict 'the wretched, naked, persecuted peasant'; the Association did not exist 'for the absurd purpose of discussing mere routine matter, but in order to wrestle with their grievances and oppressions boldly and effectually'. O'Connell advised the Association to ignore 'the farce of annually petitioning for general emancipation' as this had become a 'mockery':

> In bringing forward the abstract question particular grievances were lost sight of, their best friends were confounded and confused, and a general misunderstanding was abroad upon the subject of their disabilities... By bringing the *peculiar* grievances immediately under the notice of the Legislature – they enlisted those who were particularly afflicted, and secured their exertions.[14]

O'Connell now had the key to a successful large-scale agitation in Ireland. The 'power of common grievance' was to be utilised to build a nation-wide organisation. Eneas MacDonnell, later to be appointed as the Catholic Association's agent in London, argued in a speech in July that the people, before the Association came into being, had known no redress other than violence; the Association should instruct them in their privileges relating to petitioning parliament, 'a right of which they are ignorant of possessing'.[15]

The first and most important element, then, in O'Connell's new strategy was to expand the range of issues, grievances and questions with which the new organisation was to deal. O'Connell declared in July during the discussion on the Association's petition on the administration of justice that it was '. . . forming a new era in the history of Irish grievances. . .'[16] In the process of politicising every issue and thereby creating a mass movement, O'Connell changed the nature of the demand for emancipation from one seeking an equality of privilege for a section of Catholics to a demand for the total liberation of the whole Catholic people of Ireland from their grievances, whether these were agrarian, judicial, religious, administrative or political. O'Connell also threatened to bring 'the Catholics to act with the Reformers of England'.[17] The gentry and conservative members became thoroughly alarmed. Sheil, who was fully behind O'Connell in widening the scope of the new body, gave notice of motion in June 1823 to change the name of the Association from 'Catholic' to that of the 'National Association'.

He quickly withdrew his motion 'not from any change in his own opinion as to the propriety of the measure but from a wish to prevent disunion in the Association upon a matter of such trivial importance, but which had excited apprehensions in the minds of some members of their own body'.[18]

O'Connell now deliberately set about raising the popular expectations of the benefits which might follow Emancipation. It was a dangerous strategy, given the highly charged sectarian atmosphere amongst the people: popular songs and ballads were laced with references to the approaching overthrow of the 'heretics'. Protestants, evoking memories of 1641, feared a Catholic conspiracy to slaughter them. Prophecies circulated amongst the peasantry incorporating this theme of deliverance: those of Pastorini, derived from an analysis of the Apocalyse of St John, first publicised in 1771 by an English Catholic churchman, Charles Walmesley, foretold a violent overthrow of the Protestant churches in 1825. Pastorini's prophecies had achieved a mass circulation in Ireland by the early 1820s. This millenial strand in the folk tradition became woven into the 'Emancipation' struggle and helps to explain the explosion of popular enthusiasm which the campaign was to evoke.

The second element in the new strategy was the provision of a framework for the political action of Catholic masses as they responded to the publicising of their 'practical' grievances. To secure this O'Connell turned to the Catholic Church. It was the best possible national framework he could use. By using the Church he solved, at once, the great problem which faced any leader of a popular Irish constitutional struggle: to build a national organisation and at the same time to be able to control the mass movement at will. Thomas Wyse, from his firsthand experience, regarded the problem of control as 'one of the most difficult' as it was easy to excite

> but to keep the steam up to its original pressure, without risking an explosion on the one side, and on the other avoiding that tendency to relapse into former coolness . . . has been indeed a problem which in almost every instance of Irish politics has eluded the intellect and defied the exertion of the most zealous and sagacious patriots (*132*, I, 190).

At an early meeting of the new organisation O'Connell declared that they might with advantage adopt a regulation of the English Catholic Association and admit the Catholic priests as members of the Association 'without payment of a subscription'.[19] A 'particularly animated' discussion, on the part priests were to play in the Association, took place in June 1823. O'Connell proposed a motion to admit priests without payment and he condemned 'the supineness' of priests who would not claim their 'civic rights' as freemen. Two members, Ford and Scanlon, proposed an amendment that priests should only be admitted on the same basis as 'protestant spectators' without any other privileges. Sheil had not yet seen the importance of the Catholic clergy, and he supported this amendment 'warmly' fearing that O'Connell's motion would give priests 'a great preponderance' in the Association over the lay members. Other members, however, supported O'Connell, declaring that priests would only act in the interests of Catholics in general. At the end of this important debate O'Connell's motion was carried, without the amendment, 'by a large majority'.[20] Hence very early in the life of the Catholic Association O'Connell had added the second essential element to his new strategy. It was not immediately apparent how important this debate had been as clerical support was not tapped until the extension of the Association in 1824.

Meanwhile, the English Roman Catholics also reorganised. The subtle change in the content of 'Emancipation' being wrought by O'Connell in Ireland — from an upper-class quest for equal access to privilege to one for the liberation of the Irish people from their manifold grievances — was to widen a gulf always evident between Irish and English Catholics. The situation of the two Catholic populations was greatly different — the Irish Catholics were a vast majority whilst the English Catholics were but a small proportion of the total population in England.

The English Catholic leaders, however, were to continue to play an important role in persuading English opinion to admit Catholics to power. What Emancipation impended for most English people was the downfall of 'the Protestant Constitution'; 'no popery' had always been a potent political cry. Whether or not a traditional 'no popery' campaign would develop as Irish Catholic pressure increased remained to be seen. This depended, to some extent, on the politics of persuasion exercised by the moderate English Catholics. Such Catholics provided an appropriate contrast to their Irish co-religionists: tolerant rather than extreme, aristocratic rather than peasant, loyal rather than seditious. English Catholics had gradually advanced in English society and they were very anxious not to have their position disturbed by Irish inflexibility or violence. This new toleration depended upon the willingness of Protestants to ignore the letter of existing laws and to connive at Catholic participation. English Catholics had long courted Protestant approval and they would have accepted willingly a veto by the crown on the appointment of Catholic bishops.

The English Roman Catholic priest and historian, John Lingard, provided an example of the disingenuous character of English Catholicism. Lingard's *History of England* was published in eight volumes between

1819 and 1830 when the Catholic question was in the forefront of the political stage. His aim was to provide an accurate history which would be acceptable to Protestants and at the same time correct the anti-Catholic bias of previous histories. Lingard's method was to pander to Protestant prejudices initially and then to alter his work in subsequent editions when the 'enemy' was off-guard. His *History* was enormously successful. Later he became deeply engaged in pamphlet disputes with Protestant divines with works such as his *Defence of the Roman Catholic Church*.

The English Catholic Board, established in 1808, with Edward Jerningham as secretary, had concentrated on moderate actions designed by the gentry, who dominated it, to persuade Westminster to grant a qualified Emancipation. When Jerningham died in 1822 it was clear that a combination of gentle persuasion and securities would not carry the day. In June 1823, one month after the Catholic Association was founded in Dublin, the British Catholic Association was formed, with Edward Blount, former steward to the Duke of Norfolk, the premier Catholic nobleman, as secretary. It was to remain an exclusive body though under increasing popular pressure:

> Two visions of the future emerged, the one unabashedly popular, the other conservative and apparently self-seeking; two visions vying for the Body's favour, with proletarians expostulating upon 'the pressure of the times' and aristocrats aspiring to accommodation in the Commons and the Lords, at Quarter Sessions and County Courts, at the Bar and on the Bench (*67*, 172).

The Irish Catholic leaders knew the mentality of English Catholics. Sheil remembered his schooldays at Stonyhurst where he had met a great number of English Catholics of the highest rank:

> The number of Irish boys was about half that of the English. They were generally greatly inferior in station, though many of them were the children of the best Catholic gentry in Ireland. There existed among the natives of the two countries a strong rivalry, which was occasionally wrought up to animosity . . . The Jesuits themselves were all Englishmen, and I think that they occasionally exhibited that contempt for Ireland, which is exceedingly observable among the English Catholics who have not mixed much in the world (*114*, II, 305-6).

Relationships between Irish and English Catholics were generally uneasy and very often strained. English condescension and Irish assertiveness were a poor enough basis for a satisfactory alliance and now in 1823 the goals were diverging widely for the coming Catholic struggles. There were, of course, real links between Irish and English Catholicism — most of the doctrinal and devotional reading of Irish Catholics was, for example, produced by English Catholics. The two movements shared a liberal faith in the educability of the public mind and were sincerely attached to British constitutionalism. The Irish Catholic Association was, however, poised to develop into a mass democratic movement which would greatly overshadow its English counterpart.

The Catholic Association in Dublin received a great boost when Bishop James Doyle, of Kildare and Leighlin, published his *Vindication of the Religious and Civil Principles of the Irish Catholics* in October 1823. It appeared as a pamphlet and in extracts in the press.[21] O'Connell immediately seized upon this able tract as the manifesto of his new movement: in proposing a motion of thanks to Dr Doyle, he declared that it was the duty of the Association to pledge itself to the principles expressed in the *Vindication*.[22]

James Doyle had been educated at Coimbra University in Portugal but he drew on the English Whig political tradition and was especially fond of Locke; he clearly admired the Grattan-Curran-O'Connell tradition in Ireland and in his inaugural address to the rhetoric class in Carlow College he praised these three as the leading orators of Ireland (*36*, I, 54). Doyle admired the British constitution greatly, particularly in comparison with 'the forms of government which prevail in the countries where I have resided'. In 1822 he had issued a well-known *Address to the People* to wean people away from illegal associations but his *Vindication* was to have a comparable impact on the Irish Catholic movement as had Paine's *Common Sense* on the morale of the Americans in 1776. Doyle's short tract of seventy-one pages crystallised the political ideology of the Irish Catholics just at the significant moment when the Catholic Association was entering on a crucial debate about possible countrywide expansion. F. W. Conway, who as editor of the *Dublin Evening Post* was in some position to judge, declared that 'the *Vindication* made a greater impression on the public mind, perhaps than any writings since the days of Swift' (*36*, I, 281). By March 1824 over 8,000 copies had been distributed and some of its most striking passages were printed on placards and posted on the walls of town and village where they could be read aloud to admiring groups.

Doyle's pamphlet took the form of a letter to Wellesley, the Lord Lieutenant. He identified the real source of the Irish problem as being the 'state of the civil laws' as these 'generated' and shaped the 'dispositions of the people'. Irish Catholics, Doyle pointed out, were 'an afflicted people' of six millions with an historical experience comparable only to the Jews: indeed the Old Testament theme of Babylonian captivity runs strongly through the work. They sought admission to full equality under the Constitution '. . . as the Israelites sighed for their country, when on the banks of the Euphrates they hung their harps upon the willows and sighed, and wept, as they remembered Jerusalem'. Catholicism, he argued, was compatible with the liberties of the British Constitution which had their origins 'in Catholic times'. More recently Catholics had accepted the doctrine of the Glorious Revolution 'that the Crown is held in trust for the benefit of the people; and that should the monarch violate his compact the subject is freed from the bond of his allegiance'. He questioned 'the essential Protestantism of the Constitution' at a time when 'the whole civil constitution of Europe is new-modelled — the ideas of men have undergone an entire revolution . . .' Now, he declared, the 'essence of the Constitution is . . . to make all who live under it free and happy'. Significantly Doyle stated that it was the duty of Catholic priests, while counselling obedience to the authorities, never to cease

> whilst our tongues can move, or our pens can write, to keep alive in the whole empire, as well as in our own people a sense of the wrongs we suffer . . . Our fetters are too galling, our chains are too closely rivetted, our keepers are too unfeeling, for us to remain silent, or to permit them to enjoy repose.

Doyle shared with O'Connell a faith in progress through free institutions which was basic to the novel political thinking called liberalism. Like Thomas Moore, Richard Lalor Sheil and Thomas Wyse he was a liberal unionist who wished to make the union work on the basis of equal participation.

Bishop Doyle attacked tithes, all the penal restrictions upon Catholics, and the Protestant establishment, which he distinguished from the Protestant Church for which he professed admiration. He censured the conduct of the Irish gentry: Irish regeneration required the system of misrule be ended by a reign of equitable and just laws.

Wellesley's policy was to conduct 'the Executive Government of Ireland on principles of equity towards all His Majesty's subjects'.[23] Events had shown, during 1822, just how difficult an even-handed policy was in the Ascendancy-controlled administration of Ireland. Wellesley could not prevent his policy of 'conciliation' being perceived by Orangemen as the triumph of the Catholics over the Ascendancy. Orangemen became increasingly alienated from Wellesley's administation.

After the 'bottle riot' on 14 December 1822 a number of alleged culprits had been lodged in Newgate Jail. They were charged with conspiracy to riot but were acquitted by the city grand jury. Plunket then filed new charges of conspiracy to murder against six of them. The trial began in the Court of King's Bench on 3 February 1823 and lasted five days, ending in the acquittal of one and the disagreement of the jury in the cases of the other five. The jury was, rather predictably, dominated by Orangemen. O'Connell noted that the result would reveal to the Castle that 'it will be impossible to administer justice in Ireland' as long as the Orange faction subsisted (II, 996). While the Catholics rejoiced over White's victory in the Co. Dublin election, Protestants rejoiced over their victory in the courts.

Peel and the government in London, noting the rising party spirit in Ireland, were increasingly unsure about Wellesley's approach. On 22 February Peel wrote to Wellesley that London did not consider the 'bottle riot' to be as serious as he had himself:

> . . . we should conceal from you our real opinion if we did not attribute a considerable portion of the Jealousies, Discontent, and Party Violence, which have since arisen, to the light in which the Transactions at the Theatre have been viewed, and more particularly to the committal of the Parties concerned in them on a charge so grave as that of Conspiracy to Murder.[24]

Wellesley continued to lament that 'the great calamity under which Ireland now suffers' was 'the bitterness of party, & the perverse rejection of all means of mutual conciliation . . .'[25] The new Catholic Association could only increase party divisions; Goulburn remarked to Wellesley on 5 May, that it 'would have certainly been far more agreeable in the present circumstances & temper of Ireland not to have had to contend with or to observe such a body'.[26]

The Orange movement, in fact, was not in a particularly vibrant state in the early 1820s, having split on organisational matters (*115*, 198-9). The general thrust of government policy in the revision of the magistracy, in the introduction of stipendiary magistrates who were independent of local politics, and in organising a new constabulary force, diminished Orange influence in key areas where they had always held power. Parliamentary attention was focused on Orangemen in Ireland when Plunket responded to charges that his actions against the Orangemen involved in the 'bottle riot' had been unconstitutional. An enquiry was held into the conduct of Sheriff Thorpe, first cousin of one of the accused, who had selected the jury which had failed to find the conspiracy charge proved. Though this enquiry did not establish definite Orange interference with justice in Ireland it focused attention on the administration of justice and on the Ascendancy-dominated legal system. Some parliamentarians, like Joseph Hume, became tireless enemies of the Orange lodges, of which there were about 340 active in Ireland.

O'Connell's policy was to take advantage of the rift between the Orangemen and the Castle. On 12 June 1823 several people were killed in an Orange affray in Maghera, Co. Derry. John Lawless raised in the Association such incidents connected with Orange marches in the North which 'dealt death and havoc among the unarmed peasantry'. Some in the Association thought that these matters were not properly within the objects of the Association but O'Connell and Sheil supported Lawless in publishing such cases.[27]

In July 1823 Orange parades were subdued and there was no celebration in Dublin; there was a clash between Catholics and Orangemen in Co. Armagh which resulted in one person's death. In July the government passed an Unlawful Oaths Act directed against all secret societies including Orangemen. This resulted in the Orange Order being, in effect, dissolved and reconstituted on a new basis as Orangemen feared being placed outside the law. Under the new system the Orange lodge administered no oath but members were admitted after presenting evidence that they had at some time taken the oaths of allegiance, of supremacy and of abjuration. As many were concerned about the legal position, the autumn and winter of 1823-4 were spent in efforts to place the lodges definitely within the law. Local lodges continued to function but without the protection and direction of an effective Grand Lodge. By March 1824 the Grand Lodge, with Charles Henry St. John O'Neill, first Earl O'Neill, as Grand Master, Colonel Pratt as Grand Treasurer and James Verner as Deputy Grand Master was finally in a position to offer leadership.

The problem Orangemen faced was that demonstrations such as those on 12 July were essential for the morale and indeed the *raison d'être* of the movement but these frequently resulted in violence, and violence would now provoke legal action against the movement. Friction over policy on such matters existed between the Ulster Orangemen and the Grand Lodge of Dublin. In the spring of 1824, all forthcoming 12 July demonstrations were banned by the leadership though local processions could not be completely controlled.

O'Connell's fledgling body was allowed to grow and take flight during 1823. This resulted from the alienation of Orangemen from the Castle, their fear of becoming illegal and the government's unwillingness to smash the new organisation.

The government no longer reflected ultra-Protestant attitudes in its Irish policy. Ultra-Protestants feared the re-establishment of the Catholic religion as the predominant religion in Ireland and they were only prepared to think of 'conciliation' when Catholics knew their place under the Protestant Constitution. Thus it seemed to Lord Redesdale, a staunch upholder of Protestant Ascendancy in Ireland, 'madness to suppose that the Protestants of Ireland will submit to be restrained from commemorating the battle of the Boyne and their deliverance by William. . . . It is the watchword of their safety' (*20*, III, 263-6). The Orange or ultra policy was to make a stand for the Protestant Ascendancy in Ireland and to resist both Catholicism and liberalism. On 27 July 1823 Redesdale condemned liberalism in a letter to Charles Abbot, Lord Colchester:

> Liberality is the word of the day. That word produced twenty years of confusion and misery in France: it threatened Italy, Spain and Portugal, and produced much mischief in all those countries. It still threatens France; it annoys Germany; it has spread into Russia, and it is seriously threatening the British Empire with the overthrow of all its ancient institutions, by which it has hitherto flourished' (*20*, III, 300-1).

In contrast to these typically reactionary sentiments O'Connell relished 'the spirit of national independence and the love of liberty' evident in the struggles in Spain and elsewhere in Europe; indeed he believed in March 1823 that

> War would be *useful*, very useful to Ireland. The English cannot go to war without emancipating *us*. They cannot go to war without a general reform of abuses, without a revision of contracts — in short, without doing justice to all parties . . . the times are big with events of the deepest magnitude (II, 1002).

It was just such an eventuality that Redesdale feared; he believed that Ireland must be governed with a firm hand — if necessary 'open war' would, he felt in October 1823, be preferable to the 'secret war now carried on' (*20*, III, 302-5). Orangemen and ultra-Protestants were, of course, aware of the grievances of the peasantry but they maintained that Catholic Emancipation would not provide redress: moral regeneration of the people through scriptural education and spiritual conversion would prove far more effective.

Numerous societies such as the Hibernian Missionary Society, the Bible Society, the Irish Society and many others strove to convert the Irish people from the errors of popery: local missions and public confrontations with priests occurred throughout Ireland as the 'New Reformation' gathered momentum. Increasingly relations between Catholics and Protestants were charged with bitterness and indeed mutual incomprehension. Even moderate and liberal Protestants were incredulous when Dr Doyle, Bishop of Kildare and Leighlin and Archbishop Daniel Murray, the new Catholic Archbishop of Dublin, lent their support in pastoral letters to the concept of direct supernatural intervention in everyday life in June and August 1823. Doyle and Murray were perhaps the most liberal members of the Catholic hierarchy and the bishops most likely to attempt to lead their flocks towards a peaceful accommodation with the Protestant churches.

The occasions for Doyle's and Murray's pastoral letters were the 'miraculous' cures on two women wrought, it was said, by the agency of Alexander Emmerich, Prince of Hohenlohe, a German priest and supernatural healer. One woman had suffered from loss of speech for six years and the second, a nun, had been both paralysed and unable to speak. Both Doyle and Murray were criticised, by Protestants, for encouraging popular superstition and ignorance in order to keep the Catholic Church's ascendancy over the people.

Robert Peel, as Home Secretary, was anxious to moderate extreme views, especially among Protestants. This was, he thought, the best way to maintain Protestant privileges as he explained to Gregory, the Under-Secretary in Dublin Castle, on 5 April 1823:

> No man can feel more strongly than I do the absurdity of attempting to compel harmony and good-will by law. But depend upon it, in this age of liberal doctrine, when prescription is no longer even a presumption in favour of what is established, it will be a work of desperate difficulty to contend against 'emancipation', as they call it, unless we can fight with the advantage on our side of great discretion, forbearance and moderation on the part of the Irish Protestants. If the worst should come to the worst that forbearance and moderation will not have been thrown away' (*107*, I, 341).

The real strength of Irish Protestantism, in Peel's view, was the conviction in England that its cause was just. As a member of the cabinet, Peel was increasingly aware of the liberal drift, notably in economic and foreign policy, after the reconstitution of Liverpool's government in 1822.

'Discretion, forbearance and moderation' was just the opposite of what many Irish Protestants believed necessary. The foundation of the tri-weekly *Dublin Evening Mail* by Timothy Haydn in February 1823 is evidence of this: Haydn was a great publicist, though erratic and unscrupulous, and the *Mail* was soon 'scurrilously anti-Wellesley and anti-Catholic' (*54*, 171). Within a year it had a circulation nearly three times as large as any other Dublin paper: Protestants obviously relished Haydn's cartoons, squibs and contentious editorials. Later Wellesley's apologist wrote:

> A new paper called the *Dublin Evening Mail* was established by [the Orange] Party for the professed object of defending the Protestant ascendancy, but really for the purpose of writing down Lord Wellesley's government, and not a single number of that paper has been published without a personal attack upon his private or public conduct (*3*, III, 299).

Irish Protestants were strident because they had become acutely aware of the precariousness of their position.

The government's attempts to reform the collection of tithes in Ireland during 1823 worried both the Church of Ireland and the Protestant landholders. Tithes were a tax paid for the upkeep of the Established Church which weighed most heavily upon the poorer tenants: grasslands were exempt from tithes which were paid exclusively upon tillage, a concession to the grazier and landlord interest which was clearly unjust. Charles Grant, the former Chief Secretary, graphically explained to the Commons on 22 April 1822 the oppressive manner of tithe collection in Ireland which he described as a process of 'continual molestation of the farmer'. There was a long history of violent resistance to payment in rural areas.

During 1823 resistance to tithes was widespread, especially in the south of Ireland.[28] The Catholic Association was able to exploit the tithes question because of the widespread hatred and bitterness among Catholics who had difficulty enough paying county cess, rent and other taxes besides having to pay tithes to the Established Church in addition to their dues to the Catholic Church.

The debate on Irish tithes raised the issue of Church property and the extent to which it should be subjected to state direction. This was a delicate question with great implications for Church property in England and so it had to be gingerly handled by Goulburn, who as Chief Secretary brought forward the Irish Tithe Composition Act in July 1823. This act presaged the great ecclesiastical and political battles which were to rage for many years in British and Irish politics. The object of Goulburn's Act was to allow for the assessment of the amount to be paid in tithes in an equitable manner and to have this collected without exposing the people to the vexing proceedings of the tithe proctor. The composition of tithes was, under the Act, to be agreed upon by special parish vestries held on the application of the tithe owner or of five landholders occupying land of £20 value. Two commissioners, one representing the owner, the other the vestry, were to agree the sums to be paid by the whole parish and by each of the inhabitants according to the extent and quality of their land. The sums were to be arrived at by simple agreement or by taking the average annual amount paid for tithes during the seven years from November 1814 to November 1821, or by calculating a rate based on the corn prices during the same period.

The act made provision for voluntary composition only. An amending act in 1824 laid down that compositions reached by mutual agreement were to last twenty-one years while those based on prices and averages could be changed every seven years. Where composition was agreed it was to be paid on pasture as well as on arable land. Over the next seven years, the act was used to make compositions in over half of the 2,450 Irish parishes. The effects of the measure were politically important: clerical incomes were brought very much into the forum of public discussion and gradually a more wealthy and powerful class of farmers were enmeshed in the tithe question as pasture became liable under composition. The most flagrant abuse of the old system by which tithe proctors, paid by percentage and often open to bribery, would value crops in good years by quantity and in scarce years by price, became increasingly discredited. The act, however, had not solved the problem of peasants and tenant farmers paying dearly for the upkeep of a Church they increasingly disliked for its proselytism. Many local disputes continued to erupt.

On 9 September 1823 as the funeral of Arthur D'Arcy, a Catholic, was proceeding in St Kevin's churchyard, Dublin, the sexton of St Kevin's Church rudely interrupted Archdeacon Michael Blake to forbid any Catholic prayers in the Protestant cemetery. All cemeteries were in Protestant hands but by custom Catholic priests had recited their prayers at the funerals of their parishioners in these cemeteries. A storm blew up immediately and Archbishop Magee was blamed for the sexton's behaviour. In the Catholic Association O'Connell condemned the Protestant minister who claimed churchyards as his 'freehold': 'could he plough it and sow it? – would this be as productive as *sowing Papists*'? Moreover, this cemetery yielded nearly £2,000 a year to the minister in fees paid by Catholics. A Committee of the Catholic Association recommended in November the formation of a burial committee to purchase land for Catholic burial grounds and some years later Goldenbridge and Glasnevin cemeteries were to be opened. Meanwhile O'Connell advocated a peaceful but determined assertion of the right to say Catholic prayers at funerals: 'Let the friends of the deceased peaceably surround the priest and the body during the service; let any violence which may arise come from the preventing parties, and then the individuals to whom that violence may be used will have a distinct right of action, or may proceed by indictment against any persons who use force' (*34*, 2-7).

The Catholic burial issue and the tithes question were ideal grievances for the Catholic Association's running attack on the Irish Church establishment: they revealed the inherent injustice of the Protestant Ascendancy over the majority of the people. O'Connell declared, as he took up the tithe question in the Association, that '. . . no measure of the Catholic Association was likely to give such general satisfaction as a petition upon the subject of Tithes'.[29] A committee was appointed to inquire into tithes and at a meeting, in late December 1823, O'Connell gave a long considered analysis of Goulburn's Tithe Act, in the course of which he attacked the validity of the Act of Union which he held was a 'swingling Act' which was getting worse 'the older it grew'.[30]

O'Connell had met some resistance to his new approach from the beginning within the small body of members who attended the Association. Gradually the moderates, who feared that exposing all Catholic grievances would alienate Protestants who favoured Emancipation, were forced to withdraw or to go along with O'Connell and Sheil. It sometimes was very difficult to proceed with meetings so sparsely attended: few wanted to become involved in a continuous and systematic political mass movement. Debates on strategy were, however, increasingly important. On 1 November O'Connell had given notice of motion 'for the appointment of a Committee to extend the Association to every County in Ireland from whence an appeal for the redress of grievances – a petition – might be prepared and sent'.[31] O'Connell was now about to add the third crucial element in his new strategy: a mechanism to crystallise his policy on issues and grievances and on the admission and role of Catholic priests in the Association.

At this stage the government believed that the Association was dull rather than dangerous and that it was likely to fade from existence: it had been a nuisance rather than a threat to the established order. O'Connell prudently did not proceed with his November notice of motion to extend the Association until late January 1824. He had to convince a small number of key people to support him, and the meeting on 20 December could not proceed, despite O'Connell's reluctance to obey the rule, as there was no quorum.[32]

But by early January the Catholic leadership had returned to the attack. Sheil made a stinging attack on the administration of justice in Ireland: he attacked the government and deplored the condition of the Irish peasant. 'The common negro enjoys more practical liberty than the wretched Irish peasant, oppressed as he is by the landlord – by tithes and a Grand Jury cess . . . the philanthropists of England pity the state of the African and yet were insensible to the condition of the Irish peasant . . .' He went on to develop the theme of the 'astonishing similarity' between the state of Ireland and that of the South Americans struggling for national independence. He did not wish for separation between Ireland and England but he warned the government of 'the example of South America'. This speech was similar to O'Connell's later and more famous 'Bolivar' speech of December 1824. It implied the threat of separation and violence if grievances were not redressed by the government. Members were immediately alarmed at the tone and content of Sheil's oration; one member, Kelly, deprecated the way Sheil applied all the misfortunes of Ireland to the conduct of the administration:

It was a dangerous thing to disseminate among the people, the starving population of Ireland; he denied its truth; the over-population
and other causes had created the evils — improvident habits of the
landlords, the exorbitant rents, agents, middle-men, etc. occasioned
them . . . many who thought if Catholic Emancipation took place
there would be no more distress in Ireland were mistaken.[33]

Sheil restated his vision of the Association at the following meeting.
They were engaged, he believed, in 'the great work of liberation' and
giving a 'lesson in manliness'; the Catholic Association was not 'the substantial cause of the exasperated state of the national mind . . . but one
of the channels through which its abundance finds a vent . . .' The
Catholic Association, he declared, was sprung 'out of the national
wrongs. It is born of the public grievances.' Again members disagreed
and subsequent meetings were rancorous and disorderly. One member
argued that the Association was not formed 'for the discussion of
national grievances. Such was not the fact. It was formed for the purpose of seeking for *Catholic Emancipation*.' It was necessary to have
'tempered moderation in the discussion of their disabilities'.[34]

By the end of January 1824, a year after the organisation was first
planned, O'Connell was anxious to proceed with definite steps which
would connect the small body of activists in Dublin with the mass of
the Irish people. At this stage attendance at meetings ranged from
below ten to about thirty; these were usually joined by spectators;
many nominal members had not paid their subscription — in February
1824 there were 177 members with about fifty paid up for that year.
O'Connell let it be known that he was about to bring foward 'a proposition of great importance as well as novelty' and 'that an alteration
in the mode of managing their affairs should be adopted'.[35] This advance
publicity ensured for the meeting on 24 January a more numerous
attendance than any 'since the formation of the Association'.[36] The
government reporter noted thirty members and about thirty to forty
spectators at the meeting. Kirwan, a newspaper reporter, proposed at
this meeting that letters should be sent 'to the Catholic nobility, sons
of peers, and all who had been members of the former board' inviting
them to become members of the Association. O'Connell countered this
by arguing that

. . . Some steps ought to be taken — every parish in Ireland should be
applied to, and enquiries made in them to know how many are disposed to become members; this should be done — not by letter but
by private application . . . Every Catholic in Ireland should become
subject to Monthly Rent until Emancipation be granted; if a Rent or
even a penny a month from each were collected it would show England
that they have a deep interest in that measure . . . they then indeed

would represent the public voice and guide the public opinion . . .

Thus, as a barometer of public opinion, did O'Connell introduce his most striking innovation in political technique. Kirwan's plan was, he declared 'too narrow' and he proposed that a committee of nine be selected 'to devise the best method of enlarging the Association'. A debate took place on the alternative strategies.

The origins of the rent idea went back at least to 1811 when the Protestant, William Parnell, grandfather of Charles Stewart Parnell, wrote to Denys Scully with a scheme to 'call every nerve & sinew of the Catholic body into action by quarterly meetings of all the *Parishes* throughout Ireland'. According to Parnell it would be easy to call such meetings, to control the people, and to give 'union to the Catholic body' by raising 'generally & annually a very small voluntary contribution, if only a penny from each labourer, a shilling from each farmer & five from each gentleman' (*95*, 32-3). O'Connell recalled to the meeting on 24 January 1824:

> About the year 1812 he [O'Connell] had himself proposed, and had set on foot a temporary subscription, and in three parishes alone, he had collected seventy-nine pounds, which had gone into the funds of the Catholic Board. The collection would then have been continued under a regular organisation but that miserable disputes arose between what were called the Catholic aristocracy and the Catholic democracy and upset everything. No such result should occur now (*92*, II, 277).

O'Connell argued that the Association should have a fund 'for proceeding with such legal measures as might be found expedient for the attainment of their Emancipation'; each Catholic should pay a monthly sum 'from one penny up to two shillings' to show their interest in the cause. He stated that each parish might be visited 'or better modes might be adopted' to extend the Association.

Sheil seconded O'Connell's proposal; he argued that the 'great power' of the Catholics 'consisted in an immense mass of discontented population'. He supported O'Connell's view of the Association as a defender of 'the persecuted peasantry'; the rent would show that the '. . . proceedings of the Association had the sympathy of the public mind, that the sentiments expressed . . . had the full concurrence of the people'. He pointed out that already the Association had the support of wealthy Catholics; he named those in the room – Nicholas Mahon, Michael O'Brien, David Lynch, Cornelius McLoughlin and others – whose wealth was 'proverbial in the City'. The Association should now hold public meetings in 'the great Catholic towns of the South' where the 'moneyed interest' would also support them. Sheil noted that the success of their proceedings 'depended on the propriety of the manner adopted, and the full accordance of the national mind'. Kirwan argued that he did not see 'how the sympathy of houseless, starved wretches would serve the Association'. He was anxious to see amongst the members such men as Lord Fingall. However, O'Connell's motion was carried and the committee selected.[37] O'Connell, Sheil, McLoughlin, Mahon, Kirwan, Clinch, Coppinger, and Conway were selected, as well as Fitzsimons and O'Gorman, the chairman and secretary at the meeting.

The difficulty in implementing the novel scheme was illustrated the following week when, to O'Connell's 'considerable vexation' only six members turned up and the meeting had to be adjourned. It seemed certain that the Association would collapse before long unless the newly appointed committee could use the novelty of the rent proposal to galvanise the membership into action. Indeed, the Association was so far gone with apathy that on 4 February, the day on which O'Connell was to outline fully his complete plan for the enlargement of the Association, he had to struggle to keep the meeting in being by sending his clerk down into Coyne's bookshop to bring up three or four priests who were there; eventually there were fourteen or fifteen members present of which five or six were priests.[38]

O'Connell began by explaining the legal position of the Association and the necessity for raising funds. The printed Report of the Committee 'appointed to devise the best mode of raising a general Subscription throughout Ireland', which was published two weeks later, further outlined the political conditions whereby the Catholics had no hope 'of immediate success' unless the new plan was put into operation.[39] O'Connell explained that the plan he was about to unfold '... had long occupied his mind; it did not however originate with him but was taken from a letter published by Lord Kenmare — grandfather to the present Lord — in the year 1784 ...' Kenmare had proposed a subscription to raise £1 from each of the 2,500 parishes in Ireland. O'Connell declared that his new plan 'was infinitely more comprehensive' than this. He used population estimates to show that it would be possible to raise over £100,000 from Catholics, but he would aim to collect 'at least the sum of £50,000' every year: 'How easy', he declared, 'if only one million paid one penny per month or one shilling per year'. This estimate was based on eliciting a response from about one-seventh of the Catholic population of Ireland. O'Connell outlined the five purposes to which the £50,000 ought to be devoted.

First, it was to be used to forward petitions to parliament 'not only on the subject of Catholic Emancipation, but for the redress of all local or general grievances afflicting the Irish people'. A parliamentary agent was to be paid in London and £5,000 was to be spent under this head. Secondly, £15,000 was to be used 'to procure legal redress for all such Catholics, assailed or injured by Orange violence, as are unable to obtain it for themselves'. The printed Report refers to Orange violence 'principally in the North' and to 'Orange murderers'. Thirdly, another £15,000 was to be spent 'to encourage and support a liberal and enlightened press' in both Dublin and London in the Catholic interest. The Report referred to 'the irresistible force of truth' and thus the value of publishing 'the real principles of the Catholics'; O'Connell in his speech attacked the Irish press as being '. . . possessed of no honesty, no integrity, no principle'. Fourthly, £5,000 would be given 'for the education of the peasants' children' and further sums would be made available for 'erecting schools, building Catholic Churches, and erecting and furnishing dwelling-houses for the Clergy in poorer parishes, and ameliorating in other respects, the condition of the Catholic Clergy in Ireland'. Finally, £5,000 would be spent on supplying priests for Catholics in North America.

The objectives, outlined by O'Connell, were clearly designed to appeal to the people by offering palpable benefits in the form of publicity and legal redress with respect to their grievances. Conway later told the Association, in June 1824, that the people 'would become more anxious' to collect and subscribe 'in proportion as they should be better acquainted with the motives of its collection'.[40] The Report in February stated that 'The purposes for which pecuniary resources are wanting, should be clearly defined, and distinctly understood; they should be useful in their objects and strictly legal and constitutional in all their details'. The appeal to the Catholic clergy was very marked. The educational issue was one of the first issues which the Catholic Association was to use, early in 1824, to secure the active support of the priesthood. It was not proposed that the priest ought to be the key activist, merely that from each parish a committee of collectors would be appointed 'with the privity of the Catholic clergymen'; the priest would facilitate the publication of subscriptions at the chapel and vet the collectors.[41]

In his speech on 4 February O'Connell outlined the details for collecting 'The Monthly Catholic Rent' in each parish; he stressed the advantages of the plan which would, through constitutional means, show a 'compactness never seen before' and Catholics might 'also be enabled to get the means of being represented in Parliament'. He ended his speech by proposing two further committees of seven – one to consider the means of increasing the Association and the second to collect subscriptions and to report on 'the best plan' for collection in the various parishes. Significantly, O'Connell and Sheil were the only two to serve on both committees; their importance to the Association and the new strategy may be gauged from the fact that the very next meeting of the Association, on 7 February, could not proceed as both were absent.[42] Their leadership, especially that O'Connell, was decisive.

The Rent Report of February 1824 met considerable opposition within the Association. By the beginning of March Mary O'Connell wrote to her husband that she was 'quite out of patience with the opposition to you from Nick Mahon and his honoured nephew [Nicholas Purcell O'Gorman] . . . It is exactly such mean, paltry Catholics . . . that have kept the Catholics as they are these years back. Sheil, I perceive, is now always with you' (III, 1107). One member queried what the supply of priests for North America had to do with Emancipation.[43] Other, like Mahon, objected to the 'angry expressions' in the Report as much as to the plan itself. Mahon found it 'imprudent and rash in the extreme, to use no stronger terms, to adopt that Report hastily, and without due deliberation'.[44] Efforts were made to prevent it being printed. O'Gorman declared that the Report was the work of O'Connell alone and that it was never read to the Committee as a whole.[45] As a result of the nervousness of the moderate members the Report was printed as the Report of a Committee of the Association and signed by Daniel O'Connell; it was not issued as a policy declaration or plan of the Association as a whole and some phrases were changed to tone it down. On 18 and 24 February O'Connell managed to get the necessary resolutions agreed to implement the plan; a Finance Committee was also established. With very considerable foresight he told members that the Rent would 'set them to business' and that it would give them 'practical work' to do instead of engaging in long speeches.[46]

In the space of a year the basis for transforming the outlook of Irish Catholics had been laid; Sheil told a meeting of the Association on 27 February that he did not foresee 'Emancipation from the expectancy of any change in the sentiments of the British government, but he thought that such a mass of population possessed a power which must at last make its way and ultimately burst thro' the gates of the Constitution (*huzzas*).[47]

2

1824:
'The Grand, the Wise, the Noble Plan'

'One penny each month, is your just due,
Collected by some faithful brother
Then why should Patrick's friends refuse
In this grand plan to assist each other'.

Ballad
'The Catholic Rent or Catholic Freedom', 1824

Henry Goulburn wrote to Robert Peel, the Home Secretary, on 16 November 1823 with an assessment of the ailing Catholic Association: it appeared to the Chief Secretary that this nuisance in Dublin was about to disappear because of lack of interest amongst the members (*113*, 15-16). Yet within a year, Canning was telling Peel that the collection of the Catholic Rent had turned the Association into 'the most difficult problem that a Government ever had to deal with' (*107*, I, 345). The Church of Ireland Bishop of Limerick, John Jebb, wrote on 19 November 1824:

> Throughout all parts of Ireland the Catholic Association is omnipotent; its mandates are respected as much as the Acts of Parliament are condemned. In any district or parish the Catholic Rent needs only to be proposed, and it is hailed with acclamation . . . There is what we of this generation have never before witnessed, a complete union of the Roman Catholic body . . . In truth, an Irish Revolution has, in great measure, been effected' (*113*, 22).

How had this 'Irish revolution' occurred so swiftly?

On 18 February 1824, O'Connell, by a whole series of resolutions, established the framework of the Catholic Rent scheme. O'Connell was appointed secretary and James Sugrue, who acted as O'Connell's informal financial agent, became assistant secretary, responsible for the collection of the Rent throughout Ireland. The Association was empowered to open accounts with all the parishes, to appoint collectors, to receive monthly reports of progress in each parish, to publish the names of subscribers to the Rent, to appoint a Finance Committee and Treasurers. It was to audit and publish the accounts annually.[1]

The next four or five months were spent in laying the groundwork throughout Ireland for the collection: no steady contributions for the Rent flowed from the counties until June and July 1824.[2] Some scattered sums, especially from Dublin, were paid in by May. O'Connell arranged an aggregate meeting of Catholics in late February to ratify the new scheme. Later that day he wrote to his wife about how it had gone: 'Sir Thomas Esmonde took the chair. I never saw any meeting go off better in every respect. Stephen Coppinger made an excellent speech, so did Sheil. I spoke for full two hours . . .' (III, 1105). Within nine months — from June 1824 to March 1825 — the Rent gave the Association a fund of almost £20,000.[3] Before its collection the funds of the Association consisted of £179 in the hands of the Treasurer.[4] As Gregory observed to Peel on 11 April 1824 it was 'the most efficient mode that could be devised for opening direct communication between the popish Parliament and the whole mass of the Catholic population' (*113*, 18).

The experience of the first few months spent organising the collection modified and altered the mode of collection as set out in the February Report. Wyse notes that, at first, the collection was 'awkward and ill-organised; the amount fell far below the calculations of the proposers'. However, by the summer and autumn of 1824 the Rent collection had 'settled into a system' (*132*, I, 208-9). Two of the resolutions, proposed by O'Connell on 18 February, relate to the amount which was to be paid as Catholic Rent. The amounts are relevant to a consideration of the social composition of the support given to the Association. One resolution, following the February Report, set out that the amount of each subscription should be not less than one penny but not more than two shillings per month. 'All I ask is one farthing a week from one-sixth of the Catholics. Who is it that cannot afford a farthing a week? Yet it would make more than £50,000 if collected', declared O'Connell: he reckoned on small contributions to make the Rent a success (III, 1096). However, another resolution declared that the guinea paid by each member of the Association would form part of his subscription to the Catholic Rent. Also one general account of money subscribed was kept and, in practice, any amount of money was received as Catholic Rent. This made it difficult to extrapolate from the subscriptions of the parishes or towns either the number of subscribers or their social position. O'Connell had visualised a two-tier structure of supporters with members paying a guinea and associates paying a penny a month.

By early March O'Connell had the printed Report ready for general distribution throughout Ireland. He maintained that there could be no money collected until the Report was circulated and the organisation in each parish completed. O'Connell proposed that the Association ascertain the number of parishes in Ireland and the names of the parochial clergy who would approve the collectors. To make the legality of the measure clear he said that the names of the collectors might also be made known to the magistrates and the government. He made it clear that he saw the priests as the 'zealous guardians' of the Rent collection and he pointed out that the Rent would put down 'secret associations' as the people would be 'made sensible that there was a channel through which they would obtain permanent relief'. O'Connell repeatedly warned of the dangers of any connection between Ribbonmen and the collectors of the Rent.[5] He pointed out that through the channel of the Rent the Catholic Association would be 'informed of every local grievance that occurred in every part of Ireland . . .'

The earliest organisation of collectors took place in Dublin: O'Connell told a meeting of the Association on 3 March 1824 that twenty-four members of a confraternity had offered to collect Rent. In Waterford, a Roman Catholic society called the All Saints' Society, with eighty members 'of the working class' contacted the Association with an offer to help collect the Rent. O'Connell wrote to all the Irish Catholic bishops in early March to seek their support for the collection; he sought from them a list of the parishes in each diocese and the name and address of each parish priest (III, 1108). He also visited Bishop Plunkett of Meath and reported confidently to his wife '. . . on Sunday I travelled to Navan . . . and [spent] the day with the bishop, a very fine old gentleman of the age of eighty-six, and met a large party of his clergy. I made a harangue to the people in the Chapel and set the penny a month subscription going. It will succeed' (III, 1109). Rent started to flow from Meath in August on a regular basis.

The Rent collection very quickly became a vast operation. The Finance Committee of the Association sent huge numbers of the printed Reports, in broadside form, and great supplies of collectors' books, to most parts of Ireland. The government reporter at the Association's meetings noticed 'great piles of paper in an inner room and in the Association front room were two piles of Reports; one of them was labelled '10,000 Reports'.[6] By 20 March James Sugrue had available two types of printed books for the collectors of the Rent in each area, one an elaborate hardback ruled book and the other a simple soft-covered ruled book. These books were to be used to record the subscribers' names, the date, residence, parish and other details. Sugrue told the Association that 2,500 books would be required – one for every parish – and 1,000 were ordered to be printed forthwith. By the end of March three Catholic bishops were reported to have returned the list of parishes and priests required from their dioceses.[7] By early May O'Connell told the Association that almost all the bishops had sent a list of priests and the post towns adjacent to them. In August Edward Dwyer, the newly appointed Permanent Secretary, was requested to write to such bishops as had not responded. He prepared county and diocesan lists and sent out Catholic Rent books as the details were returned.[8]

A dramatic indication of the rapidly growing power of the Catholic Association in 1824 is indicated in the changed behaviour of Archbishop Curtis, the Catholic Primate. On 18 May 1824 Bishop Doyle published a public letter in the *Morning Chronicle*, warning the government not to rely on 'the exertions of the Catholic Priesthood'; he predicted that if 'a rebellion were raging from Carrickfergus to Cape Clear, no sentence of excommunication would ever be fulminated by a Catholic Prelate'. On 2 June Curtis wrote to Wellington, with whom he had co-operated during the Peninsular War, to condemn Doyle's 'eccentric and wild production' which had caused 'an extraordinary sensation'. Doyle will be 'put down', Curtis assured Wellington, and 'very soon, if the aggressor himself does not come forward and make speedy, full, and sincere atonement for his error'; what gave most pain to Curtis was that 'the letter in question must be offensive to government'. Curtis described how he had been 'a silent spectator' of the Catholic Association:

> They have not been joined by the chief Catholic aristocracy, or by any one of our prelates, at least so far as to go to their assemblies . . . the principal men among them were lawyers of some reputation . . . In these meetings intemperate speeches were often made that disgusted moderate men, who thought them improper, and even ill calculated to obtain the reliefs they called for . . . Petitions, complaints, and claims, however true and just in themselves, may become illegal and criminal by the improper language and manner of preparing and presenting them to government or to the legislature.

Curtis said he had cautioned the Association to this effect but even that 'gave some offence but was not without effect' (*128*, II, 272-4). On 4 June 1824 there issued from Maynooth a document, signed by five of the theological professors, setting out the Catholic position on civil obedience in response to the controversy aroused by Dr Doyle's public letter: 'we have uniformly inculcated allegiance to our gracious Sovereign, respect for the constituted authorities, and obedience to the Laws.' It was nicknamed 'the Sorbonne manifesto' because of the influence on it by Professors de la Hogue and D'Anglade, emigrés from revolutionary France who had been appointed to the Maynooth College staff. Sheil says that it was 'well understood' that the students and even the President of the College, Dr Crotty, did not agree with this declaration and that it was 'laughed at by the Irish priesthood': the reputation of Dr Doyle 'was more widely extended by this effort of antiquated divinity to suppress him' (*114*, II, 186-8). Doyle succeeded in rallying his fellow bishops to support the Catholic Association.

On 13 November 1824, O'Connell read a letter from Archbishop Curtis expressing approval of 'the temperate proceedings of the Association' and of the Rent scheme. Curtis recommended the Rent to the patronage of the clergy.[9] Curtis felt the need to explain his changed attitude to Wellington in a lengthy letter on 6 December:

> When the Catholic Association first began to meet in the course of last year, the Catholic nobility, gentry, prelates, and principal people refused to join them or frequent their meetings, that were long neither numerous nor respectable; their views were little known or minded, and very few imagined they could be of any real use for obtaining the popular measure of Catholic emancipation, or any other redress . . . Thus they would have immediately subsided and dispersed, were it not for the Orange Faction, who having first, by their violence, forced them to meet, by their daily increasing enormities and avowed inimical principles, gave them a consistency and importance that they could never otherwise have acquired, or even now retain for a moment.

Thus, according to Curtis, this 'lawless, bigoted, unrelenting faction', which hated all Catholics, gave the Association 'a fair pretext' and the Association was totally 'averse from all revolutionary or seditious dispositions' (*128*, II, 361-4). However, it was not 'the Orange faction' which had caused Curtis to change his mind between June and November: the Orange faction had been there before June 1824. The manifest support of Catholics, as demonstrated through the Rent, forced the primate to do the political thing and row in behind O'Connell. Later, on 17 December, Curtis wrote again to Wellington to assure him that he often remonstrated with the leaders of Association 'particularly on their Utopian proposal of having the Parliamentary Union of both nations dissolved and the odious mention of making common cause with the English Radicals for obtaining a radical Parliamentary reform' (*113*, 49). Curtis was attempting to keep the Catholic Church in good odour with his highly placed contact while still unable to resist the rising tide of popular and clerical support for the Association.

The co-operation of the hierarchy was essential to the Rent scheme and in November O'Connell, in gratitude, moved that £10 be allocated to each of the bishops for the purchase of religious tracts. This was accepted by the Association. By the end of 1824 O'Connell was able to claim 'the approbation of the entire Catholic Hierarchy' for the Catholic Rent.[10]

In March 1824 O'Connell and Sheil announced their intention of making 'every exertion on Circuit' to establish the Rent collection.[11] O'Connell's 'exertions' in March and April may be followed in his correspondence to his wife from Wexford, Waterford, Limerick, Tralee, Galway and Cork. These large towns and cities became key centres of support for the Rent and there is an obvious relationship between O'Connell's circuit practice and the developing heartland of his new mass movement. The meetings in the main towns during this circuit received widespread publicity in the press. At Wexford O'Connell had breakfast 'with a large party of priests' at the home of a wealthy Catholic (III, 1112). Catholics at Waterford held a public dinner at which Richard Lalor Sheil was guest of honour (III, 1113, 1125). O'Connell was drawn in triumph through Carrick-on-Suir; at Limerick he organised the Rent and spoke at a public meeting. He wrote to his wife from Limerick: 'This day I have been at home all day arranging business and writing letters on the subject of the Catholic Rent. It will certainly succeed to our heart's content. The effect will be truly formidable. It will secure the press in both countries . . .' (III, 1113). In his speech at Limerick O'Connell condemned Whiteboy activities, proselytism and the dispersal of a local Catholic funeral by the military at the behest of a Church of Ireland clergyman. William Finn told Mary O'Connell that it was 'exactly the kind of speech most calculated to make an impression on the lower orders' (III, 1118). The Catholics of Kerry held a meeting in Tralee chapel at which O'Connell's brother attended.[12] The Catholics of Galway held a meeting in the new parish chapel where O'Connell spoke for 'near two hours' and he concluded that he had a 'great triumph' (III, 1119). Sheil attended a Catholic aggregate meeting in Kilkenny which established the Rent in that city. Shortly afterwards a County and City committee was active in Kilkenny in receiving 'communications from the country parishes' from May to September 1824.[13] The Catholics of Cork held an aggregate meeting which was according to O'Connell 'the Greatest' he ever had seen: 'I spoke for two hours and made, they say, a *beautiful* speech . . .' (III, 1119). A public dinner was also held in Cork in O'Connell's honour.

Clerical support was essential to the success of the collection. The leaders of the Association attracted this support through use of the controversial issue of education. An MP, John Henry North, provided a ready pretext. North attacked the Catholic clergy of Ireland because he claimed they had neglected the education of the Irish peasantry and he implied that the priests desired to keep the people ignorant. His speech was made in support of the efforts of the Kildare Place Society of which he had been a member.[14] Early in April F. W. Conway, the editor of the *Dublin Evening Post*, raised North's speech at the Association.[15] It was an astute move politically. By assuming the defence of the Catholic clergy, Conway, at the critical stage in the organisation of the Catholic Rent, connected the Association to one of the great issues for Irish Catholicism and he opened up a remarkable correspondence between the clergy and the Association.

A week after the issue was raised by Conway, Bishop Doyle's letter, the first of many thousands of letters from priests, on North's speech was read to the Association. Doyle declared that North '. . . had made a mis-statement relative to Irish priests' neglect in educating the peasantry. In the counties of Wexford, Carlow, Queen's Co., and Kildare, a vast majority of the people under 40 years of age could read and were not indebted to the Kildare Place Society'. After discussion on Doyle's letter Conway proposed that a circular letter be sent from the Association to Catholic priests calling for a return of the schools in every parish in Ireland. The circular was published in the *Dublin Evening Post*, signed by Conway.[16] A very extensive correspondence flowed into the Association in response to the circular and the extracts from the priests' returns were published in the newspapers and provided matter for debate in the Association. By the end of April Conway was reading out so many letters from priests relative to education that members questioned the practice as it was so time consuming. Conway replied that to the public in general, 'certainly to the Catholics of Ireland and the Catholic priesthood', the letters were more important than speeches from members. The following week, O'Connell urged the necessity of having the letters read and another pile were dealt with by Conway.[17] Education provided the necessary lead into the Association for the Catholic priesthood which had been largely uninvolved before these developments.

Both the purposes which O'Connell set out for the Rent collection and the defence of the priesthood on the education issue were well designed to stimulate the priests in the parishes where their main concerns were bound to be the provision of chapels and schools in a highly sectarian local context. In May O'Connell told the Association that, in the country, some priests had offered to use their utmost efforts in the collection of the Rent provided the Association allowed them to allocate 'to their own schools and other establishments' one half of the amount received in the parishes. O'Connell advised the Association 'to acquiesce' in this.[18] Wyse observed how 'the cause of education became identified with the cause of emancipation.' It formed a principal object in the collection of 'the Rent'. There was under way in the 1820s a battle for the popular mind of Ireland, a 'tragic comic conflict' as Wyse described it: 'A flock was dragged one way, and then dragged another, into this fold and then into that: education was set up against education, school against school, teacher against teacher; and the whole intellect of the country was made the prize for contending hosts.' In June 1824 the government established a major commission to inquire into education in Ireland which reported first in May 1825 and issued the ninth and final report in June 1827. A major underlying issue in the Catholic struggle became increasingly exposed to parliamentary attention. The priest was motivated to support the Rent because he 'expected to see it return in its due season in the building of his school or the repairs to his ruined church' and thus he was '*personally* and *constantly* interested' in the Rent and in the politics and views of the Association and priests became 'the principal channel' which the Association used to communicate with remote parts of Ireland (*132*, I, 234-7). On 4 January 1825 Conway publicly commented in the *Dublin Evening Post* on how the progress of the Association had benefited from the actions of the more zealous Protestants:

> Two circumstances . . . occurred, which gave a new impulse to the Association – the ill-timed, insulting charge of Archbishop Magee, and the ill-considered but we are willing to believe, the not dishonest speech of Mr North against the Catholic clergy. The former necessarily roused the Catholic Bishops to the assertion of their religion; the latter compelled the Catholic priests to step in to the arena. The Association promptly seized on the occasion. They held out an invitation to the latter, which was as promptly answered.

Early in May the reception of the Rent scheme seemed so favourable that the Association decided to issue 'a cheap edition' of the Report setting out the Rent plan. A committee was established to do this. The actual mode of collection was still quite uncertain; O'Connell was anxious that there should be a secretary appointed for each county who would be responsible for the Rent collection. He had a motion passed to appoint thirty-two secretaries. Stephen Coppinger, a barrister from Cork, was appointed secretary for Co. Cork and O'Connell, according to the government report, sought others 'to take a County from him'.[19] These secretaries were 'to be residents of Dublin' and were to conduct the affairs of each county through 'the County Agents', the priests, and other contacts. Such secretaries were appointed for King's Co., Meath, Kildare, Waterford, and Dublin and Down. One member, an attorney called Martin Lanigan, declined to become Secretary for Tipperary though he was active in distributing rent books in the county. O'Connell was clearly trying to establish lines of 'speedy communication with all the parishes', and to share out the burden of dealing with the vastly increased business of the Association. He told the Association that Michael Staunton, who had agents for his newspaper *The Weekly Register* throughout Ireland, would forward the correspondence from the priests to Dublin.

The plan for county secretaries was not a success but was probably of some use in the early weeks when the Rent collection was being arranged and before a permanent secretary was appointed in July. Coppinger, for example, made a detailed report on the organisation of the collection in Co. Cork which became the most important county in terms of the amount subscribed.[20] By the end of June O'Connell saw that the secretaries plan was not working and that the secretarial burden required a permanent paid agent; there would be 2,500 accounts to be kept and there might be 25,000 letters to be answered. Early in July Edward Dwyer was elected Clerk of the Catholic Rent, defeating his only opponent by forty votes.[21] He proved a very capable and reliable full-time official and a devoted supporter of O'Connell. He acted as Permanent Secretary of the Catholic Association between 1825 and 1829. O'Connell and Dwyer admired each other greatly: O'Connell praised Dwyer's abilities in the Association concluding that '. . . no public body ever had a more active intelligent honourable or efficient officer'. O'Connell, wrote Dwyer, 'is a Wonderful Man, indeed, in my humble opinion, he is the greatest of the great . . .'[22]

The appointment of Dwyer and the use of newspaper proprietors and editors such as Staunton and Conway as channels of communication gave the Association a sound organisation upon which rapid expansion could be based. The newspapermen had both political and business motives in seeing the spread of their journals as a means of political communication. The work at the Association's headquarters had, previous to Dwyer's appointment, depended upon an 'open' committee of the members which had to meet daily to send out the Rent books and the copies of the Report to all parts of Ireland. The government reporter in early June noted the 'thriving state' of the Rent collection; he saw 'in the public shop below stairs piles of the "Reports" of the Association printed in the cheap form according to the copies he lately enclosed'. By the end of May 2,000 Rent books and 50,000 Reports were in circulation. By the middle of June 150,000 copies of the Report 'in a cheap form' were printed. The expansion of the Association's work and expenses were often criticised by some members, such as Kirwan, who had opposed the new strategy from the beginning.[23] In July, Kirwan proposed that priests who were not subscribers to the Association should not have a vote for the appropriation of its funds. Father L'Estrange attacked Kirwan's own contribution to the Association and O'Connell and others delivered speeches at a rowdy meeting in praise of the priests during which Kirwan was 'hissed'; O'Connell stated that one-third of the Rent had been paid in by the priests. This probably indicates the organisational importance of priests at this stage rather than the amount contributed by priests themselves.[24]

The Rent books were issued in the summer and autumn of 1824 at the rate of about a thousand a month. At the end of September another thousand books were ordered to be printed. In October the government reporter noted that 'A number of large parcels containing quantities of

Reports, Catholic Rent Collection books, etc., were prepared on the table and directed to a great many different parts of Ireland'. By this time, as the *Post* observed, the Catholic Rent measure was 'in full operation' and the success of the foundation work laid since the early spring was marked by the receipts of the Rent. In early August 1824 the Association adjourned until October but the Finance Committee continued to meet.[25] From September the Rent was averaging well over £400 per week; frequently it was almost £1,000 per week and in one week in November it was over £1,000.

The national pattern which emerged from the 1824 Catholic Rent collection was to remain for the rest of the Emancipation struggle and indeed throughout O'Connell's career in popular politics. Greatest support came from Leinster and Munster which subscribed £3,254 and £3,364 respectively; relatively little came from Ulster and Connaght, £446 and £509 respectively. Within these provincial totals for 1824 there were very significant variations: the importance of large urban centres, Dublin, Kilkenny, Waterford, Cork, Galway, and Limerick, was obvious from the figures. Co. Tipperary, with substantial towns such as Clonmel, Cashel, Nenagh, Roscrea and Thurles, was the third strongest contributor of Rent after Cork and Dublin. Wyse recalled that the Rent 'was first organised in the towns; it then spread, though slowly, to the neighbouring parishes and from thence, by degrees, to the most remote parts of the country' (*132*, I, 209).

At the local level there was much variety in the system of collection. In some parishes collectors volunteered and formed a committee. The parish or town was divided in districts which in turn were split into walks in each of which two collectors made the rounds. The parish of St Munchin's in Limerick was divided into six districts and two collectors were appointed for each.[26] As the system improved in some areas, especially in the larger towns, the activists took rooms and held weekly meetings to report progress and communicate with the Association. They also discussed 'every subject of public policy' according to Wyse: 'In the towns, the consequences were very conspicuous. The Rent proceeded rapidly; and with it a corresponding passion for political discussion, which pervaded every body and every class of society . . . But the country parishes continued more or less inert' (*132*, I, 209). Examples of meetings and discussion accompanying the Rent on a fairly continuous basis may be found in Waterford City and in counties Tipperary and Kilkenny. In Kilkenny deputations from the Catholic Rent Committee attended the chapels of various parishes in the county to organise the Rent and appoint collectors.[27] The reports of local developments in the newspapers were important as these provided encouragement, example, and a channel of communication for the activists. In some places a monthly Rent Sunday was fixed and the Rent was collected at the door of the chapel. There was no uniformity imposed on the method of collection or indeed, in many parishes, any great regularity in the return of receipts. The collection depended on local political activists including often the priest or curate responding to the Catholic Association policy of publicising local grievances or issues such as education. Many of the 'grievance' letters which survive from the parishes make it quite clear that the Rent collection was firmly associated with the securing of help from the Association to deal with particular grievances. Also visits from the leaders of the Association were important in stimulating the local response especially in the towns where the 'subsidiary association', which, as Wyse noted, accompanied the Rent, was easier to organise and where political awareness was so much more advanced.

Cork city and county subscribed the greatest amount of Rent from any county in the first phase of the Rent collection which ended in March 1825 (see Map 1). In early April 1824 a large aggregate meeting of Catholics was held in Carey's Lane chapel in order to prepare a petition to parliament and to establish the Catholic Rent. A committee of twenty-one was appointed and Jeremiah Murphy, Esq. of Hyde Park and Stephen Coppinger were chairman and secretary respectively. A number of men who became prominent in Cork politics, such as Thomas Lyons, took part in this committee; 900 subsequently signed the petition in favour of Emancipation. The Association was requested by the Cork Committee to allow them to apply half of the Catholic Rent to charitable purposes as '. . . it would induce the priesthood of this County and City to take more lively and decided part in its collection . . .' Clonakilty had a Catholic meeting in the chapel to establish 'The Monthly Rent' and according to the report 'all the Catholic property, intelligence and industry of the Town and its vicinity were present'. In June Clonakilty sent £10 in Rent which had been collected from a very poor parish in a comparatively short time. In early May Youghal held a Catholic meeting in the chapel with Richard Fitzgerald of Muckridge House in the chair. By the end of June the local secretary, John Markham, had sent £13 Rent even though the great proportion of the Catholics were poor 'especially at this season of the year'. Kanturk had a meeting of the parishioners in April with Father Edward Nagle in the chair. Nagle made a return to the Catholic Association with respect to education.

A local Catholic Committee was established in Kanturk with T. P. Vaughan as secretary. Vaughan sent a subscription to Conway for the *Dublin Evening Post* '. . . for the purpose of diffusing through this parish a more extended knowledge of the state of Catholic affairs, and

TOTAL CATHOLIC RENT FROM EACH COUNTY
IN FIRST PHASE 1824 — MARCH 1825 (TO NEAREST £)

SOURCE: DUBLIN EVENING POST — 27 APRIL 1826.

LONDONDERRY £144

ANTRIM £138

DONEGAL £76

TYRONE £66

DOWN £240

FERMANAGH £73

ARMAGH £113

MONAGHAN £195

SLIGO £165

LEITRIM £148

CAVAN £792

LOUTH £689

MAYO £293

ROSCOMMON £166

LONGFORD £168

MEATH £665

WESTMEATH £527

DUBLIN £1953

GALWAY £636

KINGSCOUNTY £549

KILDARE £567

WICKLOW £175

QUEENSCOUNTY £257

CLARE £429

TIPPERARY £1648

CARLOW £239

KILKENNY £750

WEXFORD £504

LIMERICK £548

WATERFORD £739

CORK £2825

KERRY £382

BY PROVINCE:	
LEINSTER	£7043
MUNSTER	£6571
ULSTER	£1837
CONNAUGHT	£1408
	TOTALS

thereby forwarding more effectively the objects of the Catholic Rent'. Mallow also had a meeting in the chapel and a local committee of fifteen was appointed to organise the Rent. Walter Dennelvey, the secretary of the Fermoy Catholics, wrote to the Association in June to say that they had appointed fifty-five collectors in the extensive parishes of the area. The city parishes and other areas such as Kinsale, Buttevant and Cobh were returning rent in July. In July the Catholics of Bantry held a meeting at the chapel which was very crowded; many were 'obliged to remain the chapel-yard'. The Bantry committee sent deputations to neighbouring parishes to organise the rent 'in these extensive parishes'.[28]

Thus, in a matter of months, Co. Cork was well organised from Bantry in the west to Youghal in the east and from Kanturk and Buttevant in the north to Bandon and Clonakilty in the south. The city parishes were also very active. Another aggregate meeting was held in late August in Carey's Lane Chapel and Sheil told it that the Catholic Rent was '. . . in various ways eminently beneficial, but in nothing so much as in the very mode of its collection – it called forth the exertion, the opinion of what was called the lower order of the people'. Co. Cork outstripped every other county in the level of Rent returns every month from June 1824 to March 1825 and in this period collected £872 more than its nearest rival, Dublin.

Rent collection in Dublin was sluggish until the autumn of 1824: various isolated offers and schemes for the collection were suggested in March 1824 but none were very successful. By August the lack of response in Dublin was a matter of concern in the Association. One member declared that the trifling sum collected in Dublin '. . . was a proof of the coldness and apathy of the people of Dublin towards the Catholic Rent'.[29] Attempts had been made to organise some Dublin parishes. O'Connell spoke at a meeting of the united parishes of St Mary, St Thomas and St George in July, declaring that: 'The first object of the Catholic Rent was to enable them to petition on general and local grounds. No act of oppression should occur from the Giant's Causeway to Cape Clear, but they should drag it before parliament'.[30] The interest of the Dublin parishes in the redress of local grievances was not perhaps as strong as in other areas. At a meeting of the parishes of St Peter and St Mary, an attorney called Dolan pointed out that while '. . . the leading object of the plan of the Catholic Rent was to procure justice for the people and redress of grievances', this was not so necessary in Dublin as justice was more readily obtained; there were more grievances in the country.[31] The *Post*, noting that 'the Rent languishes in Dublin', stated that this was '*solely* the fault of the collectors'.[32]

One possible explanation of the comparative slackness in the Rent is that the Dublin organisation failed to evoke as much priestly enthusiasm as manifested elsewhere. In October 1824 Edward Dwyer was directed by the Association to prepare a circular to be sent to the parish priests of the Dublin diocese soliciting their support for the Catholic Rent by having meetings called and collectors appointed. Dwyer would supply Reports, books and other requisites for the collection.[33] The Rent started to flow in the autumn when the parishes began to meet to organise it. At least sixteen parishes met and at these meetings a great number of rent collectors were appointed; for example, forty-four were appointed at a meeting in the parish of St Michael and St John.[34] Cork had surpassed Dublin in every month except March 1825 when a special effort was made in Dublin to get in all the Rent before the dissolution of the Association. A special meeting of the collectors of Catholic Rent in Dublin was called and Coppinger told them that they should adopt the Cork practice of having a person appointed to collect in each street. According to the government reporter the attendance at this meeting was 'principally of the working class of men . . .'; at a similar meeting the following week 'the great majority appeared to be needy tradesmen'.[35]

Outside of the main cities and counties where the bulk of the Rent was collected what was the immediate impact and who was involved? In Co. Longford, for example, where the actual amount subscribed was relatively small, did a local organisation evolve? The first response in Co. Longford to the Catholic Association's Rent plan came in September 1824, six months after the adoption of the Rent Report. A letter from a Mr Richard Dempsey announcing the adoption of the Catholic Rent and requiring collection books was read at the Catholic Finance Committee. Dempsey had a house in Bridge Street, Longford and in a contemporary directory is named among the gentry living in the town; he was a £50 freeholder.[36] The Catholics of Longford held a meeting in early September in the chapel and according to one hostile eyewitness 'it was composed of all the Huxtermen, Publicans, and petty fellows of the town and country'.[37] After this meeting Christopher Carbry, of Longford town, corresponded with the Catholic Finance Committee. Carbry was an extensive local businessman; he had Grocery, Spirit and General Merchandise premises in Main Street, Longford and, like many of the local shopkeepers he owned some land and was registered as a £20 freeholder and later as a £50 freeholder.[38] Dempsey and Carbry were to be in the forefront of the local Catholic struggle in Co. Longford for many years and represented the urban middle and well-to-do class which provided the local leadership in popular politics.

In October the first returns from Longford to the Catholic Rent fund were made when £11 was sent in; in November the Rent collection spread to other areas of the county. George Dowdall, a well-to-do £50 freeholder, chaired a Catholic Rent meeting in the parish of Shruel at Ballymahon where a committee of ten was appointed and the last Sunday in every month was fixed for the Rent collection. The Dowdall family were engaged in milling and farming on an extensive basis: George had over 200 acres in various parishes and his three brothers also had smaller farms. All four brothers became involved in local political activity.[39] The total rent for 1824 from Co. Longford was slightly over £50, a very modest figure in the context of almost £9,000 subscribed nationally. However the Rent collection was of paramount importance in developing a local parochial and county organisation which was in regular correspondence with national headquarters in Dublin.

In 1825 Co. Longford Catholic organisation developed quite rapidly. More parishes adopted the collection of the Catholic Rent and the first County Meeting of Longford Catholics took place. By early January Abbeyshrule and Carrickedmond parishes had been collected and they sent over £11 to Dublin. Michael Newman sent £10 for the parishes of Ardagh and Moydow. Newman was a £20 leaseholder and a fairly well-off tenant of Sir George Fetherston, the anti-Catholic MP in the county. Rev. Farrell Sheridan, curate of Granard parish sent in the sizeable sum of £31. Sheridan became a notable local political activist in the Granard area. He wrote to say that his parish enjoyed 'perfect tranquillity' despite efforts to excite 'false alarms'. There is evidence of considerable 'Protestant' opposition to the Rent Collection in the county: F. W. Conway read an extract from a letter from a Longford priest to the Catholic Association: 'My parish is small and the people very poor, but they would have cheerfully paid their mite, had not Col. Irwin Thompson, and Mr Crofton, of Longford, openly and determinedly opposed the collection'. Despite landlord opposition the Rent Collection in the county strengthened. Father Richard O'Ferrall, the parish priest of Killashee, who became very active in politics, sent £9 8s 2d at the beginning of February. Carbry was able to send another £7 2s 0d. Rev. P. O'Reilly sent £14 10s 0d from the parish of Columbkille; he was noted for political activity and as a builder of a church and school. He appears to have been held in special regard by the people. Other parishes, such as Rooskey on the borders with Roscommon and Street on the borders of Westmeath, sent in Catholic Rent. Father James O'Donoghue, parish priest of Edgeworthstown, sent the small sum of £2. O'Donoghue represented the older generation of priests; Maria Edgeworth described him as '. . . good in his kind and after his fashion – a good Catholic and a good man, keeping faith and Christian fellowship with Protestants instead of denouncing them from the altar as heretics . . .' (*99*, 487-9).

The total Catholic Rent sent in by Co. Longford between January 1825 and the dissolution of the Catholic Association in March 1825 was £118 3s 6d which compared favourably with the £50 3s 7d sent in between September and December 1824. The total Catholic Rent of over £168 from Co. Longford in the first phase of the collection which ended in March 1825 was not very impressive in a national context: there were only nine other counties with a smaller total and Louth, for example, sent in £689. But at least half of the Longford parishes had begun to be oriented to the Catholic Association and had sent in Catholic Rent and this gives the collection its great significance: it provided the framework for the politicisation of the county.

What expectations were held by Rent subscribers and by local leaders as they responded to O'Connell's appeal? The Catholic clergy clearly responded to the lead given by Dr Doyle and other bishops on issues raised by the Association, particularly education. The Catholic middle class responded to an organisation which they increasingly saw as being effective in securing them a greater share of local power and influence. The 'grievance letters' which were sent to the Catholic Association illustrate through local and often individual cases the expectations held by less fortunate social groups amongst the Catholic population.[40] From these letters it is evident that help from the Association, or personally from O'Connell, in rectifying the grievance was expected in return for rent subscriptions. The Association in 1824 and early 1825 had a policy of paying the legal expenses of specially assigned attorneys to defend cases throughout Ireland. The 'grievance letters' graphically illustrate the often defenceless and isolated condition of the poorer social groups who were in the grip of the Protestant established order in the local community.

The Association publicised the abuses in the administration of justice in Ireland: the packing of juries, the partiality of the constabulary, judges and magistrates. It attacked also the tithes paid to the Established Church; the activities of Bible societies; the Kildare Street Schools and the Orange Order; the abuses of individual landlords. In July 1824 Charles Cavanagh, attorney, Randal Kernan, barrister, John Corcoran, attorney and John Bric, barrister, were each employed by the Association to represent it and other clients at legal inquiries and court cases; their fees are recorded in the accounts of the Catholic Rent. This became a most effective way of highlighting to local people the power of the Association and the value of the Rent: for example, on 16 August Andrew Jennings was paid £20 fees for 'carrying on Orange prosecutions at Newry, in the case of McEvoy against Weir, when the latter was found guilty and sentenced to twelve months' imprisonment, and also for defending Hacket against an Orange party at Down Sessions or Assizes'. Throughout 1824 O'Connell, whose opinion on such legal matters was always given free, dispatched attorneys William Ford, Thomas Dolan, Edward Murray and others to various parts of Ireland at the Association's expense to defend or prosecute in selected cases.[41] A priest in Tullow, Co. Carlow, told his parishioners in late August 1824 that Catholics 'now begin to know their rights more accurately and feel more acutely the sense of their wrongs'.[42]

The Association received many letters complaining about reprisals against those who were involved in the Rent collection or in Catholic activities. For example, two farmers had their houses broken open by a magistrate, Rev. Mr Huleatt, in Co. Clare and their priest, Father Sheehy, wrote to Michael Staunton complaining about this and other instances of arms searches by soldiers and police in his parishes in the neighbourhood of Scarriff: '. . . They know not in what manner they may have provoked his hostility except by their activity in the collection of the Catholic Rent which has excited the enmity and *loyalty* of all the ultras but especially of the parsons.' Sheehy enclosed half notes for £8 for the Rent; he begged 'an answer as soon as possible . . . when the other half notes will be sent'. He added a postscript to say that 'This Mr Huleatt is the person who ordered the police to fire on the hurlers last year and who had the honour of some notice from your paper'. O'Connell's note on the back of the letter says that each of the persons named in the letter had an action against the clergy-man and advised that they should get an attorney and the Association 'will have notices of action prepared'.[43]

Another example was the case submitted by the inhabitants of the parish of Clonalvey, Co. Meath concerning the custody of a young girl of a mixed marriage. When the girl was four years of age she had been taken by her Catholic uncle and brought up as a Roman Catholic. In November 1824, when she was thirteen, her parents took her back but six years later she went back to her uncle and refused to return to her parents. In order to be allowed retain custody her uncle billed her parents for her maintenance and schooling. Her father obtained a warrant and the police searched the uncle's home. The parishioners sought guidance on the legality of the search. O'Connell pencilled his opinion to the effect that the father was entitled to the custody of the child until she was fourteen years old if he got a *habeas corpus* from the King's Bench and he offered counsel if this action took place. The girl, he said, should not be compelled to go to her father and the uncle might take action for the search if the pursuit of the young girl was violent. Significantly, he offered to have the girl sent up 'with any [discreet] elderly female' to Mrs O'Connell of Merrion Square who would put her into one of the convents 'where young women of her class are educated' as in another year the girl could choose for herself. O'Connell thus came perilously close to advocating the abduction of the girl to Dublin when her legal custodian was her father.[44] But cases like this reflected the grim sectarian context in which the response to the Association was made.

O'Connell and the Association leaders continued to receive shoals of 'grievance letters' in the years subsequent to the establishment of the Rent. Dealing with immediate local and often individual 'practical' grievances became an essential part of Irish popular politics. In this way the Catholic Rent was the catalyst which tranformed the popular political outlook: there was a new awareness of the context of local problems within the political system − the global demand for 'Emancipation' embraced all grievances and it was demonstrated that supporting a national agitation could be an effective means of redress.

O'Connell presented 'Emancipation' as the herald of a new order where the oppressive elements in the existing order would be eliminated. The 'spirit of legalised exertion' which he awakened created a popular political movement which was national in scope.[45] In February 1825 O'Connell wrote to his wife that the Catholic cause was '. . . daily gaining ground, and gaining it in the best way upon the popular mind. The people are becoming better informed on the subject of the Catholic claims and Catholic religion (III, 1176). O'Connell assumed the mantle of 'Deliverer' of the people from their oppression and through the Rent he united the Catholic Association with a mood in popular tradition which was permeated with the theme of far-reaching change. There was a widespread anti-Protestant millenarian strand in popular Irish Catholic culture in the early 1820s: O'Connell assumed a messianic role in the eyes of many of his lowly supporters who were convinced of the utopia which 'Emancipation' would announce. Once local immediate grievances, such as tithes and high rents, were connected to a great national political demand of an ill-defined character it was easy to believe in deliverance from all grievances. Eighteen twenty-five was foretold in *Pastorini's Prophecies* as the year of Catholic triumph over Protestant oppression, and as 1824 proceeded the scare of a Catholic rebellion grew more widespread. O'Connell displaced Captain Rock as the focus of popular hopes.

The Rent was presented to the people as the agent which would rectify all grievances and to this extent it brought a degree of utopianism into popular parliamentary politics. Goulburn in the autumn of 1824 was reporting to Peel the change in the political outlook which was evidenced amongst the people. In November he forwarded documents '. . . of somewhat an alarming character as they tend to show that there exists among the lower orders an expectation of some great event which is likely soon to occur of which when it occurs will be very favourable to the interests of the Roman Catholic religion . . .'[46] He sent some songs in particular which were circulating 'in different parts of the country' and he believed that these 'rather follow than lead the public taste'; Goulburn viewed the songs 'as some, though not the best, evidence of the disposition of the people'. One of the songs was on 'The

Catholic Rent or Catholic Freedom' which lauded O'Connell, unity among Catholics, and praised the Rent 'the grand, the wise, the noble plan':

> One penny each month, is your just due,
> Collected by some faithful brother
> Then why should Patrick's friends refuse
> In this grand plan to assist each other.

The Rent was to 'restore' the 'ancient rights' of Catholics. Raftery, the blind poet, also celebrated the Rent and advocated paying it to secure Catholic victory over the Protestants:

> I shall praise ye for ever if ye pay the Catholic Rent
> It is very little on us in the month is a farthing a week,
> And do not earn for yourselves scandal or shame (*52*, 115-23).

O'Connell tapped the collective folk memory of the Catholic people who longed for reparation of historical wrongs. This was far more potent and popular than demanding abstract prescriptive rights, as had Theobald Wolfe Tone back in the 1790s. Goulburn obviously viewed 'the new and complete organisation of the country with the Roman Catholic Association at the head of it as very formidable'.

The response of the people to the Rent showed the government the strength of feeling evoked by O'Connell's approach. Warburton wrote to Goulburn that the collection of Rent at Ballinsloe Chapel came to £20 and '... the poorest individual gave *silver* – there was not one penny of copper money in the collection'. Poor people in parishes made sacrifices in order to subscribe, as Father Corbett of Kilrush told the Association. 'Priest Corbett' was noticed by Goulburn in his correspondence to Peel for 'his zeal'. Similarly Father Duggan sent £10 from 'the wretched parishes of Moyerta and Kilballyown' where distress was prevalent and the people were counselled to rely on the Association.[47] Father O'Reilly sent £41 2s 9d from the half parish of Crosserlough, Co. Cavan, collected in December 1824 and 'the petty trader, the poor farmer already taxed beyond his means, the industrious weaver struggling to support a numerous family, the more indigent journeymen and wretched cottier' vied with each other in contributing to the Rent. The bulk of the contributions came from the quite substantial tenant farmer with about twenty acres and from the rural artisan class. Of the eighteen subscribers who sought membership of the Association in this letter from Father O'Reilly, fourteen can be identified: Peter Reilly, miller, farmer, eighteen acres; Mathew Boylan, publican, farmer, five acres; Francis Boylan, farmer, twenty-two acres; Terence Conaty, baker; Peter Callery, farmer, twenty acres; John Fleming whose father had seventeen acres; John Galligan, farmer, thirty-four acres; Patrick

Heally, aged twenty-two, son of a labourer; John McParland, wheelwright, farmer, four acres; John McCabe, farmer, twenty acres; Patrick Mulligan, chandler; Peter Sheridan, baker, farmer, fifteen acres; Thomas Smith, son of a farmer with twenty-six acres; Bryan Smith, son of a farmer, sixteen acres (*24*, 218-19). It was subscribers such as these who provided the sinews of power for the Catholic Association.

At the end of 1824 Richard Willcocks, the Inspector-General of Police, reported on the state of tranquillity in counties Cork, Waterford, Tipperary, Limerick and Kerry which formed his district. His report is revealing and important because his district was very significant in terms of the Catholic Rent collection, including as it did four of the most important counties in the whole country for rent subscriptions. Willcocks ascribed the tranquillity to the Insurrection Act, the Constabulary, the revision of the magistracy, tithe composition and the establishment of petty sessions – to good government in fact. He felt that the Catholic Association threw 'a cloud' over this improvement with '. . . the collection of the Catholic Rent, which has been very generally collected . . . and even from the meanest peasant . . . these circumstances have much agitated the minds of the farming and higher, as well as the lower classes of the Roman Catholics . . .' Willcocks stated that 'something is expected' by the people 'in return for the payment of the Rent' and he believed that 'the lower classes' looked 'entirely to their priests as their Agents to the Association for the fulfilment of their expectations whatever they may be . . .' He felt that priests had 'unbounded influence over the great mass of the population'; that they could 'in a great degree direct their movements in such a way as they may deem most advisable to obtain their ends . . .' This influence was achieved 'very lately' and he attributed it 'to the close connection' that the priests had with the Catholic Association 'and the exertions they use in the collection of the Catholic Rent . . .'[48]

In July 1824, in evidence to a Parliamentary Committee, Willcocks had charged that the younger priests in Limerick were not so anxious about tranquillity as they ought to be. This led the bishop, Dr Tuohy, and the priests of the diocese to hold a meeting to contradict this charge. The bishop issued a pastoral vindication of his priests and sixty-two priests signed the resolutions of the meeting which were widely publicised in the press. They argued that, since the only support they had was from the people, they had a vested interest in order and industry.[49] Warburton, the police magistrate, in his evidence in 1825, argued with more force that it was the Catholic Association which 'produced the tranquillity of the country in combination with the clergy' and that this demonstrated the influence and power of the Association.

He also felt that the Catholic Association gave the priests 'a much greater control than they otherwise possessed'. (*132*, I, 206). The Association undoubtedly fostered the influence of the priest in local affairs. Priests were ex-officio members; their sanction was sought for the Rent collection; episcopal approval for their participation was announced; and they were, especially in rural parishes, the local agents to whom the Association turned for assistance. However the key local leadership was drawn from prominent merchants, lawyers, shopkeepers and professional groups in the towns and from the better-off farmers in rural parishes. It is reasonable to see the fairly uniform and widespread support given by the priests to the Catholic Association as part of a total response by the whole Catholic community to the new strategy of the Association (*97*, 308-13).

The expectations of the people noted by Willcocks were also observed by others. George Drought wrote from Limerick to Goulburn in November 1824 that while his area was quiet '. . . the minds of the great mass of the people are kept . . . in a constant state of fermentation and big with expectation, that some great event is about to take place which the never ceasing activity of their priests and leading men of that persuasion to collect the Catholic Rent is too well calculated to increase'. Similarly the Chief Constable of Rathkeale reported his area free from outrage 'but the minds of all are agitated with the proceedings of the Association . . .'[50]

The Catholic Rent initiative in 1824 was decisive in transforming the prospects of the Catholic Association. By October 1824 the rapid changes in the Association's scope and force were clear to the government. It was now permanently staffed by Dwyer and two paid secretaries. The rooms over Coyne's bookshop had proved much too small for the now weekly attendance of over a hundred. At first the Picture Gallery of the Royal Arcade on Usher's Quay was used: there were about 350 present for the first meeting here on 16 October 1824. The following week there were five hundred. For the next

> All the avenues to the Picture Gallery were crowded to excess. The place reserved for spectators presented a dense and almost impassable mass of beings of all creeds and origins. Beyond the railing there were an unusually large number of the Catholic clergy, together with many Protestant Gentlemen and Ladies. At three o'clock, Mrs and the three Misses O'Connell entered the room. They were received with three distinct and enthusiastic rounds of applause.[51]

The crush of the crowd was so great at this meeting that a temporary gallery gave way. There was also an attempt by Trinity College students to break up the meeting. In November the Association took up what proved to be permanent quarters in the Corn Exchange, Burgh Quay. Here there was a large meeting room as well as offices and committee rooms, with an adjoining hotel which served as a sort of club for the members. The meeting room, an oblong hall with benches in the manner of the House of Commons, could accommodate between 600 and 1,000 people. It was to be O'Connell's Irish 'parliament' from 1824. Outside there was O'Connell's informal guard – the coal porters – whose stand was opposite the Corn Exchange. Trinity College students or others intent on disruption would have to reckon with these loyal partisans.

The Rent was the foundation upon which the future strength and work of the Association was based: it developed political consciousness and raised it to a national level, giving the Irish people a decisive parliamentary orientation. The Rent spawned all the educative measures and devices employed by the Association. Massive publicity, oratory and political meetings, the support of the priests, the gathering and articulation of grievances and the development of local political organisations all sprang from the Rent. Wyse later remarked that 'most of these measures were the children of circumstance; they were created by the moment, and were pursued from necessity' (*132*, I, 261). One speaker told the Catholic Association that 'the grand secret, the arcarium, the true philosopher's stone of Catholic politics had been ... at last discovered'. O'Connellite popular politics after 1824 always included a nationwide money subscription which provided funds for the movement but perhaps more importantly a barometer of public support for the policies being pursued. John Bric aptly described the Rent as a 'great truth-teller'.[52]

The Catholic Association used literary and oral means of political communication. The literary medium included the use of newspapers, both national and provincial, pamphlets, journals, placards, posters and other sorts of ephemera, such as ballads, on a vast scale. The oral medium was employed for mass mobilisation at political meetings both by the national leaders and by local activists. Newspapers carried detailed reports of the proceedings of the Dublin organisation and of the meetings around the country. The press was essential to such propaganda exercises as the education survey and the highlighting of grievances. Newspapers, especially editors like F. W. Conway and Michael Staunton, aided the vast postal communication network by publicising significant letters, petitions and addresses to the people as well as by helping to deal with the countrywide mail. At the end of 1824 Wellesley noted in a letter to Peel that the *Dublin Evening Post* had become the 'declared gazette' of the Association. He referred Peel to it for an account of the developments within the Association as it gave a better treatment of the events and progress of the Association than 'our manuscript reports of the proceedings' which 'are neither full nor correct'.[53] Wellesley also forwarded thirty-two issues of the *Morning Register* as background reading for Peel. The Finance Committee of the Catholic Association gave their imprimatur to the *Post* and the *Register* by deciding to print the full list of members of the Association in them.[54] The Rent enabled O'Connell to counter government subsidies to the press and thus it facilitated the revival of some degree of independence in Irish newspapers which could now attempt to be both profitable and popular.

A major feature of local political activity in the 1820s is the widespread desire to see local efforts recorded in the national press. In many parishes Rent Committees and collectors hired Reading Rooms where the people might gather to have the papers read. The people were obviously fascinated to see their local grievances and their local leaders mentioned in the newspapers. Tradesmen or farmers often grouped together to subscribe to a Dublin paper and then passed it from one to the other. A Co. Clare priest wrote in November 1824 to the Association: 'Wherever the newspaper is read, on a Saturday or Sunday, the young and the old will attend there, standing round the reader *erectis auribus*; the dance house, or whiskey-cabin, cease to have any charm for them whenever they can have a paper.'[55] The use made by the Catholic Association of the newspaper was but a part of their efforts to use the literary medium to publicise their ideas and to inculcate them into the popular political outlook. Not without good reason did the *Dublin Evening Mail* attack the Catholic Association in January 1825 as 'a permanent school for the inculcation of rebellion, bigotry, and falsehood'.[56] A great supply of political literature in the form of pamphlets, tracts, placards, addresses and other material was prepared and distributed. Polemical pamphlets recording proceedings at the Association, or at certain trials, or speeches of the leaders, supplemented handbills, broadsides, ballads and songs and major addresses to the people. In February 1825 it was even suggested that the Association ought to publish a monthly magazine containing a report of the debates and other material for general distribution.[57]

In terms of British and European politics the Catholic Association pioneered the widespread use of political meetings as the essential structure for a continuous mass popular agitation. Meetings were held at parish, county, provincial and national levels. In 1824, of the 140 parish meetings recorded in the *Dublin Evening Post*, sixty-one were in Leinster, forty-eight in Munster, twenty-seven in Connaught and seven in Ulster. These meetings mobilised the people and involved an impressive network of local leaders and committees. The parish meetings articulated grievances which were forwarded to parliament in a petition or to the Catholic Association by letter. In 1824 Irish Catholics petitioned from many areas on subjects such as burials, corporations, tithes and Orangemen. There were also many petitions in favour of Emancipation from towns such as Carrick-on-Suir, Clonmel, New Ross, Wexford, Limerick, Galway, Cork, Newry, Monaghan and Waterford.[58] This great use of public petitioning and grievance letters oriented the people to national and parliamentary politics: electoral consequences followed inevitably upon this mass political participation.

By October 1824 Goulburn had realised the electoral implications. He told Peel: 'It is not concealed . . . that whenever an election shall take place the people will be placed in opposition to their landlords and such members only returned as shall please the Association' (40, 389). As early as August 1824 the *Dublin Evening Post* had spelled out the possibilities inherent in the forty shilling franchise and how it had been successfully used in Co. Dublin.[59] In December 1824 Sheil announced that he would move on the first opportunity an address calling on Roman Catholic freeholders to register their freeholds and to give their votes at the coming election to no candidate who was not pledged to support Emancipation.[60] In January 1825 Kirwan moved that this address be prepared and that a committee should commence work preparatory to the next election but O'Connell had action on the franchise suspended due to his negotiations in London for Emancipation: the motion pressing the immediate registration of forty shilling freeholders was withdrawn at his request.[61] But the Catholic Association had already presented the government with a major anxiety.

During 1824 links with the pro-Catholic efforts in Britain were considerably strengthened by O'Connell and the Association. Important business of the Catholic Association was inserted in English newspapers at advertisement rates; certain pro-Catholic papers received subsidies from the Catholic Rent and later the *Truth Teller*, an English paper wholly devoted to the Catholic cause, was established.

In November, Eneas McDonnell was appointed the Association's London agent, his job being the maintenance of links with English Catholics and the organisation of the Catholic lobby at Westminster. The English Catholic Association formed branches amongst provincial Catholics in Manchester, Liverpool, York, Sheffield and other places. These local branches, like the Association in London, repelled attacks in the anti-Catholic press and supported the pro-Catholic propaganda effort. They helped organise petitions to parliament.

Thus there developed during 1824 a multi-dimensional pro-Catholic effort in both Ireland and England. One important dimension was that of literary endeavour in favour of the Catholic claims. In April 1824 Thomas Moore published in London his first important book of prose, the satirical *Memoirs of Captain Rock, the celebrated chieftain with some account of his ancestors*. Written in his triple capacity as a Whig, an Irishman and a Catholic, Moore produced a superb political 'tract for the times'. Under the transparent disguise of tracing the history of the Rock family, the leaders of popular disturbance in Ireland, Moore reviewed with bitter ironic power the history of English misrule in Ireland. He attacked the proselytising educational societies, tithes, and the Anglican Church 'as by law (and constables) established in Ireland!' His work, a most readable and comprehensive arraignment of mis-government in Ireland, created an immediate sensation and rapidly went into a number of editions; long quotations were carried in *The Times* and the *Morning Chronicle*. This angry indictment of the penal laws made a tremendous impact on educated English opinion, all the more so because of Moore's pre-eminent position in literary and liberal circles.

Moore had toured Ireland in 1823 and had been shocked by the misery and pitiful condition of the people. He wrote the *Memoirs* as, in effect, an historical vindication of the Irish people, drawing parallels between historical events and the contemporary situation. The main thrust of the work was that it was the rulers, not the ruled, in Ireland who required to be instructed and converted; that as long as the Catholic people of Ireland were refused justice so long would Rockism reign. Moore's facts and views were based upon recognised histories, parliamentary papers and such famous authors as Burke, Swift, Curran, Grattan, Bolingbroke, Milton, Molière, Hume, Spenser and Rabelais. Moore established in the minds of many the contours of the Irish his-torical consciousness succinctly captured in the quotation, 'You may trace Ireland through the statute-book of England as a wounded man in a crowd is tracked by his blood'. It was apparent from his work that moderation could not be expected from a people kept constantly upon the rack of oppression. He was very bitter against the Orange faction which he accused of 'manufacturing' Irish rebellions, such as 1798, '. . . the prompter's book and stage direction are still at hand in the archives of Dublin Castle, whenever an able Orange manager shall be found to preside over a renewal of the spectacle.' Moore's impact can be gauged from Lord John Russell's reaction: 'Success! Success! Your Captain is bought by all the town, extravangantly praised by Lady Holland, deeply studied by my lord, and has given all the Orangemen the jaundice with spleen and envy' (*113*, 83). Together with the advocacy of the Catholic cause in the *Edinburgh Review*, where Francis Jeffrey, Sydney Smith and Henry Brougham discussed the issue, the ultimate effect was to place the defenders of the Protestant Constitution even more on the defensive intellectually. In Ireland, where the work was greeted as a triumph, it was a major encouragement to the Catholic leaders at a delicate moment in the genesis of the Association.

One of the other important works widely distributed in Ireland at this time was William Cobbett's *A History of the Protestant Reformation* published, like Moore's *Memoirs*, in London in 1824. Cobbett and O'Connell were by now co-operating in publishing pro-Catholic propaganda (III, 1147). Cobbett challenged the popularly accepted version of the events of the Protestant Reformation. His interpretation of the events which led to the break with Rome and the Establishment of the Protestant Churches in England and Ireland was that 'it was an alteration greatly for the worse; that the "Reformation", as it is called, was engendered in beastly lust, brought forth in hypocrisy and perfidy, and fed and cherished by rivers of innocent English and Irish blood . . .' In Cobbett's view greed for the great revenues owned by the medieval Church had been the great motivating force behind the Reformation:

> They never told us, and they never tell us, that this Catholic religion was the only religion known to our forefathers for nine hundred years. If they had told us this, we should have said that it could not possibly have been so very bad a religion, and that it would be better to leave the Irish people still to enjoy it; and that, since there were scarcely any Protestant flocks, it would be better for us all, if the Church revenues were to go again to the original owners.

Cobbett's *History* traced the development of the Established Church from Henry VIII to the end of eighteenth century. He argued that parliament had the power to take away one church's property and tithes and to give it to another church, since it had done it before. This partisan and passionate work did an important service to the Catholic cause by combatting the predjudices of 'Protestant' history: it referred again and again to the great injustices suffered by the Catholic people in Ireland; a plea for tolerance and understanding for the Irish Catholic people ran through the book. It greatly stimulated and encouraged Irish Catholics.

Throughout 1824 the divided Irish government observed the rapidly developing Catholic Association. Wellesley felt by March 1824, 'without support or countenance' as he told Plunket privately, that he had 'to submit to the kicks of the ass and the dirt of the monkey': his responses to the dressing the statue of William III, the 'Bottle' riot, the Orange and Ribbon confederacies had not brought him any kudos on his 'mock throne':

> I am indeed most unhappy here — degraded, vilified, and object of scorn and detestation, without protection or even care; anxious to save the country; able to save it as far as relates to my own powers; frustrated, baffled, and betrayed by all my own agents; encompassed

by traitors even at my own table; the whole machinery of my own government working to my destruction; and in England not the slightest symptom of a disposition to give me support or credit . . . I pant for release (*110*, II, 145-6).

Redesdale told Colchester on 16 April 1824: 'The first effort of a wise Government should be to Anglicise and Protestantise Ireland . . . Conciliation is out of the question. Protestantism must be strenuously supported, or it will be lost in Ireland' (*20*, III, 323-4). Protestants could not imagine an accommodation with Catholics: they knew only victory or defeat. Wellesley's administration was assailed from the two sides – for truckling to Catholics by Protestants and for faint-hearted and dilatoriness in securing Catholic concessions by Catholics. Wellesley's manner, approach and policy was leaving his administration divided and stalled. The speed and novelty of the Catholic Association's rise in 1824 was completely unforeseen and Irish policy continued to drift throughout the summer and into the autumn.

By October and November a potentially revolutionary situation appeared to have developed and the military establishment of over 20,000 troops was reviewed, although not immediately augmented. The constabulary of over 4,000 men, also trained in the use of arms, was another instrument available to support the government should a real crisis occur. It took the government some time to realise that the Catholic Association's power was a new phenomenon and not in any way to be dealt with as 'Captain Rock' was dealt with. Force of argument, not force of arms, was the weapon of the Association. Yet the nagging worry always remained: could O'Connell, even if he wanted to, control the violent and volatile masses?

Something would have to be done, but what? Prosecutions would not lessen the influence of the Association but would perhaps help to remove the impression that the government connived at its activities. The existing law could be enforced but only if the Association violated it and evidence could be produced to justify a verdict in the court. New laws could be passed either of a general nature or specifically aimed at the Association. A general law would probably be evaded and any law would be subject to criticism as an attack on constitutional liberties. Peel wrestled with the technical difficulties of framing such a law, having become convinced of the need for a parliamentary declaration against the Association. But he realised that 'it may not drown such practised organs as those of Mr O'Connell and Mr Sheil' (*107*, I, 369).

Wellesley favoured a preliminary enquiry in a parliamentary committee before final decisions on fresh coercive legislation were taken. Peel favoured as strong a measure as possible on the authority of the government and on 14 December the cabinet agreed with this approach.

Peel, Goulburn and the legal advisers got to work on a new bill to be ready for parliament in February.

The government was thoroughly alarmed by the Catholic Association. Peel, in early November, was unsure of the correct response as he set out the options in a long letter to Goulburn raising the question of the need for a new law. Wellington had been very pessimistic in a letter to Peel on 3 November: 'If we cannot get rid of the Catholic Association, we must look to civil war in Ireland sooner or later' and though he believed the military could restore control he questioned whether they would be better situated afterwards: 'I think not', he concluded. The king threatened to withdraw his consent to Catholic Emancipation being regarded as an open question in the cabinet if the developments which 'may fairly be termed intended rebellion' were not checked in Ireland. Goulburn, very conscious of the real alarm amongst Irish Protestants, saw the danger more in 'a sudden ebullition of fanatical fury in particular places' than in a 'premeditated plan' (*107*, I, 346-53). Redesdale wrote to Eldon on 31 December 1824: 'If a revolution were to happen in Ireland, it would be in the end an Irish revolution, and no Catholic of *English blood* would fare better than a Protestant of English blood . . . and the great motive of action *will be hatred of the Sasenagh* [sic] . . .' (*124*, II, 530-1).

Then, at an Association meeting on 16 December, O'Connell made his famous 'Bolivar' speech. As reported next day in *Saunders' Newsletter*, O'Connell had 'hoped Ireland would be restored to her rights — but, if that day should arrive — if she were driven mad by persecution, he wished that a new Bolivar may be found — may arise — that the spirit of the Greeks, and of the South Americans may animate the people of Ireland!!!' The Irish government decided on the basis of this report to charge O'Connell with having uttered seditious language. They did so on 20 December without referring the matter to Peel. In London the Foreign Secretary, Canning, was proposing to recognise the new South American republics which had resulted from Bolivar's revolts. Canning was trying to secure the king's and the Tory party's consent to this. O'Connell's prosecution might point to an embarrassing contradiction if Bolivar's example was seditious in Ireland but worthy of recognition in the proposed treaty with Colombia.

To Peel the meaning of O'Connell's words were clear. He informed Wellington that they were merely code for: 'I hope the people will rise in arms against their lawful government'. Wellington saw more difficulty than Peel:

> Mr O'Connell is charged with sedition, by exciting the people of Ireland to rebel after the example of Colombia, and holding out hopes of their finding a Bolivar. The King says you must prosecute

this man in earnest. If you hold that the people of Colombia have been guilty of no crime, and that Bolivar is a hero and no rebel, then you ought not to prosecute O'Connell. If the contrary, then you ought not to make any arrangement with that country . . . we are going to bring rebel Bolivar and the rebel state of Colombia into diplomatic relation with his Majesty, at the very moment in which we prosecute Mr O'Connell for holding them up as examples to the people of Ireland (*128*, II, 383-6).

Peel believed it necessary to support the Irish government's actions however unfortunate and Wellington agreed, noting, however, that it was not the right moment to recognise Bolivar. 'We are in that happy state in Ireland', Wellington remarked to Peel on 30 December 1824, 'that it depends upon the prudence and discretion of the leaders of the Roman Catholic Association whether we shall have a rebellion there or not within the next six months' (*128*, II, 385). In Dublin another decision was taken, again without consulting the Home Office, to prosecute a prominent Orangeman, Sir Harcourt Lees, for calling on the Protestants in Ulster to arm themselves against Catholics.

On 3 January 1825 Plunket presented bills of indictment against O'Connell to the Dublin City Grand Jury. The press reporters questioned refused to co-operate and S. N. Elrington, the reporter for *Saunders' Newsletter*, replied that he had been asleep during O'Connell's speech and had only written what another person had told him. By a majority of 15 to 8 the Grand Jury threw out the indictment. The Protestant Grand Jury believed that embarrassing Plunket was more worthwhile than punishing O'Connell. If Plunket could not succeed in any prosecution perhaps he might be removed. Before the trial O'Connell had noted that Plunket was 'detested by everybody' so it would not be a surprise 'if the bills are thrown out' (III, 1147). The government was faced with a novel democratic organisation rather than a revolutionary movement. As Sheil pointed out in the Catholic Association, in Ireland, 'the rebel against the law would revolt against nature':

Providence appears to have pre-ordained the junction of the two countries, and without arms, without organisation, without concert, with nothing but an undisciplined multitude for the accomplishment of this object, what could the leader of a rebellion expect to achieve? And where is he, where is the Cataline, or rather the Spartacus, who is to head this servile war? Is he to be found among the wealthy burghers of the metropolis? Or are we to seek the great disturber among the Bishops of the Association? . . . Or is it my Lord Kenmare, with his fifty thousand a year, who is to shake the dire dice-box in this desperate game, and commit to the hazard of revolutionary confiscation? But perhaps, it is among the lawyers that this regenerator is to be found ... The lawyers! It might as well be imagined that we would pull down the dome of the Four Courts on our heads as to subvert a Government, in whose ruins we could not fail to perish.[62]

O'Connell would not contemplate rebellion and neither would his associates, with 1798 vivid in their memories. Admission to, not destruction of, the British Constitution was their goal.

3

1825:
'Events are not yet Ripe'

'I look upon the session till Easter as monopolised by the
grievances and distractions of Ireland'.

George Canning,
15 February 1825 (*49*, 394)

By late 1824, the Catholic Association had rivetted parliamentary
attention upon Ireland and Catholic Emancipation. Ireland was for the
Whigs 'the great object of our attack' (*87*, 178). This brought on a crisis
which threatened to smash the Liverpool government in the spring of
1825. Anticipating that the focus of action was switching to London,
the Association had already appointed O'Connell, Sheil and John Bric
to go there on a 'mission' to represent directly Irish Catholic interests.
O'Connell was still embroiled in the 'Bolivar' prosecution and the
delegation did not travel immediately.

The King's Speech in February, expressing 'ardent wishes for [the]
speedy annihilation' of the Catholic Association, made it clear that the
government was intent on repression rather than relief. On 15 February
a much larger deputation under O'Connell crossed over to London in
the hope of being allowed to defend their campaign for Emancipation,
perhaps by pleading their case at the Bar of the House of Commons.
This hope proved vain, but at least they were able to consult frequently
with parliamentary advocates of Emancipation. In his new guise of conciliator, O'Connell played a central rôle in the preparation of an Emancipation measure attractive enough to succeed in the Commons.

The government left the construction of the bill designed to suppress the Catholic Association chiefly in the hands of Goulburn. As an
extremist, Goulburn would have preferred a bill directed solely at the
Catholic Association but the government, wishing to appear impartial,
insisted it should apply to the Orangemen as well. On 10 February 1825,
Goulburn introduced his Unlawful Societies in Ireland Bill. It proposed
to make it unlawful for an organisation, such as the Catholic Association,
to exist and for meetings of Catholics or others to last longer than fourteen days. The bill was to be in force for two years with the possibility
of re-enactment. Goulburn would have wished it to be permanently on
the statute book.

In parliament the debate turned into a long discussion on the Catholic question. It proved to be the longest debate within memory on a bill which had been recommended in a King's Speech (*15*, III, 88). Goulburn attacked the Catholic Association because it evaded the Convention Act of 1793: it imitated the forms of parliament though it had not appointed a Speaker because, as Goulburn drily joked, no one was found in it who would be silent. Within the Association there was 'no competition of opinion: no opposing voice was heard' yet there were to be found in it men who had been 'familiar with the traitors of old times – Tone, Russell, and Emmet . . .' The Catholic gentry and aristocracy had been coerced to support the Association though they were really alarmed at it. The Catholic Rent was a tax outside parliament and the priests were used and abused in having to co-operate with its collection. It was however the interference of the Catholic Association with the ordinary administration of justice of which he mainly complained. The Association had poisoned the administration of justice with the bitterness of political discord: 'If the system was allowed to continue, a court of petty sessions in Ireland would be rendered merely a theatre for the exhibition of the talents of a Catholic Associator; and the magistrates composing it would be perplexed with subtleties having nothing to do with the real merits of the cases before them.' Goulburn pointed to an 'Address of the Catholic Association to the People of Ireland', issued in December 1824, as a libel on the legal system because it stated that the innocent had suffered during disturbances; it also included the phrase 'by the hate you bear the Orangemen' in circumstances where Protestant and Orangeman were synonymous in many parts of Ireland. This had been read by many priests from their altars. Goulburn did not once refer to the suppression of Orange societies but he pointed to the danger of a rival Protestant Association arising if the Catholic Association was not surpressed.[1]

Speakers in favour of Catholic Emancipation pointed out the profound sense of injustice amongst Irish Catholics. Sir Henry Parnell, in particular, spoke in favour of the Association: it was not guilty of 'unconstitutional conduct' and it had been necessary for the Association to interfere in the administration of justice; he gave examples of attorneys, like Mr Bric, obtaining justice for Catholics such as the dismissal of a chief constable of police at New Ross. 'Nothing is so important', declared Parnell, 'for the peasantry of the country as to have some protection and some security that the laws shall be fairly administered by the magistrates.' He maintained that the Rent collection was not dominated by the priests but managed by a parochial committee: '. . . in no case out of some hundreds that I have read, have I ever found the priest appointed to act as treasurer,' he argued, 'in point of fact, the priest has nothing more to say to the business than any other person, and either supports or opposes the plan, as he thinks proper.' The real cause of alarm which had developed in Ireland in November 1824 was not found in the Association, which had been adjourned between July and October. Parnell maintained that the efforts of Bible societies, such as the London Hibernian School Society, in places like Clonmel, Waterford and Loughrea, and their local confrontations with Catholic clergy, led Catholics to believe that there was a general and systematic plan to put down the Catholic religion. 'It was by these numerous meetings, the publishing of the whole of the speeches, and the strong doctrines set forth by both sides, that by the beginning of November a universal alarm prevailed throughout Ireland.' These 'Bible fights' continued at Carrick-on-Shannon and Carlow in November and December but when such meetings ceased alarm also ceased. Parnell traced the origins of these sectarian tensions to

> the celebrated, but most injudicious charge, of the Archbishop of Dublin. It is quite inconceivable to what an extent this has excited soreness and passion among the whole Catholic body. It is to this that is wholly to be attributed the appearance of the bishops and priests as the warm supporters of the Association and the Catholic Rent; their stirring in politics can be most accurately traced to this event.

Parnell warned that the 'most extensive change' in 'the Catholic mind of Ireland' had occurred and that suppression of the Association would inevitably lead to confusion and rebellion. The Union, passed in 1800, still existed 'only on paper': 'there is no cordial national union. Ireland is still in feeling and in fact a country foreign to England. The people form a clear notion of a distinct Irish nation and a distinct English nation.' Parnell pointed out that the Irish people 'do not live as the people of England, perfectly obedient to the laws' in villages under a parish constable 'but they live hutted over the whole face of the country, free from almost all control and superintendence'. Hence the danger of open rebellion, Parnell continued, because if any fixed determination to make a popular effort should seize possession of their minds, in vain would the Catholic nobility, the Catholic lawyers, and even the Catholic priests try to stop it. Such was the opinion current amongst the best informed resident gentlemen of Ireland: 'the conversation of all private society dwelling so much upon it. What happened in the year 1641 is constantly spoken of . . .'[2]

Other speakers attacked the very notion of political associations: 'Where were these Associations to end?' Peel demanded to know 'why might not the country expect an Association for the purpose of obtaining parliamentary reform?' [*cries of 'hear, hear!'*][3] Peel also made it clear in the debate that the Unlawful Societies Bill would include the Orange lodges. The Grand Lodge accordingly held a final meeting in

Dublin on 18 March 1825. Orangemen now had to rely on the personal influence of ultra peers and the inflexible stance of the crown to resist Catholic advance. Until late 1828, when there was a revival of the Irish Orange movement, there was no effective organisational link between the popular Protestantism of Ulster and the ascendancy opponents of Emancipation throughout Ireland.

Plunket repeated the charge that the Catholic Association had assumed the functions of parliament, while Canning launched a major onslaught on the Catholic organisation:

> Self-elected − self-constructed − self-assembled − self-adjourned, − acknowledging no superior, − tolerating no equal, − interfering in all stages with the administration of justice, − denouncing publicly before trial individuals against whom it institutes prosecutions, − and rejudging and condemning those whom the law has acquitted, − menacing the free press with punishment, and openly declaring its intention to corrupt that part of it which it cannot intimidate; − and lastly, for these and other purposes, levying contributions on the people of Ireland.

Both Plunket and Canning put forward long but not totally convincing defences of their participation in a government that refused to introduce legislation for the Catholic question. Canning pointed out that there was in England 'a great inert mass of opposition to the Catholic question, which can only be worn down by degrees, and which must be dealt with gently and considerately'.[4]

The Radicals, led by Sir Francis Burdett, supported Emancipation and generally approved of the Association, as they believed it would be an ally in their fight for parliamentary reform: 'It was a contracted view of this question to call it an Irish question', declared Burdett who called it 'an English question, the most important of any which had been brought under the consideration of government since the Revolution'.[5] The Radicals were to be sorely disappointed in O'Connell, who for opportunistic reasons declined to support reform and even endorsed a measure of disenfranchisement. The opposition Whigs under Grey sympathised with the Catholic Association to a limited extent and were mainly in favour of Emancipation. Henry Brougham stoutly defended the Association, declaring 'I am the advocate of the right of the Irish people to meet, to consider, to plan, to petition, to remonstrate, to demand . . .'[6]

The government majority was made up by rabid anti-Catholics known as the ultras, who were to find an unlikely hero of conscience in the Duke of York, and by pro-Catholic Tories in government. The ultras denounced the Association as a revolutionary seditious organisation which would dissolve the Union and supplant the Established Church.

George Dawson, MP for Londonderry and brother-in-law of Peel, declared it was the objective of the priests 'to overthrow the Protestant Church and establish that of Rome in its stead [*cheers*] ', while Charles Brownlow argued that the Roman Catholic faith was founded on ignorance and it was afraid of education. The Catholic Association, he maintained, would not be satisfied with mere Emancipation but would seek Church property as well.[7] Colour was lent to their overheated imaginations when Peel accused the Association of approving of Hamilton Rowan, 'an attainted traitor', of 1798. Sheil later remembered sitting with O'Connell on 18 February observing the debate in the Commons on whether the representatives of the Catholic Association could be heard at the Bar of the House, and how Peel

> pronounced his invective with great and very successful force. He became heated with victory, and, cheered as he was repeatedly by his multitudinous partisans, turned suddenly . . . and looking triumphantly at Mr O'Connell, with whom he forgot for a moment that he had been once involved in a personal quarrel, shook his hand with scornful exultation . . . (*114*, II, 41).

John Cam Hobhouse, the Whig MP, recalled that Brougham embarrassed Peel by pointing out that Rowan was a magistrate who was received at the Castle; Hobhouse thought that never did a Minister get 'such a whipping': Peel 'looked so red and so silly, and all those who had cheered him looked so red and silly, and we so roared and cheered our champion . . .' (*15*, III, 88-9). Later it transpired that Rowan had not in fact been admitted to the magistracy.

The pro-Catholic Tories wanted to suppress the Association as a menace to orderly government which, as Canning had argued, threatened the prerogatives of parliament itself. Suppression, they believed, would serve as the prelude to an eventual settlement of Catholic claims.

There was never any doubt as to the outcome of the debate. O'Connell wrote to his wife: 'We have little to expect from such a crew of miscreants' (III, 1168). The Unlawful Societies Bill passed by 155 votes on the first reading, 146 on the second and 130 on the third and easily passed through the more anti-Catholic Lords. It received the royal assent on 9 March 1825.

O'Connell was now in a difficult tactical position. He proposed to stay in London, at considerable financial cost to himself in lost earnings, in the hope of seeing a Relief Bill for Catholics introduced in the House of Commons. But there was no question of it being anything other than an incomplete measure: a Bill which would fully have satisfied the Association's demands was simply unrealistic, given the political complexion of parliament. As early as 16 February he was warning his wife that he might expect only ingratitude from the public for his sacrifice in London (III, 1168). He anticipated his vulnerability to the advocates of 'unqualified Emancipation' once he exposed himself by negotiating for the sort of Relief Bill which might actually have a prospect of success.

O'Connell began his efforts by trying to convince sufficient MPs that Catholics could be conciliated and that they did not wish to threaten or bully Westminster. The dangerous demagogue of the 'Bolivar' speech was transforming himself into the delicate diplomat. Sheil later recalled the moment. O'Connell, 'upon whom every eye was fixed' (on his first night at the Commons he saw Charles Manners Sutton, the Speaker, 'measure me with his glass' [III, 1169]) affected 'a perfect carelessness of manner; but it was easy to perceive that he was full of restlessness and inquietude under an icy surface. I saw the current eddying beneath' (*114*, II, 35). O'Connell was little impressed by the House of Commons: 'The fact is, they are always careless about Ireland till they want us' and 'after all, what is it to them, if we are crushed?' (III, 1169, 1172). At first he found an 'English coldness' about the political leaders, even Sir Francis Burdett. However, Burdett greatly improved on acquaintance.

O'Connell started his 'mission' with 'a long conference' with Burdett who had been chosen by the Association as their spokesman in the House when a Relief Bill was to be introduced. He also engaged in a round of meetings and public dinners to influence public opinion in London: 'We receive every compliment imaginable. Crowds of peers and parliament men pouring in upon us. I am made the "spokesman" of every meeting. I have no doubt but this visit will do the "cause" some good if it were in nothing else but in showing us what a base and vile set the House of Commons is composed of' (III, 1172). In his letters to his wife O'Connell revealed private thoughts which he kept well disguised from public view. Sheil, in fact, believed O'Connell's compromise on the Relief Bill was due to the contrast between 'the din of popular assemblies' in Dublin and the 'dazzling' splendour of English high society, and that an Irish provincial inferiority complex affected O'Connell and his deputation. Cobbett also claimed that he had warned O'Connell: 'The very first words I said to him', wrote Cobbett in August 1825, 'were these: "Well, Mr O'Connell, let me beseech you to bear in mind that you are come into hell, and that you have, of course, devils to deal with".'[8]

It is clear from his letters that O'Connell was delighted to be at the centre of things. He exclaimed in a letter home: 'I had no motion of such splendour' and he described Norfolk House as 'magnificent' (III, 1182). But he also recognised the dangers of 'flattery', even when he sat between the Duke of Devonshire and Earl Grey at the Duke of

Norfolk's dinner. He told James Sugrue with a characteristic shrewdness that 'while others of the deputation were complimenting – as they ought to do – great folks, my study has been directed towards the middling classes . . .' (III, 1177). In evidence to the Select Committees established to inquire into Irish affairs and in negotiations with politicians, O'Connell told them what he believed they wanted to hear: his objective was to win his way 'with the people and with the House, in spite of Peel and the Orange faction' (III, 1178).

O'Connell had his reward when Sir Francis Burdett's motion to consider the Catholic claims was passed by thirteen votes on 28 February. O'Connell had agreed to certain 'securities' for the Protestant Constitution. In particular, he supported the celebrated 'wings' of the 1825 Relief Bill, so called because they would help it to fly successfully through parliament. The first 'wing' was the payment of the Catholic clergy out of state funds and the second was the disenfranchisement of the Irish forty-shilling freeholders. The first was designed to secure the loyalty of the Catholic Church to the crown and state and the second to ensure that whatever Catholic MPs were elected would not have to depend upon the votes of 'the mob'. O'Connell's strategy depended upon convincing Lord Liverpool to 'take up the question' and upon an acceptance by Irish Catholics of 'the wings'. The hope was that the less rabid ultras would accept this 'Emancipation' as a resolution of the serious and long-standing political problem, accompanied as it was by sufficient 'securities' for the Establishment and had as a 'propeller' the suppression of the Catholic Association and Orange lodges under Goulburn's Act.

In early March O'Connell was bouyant because he believed Liverpool would allow 'Emancipation': it seemed inevitable. That was O'Connell's great miscalculation. When Liverpool questioned O'Connell on 9 March in the Select Committee of the Lords, O'Connell misread the situation badly in his letter to his wife. 'Lord Liverpool would be *pleased*, I think, at Emancipation. His examination of me was very courteous, and you will be surprised to hear that the Duke of Wellington was even kind'. It was widely rumoured that Liverpool had weakened on Emancipation so much that O'Connell reported that it was 'scarcely doubted even by our enemies and not at all by our friends' that Liverpool and Wellington would support the Bill (III, 1184). Thus O'Connell believed he had triumphed. 'In short, we have won the game. . . . If I had not been here, nothing would have been done. I *forced* Sir Francis Burdett to bring on his motion' (III, 1180). The voluntary suppression of the Association before Goulburn's Act became effective would 'work wonders' according to O'Connell and he publicly declared that it had been 'permitted to me to draw the rough draft of this Bill'.[9] John Cam Hobhouse noted in his diary on 9 March 1825: 'Burdett is preparing, in conjunction with

O'Connell and Plunket, the Catholic Bill. The greatest harmony reigns between the three, and also the great Whigs' (*15*, III, 93).

O'Connell had to head off any premature condemnation of 'the wings' especially in Dublin during his absence and he gave directions to this effect. On its dissolution on 18 March 1825 the Catholic Association resolved that O'Connell 'continues to enjoy the *undivided* and *undiminished* confidence of the Catholic Association'.[10] He ensured the support of the bishops through the delegation of the five Catholic prelates from Ireland who were in London to be examined by the Select Committee of the Commons: Curtis of Armagh, Kelly of Tuam, Murray of Dublin, Doyle of Kildare and Leighlin as well as Magauran of Ardagh. Thus he believed, by 14 March, that 'the machine' was 'working well in all its parts and carrying us on daily to Emancipation'. O'Connell, by mid March, still believed '*the game is won*' and that it was 'only the manner of playing it that makes any difference' (III, 1191). John Cam Hobhouse noted in his diary on 12 March the great talk that was current that the Catholic question would be carried in the Lords. He dined with O'Connell at a party on 13 March recording these impressions of the Irish leader:

> O'Connell very pleasant, natural, and easy. He is not what is called a man of the world, or with the airs of a town-bred gentleman. He wears a curly wig (black), and in the street a furred mantle. The Irish tell me he is vain . . . but all confess him to be a most powerful speaker, and a very learned lawyer, and a most diligent student. He rises very early in the morning (*15*, III, 94).

O'Connell believed he had succeeded in winning Catholic Emancipation, in 'carrying this great measure in a manner which will leave our religion untouched whilst it not only increases our liberties but at this moment will actually inundate Ireland with English capital'. The provision for the clergy 'would bring about £250,000 a year of English money into Ireland' and there was 'not to be the least interference of the Crown with any kind of appointment in our church' (III, 1185). On 15 March O'Connell believed that the cabinet ministers were 'at work' and he expected 'within a week' resolutions of both Houses in favour of Emancipation. He attended the Duke of York's levée 'and was received with the greatest kindness. He even joked with me on the advantage my profession gave me in my long examination before both houses . . .' (III, 1188). O'Connell continued to work on certain MPs such as Charles Brownlow and George Dawson, not without some success as Brownlow was shortly to announce his conversion to Emancipation (III, 1184, 1205). On 21 March O'Connell, well satisfied, set out for a few weeks sojourn in Ireland before the critical debate on the Relief Bill came on in the middle of April.

By this stage the Catholic question dominated Westminster politics and public agitation throughout both islands. Anti-Catholic petitions, in many cases sponsored by Anglican clergymen, flooded in; Methodists took an even stronger anti-Catholic stance than did Anglicans but the older dissenting denominations remained largely pro-Catholic. O'Connell had taken the trouble to dine on 11 March with 'the liberal Dissenters, if liberal I can call them' (III, 1184). The Methodist missionary involvement in Ireland, where they confronted a renaissant Catholic Church, was a principal cause of English Wesleyan anti-Catholicism and it helped to align the English Methodists with ultra-Tory politics. Catholicism was perceived as spiritual slavery by many Methodists. This was exemplified by the Methodist MP Joseph Butterworth whose opposition to Catholic Relief in 1825 was heavily coloured by missionary reports from Ireland. Methodists did not like the comparisons which were drawn between their organisation and that of the Catholics (*46*, 39-40). The prospect of Emancipation brought on a virulent 'no-popery' clamour which considerably stiffened parliamentary resistence to the Relief Bill.

O'Connell was a realist and recognised the great difficulty of getting even a qualified and limited Emancipation measure approved. If friends of Emancipation such as Sydney Smith, for example, were in favour of securities how much more worried would opponents be of this great constitutional change. Smith was in a minority of one at a meeting of Anglican clergy in Yorkshire on 11 April 1825 when he spoke only in favour of a 'qualified' Emancipation:

> I mean eligibility of Catholics to all civil offices, with the usual exceptions introduced into all bills – jealous safeguards for the preservation of the Protestant church, and for the regulation of the intercourse with Rome – and, lastly, provision for the Catholic clergy (*121*, IV, 362).

English popular opinion tended to see Catholicism as unchanged from the religion that persecuted Protestants, that was unfriendly to liberty, that sought supremacy of a foreign power in English affairs and that was based on false theology and dubious morality: 'no popery' was a popular slogan in most English constituencies.

On the Irish front, John Lawless published a letter in the *Freeman's Journal* on 18 March which attacked O'Connell for accepting disenfranchisement and the provision for the clergy. He even attributed base motives to O'Connell who, he claimed, was selling the people for a silk gown. This was the first shot in what became a major controversy within the Catholic movement in Ireland throughout 1825. O'Connell also lost the support of English reformers such as Cobbett on account of the 'wings'. Cobbett pilloried O'Connell in *The Political Register* for his deception, arrogance and vanity: 'Irishmen', he wrote in an Open Letter to the Freeholders of Ireland,

> when you were paying, or giving your pennies under the name of 'Catholic Rent'; and when many persons, Protestants as well as Catholics, were contributing to the same fund, did you, or did they, imagine that the money was to assist in obtaining you a *loss of your right to vote*? Did you or did they, ever dream that 'Emancipation' could possibly mean *disfranchisement*?[11]

Cobbett was more interested in parliamentary reform: he did not 'wish to see rich Catholics let into power, while poor Catholics are deprived even of the rights that they now enjoy'. He believed O'Connell was not 'the victim, but the practiser of duplicity' in these negotiations (*117*, II, 467). On both fronts, then, O'Connell's strategy was under mounting attack but most critically in England. When O'Connell returned to England in mid-April he began to fear 'the coldness and apathy of our friends the Whigs' who for party purposes would desert his cause (III, 1204).

In this uncertain climate Burdett introduced the Relief Bill to emancipate Catholics: it contained a provision for control of Catholic ecclesiastical appointments by the government and it provided a modified version of the Oath of Supremacy for Catholics. The Bill was to be accompanied by separate measures for the disenfranchisement of the forty-shilling freeholders in Ireland and for the payment of the Catholic clergy. It was certainly a 'qualified' Emancipation, but the veto aspect was considerably modified and O'Connell, hoping for success, and with no alternative readily to hand, did his best to quieten the apprehensions of the Irish Catholics and to ease Whig difficulties with disenfranchisement. O'Connell wrote that the Disenfranchisement Bill was 'a very hard card to play. If we concede the freeholds, we shall get over many enemies but we shall perhaps lose some who at least call themselves our friends. *Thus* are we circumstanced for the present' (III, 1207). O'Connell was acutely aware of the new legal difficulties of agitation after Goulburn's Act and he had not been convinced that forty-shilling freeholders were able freely to vote according to conscience. He satisfied himself that state payment for the Catholic Church was better than the voluntary support system.

The Relief Bill was introduced on 19 April for its second reading and it passed by twenty-seven votes. The debate produced the remarkable speech of Charles Brownlow, the Co. Armagh MP who had become converted to concession of the Catholic claims. He believed that the Roman Catholic religion was now free from past objections 'because it has freed itself from the corruptions of the Roman Curia' and that the Pope was now only a spiritual leader. Also the landed interest of Irish

Catholics had increased so much that Catholics no longer sought to overturn the land confiscations of the seventeenth century. The evidence of the State of Ireland Committees of the Lords and the Commons in February and March was beginning to have an effect on Catholic debates. George Dawson, the Londonderry MP and brother-in-law of Peel, declared that the evidence given to the Select Committees

> will lead you into the cabin of the peasant in every part of the country; into the house of the landlord; into the mysterious recesses of the land agent and the tithe proctor; into the halls of justice, whether at assize, quarter sessions, petty sessions, or manor courts; it will lead you into the Protestant church, the Presbyterian meeting-house and the Catholic chapel . . .[12]

As a contemporary reviewer of the evidence of these Irish Committees pointed out, Ireland was exposed to 'the gaze of all mankind'.[13]

The evidence of Bishop Doyle to the Select Committees of the Commons and Lords presented an image of a liberal Catholicism extremely anxious to be accommodated within the 'admirable' British Constitution.

> I am convinced in my soul — I never spoke without sincerity, but I never spoke more from the fullness of my heart than I do at this present moment — that if we were freed from the disabilities under which we labour, we have no mind, and no thought, and no will, but that which would lead us to incorporate ourselves fully and essentially with this great kingdom; for it would be our greatest pride, to share in the glories and riches of England.[14]

He informed the Lords Select Committee on 21 March 1825 that Emancipation would end the 'extreme difficulty' priests had: 'one in which we are endeavouring to conciliate the upper orders, and to keep quiet the feeling of the lower orders'. Bishop James Magauran of Ardagh told the Commons Select Committee that the lower orders felt like 'an excluded caste' and while they could not define Emancipation they were 'very anxious to be relieved from this kind of slavery which they were not able to explain': the Catholic Association had articulated for the people their sense of oppression and injustice.

Sheil and Lord Killeen gave evidence amounting to support for the removal of the franchise of the forty-shilling freeholders. Killeen argued in favour of a £5 qualification accompanied by Emancipation though his mind was not 'quite made up on the subject' whilst Sheil declared that '. . . the mass of the peasantry should not be invested every five or six years with a mere resemblance of political authority, which does not naturally belong to them, and which is quite unreal'. Sheil did say he was not well acquainted with rural elections and that he gave an urban view. O'Connell's view was that in general the peasantry were driven 'in droves of freeholders to the hustings: they must obey the command of their landlord; it is only in cases of peculiar emergency and where their passions are powerfully excited, that a revolt against the power of the landlord can take place.' Co. Dublin in 1823 afforded 'no illustration of the rest of Ireland; it stands on its peculiar grounds'.[15]

O'Connell in evidence to the Lords Committee presented an image of the wealthy Catholic mercantile and landed classes committed to the established order of law and property and wishing to be given equality within the United Kingdom: '. . . to my certain knowledge the Roman Catholics of Ireland are as sincerely attached to the succession of the Crown in the present Royal Family, and to the principles of the Constitution, and to the connexion with Great Britain, as any Protestant possibly can be.' O'Connell stated that forty-shilling voters who went against their landlords were 'generally ruined by it' and he found it 'extremely difficult to reconcile oneself to the misery' produced through landlord reprisals. The Catholic Rent could not be used to protect such voters and he would be happy to exchange the forty-shilling franchise for Emancipation.[16] Colchester, the ultra peer, recorded his impressions of O'Connell before the Lords Committee in his diary on 9 March:

> O'Connell appears to be about fifty-three or fifty-four years of age, a stout built man, with a black wig, and light-coloured eyebrows, above the middle stature, pale countenance, square features, blue eyes . . . his whole deportment affectedly respectful and gentle, except in a few answers where he displayed a fierceness of tone and aspect (*20*, III, 372).

O'Connell admitted to the Commons Select Committee that the tenants valued the forty-shilling franchise as they 'feel it makes them of importance; they must once in seven years, be courted, and in the meantime be attended to . . . for it gives, where it is bona fide, a term, a life; and in Ireland, where land is so valuable to the peasant having a long tenure is always valuable'. O'Connell did argue for an extension of the franchise to all householders 'if the thing were well managed' but stated that his 'crude opinion' at present was for a five pound franchise though this was 'not a very decided' opinion.

O'Connell revealed in his evidence an almost total ignorance of the north of Ireland:

> Were you ever in the county of Antrim? *Never.*
> Were you ever in the county of Down? *I cannot exactly say; if I was, it was only passing to Monaghan.*

Were you ever in the county of Derry? *No.*
Were you ever in the county of Armagh? *Never.*
Were you ever in the county of Fermanagh? *Never.*
Were you ever in the county of Donegal? *Never.*
Were you ever in the county of Tyrone? *Yes; passing from Monaghan to Athlone.*

He admitted his information on the north was 'necessarily rude and indistinct'; in fact he believed there was no county in Ireland 'in which the majority is not Catholic . . .'[17] He had a very poor understanding of popular Ulster Protestantism and a dangerous blindspot in gauging Ulster reactions to the Catholic movement.

On 23 April the Disfranchisement Bill was introduced by E. J. Littleton, a Canningite. O'Connell wrote that day:

The fact is, there floats amongst the individuals in the House a great portion of real substantial bigotry. It really is bigotry which stands between us and Emancipation but we are quite sure of going through the House of Commons and we must as rapidly as possible take our measures for assailing the House of Lords (III, 1207).

But it was already too late. On 25 April the Duke of York made his momentous declaration in the Lords against the royal assent ever being given to a Catholic Relief Bill. Pointing out that there was a great difference between toleration, participation and Emancipation, the Duke asked how could Catholics in the Commons legislate for the Established Protestant Church? He read out the Coronation Oath with its obligation to maintain 'the Protestant reformed religion established by law' and observed that he could not relieve himself from such obligations were he in such a position as his brother. After noting that the Catholic agitation had caused severe illness and ten years of misery to his father, George III, he concluded that '. . . these were the principles to which he would adhere, and which he would maintain and act up to, to the latest moment of his existence, whatever might be his situation of life — so help him God!'[18] The Duke apparently had become aware of O'Connell's part in drawing up the Catholic Bill, 'for he heard Lady Jersey say so *out loud* to the deaf Duke of Devonshire at dinner' and this was unlikely to soften his resistance to the measure (*15*, III, 95-6).
Catholics now understood that George IV's expected successor would be as adamant for 'bigotry' as were his predecessors: anti-Catholics rejoiced and called for his speech to be printed in letters of gold. George IV's own attitude was stiffened and the spirits of the pro-Catholics were considerably dampened. For a while O'Connell hoped

that 'the ferocious speech' would do the Catholic cause good and he attended the king's levée two days after the speech but he realised that the crisis had arrived (III, 1211). The second reading of the Disfranchisement Bill had passsed on 26 April by forty-eight votes and on 29 April a resolution on the state payment of the Catholic clergy was passed by a similar margin.

The Whigs were divided over the Disfranchisement Bill and over the provision of state payment. This weakened the pro-Catholic effort. For the cabinet, however, the 'wings' presented more serious difficulties. All the pro-Catholic cabinet ministers in the Commons except Canning, who was absent through illness, had supported the 'wings' and their anti-Catholic colleagues were alienated by this gratuitous break of the 'open' system which only obliged voting for the actual Relief Bill. The 'wings' in fact gained little support for the Catholic Bill and, as John Cam Hobhouse noted, something 'was lost by the sacrifices'. Hobhouse himself disliked the Disfranchisement Bill but did not wish to risk the Relief Bill so he did not vote at all on the Disfranchisement Bill (*15*, III, 96-8). Liverpool became extremely alarmed as he considered it inevitable that his government must break up and that it would have to be succeeded by a pro-Catholic ministry which would then carry Emancipation. Liverpool's role now became crucial in the crisis. On 1 May O'Connell wrote to his wife: 'We have arrived at a most critical period in our affairs and if we are not now successful it is not known when we shall. Our prospects are indeed daily brightening. Certainly the Lords are now completely at the disposal of Lord Liverpool' (III, 1215). On 3 May he recognised that 'one word from him certainly carries it' and on 4 May that Liverpool 'now holds our fate in his hands' (III, 1216, 1217).

The government's survival was in the balance. Liverpool and Peel had declared at a meeting of ministers that they would resign rather than be a party to the sort of compromise on the Catholic question which now seemed unavoidable. Liverpool on 4 May wrote to the anti-Catholic peer, Bathurst '. . . the *crisis* cannot be averted for many months. I should be forced out, if not by any direct act of my colleagues, by the circumstances of the Government. When the *crisis does come* the *Protestants* must go to the *wall*' (*80*, 60). Next day O'Connell correctly reported to his wife that the cabinet was 'extremely divided' and that 'Lord Eldon and Peel are endeavouring to throw out Canning but the latter is supported by Lord Liverpool. If this controversy shall end in favour of Canning it may give us Emancipation at once so that our fate is in the scale . . .' O'Connell felt that public opinion was in favour of the Catholics but it was clear that internal cabinet politics were to be decisive (III, 1218).

Bathurst and Wellington devoted themselves to keeping the government in being so as to avoid a coalition of Canning and the Whigs which would be committed to carrying Emancipation. Wellington urged strongly that rather than forfeit office the ministers should agree to a Catholic settlement on the basis of compromise: he had formulated a plan whereby Catholic Relief would be passed in return for a concordat with the Pope which would give the crown partial control over the appointment of Catholic bishops.

It is important to note that Archbishop Curtis was indicating to Wellington on 21 May that he did not wish for any Emancipation 'that government may think unsafe to grant, or which a great proportion of other denominations of Christians, particularly those of the Established Church, may still continue to oppose, as inimical to the true interests of Church or State, whether well or ill understood by them'. Curtis did express fears about the consequences of rejection of the Relief Bill in the Lords, particularly after the state of Ireland had been exposed in the parliamentary enquiries (*128*, II, 451-3). Wellington's scheme was only to be activated if Liverpool and Peel could not be persuaded to remain in office as anti-Catholics. Bathurst reminded Liverpool that his government was formed upon the 'open' system and Liverpool ought not to resign over the issue which was central to that system. 'Your Government was formed upon it: your friends have trusted their political fortunes upon it, and you now without notice turn round and consider it as a vital question' (*80*, 59).

Peel was told by Wellington that his resignation, which would precipitate Liverpool's, was 'completely throwing up the Protestant cause'. By 6 May O'Connell had heard that Liverpool expressed 'an opinion perfectly hostile' towards Emancipation 'Well, well', he mused to his wife, 'let them abide any evil consequences that may ensue. We are not to blame . . .' (III, 1219). Next day he recognised that 'our prospects are clouded' and that the Bill could only be saved in the Lords 'by a miracle or the exertion of popular sentiment'; O'Connell now realised the damage the Duke of York had done on 25 April:

> That vile villain, the Duke of York, *they say* made no impression but the House of Lords is after all so sorry and sad a gang that, sweetest, we have little to hope from them for honesty or liberality while the heir apparent or presumptive chooses to take a stand for folly, bigotry and knavery, and then indeed, darling, they say the Royal Duke is quite at home. His conduct with Mrs Clarke, etc. is as familiar as day and his tradesmen are, they say, unpaid, his debts of honour undischarged, and with honesty and morality on a par with those of the vile women who infest the midnight streets. This royal rascal has scruples of conscience forsooth!!! (III, 1220).

On 10 May the Relief Bill passed by a relatively narrow margin of twenty-one votes on its third reading in the Commons. It was, as O'Connell realised, *'now* or never': a postponement would not involve passage in 1826. But he wrote gloomily on 13 May '. . . every hour seems to lessen our prospects. Lord Liverpool appears too much of an old woman to take any active or decided part and thus we are to be left to the mercy of the Eldons and Peels . . .' (III, 1228). The Lords debate took place on 17 May before a large audience. Colchester in the debate declared that Catholics aim

> to begin with the destruction of our church property and its endowed establishment. Equality of rights they say, but domination they mean. And nothing less can result, whatever they may profess to begin with, than the gradual re-establishment of their own church in Ireland; practically destroying that fundamental article of the union, which has established one Protestant Episcopal Church for England and Ireland; and finally dissolving in both countries the whole connexion of a Protestant church and Protestant state, which forms an essential principle of the British Constitution.

Anglesey, though he said he was generally favourable to Catholic claims, 'would not give them anything at the expense of the Protestant Establishment'; he would prefer to face rebellion with the sword. The Earl of Longford could not at all see why Catholics were to be admitted 'to a participation with Protestants of certain civil rights and political power in a free Protestant country'. Catholicism, according to Longford, always interfered with 'the general transactions and ordinary business of life' and Protestant security required Protestant ascendancy; this was necessary for the well being of the empire. Liverpool expected that the bill would be rejected by a narrow majority such as would not justify further resistance to the claims of Catholics. He was anxious to emphasise that his own conscience would not allow him to participate in a pro-Catholic ministry and he therefore made a more inflexibly anti-Catholic speech than any which had yet come from him. Sounding like an ultra, the Prime Minister was unyielding in his condemnation of Catholic relief mainly on religious grounds. He gave no hint of compromise.[19] The consequences of his observations surprised Liverpool. He thought he was making a final personal protest against the inevitable grant of Emancipation. In the event he helped to rally the anti-Catholic resistance of the Lords so effectively that when the peers divided a little before six in the morning after two nights of debate the Bill was thrown out by forty-eight votes, about twenty more than he had expected (*20*, III, 385-6).

The 1825 crisis was over: the pro-Catholic effort ended in failure, although it had been a close run thing. Next day O'Connell wrote to his wife. He had spent eight hours 'standing in the thickest crowd imaginable, for the spectators in the Lords have no place to sit' and he had not got to bed until six in the morning: 'I could not write yesterday. This day I have nothing to say or sing but defeat. Blessed be God. We must begin again . . . Ireland in the meantime is condemned to more tyranny and distraction . . .' (III, 1231). The government would now be able to carry on with the status quo: O'Connell lamented amidst public rejoicings by the anti-Catholic mobs and the ringing of church bells.

The only question now was what would the pro-Catholic members of the cabinet do in the face of the defeat. Canning declared that the Catholic question must now be settled one way or the other: the cabinet would find it impossible to continue if Canning stuck to this line. Liverpool believed that he would have to inform the king that the formation of an exclusively anti-Catholic government was 'absolutely impracticable, whereas the formation of a government upon the opposite principle . . . is within his power' (*80*, 62). However, at a cabinet meeting on 20 May it became clear that Canning had no intention of sacrificing office in order to make an extremely risky attempt to set up a pro-Catholic government. By 23 May O'Connell believed it 'quite imaginary or at best a delusive hope' that Canning would turn out Liverpool, Eldon, and Peel by a junction with the opposition' (III, 1235). Canning declared himself at liberty to propound the Catholic question in the cabinet whenever he thought proper. Henry Hobhouse, the Under-Secretary of State in the Home Office, noted this in his diary, and remarked:

> Observe how he labours to keep well with the Catholics by declaring that it is conducive to their interests that he shd. retain his place. If he had resigned (as he ought in consistency to have done, after being foiled in the purpose for wch. he summoned the Cabinet) it is doubtful whr. he would have been followed even by his friend Huskisson, much less by Robinson. Wynn perhaps wd. have taken that step (*2*, 116).

Canning maintained he would refuse to support fresh penal enactments by resigning if Ireland should be agitated in future as a consequence of the refusal of the Catholic claims. His stand, as John Cam Hobhouse shrewdly observed on 27 May, 'is as much like a fall as possible' (*15*, III, 103-4). Canning in fact still supported the 'open' system and the danger to Liverpool's government had completely passed by the end of May.

O'Connell now reflected on 'total defeat' and on the 'scoundrel Lord Liverpool and that greater rascal, if possible, the Duke of York'; he wrote to his wife, 'Never certainly was anything more complete and *for the present* we are without hope . . .' and his mind turned to renewed agitation: 'We will attack the rascals in every quarter that the law will allow, and they shall be disappointed in their expectation of putting down the Catholics of either country.' At public meetings he resolved to make violent speeches: 'I have no notion of mincing the matter with Lord Liverpool. He is a public enemy and must be hunted down like a wild cat' (III, 1232, 1233). The inpenetrable anti-Catholic barrier was the Lords and the crown, which was why Canning accepted that the 'open' system must therefore continue for an indefinite period. Grey, the Whig leader, sagely observed to Lord Holland in September 1825: '[The] question will never be conceded except to an irresistible necessity; & for this, events are not yet ripe' (*79*, 482). There is evidence that from 1825 onwards Peel and Wellington began to consider seriously how the 'inevitable' Catholic Emancipation might be passed in such a way as to secure the Protestant Constitution. Wellington wrote in December 1825 a detailed private 'Memorandum on the Case of the Roman Catholics in Ireland' in which he set out the advantages of a timely settlement whilst the Lords majority, 'our only resource, remains undiminished and unimpaired'. Both men recognised that the course of liberal thought was gradually eroding the exclusive Protestant position. Wellington favoured a concordat with the Pope which would contain safeguards for the Protestant interest. He identified the priests, nobility, lawyers and propertied gentlemen of Catholic Ireland as 'a sort of *theocracy*' which governed the people and which was 'in strict communion with the Church of Rome'. The laws imposing disabilities on Catholics had not 'answered their purpose' and a new arrangement was called for (*128*, II, 592-607). This flexibility of approach was kept hidden from public view and no leadership was provided by either man for public opinion. The deadlock could only be broken by a vital extra-parliamentary movement, an 'irresistible' Irish demand, if the heart of the Protestant Constitution was to be penetrated. O'Connell noted: 'We have nothing for it but to keep up the fire of agitation as much as we possibly can' (III, 1235).

O'Connell's position after the failure of 1825 was serious indeed. He had staked his reputation on the Relief Bill and the 'wings'. As Thomas Wyse noted, it was the failure to achieve Emancipation in 1825 which 'threw a slur on the negotiators', for success 'would have redeemed a host of errors and sins' (*132*, I, 220). On the parliamentary front nothing was to be expected; in June 1825 parliament was approaching the end of its sixth session and a dissolution was expected for if it ran another session it would be the first parliament since the Septennial Act to run its whole legal period. The government pro-Catholics feared an election and Canning gave a commitment to Liverpool to suppress discussion of the Catholic question in the next session between February and May 1826. Grey and the Whigs argued vehemently against suppression of the question; Grey remarked to Brougham: 'It may be convenient to *us* to have no Catholic Question; but is it equally good for the Irish? Have they ever got anything except what has been extorted in the hour of distress? Is it not then *their* interest, to keep alive & to inflame a spirit of discontent for that reason?' (*14*, II, 473-5).

Inflaming a 'spirit of discontent' was difficult for O'Connell who had indulged in a dangerous game of compromise in London without getting a mandate in Dublin; he was apparently committed to a qualified measure of Catholic Emancipation which at once alienated English Radicals, such as Cobbett, and Irish Catholics. His support for disenfranchisement, in particular, brought down a whirlwind of protest on his head. It was represented as a betrayal of the people who had so nobly paid the Rent. Lawless tabled resolutions for a Catholic meeting condemning O'Connell, while Mahon organised a group, nicknamed 'the Bridge Street Gang' by O'Connell, to support Lawless. The 'ingratitude' O'Connell had expected for his efforts in London turned out to be furious public opposition.

While in London O'Connell had directed his friends in Dublin; these now arranged for a public reception for O'Connell to counteract the hostility. He wrote to his wife on 27 May: 'We must immediately form "the New Catholic Association". I have it all arranged. They shall not get one hour's respite from agitation, I promise you ... I never was *up* to agitation till now' (III, 1239). O'Connell arrived back on 1 June and was met at Howth with a public procession; he was followed by an immense crowd to Merrion Square where he spoke from the balcony of his house. After flattering the crowd, he declared that '. . . the time was near at hand when Catholic rights would be constitutionally obtained [*cheers*]'.[20] On 8 June an aggregate meeting to consider the position of the Catholic cause was held in St Michan's Church, North Anne Street. The crowds assembled hours before the meeting was due to start and the *Dublin Evening Post* estimated that between six and seven thousand people were present. O'Connell appeared at this crowded meeting in a uniform for 'the New Catholic Association': a blue frock-coat and black velvet collar, buff waistcoat and white pantaloons. Thus personally symbolising a renewed campaign O'Connell discreetly avoided all reference to the obnoxious securities, having already ensured that a majority of the meeting would oppose the Lawless motion condemning the 'wings'.

The crowd was on O'Connell's side. Lawless was received with general hisses and O'Connell asked that he be heard, observing: 'if he shall have said anything mischievous you may be sure, I will not fail to answer him'. Coppinger, Mahon and Lawless wished to reiterate Catholic commitment to a full and unconditional Emancipation and to condemn the 'wings'. The clear implication was that O'Connell and the deputation had acted incorrectly. Lawless stated that he wished to call Catholics back 'to their old and honest principles' and declared that the question had been thrown back for twenty years 'by the unfortunate credulity of the last three or four months'. The crowd got so excited, shouting 'off! off', that eventually Lawless was inaudible. O'Connell, with the crowd behind him, was more effective in mob oratory: "Tis true we have been defeated, but we are not dismayed; we have been betrayed, but we are unconquered still [*cheers*] . . .' He pointed to the fifty-three Protestant peers whose resolutions favoured Emancipation and to Brownlow's conversion; he entertained the crowd at the expense of the Biblical Protestants and by abusing Lord Liverpool. He promised the revival of the Association and the Rent: 'Let us rally and unite round the standard of liberty', he cried. 'I have promised in England that there shall be a new Catholic Association. I have promised that there shall be a new collection of the Rent'. After the meeting O'Connell's horses were taken from his carriage and he was drawn in triumph by the crowd to Merrion Square.[21]

O'Connell's movement was legally suppressed and internally divided. His attitude to legal suppression had been articulated in early January when Goulburn's Bill had been rumoured. He had then challenged the government to frame a statute capable of stifling the Catholic protest:

> Well, should they be displeased at the formation of this room, or our meeting in it, why we can build another; if they object to the denomination we have given ourselves, why we can change it with that of board, or committee, or even directory. If they prohibit our meeting, surely they cannot prevent our assembling to dine together. This Association is the creature of the Penal Code, and as long as Catholic disabilities exist, so long must some organ have its being through which to convey our complaints, to proclaim our grievances and to demand their redress (*92*, II, 469).

O'Connell now had to explore carefully the loopholes in Goulburn's Unlawful Societies Act. It was only legally possible to constitute a society to manage such of their affairs as had no relation to redress of grievances or any alteration in the existing laws. Petitioning and political matters had to be dealt with in separate and aggregate meetings of no more than fourteen days duration. The life-blood of the old Association — the Rent — ceased to flow with the dissolution of the Association in March 1825. At the same time, O'Connell had advised that the collection of the Rent should cease 'in all quarters' until he advised otherwise (III,

1189). It did not recommence until June 1826. Even allowing for O'Connell's legal ingenuity it was clear that the government had dealt a major, perhaps fatal, blow to his mass agitation.

O'Connell had to construct a new organisation and to restore his popularity throughout the provinces. In late June a Catholic meeting in Dublin elected a committee of twenty-one 'to consider whether a permanent body can be formed without any violation of the existing law'.[22] In July the plan of the New Catholic Association was announced.[23] The New Catholic Association was for the purpose of 'public peace and harmony' and to encourage 'a liberal and religious system of education', to conduct a census of the Catholic population, to promote a liberal and enlightened press and to pursue public charity 'and other such purposes as are not prohibited by the said Statute of the 6th Geo IV, Chap. 4'. The stated purposes and organisation of the new body effectively put it beyond reach of the law but the work of the old Association was only able to continue upon a restricted basis. Grievances received after March 1825, for example, did not receive the help afforded by the old Catholic Association, as O'Connell had to watch the legal restrictions very carefully. Catholic meetings 'on the subject of Catholic grievances' could meet in the counties and O'Connell exploited this fully to restore his authority and to keep the agitation alive.

In Wexford, for example, on the afternoon of 20 July, O'Connell embarked at Ferrycarrig and sailed the two miles down the river Slaney to the town in a procession of some fifty boats where he was guest of honour at a public banquet:[24] 'nothing could equal my triumphant entry *by water* into Wexford. The dinner was splendid, everything went off most admirably', he wrote home (III, 1243). Catholic meetings in Waterford, Carrick-on-Suir, Limerick, Kinsale and Dungarvan had already rowed in behind O'Connell.[25] The last six months of 1825 was marked by the absence of parish meetings, as the old Association had been the focus of local petitions and grievances but there were twenty-two county meetings as well as a number of town meetings.

In August 1825 Catholics in Co. Longford, for example, requisitioned a county meeting to petition parliament for Emancipation.[26] This county meeting, which took place on Saturday 24 September in the chapel at Longford, was important for local political development. It established a popular political organisation on a county basis for the first time — an organising committee for the meeting — which built upon the parish organisation evolved in the Rent collection. This Longford meeting also brought Bishop Magauran out in open support for the Emancipation campaign at local level which signalled a more strident clerical participation in the county noticeable in the years after 1825 in priests such as Father Felix Slevin, secretary to the meeting.

Bishop Magauran, in fact, proposed the resolution in praise of O'Connell, 'the steadfast and indefatigable advocate of our rights, and that at a time when his character is assailed by those who wish to create dissension and disunion amongst the Catholics of Ireland, we consider it out bounden duty to assure him that he is entitled to, and possesses, our unlimited confidence'. Later at the dinner, after the meeting, Magauran stated that he had been influenced to realise the necessity for clerical participation in politics when he had gone to London with the other bishops: he was now resolved 'to lend his assistance to the laity'.[27]

The laity in Co. Longford were, indeed, the prime movers: the rural and urban middle- and upper-class Catholics in the county had been roused to organise for their cause. There were about twenty chief activists and these can be identified by social position and occupation. In addition to Richard Dempsey, Christopher Carbry and the Dowdall family, already noted for their activities in the Catholic Rent collection, men like John C. Nugent, a landowner and £50 freeholder of Killesorna, Granard; J. D. Brady, who owned an estate of over 2,000 acres at Springtown, Granard; and Colonel Myles O'Reilly supported the meeting. The organising committee claimed to have obtained the signature of 'almost every Roman Catholic of respectability in the county' to call the meeting: of those who signed the requisition and who spoke at the meeting – in all about twenty – eleven were £50 freeholders in the county and five others were £20 freeholders. There were also prominent Longford business and professional interests such as were represented by Simon Nichols, an apothecary, surgeon, and £50 freeholder; Christopher Reynolds, attorney and £50 freeholder; in addition to the well-to-do Christopher Carbry. There were also a few large tenant farmers such as Edward Rooney and Valentine Dillon (*99*, 499-501).

The county meeting was an important occasion for the mass of the people also:

> A space near the altar was appropriated for the accommodation of the Gentlemen who took an active part in the proceedings. The aisles and galleries of the Chapel, which is, we understand capable of accommodating two thousand persons, were completely occupied by the crowds of peasantry who thronged in as if to show that *they* felt deeply their degrading condition.[28]

This was the first major political mobilisation of the people in Co. Longford for a parliamentary objective. This Longford pattern was replicated in the twenty-two counties which held such meetings before the end of 1825.

In this way O'Connell restored his political fortunes. His personal fortune also recovered. He had suffered a financial loss of about £3,000 due to his absence from the courts when in London between February and May (III, 1241). However, the death of his uncle in February enabled O'Connell to recover from this lost income as he now inherited Derrynane House and one-third of Hunting Cap's financial assets (III, 1159). O'Connell also attended to his legal duties assiduously on his return, taking cases wherever he could. As there was no prospect of parliamentary movement on Emancipation for perhaps two years it was in O'Connell's interests to ride out the storm of abuse over his compromising negotiations throughout 1825.

O'Connell faced sporadic revolts and some organised attempts to inflict a public defeat on him. Some wished to remove him from his dominant leadership position. The Bellews, one of the most prominent Catholic gentry families in Ireland, opposed O'Connell. Sir Edward Bellew had proposed the ballot procedure to elect the committee of twenty-one to consider the formation of the new Catholic organisation; O'Connell objected to this procedure but a ballot was held. Sir Edward was not, however, returned amongst the twenty-one elected but O'Connell was also well down the poll.[29] William Bellew, the barrister and brother of Sir Edward, then published a legal opinion against forming a new Catholic Association. William Bellew had been one of the first Roman Catholics called to the Bar and he represented the Catholic gentry amongst the legal fraternity. He was an aristocratic figure with a deep respect for the law: according to Sheil he at one time 'monopolised the whole Catholic business' and knew the situation of every Catholic family of importance in Ireland (*114*, I, 143-56). O'Connell was furious and published a letter to the Catholics of Ireland on 28 June strongly attacking Bellew who, as a pensioner of the Castle, was in the pay of the government. Bellew had received a pension in lieu of promotion to the position of assistant barrister. 'The under-growl of poor Jack Lawless, and his few foolish partisans may be, as it has been, a mere source of laughter and ridicule. It might tease for a moment but it could do no permanent harm. But Mr Wm Bellew stands in a very different situation'. O'Connell stated that as soon as parliament rose the New Catholic Association would commence. Stigmatising Bellew as a 'Castle' Catholic effectively neutralised his opposition in popular eyes.[30] O'Connell had to defend a poor case by claiming that he had had the consent of the Irish bishops in London for the clerical 'wing' and by acknowledging that his sacrifice of the forty-shilling freeholders had been a mistake. His vindication rested upon his long record in the Catholic cause.[31] O'Connell skill in popular politics and his ruthless attacks on less able opponents ensured his survival during these critical months.

In the summer of 1825 Dublin was in a novel mood of silence, as Goulburn reported to Peel on 22 July: 'The general opinion is that

there will be very little done in the way of mischief until after the cir-
cuits or even until the opening of the law courts in November ... quiet
is good for O'Connell's embarrassment at present' (*113*, 25). Shortly
after this Archbishop William Magee wrote to Lord Colchester on 5
August wisely discerning the meaning of the silence:

> It happens indeed that there is nothing to communicate but the
> one great miracle, that we are quiet. For several years I have not
> witnessed the appearance of so much tranquillity as this country
> presents at this time ... Our great agitators are at this time on cir-
> cuit. This, and the serious divisions existing amongst the leaders,
> afford us a respite from turmoil. When the demagogues, civil and
> ecclesiastical, have shaken hands, and a plan of operations has been
> fixed on, we may then have something more to talk of.

Magee gave Colchester as one extraordinary proof of 'the degree of
quietness' that he was allowed 'to walk abroad unmolested by rude
expressions or menacing looks'. (*20*, III, 402).

There were several new stratagems proposed for the New Catholic
Association; these included a 'census' of the population to use the over-
whelmingly superior numbers of Catholics as a propaganda weapon.
Sheil proposed this in June 1825:

> Forty-eight non-contents [in the House of Lords] have produced
> seven millions of malcontents. That we are malcontents, they admit
> — that we are seven millions, they deny. What, then, is to be done?
> Let there be a census of the Catholics of Ireland. 'Do not dress your
> slaves in a peculiar garb', said a Roman statesman, 'lest they should
> learn their own strength'.[32]

At the Meath Catholic meeting on the banks of the Boyne on 28
August 1825 Sheil declared:

> A census must be taken. Every parish must meet on the same day —
> and a great convention must be summoned. Let the Catholic pre-
> lates, the chief of the Catholic clergy, the nobility, the gentry, the
> great agriculturalists, the merchants, and the members of the liberal
> professions meet. Let the Peers and leading Catholics be invited to
> unite themselves with this National Assembly. The eyes of the
> empire would be fixed upon its deliberations. Its setting may be
> continued for fourteen successive days ... when liberty is spreading
> its illuminations to the extremities of the world ... while South
> America is starting into freedom, Ireland should still continue en-
> slaved? (*119*, 371-2).

There was a growing Irish-American response to the Irish Catholic movement: in the summer of 1825 Irish-Americans in several cities began

organising support for O'Connell and the Catholic Association. The New York Friends of Ireland formulated an address requesting Latin American assistance for Ireland. Many major American newspapers both endorsed Catholic Emancipation and fully covered the issue (*88*, 354-62). Sheil's words had some substance. For the next three years census returns from parishes came in but while never completed the returns made excellent propaganda at public meetings. The simultaneous meetings proposal was not implemented until 1828. To achieve this the new apparatus would need to use priests much more than had been the case in the old Association.[33]

O'Connell and Sheil proceeded with great caution, making no attempt to implement such major proposals or to collect the Rent afresh. O'Connell concentrated on his own heartland in Munster and Leinster and to this end two major provincial meetings were held as rallies, one in Limerick in October and one in Carlow in December. These provincial rallies became a feature of the new agitation: in all eleven were to be held before 1829. They took the form of annual conventions and they necessitated considerable organisation and preparation. For the first Munster provincial meeting at Limerick the committees from the various counties met first in Limerick. The secretaries of the different counties then formed a central committee. This committee then 'convened the principal gentlemen of their respective counties' in order to gain their assent for the resolutions prepared by the central committee. Then the committee issued a circular letter to 'the most respectable individuals' through each county secretary and the replies were sent to the central secretary at Limerick who made the arrangements for the meeting and the dinner.[34]

The Limerick meeting in October turned into a rally for O'Connell, as he recounted to his wife:

> The provincial meeting has gone off admirably. We had no less than six Protestant speakers . . . I got a flaming address from the *trades* of Limerick. They made a procession in the streets to the chapel and accompanied me back again. I spoke for something less than an hour and was as well received as it is possible for anybody to be. The crowd was immense. We had gentlemen in numbers from all the counties in the province (III, 1253).

Such a meeting added colour, glamour and excitement to an agitation badly shaken by events of 1825: huge processions with symbolic green branches and festoons, circles and other emblems contributed to the sense of occasion and spectacle. Wyse specifically points out that the role of the clergy at provincial meetings gave a 'sort of religious sanction' to the cause (*132*, I, 228).

Shortly after this triumph O'Connell dealt with further criticism for his 'wings' compromise. The Catholics of Co. Louth had met in the Catholic chapel of Dundalk on 17 October and Anthony Marmion, the secretary, proposed the censuring of O'Connell, accusing him of having acted on 'corrupt and personal motives' but this motion failed. O'Connell none the less wrote, as he told his wife, 'a long and tame answer' to the Catholics of Louth on 31 October, going through the charges at length.[35] He could not afford to show his anger in public. His spirits were revived by the stir caused by Wellesley's marriage to a Mrs Patterson. She was a strict Catholic and the ceremony was performed by Archbishop Murray attended by two priests on 29 October. This outraged the Orangemen and O'Connell reflected on his pleasure at 'the discountenance which a Catholic vice-queen would necessarily throw upon the *ribaldry* of the oppressing faction' (III, 1258). Mrs Patterson had already seriously embarrassed Saurin when he did not realise she was a Catholic:

> She dined some days ago with Saurin and somebody introduced Catholic politics. Saurin at once damned Pope and Popery to the lowest pit of Hell. She said nothing at the time, but before dinner was quite over she took occasion to mention her being a Catholic just as a matter of course. You may judge of Saurin's confusion. He said nothing but next day she got from him a long apology which of course she disregarded (III, 1255).

Restored in spirit O'Connell began to agitate in Dublin as he wrote on 1 November. 'We are beginning to agitate again. Tomorrow we will hold a little aggregate and if that shall succeed we will hold one every Wednesday. The New Association will meet on Saturday so that I hope the effect of the anti-association bill will be to give us two meetings in the week in the place of one' (III, 1258). O'Connell now stated that he was prepared to recommence the collection of the Catholic Rent which he believed could be managed legally.[36] No immediate steps were taken, however, on such a collection.

The next major test of O'Connell's control over the Catholic movement was the provincial meeting arranged for Carlow on 15 December. William F. Finn, O'Connell's brother-in-law, condemned the 'wings' at the Carlow aggregate meeting on 28 November though he was careful to say he was not attempting to censure O'Connell. Finn was the son of a rich Carlow merchant who owned Finn's *Leinster Journal*: he had married O'Connell's sister Alicia in 1812. However, a major anti-O'Connell effort was made. In early December Mary O'Connell wrote to her husband:

> Were I in your place I would not go a step to the *Carlow* meeting and, what is more, I would give up Catholic politics and leave the

nasty ungrateful set to sink into insignificance. Of course Finn must be at all times opposed to you, and *Master* Sheil, I think, is wheeling round again. Leave them all *there* and in a short time make a fortune without sacrificing your time and your health (III, 1268).

On his way to the Carlow meeting O'Connell knew he had a battle on his hands:

There is a most violent party raised against me. What a world we live in! The object probably is to drive me off the stage of Catholic politics . . . It would be a great triumph to them if they could drive me off. Obloquy and reproach have been the certain salary of those who in every age or country have honestly struggled for the welfare of their native land (III, 1269).

Shrewdly O'Connell arranged a public presentation of a salver and an address from the Wexford Catholics on the morning of the meeting.

Bishop Doyle, whom O'Connell claimed had concurred with the 'wings' in London, had shown in July that he did not sanction O'Connell's acceptance of them; he declared he would have resigned as bishop rather than accept Treasury money.[37] Doyle now seemed to oppose O'Connell by his part in the preparation of resolutions condemning the 'wings' for the Carlow meeting; he described the measure for clerical provision as a 'paltry bribe' at Carlow College on the evening before the provincial meeting.[38] O'Connell could not afford to alienate such a key figure in the Catholic hierarchy and he sought quickly to re-establish Doyle's support through an intermediary, Rev. Dr Jeremiah Donovan, a professor in Maynooth (III, 1273).

O'Connell defeated 'William Finn's three weeks of organisation' through his appeal to the people, as he told a worried Mary who had been anxious to hear 'the result of your *trial*' at Carlow (III, 1270).

At Carlow, darling, at Carlow where we were to have been defeated and put down for ever . . . at Carlow *we were triumphant*. We beat the Wingers out of the field. O'Gorman was most heartily hissed and all but pelted to pieces. I never, darling, will forsake the people. The good sense, the good feeling of *my* poor people . . . They would not listen to the Wingers and their fantasies. It would do your heart good if you were to know how harshly the Wingers used me in the first instance, to see their total defeat by the people. They really thought they had nothing to do but to declaim that they were the friends of the people and that I was their enemy . . . In short, darling, I never in my life was so delighted with any meeting (III, 1271).

The Carlow 'trial' was crucial. It enabled O'Connell to restore unity on the formula of 'unqualified Emancipation'. He avoided a formal condemnation of the 'wings' which would have implied rejection of his London position. He was determined that the 'wings' would not split the Catholic movement, as the Veto controversy had done a decade earlier.

The 1825 experience was to prove central to the Catholic struggle and indeed to the evolution of Irish popular politics. O'Connell now became convinced that Emancipation could only succeed without securities, as he explained to Pierce Mahony in September 1828:

> I have at my side the experiment of 1825, at which time I am con-
> vinced we should have had Lord Liverpool compelled to grant
> Emancipation if I had not foolishly acceded to the securities called
> 'the Wings'. In fact we were carrying the Emancipation bill not by
> reason of the political wisdom of the Ministry but from the appre-
> hension entertained of the resentment of the Irish nation in con-
> sequence of the suppression of the Catholic Association. The course
> I should have taken was to have kept up that salutory apprehension
> and I could easily have done so but, instead of *that*, I listened in an
> evil hour to the suggestions of Mr Plunket, etc. who said that if we
> conceded 'the Wings' by way of security, we should certainly carry
> the bill. Now, it would have been impossible to obtain a public
> sanction to 'the Wings', so I gave mine and succeeded. I was the only
> man, I believe, who could succeed in causing a perfect silence to
> reign amongst the universal Catholic body. I procured for this pur-
> pose public tranquillity. The Ministry saw that I had appeased the
> storm, they considered that the danger was passed and the House
> of Lords scouted our Emancipation bill . . .

In fact O'Connell was abused for betraying popular rights for the sake of personal ambition by Peel, Cobbett and Irish Catholics such as Lawless. O'Connell resolved never to be 'deceived' again: 'We shall never be emancipated but as we were relieved in 1778, 1782, and 1793, that is, when it becomes *necessary* for the English Government to do something for Ireland' (III, 1485). From 1826 he concentrated on creating that necessity for Emancipation.

4

1826:
'The Whole Nation in One Cry'

'It will be a *battle* . . . which . . . will decide the Catholic Question . . . The election of Mr Stuart must be considered as the harbinger of Civil Freedom in Ireland.'
Dublin Evening Post, 28 March 1826

'A darker cloud than ever seems to me to impend over Ireland, that is, if one of the remaining bonds of society, the friendly connection between landlord and tenant, is dissolved.'
Sir Robert Peel to Sir George Hill,
16 July 1826 (*107*, I, 412-13)

On 16 January 1826 a 'Catholic Association for 1826' was established for a period of fourteen days. This temporary 'Association' brought a new degree of unity amongst Irish Catholics after the damaging dissensions caused by the 'wings' controversy in 1825.[1] The keynote of the future was sounded by Thomas Wyse, a new leader from Waterford. Wyse had the foresight to envisage the Catholic organisation being transformed into a vast electoral machine. He stressed the importance of involving the lower classes in politics, arguing 'that the common people should meet together as much as possible upon constitutional subjects'. He declared to the Association members going back to their respective counties that they had the means 'of bringing up the whole nation in one cry . . .'[2]

The Catholic cause was in some difficulty in early 1826. The Protestant ultras could look forward to raising the powerful 'no popery' cry in the forthcoming general election. This could destroy the overall balance of support for Emancipation in the House of Commons and undo the long patient work of the British Catholic Association and others in the development of a public opinion favourable to the Catholic cause. Besides, liberal Tories like Canning had agreed to defer discussion of the Catholic claims in the Commons in 1826. Parliament met at the beginning of February with every prospect of a turbulent session. As Henry Hobhouse observed, the commercial distress, the Corn Laws and the Catholic question all afforded possible matter of 'angry debate'. However, except for the presentation of petitions, the Catholic question was 'not stirred' (*2*, 120).

The parliamentary stalemate revealed how dependent the Catholic movement was on liberal Protestants. Here O'Connell saw the need to rally support. In June 1825 sixty-five peers, all describing themselves as 'Protestant peers possessing property in Ireland', had given their assent to resolutions, drawn up at Buckingham House, London, advocating Emancipation. The Dukes of Devonshire and Buckingham, the Duke of Leinster, Lords Lansdowne and Fitzwilliam, as well as Donoughmore and Charlemont led these peers in calling for civil equality for Catholics. The sixty-five peers warned, in the wake of the Lords' rejection of Burdett's Catholic Relief Bill, that it was expedient 'to confer with advantage what cannot be refused with safety and to adopt in peace a measure which may be forced upon us in war'.[3]

This public show of support softened the bitter disappointment of 1825. At a Catholic meeting on 23 November 1825 O'Connell arranged to issue invitations to the sixty-five Protestant peers, to such Irish MPs as supported Emancipation, to 'those amongst the Irish Protestant Gentry who have distinguished themselves for liberality', to the Anglican bishops of Norwich and Rochester, and Rev. Sydney Smith, Rev. William Shepherd and John Wilks.[4] On 2 February 1826 the Catholic Association gave a great dinner to these 'friends of civil and religious liberty' which was described as 'by far the most sumptuous dinner we ever witnessed . . . All the Catholic Noblemen, Baronets and Gentlemen now in Ireland were present'.[5] A minority of the Irish MPs invited actually attended but some, like Sir Edward O'Brien, MP for Co. Clare, had the excuse that they were attending the opening session of parliament in London and so could not be in Dublin. Like O'Brien, many Irish MPs believed Emancipation 'would be no less an act of policy than of justice' but they were not particularly keen to be closely identified with O'Connell and the Association (III, 1278, 1280).

O'Connell, in his evidence to the Select Committee on the State of Ireland of the House of Lords in March 1825, had defined a 'liberal Protestant' as one who had declared an opinion favourable to Catholic claims or, in practice, every person not known to be unfavourable. Earlier he had described a 'liberal Protestant in Ireland' to the Select Committee on the State of Ireland of the House of Commons as

an object of great affection and regard from the entire Catholic population; amongst ourselves we always talk of him as a protector and friend; a Protestant who is not an Orangeman is spoken of as a stranger merely would be, but without feelings of hostility; the Protestant who is an Orangeman is considered as decidedly an enemy, and the extent of that enmity depends upon the peculiar education and habits of the individual who speaks of it; the peasantry speak of them as of Exterminators . . .

Catholic Emancipation was still perceived even by Catholics as a great potential achievement of liberal Protestantism. The Grattanite tradition was drawn upon by both Protestant and Catholic liberals who wished to unite through equality the Irish Catholic and the Irish Protestant into a common citizenship under the Constitution.

Famous Irish Protestant writers, such as Lady Morgan and Maria Edgeworth, favoured Catholic Emancipation as did many landed Protestant families. For Maria Edgeworth the ideal instrument for reforming Irish conditions was an enlightened liberal governing class. She believed that the Irish landed gentry should take their duties much more seriously. If Catholic Emancipation was achieved under their benign auspices Maria Edgeworth believed it would be a panacea for Ireland's social and political ills: 'Catholics *can* and should have equal rights', she declared, 'but *must* not have a *dominant* religion' (*51*, 37). Edgeworth admired men like Henry Petty-Fitzmaurice, third Marquess of Lansdowne, a moderate Whig, who owned vast estates in Co. Kerry and the great Whig house, Bowood, near Calne in Wiltshire. Lansdowne was Thomas Moore's friend and patron. Maria Edgeworth corresponded with Thomas Spring-Rice, the Limerick City MP, a Whig reformer, who claimed that 'the safety of the Protestant Establishment in Ireland requires Catholic Emancipation' (*51*, 44). Thomas Spring-Rice, like other liberal Protestants, feared the dangers of an Irish 'democracy' developing if Emancipation were not conceded. Spring-Rice wrote a pamphlet entitled *Catholic Emancipation considered on Protestant Principles* in which he said the British Constitution was being threatened by 'a republic of agitators'. He declared: 'The refusal is that of England; the demand being that of the Irish nation . . . England and the Union are fast becoming words of reproach amongst us'.[6]

Lady Morgan's literary and political salon of the 1820s at No. 35 Kildare Street, Dublin was influential in promoting the Catholic cause as were her popular novels and writings. There were valuable social occasions where the Morgans and the Wellesley administration brought together both Catholics and Orangemen. For example, in March 1826, O'Connell, Lord Killeen, and the Morgans attended a private party in Dublin Castle with Colonel Blacker, described in Lady Morgan's *Diary* as Grand Master of the Orange Lodge, 'the roaring lion'. Henry Joy, 'the *oriflame* of every species of intolerance and illiberalism' was also present, as was John Doherty 'the ministerial *enfant trouvé* (*47*, II, 225). In this way liberal Protestants provided a 'bridge' between Catholics and Orangemen and helped to soften asperities and to further the social and political acceptability of Catholics.

Most liberal Protestants simply wished the Catholics cause success in the passive way Thomas Wyse describes:

The liberal Protestant sat quietly looking on — read his article in the

Edinburgh Review or the *Morning Chronicle* — prophesied that some time or other the question would be carried — regretted the obstacles which the Catholics had thrown in their own way — trusted to the gradual illumination of the lower classes in England, and then sipped his tea, and proved to his *own* satisfaction that he had fully done his duty (*132*, II, 12).

In Ireland time was running out for such complacent liberalism: up to 1826 Catholics needed sympathetic Protestant parliamentary representatives, 'Friends of the People', as they were termed. But what if 'the People' themselves were to display a novel potential for independent political action?

The significance of the 1828 general election in Irish popular politics lies in the nature of the electoral system after the Act of Union. Since 1800 Ireland sent to the parliament of the United Kingdom 100 MPs. The balance of representation was weighted heavily in favour of the thirty-two county constituencies which had two seats each. The remaining 36 MPs represented cities and boroughs and the University of Dublin.

Boroughs had one seat each, as had the University, but the cities of Dublin and Cork had two seats each. Many of the boroughs were immune to contests of any kind being in the nomination of a local magnate. The more 'open' boroughs were also effectively controlled: there were only six boroughs which had a polled contest, with electors actually casting votes, in the 1818 general election and only seven in the 1820 general election. Conditions for eligibility to the franchise in the boroughs varied but the numbers of voters were almost always very small: 155 voters, for example, cast their ballots in the Kilkenny City election in 1820 while 205 voted to decide the Mallow election. In places like Limerick City and Galway City perhaps up to 1,000 people were eligible to vote while in the exceptional case of Cork City perhaps up to 3,000 had the franchise. Boroughs were almost totally outside the realm of popular electoral revolts.

Unlike their English co-religionists the Catholics of Ireland had been admitted to the parliamentary and municipal franchise in 1793. Few of them gained the municipal vote due to Protestant control of the corporations. The only potential political effect of Catholic votes lay in the counties. Representation here rested on freehold property. Such property was deemed to be that which was owned and held for an indeterminate period, because it was owned in fee simple or leased for a term of life. A man with freehold property was supposed to be 'independent', and therefore non-freehold property could produce no voters.

An anomaly arose because of this distinction in that a man with a lease for one life was a freeholder while a man with a lease for a period of time, even 999 years, was not. The Irish electoral system involved periodic registration of different categories of freeholders: £50, £20, £10 and forty-shilling freeholders.

Landlords controlled the representation in the counties and where contests occurred they were fought out between county landed families usually on a local basis with little enough attention being paid to the great issues dividing politicians at Westminster. Landlords expected their tenants, who were registered as voters, to vote for them and they formed coalitions where necessary with other landlords to secure sufficient backing to be elected. Mostly it never came to an actual poll, the result being obvious from past experience or from the preliminary canvass. In 1818 eight counties had a poll while in 1820 only in three counties did voters have to cast their votes. Many counties after 1800 had never been polled and others had only had one or two contests in that time. Co. Dublin and Co. Leitrim were noted for frequent polls due in part to the lavish expenditure of the wealthy White family in pursuit of parliamentary seats.[7]

Despite the infrequency of voting it was still important for landlords with a political interest to ensure that as many of their tenants as possible were registered to vote: having an obvious preponderance of voters deterred potential candidates from bringing an election to a poll. If a landlord was able to contribute a sizeable number of freeholders to a successful candidate he had an important claim on the local patronage exercised by the MP. It had become common practice to grant leases for terms of life with an alternative of terms of years. Leases could be worded so as to create a freehold interest by the insertion of terms of life as required. In this way forty-shilling freeholders were created to bolster a landlord's political interest in the county representation. In 1820 an Election Act simplified the registration procedure for such voters and according to critics of this Act numerous squatter tenants and 'fictitious' voters were admitted to the franchise. The forty-shilling freeholder had to swear to a forty-shilling interest in his 'freehold' after his rent and other charges were paid.

Potentially the forty-shilling freeholder franchise might achieve a very large Irish electorate. Such preponderant Catholic voters, if organised, could pose a devastating threat to Protestant and landed control in Ireland. However, in practice the right of these voters was largely abstract as they were never asked to exercise it at all. The franchise did confer some economic advantage on tenants where landlords allowed some indulgence, in matters of subdivision of land or in rent concessions, for political reasons. Some landlords undoubtedly engaged in what Edward Wakefield called 'political agronomy'. The vote could, however, be a disaster for the tenant if he was pressured to resist his landlord's claims on his vote: eviction for disobedience or other 'punishments' were inflicted. At no time was the forty-shilling franchise exercised by more than some thousands in those counties which had contests. For example, it was estimated that 5,200 freeholders were capable of voting in Co. Westmeath but perhaps half that number actually voted in a hotly contested election in 1826.[8] In the 1820s the Co. Louth electorate was about 3,000 voters but perhaps less than one-third of that number, 930 votes, were actually cast in a very close fought contest (*84*, 136-7, 150). Mostly candidates were elected on relatively small numbers of votes where the infrequent polling occurred: the highest polling candidate in the 1818 general election was Richard Butler, Viscount Caher, with 5,331 votes in Co. Tipperary, an exceptionally large county. The highest polling candidate in the 1820 general election was Richard Hobart Fitzgibbon with 4,195 votes in Co. Limerick. These were very much the exceptions.

When an election was called landlords had to assess the relative strengths of the various contenders in terms of registered voters. By law voters had to be one year registered before they could actually vote. Each county voter had two votes — one for each seat — but they might exercise only one, if they wished, as a 'plumper'. The votes were declared in public in an open ballot over a period of days. Each barony sent in its voters to its own open booth in the county town. Before such voting at the hustings a number of stages took place. Candidates issued election addresses calling for support and announcing their intention of seeking election. Then followed a period of canvassing of the landed interests in the county. This canvass would take some account of the freeholders' general interests: a majority of the Irish MPs supported Catholic Emancipation, reflecting the increasingly important 'Catholic vote' for liberal Protestant candidates. By 1820 there existed in eighteen of the twenty-three counties outside Ulster distinct Catholic interests which supported the candidate or candidates in favour of Emancipation. After the canvassing nominations were made at the hustings with public speeches and then, if necessary, polling commenced.

Irish county elections were notorious for violent local affrays between rival landed interests: riots and disorder generally accompanied a contested election. Mobs of non-voters, well primed with free liquor by their patrons, were frequently employed to intimidate the electors. Corruption was common: it could occur in the form of personation, false swearing of the required oaths or through simple bribery in close contests. Where tenants were caught in a contest involving pro-Catholic and anti-Catholic candidates their dilemma might indeed be cruel. Economic reasons for obeying the landlord had to be weighed against loyalty to Catholicism. Many chose not to vote at all in this situation if they could avoid it. The final episode in an election was the 'chairing' of the successful candidates through the town and the holding of victory celebrations.

The general election of 1826 was a challenge to the Catholic Association to demonstrate popular support for Emancipation. Could they bring 'the whole nation in one cry' for Emancipation? The government had always worried about the implications of Catholic voters being directed by the Association. 'The Protestant interest in this country is the support of the government', Goulburn had written worriedly to Peel in September 1825. 'I ought rather to say, of government and of British connection, and wherever that shall be defeated, as it will be in many instances, you will have an immediate political opponent' (*40*, 395). At this time Goulburn anticipated contests in eight counties, possibly even eleven, and he was convinced that in some of them — Waterford, Mayo, Kilkenny and Cavan — the influence of the priesthood would be brought to bear on the electorate in opposition to 'the Protestant interest'.

As early as August 1824 the *Dublin Evening Post* had pointed out that the forty-shilling franchise gave 'an importance to the Catholic population of Ireland which it did not possess since the Revolution'. It cited Sligo and Dublin as counties where 'this importance has been felt' as in these counties forty-shilling voters had deserted their landlords: the *Post* pointed to these 'lessons' for parliamentary candidates 'hereafter' who would be forced to declare for Emancipation or face defeat. In September the *Post* suggested that a test for parliamentary candidates might be whether they had supported the Catholic Rent.[9] In October 1824 Goulburn wrote to Peel that 'It is not concealed that whenever an election shall take place the people will be placed in opposition to their landlords and such members only returned as shall please the Association' (*40*, 388-9).

The rôle which the priests would play in the general election gave particular concern to the government in Ireland and when the election occurred the Association did indeed call upon the priests to do 'their duty in the present crisis' as citizens and as local leaders. O'Connell called for archdiocesan and diocesan meetings throughout Ireland and the *Post* published a long defence of the rôle of priests in politics.[10] Before these elections the Catholic leaders did not really believe that they had the considerable resources necessary to mobilise on a widespread national scale the forty-shilling voters or that the forty-shilling voters could be a reliable source of electoral support due to landlord influence and control. O'Connell had been prepared to sacrifice the forty-shilling franchise in 1825 as part of the negotiations for Emancipation: he was not convinced of the national possibilities in the popular electorate under existing electoral conditions.[11] Other informed observers were convinced, however, that if it came to a direct collision of appeals to the forty-shilling freehold voter Catholicism and the priests would beat property and the Protestant landlords.

There were no precedents for a national political organisation centred upon electoral politics. O'Connell had been quite prepared to warn hostile MPs of his influence at the polls but he had not yet conceived of a national electoral organisation. General Elections had been conceived more in terms of a series of local contests: thanks to the Association, 1826 was to mark a major advance towards the concept of general elections as confrontations between national parties on national issues. The Catholic Association policy in 1826 was to contest only where the Catholic would 'gain a vote in the House of Commons by a change of men . . . if a change in the representation will not produce such a result we leave the County politics to be decided by County interests — by piques, by family influence, and by those numerous motives which govern men in such circumstances'.[12] In 1824 the Catholic Association had begun to consider possible preparations for the expected general election but the negotiations in London, and the subsequent internal divisions in the Association following the 1825 crisis, meant that little work had been done at national level for the general election. It was left almost entirely to local initiative in the counties to make preparations for electoral revolts: it is at county level, especially in Waterford, that the significance of 1826 may be discerned.

The Catholic Rent collection in Co. Waterford had transformed attitudes to local politics. The well-to-do John Matthew Galwey is a notable example of this change. He was a Catholic with a number of business interests; he was a wine merchant, shipowner, land agent and owner of an estate in Cork. In March 1824 Galwey withdrew his name from the list of Rent collectors as he felt that 'party business of any kind is injurious to the country' and he advised Catholics to have 'patience'.[13] Yet, Galwey became a noted local leader in the 1826 contest and went on to become a Repeal MP for the county in 1832. His progression in popular politics was typical of middle- and upper-class Waterford Catholics.

The political struggle in Co. Waterford began in the summer of 1824.[14] Henry Villiers Stuart, a young wealthy landlord, who had just attained his majority, decided to make Dromana his principal residence in July 1824; by August he was on the Grand Jury and giving a lavish entertainment to three hundred guests at Dromana.[15] Early in 1823 Stuart had been praised for his relief to the poor in the parish of Aglish.[16] Already he was being mentioned as a possible candidate in Waterford

(*4*, 83). At the end of 1824 he joined the Catholic Association and sent in a subscription of £20.[17] As a resident landlord, who could claim he spent £20,000 each year improving his estate, Stuart was the ideal liberal Protestant candidate for local Catholics.[18]

In October 1824 Waterford Catholics held a large meeting 'to counter-act the Bible Societies' with the bishop, Dr Kelly, in the chair. The leaders of the Waterford Catholic movement were landed, professional and commercial men, such as John Leonard, who chaired meetings of the Waterford Chamber of Commerce; Thomas Meagher, a wealthy Catholic merchant; and Roger Hayes, a barrister of King St, Waterford. These were ably assisted by Father John Sheehan, the most active priest in the local Catholic Association.[19] The October meeting sought not merely a restoration of Catholic rights but, according to Meagher, 'to preserve inviolate the purity of their true and ancient faith' [*very great applause*]. Several Protestant evangelical societies such as Waterford Auxiliary Bible Society and the Waterford Church Missionary Society had become active in Co. Waterford at this time.[20]

By the end of 1824 the Catholics in Waterford were organised and conscious of a wide range of issues upon which they might fight. Villiers Stuart was making himself available as their champion in the coming election, and there was considerable local liberal Protestant support for Catholic Emancipation. In February 1825 twelve Protestant magistrates and thirteen other Protestants of note signed a County of Waterford Protestant Petition in favour of Catholic Emancipation.[21] The spring of 1825 was marked by increasing Waterford contributions to the Rent until the collection had to stop in March. In June the Waterford Catholics held a large aggregate meeting at which a com-mittee of five people was established to further the registry and to devise the best mode of securing the proper representation of the county; a similar move was made in Carrick-on-Suir at another aggregate meeting.[22]

In late July the Beresfords began to take note of Catholic activity. The Beresford family represented one of the wealthiest and most power-ful interests in Ireland: to a unique degree they symbolised the Protestant Ascendancy. Lord John George Beresford was Archbishop of Armagh and Primate: the head of the Established Church in Ireland. Lord George Thomas Beresford held the Beresford seat in Co. Waterford which the family felt was its by proprietorial right. The Beresford name was synonymous with Protestant control and patronage and had been so for as long as anyone could recall. Now, in August 1825 the Marquis of Waterford, father of George Thomas Beresford, warned the Grand Jury about the Catholic moves. At this time the Catholics of Waterford gave a dinner to the twelve liberal Proestant magistrates who had petition-ed in favour of Emancipation in February. Sheil spoke at the dinner and the health of Henry Villiers Stuart and the prospect of his return was toasted.[23] According to Thomas Wyse this dinner 'was the seed of all the after events' (*132*, I, 263).

The groundwork had been laid during 1824 both by Stuart and by the Catholic activists. It was apparent that the great 'discordancy between the electors and the elected', as Wyse termed it, could be ended by a challenge to the Beresfords; this dinner marked an alliance between the liberal Protestants and the well-to-do Catholics in the county. The initial electoral revolt in Waterford came from the gentry and middle classes, both Catholic and Protestant, against the dominance of the Beresfords. The gentry 'had hitherto acquiesced' in the division of the county between the Duke of Devonshire and the Marquis of Waterford; in 1825 they 'determined that their opinions *should be heard* and they lost no time in looking about for a member who could and would express them' (*132*, I, 267).

In the middle of August 1825 Thomas Wyse arrived in Waterford having spent almost ten years on the continent.[24] Wyse was a very accomplished representative of the Irish Catholic gentry. He was a master of several languages, and interested in artistic and literary matters as well as antiquities. He became the first historian of the Irish Catholic movement and his family had a long and proud involvement in Catholic affairs since the 1750s. In 1821, he had married Letitia Bonaparte, a niece of Napoleon. His political views were sophisticated especially in the context of the rowdy debates of the Catholic Association: he was passionately interested in the political education of the Irish people and was a serious liberal and reformer. Sheil provides a good contemporary description of Wyse:

> His person is small, and rather below the middle size; he has, however, an exceedingly gentleman-like bearing, which takes away any impression of diminutiveness. He holds himself erect, and seems a little animated by a consciousness that he belongs to an ancient family and is owner of the manor of St John. He is exceedingly graceful in his manners, and at once conveys the conviction of his having lived in the best society (*114*, II, 340).

Like Sheil, Wyse was a product of Stonyhurst and Trinity College, Dublin. Wyse was quickly caught up in Catholic affairs in Waterford. He revealed a real talent for political organisation, becoming chairman of the committee supporting Stuart; later Wyse recalled that at this stage 'the enthusiasm' was confined 'to the upper and middle classes (*132*, I, 268).

In September the *Dublin Evening Post* pointed to the great rôle which the Catholic clergy might play in the election and to 'the intense interest' in the forthcoming battle: 'Waterford will be the test', it declared.[25] The dissolution of parliament was expected in October and Beresford issued an election address on 21 October attacking his 'juvenile antagonist'.[26] Had there been an election at this time Stuart would have won, as he had ensured a majority of the votes on the registry books: 'the house of Dromana would have vanquished in fair feudal lists the house of Curraghmore', as Wyse observed. With the general election deferred until 1826 the Beresfords were given time to rally and the result was that a novel appeal had to be made to the people (*132*, I, 269-70). From late 1825 to June 1826 the contest developed remarkable and original proportions. The right of the holder of the franchise to exercise it 'freely' became a central issue as the Beresfords fought tenaciously to control the county.

Attempts were made from early October 1825 by Stuart's supporters to get the Duke of Devonshire's support for both Stuart and Richard Power, who had been a Whig MP for Co. Waterford for many years; the Duke maintained his support for Power but declared his neutrality between Stuart and Beresford. The Waterford Catholics sought to have Devonshire's full backing for the Emancipationist cause.[27] The Duke in fact expected his forty-shilling freeholders to vote as he put it 'singly for Mr Power'. The Catholics 'acquiesced' in this 'temporary disenfranchisement' until June 1826 when O'Connell helped 'to put an end to the absurd notion of neutrality'. There were about 400 voters 'belonging' to the Duke of Devonshire. According to O'Connell, Devonshire agents 'acted a most treacherous part' towards Stuart's committee who 'were afraid openly to attack these voters' because of the Duke's neutrality. O'Connell deemed this 'all sheer nonsense' and in the subsequent popular enthusiasm Devonshire's voters were won over (III, 1312, 1314).

Thomas Wyse came to the fore at the Munster provincial meeting in late October 1825 at Limerick when he presided at the dinner and made a noted speech. This meeting was quickly followed by an aggregate meeting of the Catholics of Waterford in the Great Chapel in early November where Wyse made another speech and was amongst the most prominent organisers.[28] In the last half of 1825 he had emerged as the outstanding local leader in Waterford.

Early in January 1826 the Waterford Catholics held another large meeting representative of the county and city in the Great Chapel. Richard Power O'Shea, of Gardenmorris, a member of the local gentry at Kilmacthomas, was chairman and Father John Sheehan was secretary.[29] Amongst the other prominent participants were Robert Power of Whitechurch, a brother of the MP Richard Power, and members of the Waterford gentry such as Patrick Power of Tinhalla, Nicholas Power of

Faithlegg, Pierce George Barron of Belmont, Cappoquin, Alexander Sherlock of Killaspy House, William Power of Dunhill Lodge, Patrick Power of Bellevue, and Henry Winston Barron and William Winston Barron; amongst the well-to-do business and professional men at the meeting were John Archbold, John Leonard and Roger Hayes.[30] This important meeting, while it sought 'unconditional and unqualified Emancipation' was mainly concerned to pledge support for 'the two liberal candidates' in the county at the coming election, as well as for Sir John Newport, MP for the City of Waterford.

With the county gentry fully mobilised the Waterford activists pursued their electoral campaign by holding a large dinner for Villiers Stuart in Morrison's Hotel, Dublin. The dinner was given by 'The Friends of Civil and Religious Liberty and Purity of Election'.[31] Lord Killeen took the chair and about 150 attended including 'most of the Gentlemen active in Catholic politics'. This Dublin meeting was clearly intended to highlight the national importance of the contest in Co. Waterford. O'Connell spoke at the meeting expressing confidence in Stuart's cause. Sheil advised close attention to the registries in Waterford. The situation was becoming less favourable to Stuart because of the strong Beresford counter-effort from late 1825. The Beresfords were at work on the various estates to influence the tenantry and register their voters.[32] George Wyse wrote to his brother to ask him to bring Stuart to Waterford as quickly as possible:

I think he is *much* wanted . . . there appears to be great disorganis-ation or want of system in the operations of the Committee — All the subordinate agents (who should be attended to) loudly complain of being neglected — no adequate supply of money — whilst the opposite party are most lavish — of late their distribution has been enormous . . .

George wished to hold a meeting of the entire committee in Waterford to rectify 'the disordered machinery'; there was 'a vast deal to do' — even the library and the newsroom, which had developed from the Catholic Rent collection, were 'on the wane'.[33]

From early 1826 a great socio-economic and political confrontation was developing in Co. Waterford and the outcome was clearly seen to have great national significance: 'It will be a battle . . . which . . . will decide the Catholic Question . . . The election of Mr Stuart must be considered as the harbinger of Civil Freedom in Ireland' declared the *Dublin Evening Post* on 28 March 1826. Success on both economic and political levels was to be gained only by very thorough organisation in the county and city. It was necessary to spend great sums of money to combat the economic sway of the Tory camp. Wyse notes that the agitators took care first to provide 'a proper organisation. The system they adopted . . . was simple but all-powerful' (*132*, I, 285). A general committee was established in Waterford which consisted 'nominally of many members' though only a few were very active; branch committees were established in the seven baronies in the county and priests were honorary members of these baronial committees. This outline structure very quickly suggested to Wyse the formation of a more permanent association to secure 'the proper representation' of the county and he planned this even before the election of Stuart.[34]

Each baronial committee had two local agents who furnished weekly reports and the baronial committees in turn made similar reports to the general committee in Waterford. The selection of the local agents was very important and great care was taken: Nicholas White was recommended as agent because he had experience of an election in Co. Tipperary and because he had 'local knowledge of two baronies, Middlethird and Upperthird' and he spoke Irish.[35] Valentine Devereux was suggested as agent for Gaultier because he was 'a determined man' who 'knows all the people about Passage and is known by them'.[36] Another agent by the name of Cahil proved to be 'a most active and efficient agent': Cahil was able to procure promises from 'a great proportion' of the forty-shilling freeholders in Upperthird. Cahil attended the tenantry of Lord Waterford from the parishes of Rathgormuck and Clonea as he knew them all personally. He was important in maintaining these for the Stuart cause and attempts were made 'to corrupt' him by the Beresford agents.[37] These key local agents for Stuart's campaign were paid a salary.[38] Each parish priest, local agent and baronial committee kept registry-books as they watched over the registry sessions and examined their areas.[39] It was possible from these shortly before the election to compile '. . . an analytic view (which scarcely presented a single error when brought to the test of experience) of the temper and dispositions of the entire county' (*132*, I, 285). Rudolphus Greene, an attorney in Dungarvan, was employed to investigate the legality of each registered voter according to a resolution of the general committee in early May.[40]

Detailed preparations were made with respect to travelling arrangements for the election, the treatment of the voters, the organisation of poll-agents and tally-rooms. The general committee had made arrangements in April with Charles Bianconi to supply the necessary transport.[41] During the election every sort of conveyance was needed to transport voters and detailed preparations were necessary: for example a request came to transport 300 fishermen from Dungarvan to Waterford.[42] Communications were aided by the appointment of a number of couriers, flagbearers and a trumpeter. These men attended to dispatches, announced the coming of the freeholders, regulated the processions and attended the freeholders from the suburbs into the town.[43] Premises were rented as tally-rooms near the court house.[44] Poll-agents were hired to help bring the freeholders to poll.[45] Wyse concludes that the local machinery 'worked admirably'. The general committee was nicknamed the 'Young Committee' as 'not one of its members had been engaged in an election warfare' before 1826; Wyse and the other local leaders pioneered the 'crusade' which involved 'an almost individual appeal to the forty-shilling constituency of the county' (*132*, I, 286-9). They built the organisation upon the basic framework which had evolved in the county to collect the Catholic Rent and they utilised the clergy and chapels in the campaign.

It was a novel election and many of the pro-Stuart leaders had qualms about the nature of the campaign. Henry Winston Barron, a prominent Catholic landowner and newspaper owner wrote to Wyse announcing that parliament was to be dissolved:

> You should have all the rent committees officially informed of this and they should sit *daily* until the Election. The sub-agents should be very active in making the returns and *every freeholder should be personally canvassed* by the priests. I am free to confess that I do not think this is a legitimate or constitutional way of carrying on an election but we are not placed in a legitimate or constitutional position. Argument and reason are of no avail with our opponents and are in fact completely thrown away. We are therefore compelled, however unwitting, to make use of other means . . .[46]

Wyse, himself, though he has defended the rôle of the priests in his *Historical Sketch*, obviously disliked priests having any more influence than any other citizen (*132*, I, 284). Like Barron, however, Wyse believed that, in 1826, all the power which the Catholics possessed must be mobilised to achieve victory.

A number of the committee were deputed to address each parish, in rotation, on each Sunday, for two months prior to the election: the activists argued that the Bribery Oath prevented Catholic voters supporting Beresford because, in all conscience, they must disagree with his views on their religion and hence their support must be based on material reward. The priest lent the weight of his authority to this and it was disingenuous for Wyse to state that the arguments which the priests used 'had no connexion with their spiritual power'. Beresford maintained that the priests and Dr Kelly had declared it a mortal sin to vote against Stuart and he ascribed great influence to the Catholic bishop. According to Beresford the priests suspended the celebration of mass in a parish if the parishioners did not agree to support Stuart and Beresford supporters were 'shut out from all society and intercourse' and were verbally abused as 'mad dogs'.[47] The *Dublin Evening Mail* on 5 June 1826 referred to 'the crusade' of priests in Waterford against Beresford.

As Wyse notes the clergy were divided into two parties, the old and the young: it was with great reluctance that the older priests engaged in electoral politics and they only responded to the great upsurge of public opinion. The younger priests 'were of a very different temper . . . they were full of the spirit of the times . . .' Wyse indicates that the accession of the bishop, Dr Kelly, was important to the liberal party but he maintains that it was the people who 'kindled' the priests and not the priests who led the people. The great torrent of public opinion hurried the priest along and he 'had only to decide whether he should ride on its surface, or be buried altogether beneath the stream' (*132*, I, 282-4). The lay agitators were undoubtedly the most important in the contest in Co. Waterford but the priests were invaluable lieutenants.

Thomas Wyse undertook the principal management of the Stuart campaign and he went on a five week tour of the rural parishes in the county, accompanied by Father Sheehan, who, when necessary, translated his speeches into Irish. Wyse's great theme was that landlords had no right to force their tenants to vote according to landlord decree. The Beresfords had attempted to secure the tenants of Viscount Doneraile but Wyse drafted an address for them in which they acknowledged their duties to 'a kind and considerable landlord' but they pointed out that these duties did not include '. . . the duty which the freeholder has to discharge at the hustings. If we are your tenants, we are also the electors of a free state, and entrusted with the elective franchise not for the exclusive benefit of the landlord, but for our own benefit and for that of our fellow countrymen'.[48]

The Tory viewpoint was that their freeholders 'belonged' to them and they did not conceive that the freeholders had a constitutional right to act 'out of the range of this dependence'; Wyse mocked this 'divine right of landlords' (*132*, I, 267-70). The economic power of the Tory party was their 'sheet anchor' as George Wyse told Thomas.[49] The Stuart committee had to mount a huge financial effort to combat this Tory advantage. From the early spring of 1826, well before the election, Stuart supporters were suffering in terms of employment and in other ways because of Tory reprisals.[50] As this developed Wyse and his committee had to supply alternative employment, remuneration and even houses in order to prevent the economic power of the Tory party becoming the decisive factor; as one priest put it, '*Patriotism may fill a man's heart, but cannot fill the belly*'.[51] The Beresford party also offered carrots as well as sticks to doubtful voters. Their agents distributed meal and money and succeeded in gaining some tenants in this way.[52] They opened a shop in Dungarvan where every sort of clothes were given on credit and every effort 'to corrupt the people' was made. There was a thin line between bribery and the more normal 'treating' of voters; it was essential to provide economic or material rewards to the voters either when they sought them or needed them in such a close contest. Both sides were thus competing in an economic struggle and the voters were quick to see the market value of their vote. Undoubtedly some sense of security had to be given for opposition to the landlords.[53]

John Matthew Galwey, who acted as treasurer on the Stuart committee, wrote in early June that 'there is not a freeholder of Lord Waterford's in the parish of Abbeyside that would not vote for Mr Stuart if the poor people saw any chance of getting a house if they were turned out of their cabins . . .'[54] Another activist told Wyse that the Stuart workers were 'most anxious to be enabled to *show* the people that they can protect them'.[55] The Tories expected to break up the Stuart organisation 'by the timely scattering of a few handfuls of gold-dust' (*132*, I, 269). However, the liberals showed great economic resourcefulness and spent freely. Although J. M. Galway, as treasurer, was very concerned about the high cost of the campaign, he nevertheless had houses built for the people who feared eviction from six acres and he also gave employment: '— *this is what will Carry the Election* — the poor devils only want to be assured if they are turned out of their houses by the Duke or Lord Waterford they won't be left with their children on the High Road (as they say themselves)'[56] The Tories tended to regard the canvassing of their tenants as an 'encroachment of the rights of private property' and they made every effort to magnify minor clashes into events of major proportions to indicate the extent of the 'insurrection'. As a result of the Kilmacthomas 'riots' the Tory magistrates imposed a stipendiary magistrate which involved the local inhabitants paying for the appointment.[57] In fact, despite the very extensive political agitation and excitement, the county remained relatively free of outrage. Major Carter, the stipendiary magistrate at Kilmacthomas, reported in May that the peasantry were 'under considerable agitation, from the conflicting feelings, under which they find they will be obliged to vote at the ensuing election: temporal interest inclining them for one candidate and spiritual influence directing them to the other'.[58] The economic resources of the liberals were indeed liberally expended but the price was enormous: a great national effort, through a New Catholic Rent, was needed to sustain the pro-Stuart voters and the debts were to remain a big problem for years after 1826.[59]

An important aspect of the popular struggle was the rôle of the local press. A number of local newspapers were devoted to party interests and indeed like the *Waterford Mirror* and *Waterford Chronicle* were set up or bought for electioneering purposes. The *Waterford Mail* served the Protestant and Tory interest. The *Waterford Chronicle* was taken over by Philip Barron in 1825 and it became the outstanding local liberal paper in the region (*91*, 8-10). The *Waterford Chronicle* stressed the importance of a liberal local press and endeavoured to serve Tipperary, Kilkenny, Wexford as well as Waterford. It established an agent and office in Wexford and in other towns and was 'particularly anxious' to be circulated amongst 'the Farmers and the Poorer Classes'; it favoured a scheme for establishing news-rooms in every townland for farmers and labourers to be called 'The Forty-Shilling Freeholders' Reading Room'. It employed reporters to cover meetings in the south-east.[60] In 1827 a *Weekly Waterford Chronicle* was published as it was found that a subscription to a three-day paper was beyond 'farmers and other classes' who 'feel the deepest interest in the passing political events of the day'; the weekly edition was in addition to the three-day paper. The *Chronicle* was imbued with liberal Catholicism. The design at the masthead summarised its political stance: against the background of a rising sun and harpist symbolising Ireland was inscribed 'public spirit' springing from the Treaty of Limerick and 'Magna Charta' [*sic*] which were symbols of Catholic and liberal constitutional rights. Grattan's motto, 'Emancipation would give a Constitution to the People, and a People to the Constitution' was placed underneath the design. The contents were a powerful mixture of virulent anti-Beresford propaganda interspersed with much important guidance and information for the Stuart supporters; the paper was an invaluable channel of communication for the liberal organisation. Major Carter, the stipendiary magistrate, recognised the *Chronicle* as a very important medium in popular politics and he felt that it tended 'to exasperate unjustly the minds of the peasantry against the Constabulary Force' which it termed the 'armed Orangemen of the present day'.[61] Significantly the *Waterford Chronicle* overtook the milder *Waterford Mirror* in 1825 in terms of circulation and it maintained a large circulation and lead over its local rivals.[62] The Barrons demonstrated that the provincial press was 'a powerful engine' in the Catholic and liberal interest and leading activists paid tribute to the rôle of the *Chronicle* in the 1826 election.[63]

By June 1826, when the writs were issued, the liberal organisation was thoroughly prepared for the election. The campaign had covered the estates and parishes of the county. National attention was focused on Waterford as 'the most important contest' in Ireland.[64] A Beresford win was expected as they had a majority of more than 600 over Stuart by June 1826 on the registry books (*132*, I, 274). The *Dublin Evening Mail* declared that 'the great struggle between the Landed Interest and the influence of the Church of Rome is to be decided at Waterford'.[65]

The campaign was deeply sectarian. The Beresfords were attacked as 'the blood-hounds' and 'Orange Blood-suckers' who had exploited and oppressed the Catholic people. They were represented as heretics and enemies of the Catholic religion. The anti-Beresford propaganda and the popular slogans such as 'Down with the Pitchcaps', 'Down with Claudius and the Triangles' were redolent of 1798. Yet Wyse admits that Lord George Beresford, who had little political talent, was 'an exceedingly friendly and kind man in social life'. John Claudius Beresford was certainly unpopular because of 1798 punishments but another Beresford, Lord Tyrone, had been known in 1798 as the 'Croppy Colonel' because of his humanity during the rebellion (*132*, I, 265-6, 272-3). As the campaign gathered momentum and enthusiasm the minds of the freeholders must have been filled with a mixture of historical memories, promises, threats, religious beliefs, wild expectations and political idealism. They were caught up in an historic encounter the crucial significance of which they can hardly have completely grasped.

On 9 June Stuart wrote to O'Connell inviting him to Dromana for the election. On 18 June O'Connell began a tour with Stuart of the strong Beresford centres in the county such as Kilmacthomas. O'Connell described it for his wife:

... we heard an early mass at Waterford and then started for Dungarvan. We breakfasted at Kilmacthomas, a town belonging to the Beresfords but the people belong to us. They came out to meet us with green boughs and such shouting you can have no idea of. I harangued them from the window of the inn, and we had a good deal of laughing at the bloody Beresfords. Judge what the popular feeling must be when in this, a Beresford town, every man their tenant, we had such a reception. A few miles farther on we found a chapel with the congregation assembled before mass. The priest made me come out and I addressed his flock, being my second speech. The freeholders here were the tenants of a Mr Palliser, who is on the adverse interest, but almost all of them will vote for us. We then proceeded to Dungarvan on the coast. There are here about four hundred voters *belonging* to the Duke of Devonshire. His agents have acted a most treacherous part by us, and our Committee at Waterford were afraid openly to attack these voters lest the Duke should complain of our violating what he calls his neutrality. But I deemed that all sheer nonsense, and to work we went. We had a most tremendous meeting here; we harangued the people from a platform erected by the walls of a new chapel. I never could form a notion of the great effect of popular declamation before yesterday. The clergy of the town most zealously assisted us. We have, I believe, completely triumphed ...' (III, 1312).

The state of public feeling convinced O'Connell that Stuart would win though prior to his tour he had hardly dared to expect victory; he believed in victory because the priests had 'gained over a sufficient number of the *adverse* voters' to ensure a decided majority (III, 1314).

It became a religious obligation to support Stuart and this obligation was reinforced by the popular enthusiasm — both 'shame and emulation' stimulated, as Wyse noted, the voters in the great 'crusade'. The Bribery Oath was made a test of conscience and those Catholics who voted for Beresford were warned that their names would be published frequently and that they would be shunned.[66] O'Connell condemned the Catholics who voted for Beresford on the first day as 'miscreants' and he publicly castigated them as enemies of their religion: '. . . The mothers who bore them ought to mourn for the hour that gave them birth; the wives from their sides should leave them . . . [*Deep groans agitating the crowd*] . . .'[67] Beresford in his election petition alleged that his voters were turned out of the chapels in the presence of the congregation and were publicly cursed by name and they were 'halloo'd at as a "Mad dog"' and, in modern parlance, boycotted. He declared that the freeholders were refused Church rites if they supported him and they faced 'actual ex-communication'.[68] A certain degree of religious and political fanatic-ism was certainly aroused: a squib was circulated reporting the 'Sudden, Awful and Horrible Death' of a Catholic who took the Bribery Oath and voted for Beresford.[69] Given the usual, and often murderous, violence which accompanied county elections in Ireland, the Waterford election was remarkable: O'Connell observed to his wife: 'Here, where passion and party spirit run highest — here, where the feeling of triumph over faction is at its height, we have not the slightest species of dis-turbance. We have kept the people perfectly tranquil . . . Nothing can provoke them to any, even the slightest breach of the peace' (III, 1321). As the *Dublin Evening Mail* remarked, all eyes turned towards Waterford for the election. In the city itself and throughout 'all the suburbs and several of the streets in the interior', the houses were hung with green boughs and banners and the Tree of Liberty was planted in some of the streets.[70] O'Connell was proposed as a candidate — the first Roman Catholic to be nominated since the penal era — in order that he might speak. He delivered, in Wyse's opinion, 'one of the most truly eloquent harangues'; Wyse believed that he would have been elected had he not withdrawn as pre-arranged (*132*, I, 276-7).

Very quickly it became obvious that the Beresfords faced a humili-ating and historic rout. At the close of the poll Power, the elderly and mildly liberal MP had 1,424 votes; Stuart had 1,357; Lord George Beresford had only 527: it proved unnecessary to poll most of the voters on the pro-Stuart and Stuart estates. Defeat for the Tory land-lords 'came in every shape of mortification' as attempts to 'coup' voters in Waterford failed and those 'who had received bribes, held up the notes in open court' (*132*, I, 278). A huge victory celebration was held in Waterford with each barony parading under its own banner with appropriate mottos and slogans.[71] The county remained for many months in a state of 'feverish' excitement and the liberal leaders and the priests had to exercise 'a powerful control'.[72] It was a shattering experience for the Beresford interest, the very symbol of the Protestant Ascendancy in Ireland. The total discomfiture of the losing party was apparent to all: it was suddenly found that what they had always re- garded as their legitimate rights were snatched from them by what they regarded as priestly influence and mob intimidation. Where would it end? What was next? One Waterford landlord wrote on 24 June:

> Men who in the year 1798 with exemplary loyalty assisted me to keep Rebellion out of these parishes, and in the last year resisted to a man the payment of the Catholic Rent, although called upon by the priests from the altar to contribute, have been now compelled to bow to this Popish Inquisition . . . none but my five Protestant tenants have been polled out of this large estate, and Lord Doneraile who has upwards of an hundred, has not been able to bring to the poll more than his seven Protestant tenants, and I understand all the remainder have polled against him, as have even Lord Waterford's own tenants (*113*, 96).

It had been the most remarkable popular triumph since the Union and a crushing demonstration of Catholic electoral power.

The great defeat of the Protestant Ascendancy in Co. Waterford had been well planned long before the general election was called. It was the centrepiece of an election which formed, as the *Dublin Evening Mail* put it, 'a crisis in the history of Ireland, next in importance to the Union'.[73] There were dramatic contests in other counties which were all the more shocking for being more sudden and apparently less organ- ised than Waterford. There were major revolts by Catholic freeholders against landlord control and in favour of Emancipation in counties Louth, Monaghan, Westmeath and Cavan. In many other counties Eman- cipationist MPs already in control were returned and Catholic influence was seen to be effective. Charles Brownlow, despite his public con- version to Catholic Emancipation, was re-elected in Co. Armagh on 29 June after a contest. In Co. Dublin White and Talbot were also re- elected after a contest. In Co. Mayo John MacHale, as co-adjutor Bishop of Killala, was credited with the defeat of Denis Browne; the county returned two MPs in favour of Emancipation without a poll. In Co. Limerick, where there was a contest, both victors were 'Emancipators' while in Roscommon Catholic interests united to return Arthur French, again without a contest. In Co. Westmeath there was a notable contest where freeholders deserted the landlords to support the Emancipationist candidate Tuite who was successful by the narrow margin of twenty-four votes. Co. Kilkenny had its first contested election since the Union with a thirteen-day poll, though Pierce Butler a prominent supporter of the Catholic Association was unsuccessful (III, 1194).

In Co. Kerry there occurred a most violent election. Police and troops opened fire on a stonethrowing crowd in Tralee, killing five persons and wounding about a dozen others. O'Connell, who was not present, due to the Waterford and Dublin elections, was informed by his brother John that there had been no need for such a display of force. Col. James Crosbie, MP since 1812 and strongly in favour of Emancipation, lost his seat to the Hon. William Hare. O'Connell had advised Crosbie that the polling was illegal: the Sheriff had postponed polling, it was said, to suit Hare who was regarded as a trimmer, at best, on the issue of Catholic Emancipation. O'Connell felt bitter about the Sheriff's conduct:

> The sheriff ought certainly to be hanged; but if he escape the gallows
> — which God forbid! — he will be imprisoned for months in Newgate.
> There were five Catholic peasants justly hanged for the horrid
> murder of one Protestant at the cross of Shinah. It was quite just
> that it should be so. Shall it be said that five Catholics shall be basely
> slaughtered in the streets of Tralee without retribution or atone-
> ment? I think it impossible. The sheriff who ordered the firing and
> the officers, soldiers and policemen who fired are all guilty, accord-
> ing to the coroner's inquest, of wilful murder . . . (III, 1320, 1322).

In Co. Galway another violent election occurred with strong sectarian undertones. In 1820 James Daly and Richard Martin had been returned without a poll. Martin, known as 'Humanity Dick' because of his interest in animal welfare, was an old friend of the Catholic cause. Now over seventy, he had voted for the Catholic Relief Bill of 1778, was a close relative of Trimleston and Gormanston and had spoken in the Catholic Association as the oldest parliamentary advocate of Emancipation. He was challenged in 1826 by the anti-Emancipationist James Staunton Lambert. Subsequently the election was the subject of an investigation by a Commons Select Committee which concluded 'that an organised system of rioting prevailed throughout the late election for the County of Galway, by which houses were destroyed, several persons lost their lives, and others were greviously injured . . .' It appeared to the Select Committee that the authorities in Galway neglected their duty to protect Lambert's voters. Lambert was held out before the mob as a 'Protestant rascal' and Martin's partisans obstructed his freeholders as they sought to vote. Major Warburton, who was in charge of the police in Galway, said there was 'a continued scene of riot' during the election.[74]

Martin's daughter Harriet wrote a novel called *Canvassing* describing this Galway election in colourful but quite accurate detail in the light of the evidence given to the Select Committee. The popular excitement is neatly encapsulated in the saying that 'the fighting candidate has always the best chance, you know, of being the sitting member'. Non-voters, drivers, butchers, grocers, waiters, grocers' boys, ostlers, carmen, beggars 'and such like gentry of the town' were keenly interested and involved in the election. Priests played a very important rôle both in calming the mob violence and in guiding the voters.

The priest was up against the proprietorial feeling of landlords. As one landlord put it, 'I take care that nobody dare meddle with a free-holder of mine, or I'd put a bullet through his head, and distrain every beast belonging to the tenant who dared even to think of voting according to his own vagaries'. The priests did watch the voters carefully and there were examples of voters, who, torn between the two, fled the hustings. Harriet Martin records the following exchange between a priest and a freeholder at the poll:

'My blessing to ye! Phanick O'Dea!' said Father John, 'how long is it since you turned Protestant?'

'Me turn Protestant, is it Father John! The Lord save us!' And Phanick crossed himself reverentially. 'Sure I'm no Protestant, nor one belongin' to me; the heavens betwixt us an' harum!'

'If you arn't a Protestant, and a bitter black one, too, how do you come to vote for the Orange candidate, my man?'

'Avoch, Father John, sure it isn't of our own will we're voting! didn't Pat Sullivan threaten to burn the houses over our heads, and banish us the place, if we didn't vote the way we were ordhered? An' how would we stand in country, Father John, if we didn't? always in arrares of rint, you know.'

The freeholders found their newly accorded liberty of thinking and acting for themselves a perilous as well puzzling privilege:

'Do you want to deny your religion, ye unfortunate misguided cratures?' Father John cried. 'Oh that ever I should live to see a man of my flock voting for an Orange candidate and Protestant Ascendancy; and the downfall of their own ancient thrue and holy religion! and when I'll be witness agin ye at the last day, that I warned ye, but that ye wouldn't give heed to me, how will it be with ye then boys?'

While many freeholders must have dreaded their forced choice at the hustings, for others it was a festive and exciting occasion.

The eventful morning came, and the whole town was alive at the dawn of day; crowds of partisans of all ages and ranks gathering round the committee-rooms of the opposing candidates; election-eering agents, oratorizing, explaining, or mystifying, as suited their purpose; looking over certificates, and 'making Pat Conny sinsible he was only to be Pat Conny the first time he voted, but Dennis Sheeran, the second time, in regard of poor Dennis not being convenient just then, because he was buried last week' . . . and other trifling, though necessary arrangements, for the proper carrying on of their employer's interests; and the voters were eating, drinking, shouting, laughing, and whirling their ferrals to give them 'the real fighting touch' . . . to keep up the honour of 'the family', and make as much riot as possible.[75]

The result of the Galway contest was the election of James Daly with 6,206 votes and Richard Martin with 3,719 votes. J. S. Lambert received 3,635 votes but as a result of his petition he was later declared elected on 11 April 1827. Martin was unseated.

In contrast to Waterford, the revolt of the Catholic freeholders against their Protestant landlords in the Louth election of 1826 was sudden and wholly unexpected. Before 1826 the Catholic vote in Louth was regarded as something which could safely be employed as a pawn in the old game played exclusively by Protestant proprietary interests. The first intimation of a contest occurred in October 1825. Anthony Marmion, secretary to the Catholics of Louth, issued a printed circular letter calling upon the freeholders of Louth to unite behind 'one or two liberal candidates' who would support civil and religious liberty in parliament. However the Catholic gentry headed by Sir Edward Bellew, or the Protestant 'independent' interest headed by the Balfours and the Bellinghams did not respond. Blayney Balfour was strongly pressed to stand as an Emancipationist but he declined to do so in early June 1826:

. . . the Protestant gentry were regarded as omnipotent. For upwards of half a century, the Jocelyns and the Fosters had returned two members to parliament, and divided the county, like a family borough, between them. A strong and apparently indissoluble coalition had been effected between Lord Roden and Lord Oriel; and it was supposed to be impossible to make an effectual opposition to the union of Orangeism and of Evangelism, which the wily veteran of Ascendancy [Oriel], and the frantic champion of the New Reformation [Roden], had effected (*114*, I, 168).

Louth had been through elections without a poll for over fifty years. The candidates who appeared to have another walkover in 1826 were John Leslie Foster, a friend of Peel, and Matthew Fortescue of Stephenstown.

The election was fixed for 21 June; at a late stage, the Catholic cause was championed by the unpromising Alexander Dawson of Riverstown, Ardee. Though a candidate of undoubted respectability, educated as a barrister, Dawson was in his mid-fifties and he had only a small property in the county. The contrast with Waterford, where both combatants, Beresford and Stuart, brought hereditary rank and vast opulence to the contest was marked. Dawson was a total surprise as a radical and Catholic leader. He indeed held radical views as he later made clear in a speech in the parliamentary constituency of Westminster, 'the classic territory of the Radical or Reforming Party' as Gustave d'Eichthal observed when he heard Dawson speak to a receptive audience in this vein in May 1828:

> What do they matter to us, transubstantiation and all the substantiations in the world, purgatory and Papacy, and all these fads! Let every man go to Heaven in his own way and let us attend to matters temporal. Let us concern ourselves with the taxes, the government, the finances and the industry of this world. And let us leave the priests to settle their quarrels as they will (*112*, 31).

Of course such indifference to religion was not made evident in the Louth constituency in 1826. At first Sir Edward Bellew and the Catholic gentry held aloof from Dawson but the overwhelming support amongst the Catholic rank and file forced Bellew and others in behind him, and indeed they contributed much to his funds.

The Emancipationist campaign was financed by the Catholic tradesmen and merchants of Dundalk and the subscriptions raised in the parishes of the county. Archbishop Curtis sent a pro-Dawson circular to all his priests. A sum of £2,174 was quickly raised. The local priests took the lead in whipping up popular enthusiasm for Dawson and on 15 June the Catholic Association itself took up the Louth election. By 22 June Nicholas Markey of Welchestown could write to O'Connell in Waterford that 'the fight is begun and victory certain'. Louth he reported 'after slumbering 55 years is again awake and determined to be free'. Sheil had been sent by the Association to Louth and his speech 'astonished *all parties* but when he announced himself a *freeholder* of the County, I cannot describe to you the effect it produced'. Markey went on to describe Dawson's entry into Dundalk accompanied by about 5,000 people as 'splendid': 'You may judge of the state of our *opponents* when 20 sovereigns was offered last night in my neighbourhood for a single vote although not a man has polled yet – Public spirit is at such a pitch, *no money* will tempt them' (III, 1316). Sheil saw the vast multitude 'descending with banners of green unfurled to the wind, and shouting as they moved along': Dawson was seated in an old gig wearing 'an old frock-coat covered with dust, and a broad-brimmed weather-

beaten hat which surmounted a head that streamed with profuse per-
spiration; his face was ruddy with heat . . . he did not seem to be . . .
at all conscious of the boldness of the enterprise in which he was embarked . . .' Dawson's appeal was to the middle classes and he relied
on the spirit of agrarian revolt amongst the forty-shilling freeholders.
No means of persuasion or terror were spared by either side in bringing the freeholders to the poll (*114*, I, 169-74).

Sheil indeed stirred things up: after mass on Sunday, 25 June, outside Dundalk church he compared the landlords' claim to direct the
votes of their tenants to their claim in feudal times to sleep with every
newly married bride on their estates: 'I tell you that your landlords
have no more right to ask you to vote against your religion and your
conscience than they have to ask you for the virginity of your children . . .'[76] In a famous phrase he described the election for the tenants
as a choice between the cross and the distress warrant. The alliance
between Fortescue and Foster came under great strain. Fortescue wrote
asking point-blank for Foster's second votes but John Leslie Foster
wrote to his uncle Lord Oriel as early as 15 June that '. . . the first laws
of self-preservation made it absolutely necessary that you should say or
write nothing about your second vote until you have had full communication with me in person' (*84*, 144-5).

Foster would depend on those second votes of the tenants as he
could not command the first vote. On the first day of polling, 24 June,
and possibly on the second, 26 June, Foster and Fortescue gave each
other some assistance. Thereafter, when it had become apparent that
Dawson was going to win and that the only contest was for second
place, Foster and Fortescue began to throw every possible impediment
in each other's way.[77] Only six of Oriel's tenants gave their second
votes to Fortescue, and only ten of Lord Roden's gave theirs to Foster
when he had been promised Roden's 250 votes (*40*, 396). The extent
of the divisions between the anti-Catholic ranks was unparalleled. Foster
was extremely exposed, more so than Fortescue, because of the Foster
family's long and consistent opposition to Emancipation going back to
1782. Foster himself was the ablest Irish opponent of Emancipation in
the Commons. His defeat was averted only by the slowness of the
leaders of the Dawson campaign to resort to the fairly obvious tactic
of giving their second votes to Fortescue. The result of the election was
Dawson 862, Foster 552, and Fortescue 547. Foster did not attend the
declaration of the result and Sheil considered his flight as 'most in-
glorious': the Catholic orators boasted that he did not dare to meet
them:

Having fled from Dundalk, where Mr Dawson was chaired, he caused
himself to be put through a similar honour in his uncle's demesne;

all the vassals and retainers of Lord Oriel, who could be procured, were collected together, and Mr Foster having been placed upon the shoulders of four stout Protestant tenants, was conveyed through the village of Collon, amidst the plaudits of the yeomanry, the hurrahs of the schoolmaster, the sexton, and the parish clerk, and the acclamations of the police' (*114*, I, 181-2).

It was the end of Foster and Protestant dominance in electoral politics in Co. Louth.

Foster would certainly have been beaten if the right tactics had been applied in time. Apparently Sheil advocated concentration against Foster but Marmion, the most important local organiser, preferred Foster to Fortescue. However, Archbishop Curtis believed Sheil spared Foster because of 'the humble and urgent entreaty made to him and party publicly on the hustings by Counsellor North, brother-in-law to Foster' (*113*, 98). Sheil, however, points out that in the local context Fortescue's associations with religious antipathy towards Catholicism as Lord Roden's candidate were more important than the symbolic significance of ejecting Foster from the Commons (*114*, I, 178-9). A contributory factor to the near defeat of Foster was that over one hundred of their own freeholders were found to be improperly registered. Foster, shocked, explained the result to Peel:

> Very many Protestants were forced to vote against me by the threats of assassination or having their houses burnt . . . When the poll commenced all the priests of the county were collected and distributed through the different booths, where they stood with glaring eyes directly opposite to the voters . . . At the close of the election the Catholics threw in their votes to the other Protestant merely to get me out, but they were a little too late in the manoeuvre . . . the tenantry [are] sullen and insolent. Men who a month ago were all civility and submission now hardly suppress their curses when a gentleman passes . . . I begin to fear a crisis of some kind or other is not far distant (*113*, 97).

Foster forecast an Emancipationist landslide at the next general election in Ireland unless the franchise was raised to £20; on the forty-shilling franchise, if Emancipation were granted, he estimated that 60 Irish constituencies would return Catholics and Louth would return Sheil.

In 1826 the great weakness of the Catholics in Louth had been lack of preparation; they had no candidate until ten days before the poll began and their victory was due to local initiative rather than national direction. Even the Catholic gentry only joined the cause belatedly to save themselves from complete discredit. The Bellews did not regain their position of authority until 1831. Louth contrasts with Waterford in the lead up to popular victory. In Waterford the most striking feature of the election was the good order and discipline of the Catholic voters whilst in Louth as in the other constituencies in Ireland in which the Catholic vote played a decisive role in 1826 violence and disorder was symptomatic of the spontaneity of the campaigns. If Catholic preparations had been better laid they might have secured both seats in Louth and would have increased this prospect in a higher poll. The Louth poll of 930 in 1826 on a registered electorate of at least 2,800 was very low indeed. It is likely that many voters avoided the choice between the distress warrant and the cross by staying away. With more time for Catholic preparation and drilling of the voters this was unlikely to be the case next time round (*84*, 150). 'The question simply comes to this', declared the *Dublin Evening Mail* on 26 June, 'and we rejoice that it has so resolved itself: Is Ireland to be governed by the Popish Priests, or is it not?' Given the Catholic successes the *Mail* insisted that 'the Priests have gone too far . . . the present Elections have afforded a proof which must put at rest the question of Catholic Emancipation and lead to the abolition of the Forty-Shilling Freeholders'.[78] The writing was on the wall for Protestant domination of the existing electoral system: by the beginning of 1827 even old Lord Oriel had become convinced of the need for concession; by the middle of 1828 Foster had decided it would be futile for him to contest the seat again.

'In every county but one — Cavan — where there has been a struggle, the Orangemen have been worsted', exulted the *Dublin Evening Post* on 3 August 1826. The Tory monopoly was challenged in Cavan unsuccessfully by Robert Henry Southwell, of Castle Hamilton. Southwell was a popular landlord with a record of support for Catholic Emancipation. He was joined by Charles Coote of Bellamont Forest in opposing Henry Maxwell and Alexander Saunderson. Southwell and Coote were both in financial difficulties and this limited the campaign against the Tories (*25*, 18).

O'Connell visited Cavan on 11 June to stimulate the campaign in support of Southwell: polling was fixed for the week of 20-27 June.[79] The flying visit by O'Connell failed to initiate a sufficient revolt in Cavan and the Catholic Association might have done a great deal more there to detach the Catholic vote from Maxwell and Saunderson who probably received about 1,400 Catholic votes. The Cavan activists had been shaken by 1825 and O'Connell was not fully trusted because of his apparent willingness to ditch the forty-shilling freeholders. A further difficulty for the Emancipationists in Cavan lay in having both Southwell and Coote in the race. O'Connell had said in Cavan on 11 June: 'I apprehend and fear that if too much exertion is made for Mr Coote, they would be grasping at too much and lose both Coote and

Southwell'.[80] In Cavan the voters were asked to vote for both Southwell and Coote against Maxwell and Saunderson and there was not the same room for compromise as in Louth, Waterford, Armagh and elsewhere. In addition, Saunderson's views on the Catholic question were rather more uncertain than those of Maxwell and this provided some escape for Catholic voters when the pressure was applied. The result of the poll on 28 June was Maxwell 2,854, Saunderson 2,673, Southwell 1,917 and Coote 1,901.[81] Given that Cavan had not been polled since the Union the Tories took little comfort from the result. With better organisation and more resources a future election might bring victory for the Emancipationists.

Like Cavan, Monaghan was a constituency with a fairly mixed population and electorate, where the Orangemen were powerful and Emancipationist policies were not necessarily popular politics. Yet in 1826 the Emancipation issue played a dramatic and decisive part. The return to his extensive estate of Evelyn John Shirley, described by the *Dublin Evening Mail* on 11 January 1826 as 'an Englishman, and until within the last two years an absentee', changed the electoral balance in the county. By registering freeholders and by seeking election, Shirley upset the control of the seats by Charles Powell Leslie and the Westenra family.

Monaghan Catholics took an interest in the election only at a late stage. They had held a large meeting in January chaired by the Bishop, Dr Kernan, and there was no reference to electoral politics except that the 'error' of O'Connell in relation to the 'wings' controversy was acknowledged.[82] As the election approached, however, a Catholic opportunity presented itself. There were three strong candidates: Charles Powell Leslie, Henry Robert Westenra and Evelyn John Shirley. The fourth candidate, Walter Taylor, was not really in the race. The Catholic objective was to defeat Leslie of Glaslough, who had held one of the two Monaghan seats since 1801. Leslie was Colonel of the Monaghan Militia and one of the most powerful men in the county; he was noted for his anti-Catholic stance. Westenra, who had been MP for the county since 1818 had opposed Emancipation, but his father, Lord Rossmore, supported the Catholic cause. Shirley, with his large base in the barony of Farney and his active registration of his freeholders, was certain of election. He was reputed to be of liberal views and to be more popular than most landlords. The contest was between Leslie and Westenra and the key lay in the second votes of the Shirley voters.

O'Connell now intervened in a sensational fashion. He sent a circular canvassing letter on 6 June to the Catholic priests of Monaghan condemning Leslie in very strong terms and seeking support for Westenra. Westenra's claim on the Catholic voters lay mainly in the support his father had given to Emancipation. O'Connell put it like this to the priests: 'Mr Westenra himself cannot perhaps be expected *at this moment* to declare in favour of Emancipation – but I have reason to assure you in confidence that he will not give any pledge to vote against the measure . . .' This hint was enough. The objective, in any event, was to prevent Leslie's return.[83] The Orange and Protestant party were appalled at O'Connell's open invitation to the priests to sway the tenants to vote against the commands of their landlords. One chorus in favour of Leslie went:

> For we are true blue,
> And Orange too,
> And will never consent to see,
> O'Connell Dan, return the man,
> Who'd blindly vote for Popery.

John Bric was sent by the Catholic Association to support Westenra who was declaring that he would go into parliament untied to any party. Those who cried out for Catholic Emancipation and those who insisted on keeping up the Protestant Ascendancy could, if they wished, find it possible to vote for Westenra. He was adopted by the Catholics as a means of defeating Leslie.

Leslie's great local influence was pointed out in a handbill to the Catholic voters: 'He got himself made Colonel of the Monaghan militia; he influenced the appointment of Sheriffs, Magistrates, Revenue Officers, Postmasters, and even of Petty Constables. In short, his was the hand that distributed the favours of power.' He had used this influence to exclude Catholics from everything. The stormy election began on 24 June in Monaghan town with a riot, as a result of which three people died. Bric toured the chapels of south Monaghan and received the ready support of the bishop and the priests. Shirley and Leslie formed an alliance as to second votes which they were to direct to each other. It was crucial for Westenra to secure the second votes from Shirley's freeholders. Would they go against their relatively benign and popular landlord? The closing days of the campaign concentrated on the Farney area where the election was to be lost and won. The Catholics issued the following handbill:

> MEN OF FARNEY
> Catholic Freeholders of Farney,
> Are you Men or are you Slaves? –
> Natural beings, or below the dignity of
> human nature? – Why suffer yourselves
> to be imprisoned like murderers and pickpockets,
> or impounded like Cattle? – Burst the
> bonds of Slavery, and assert your independence.
> – Enjoy your liberty and walk the street

like other men. — Vote not for the man
who is sworn to Vote against you.[84]

Shirley requested each of his tenants by letter to give their second votes
to Leslie. But the huge popular excitement and the Catholic appeal was
successful: sufficient voters refused direction from their landlords. The
result was as follows: Shirley 1,889, Westenra 1,502, Leslie 1,240,
Taylor 170. Leslie was defeated and lost a seat held by his family since
the 1780s. Westenra gave a great victory celebration; later he did, in
fact, support Emancipation.

Eighteen twenty-six is the great turning point in Irish popular politics:
Sheil hardly exaggerated when he declared that Ireland 'has been to a
certain extent revolutionised' because the Catholic Association had
'awakened the people to the noble consciousness of their religious and
political duty; we have taught them how to know their rights . . .' The
Dublin Evening Mail admitted on 5 July 1826 that what had been done
in Waterford, Louth, Monaghan, Westmeath, Dublin and Armagh could
be done in every county in Ireland and also in boroughs where Catholic
voters outnumbered Protestant voters. Sheil forecast that the Catholic
Association would be in future 'master of the representation of Ireland'[85]
The *Dublin Evening Post* called for a 'Historical Collection' to be made
concerning the Irish elections of 1826 as 'a revolution, greater than ever
took place since the Elective Franchise was conceded to Ireland, has
occurred in the public mind'.[86]

The general election had indeed indicated a widespread and decisive
shift in Irish parliamentary politics. Out of the thirty-two county con-
stituencies about half had been affected by the Emancipation struggle:
thirteen counties were contested to a poll and counties like Cavan,
Kilkenny, Louth and Monaghan had the first poll of electors since the
Union. In eight counties there were highly significant contests: Armagh,
Cavan, Dublin, Kilkenny, Louth, Monaghan, Westmeath, and Waterford.
O'Connell could claim six county victories in Waterford, Louth,
Monaghan, Westmeath, Armagh and Dublin. He declared that he would
not now accept Emancipation 'coupled with any conditions that would
tend to deprive the forty-shilling freeholders of the elective franchise
[*cheers*]'.[87] Given that many counties had already Emancipationist
MPs in at least one of the seats, the next electoral move by the Catholic
Association would be to try and secure both seats for the cause.
Perhaps they would also oppose those who, even if they favoured
Emancipation, supported the government which refused to take up the
Catholic question as a cabinet measure. In 1826 the policy of the
Association had been not to disturb Emancipationist candidates whether
they were supporters of the government or not.

Sir Robert Peel quickly realised that the Irish results had changed the terms of the debate on Emancipation but he pondered their precise significance. On 16 July 1826 he wrote to Sir George Hill, the Londonderry MP: 'A darker cloud than ever seems to me to impend over Ireland, that is, if one of the remaining bonds of society, the friendly connection between landlord and tenant, is dissolved.' He speculated that 'a powerful reaction' might set in to the priests who had carried the tenantry in some counties by 'a *coup de main*'; this might take the form of disfavour shown to tenants by landlords even if such landlords did not enforce their full legal rights. 'Six or seven years is a long interval of sobriety after the drunkeness of the election', thought Peel. 'It is however a difficult matter to speculate upon.' The true policy for Irish Protestants, he felt still, was 'to forbear, above all, to refrain from demonstrations'. O'Connell immediately called for the revival of a 'New Catholic Rent' specifically to aid those freeholders liable to the wrath of their landlords.[88] The *Dublin Evening Mail* admitted on 10 July that 'a frightful retaliation' had commenced on the part of the landlords whose tenants had disobeyed them. The *Mail*, of course, thought this entirely understandable: if tenants sought to be 'independent', they ought not to wish to be in a landlord's debt. Louth, Monaghan, Waterford, Westmeath and Cavan were the principal recipients of the aid of the Catholic Association from the New Catholic Rent: by the end of 1826, out of a total of £5,680 collected, nearly £3,500 had been spent in these five counties which themselves had subscribed over £1,500 of the £5,680 (*99*, 257).

Peel pondered whether the Catholic successes would be lasting in a letter of 16 July to Leslie Foster, his associate who had had such a narrow escape in Louth:

> The old question still remains: Are these things the mere effect of artificial distinctions and disqualifying laws, or is there a deeper cause for them in the spirit of popery, in a state of society in which the land belongs to one religion, and the physical strength to another, and in a bigoted priesthood so independent of all authority that it would be almost better they should be dependent on the Pope?

Peel confessed, with a rare disclosure of his inner doubts, that it would be 'a greater relief to my mind than I can hope to enjoy' to be persuaded that the removal of the present disqualifications would be a cure 'for the present evils, and at the same time leave Ireland under a Protestant Government' (*107*, I, 412-14).

Significantly O'Connell had declared in his letter to the Catholics of Ireland on 10 July 1826 (calling for the collection of the New Catholic Rent) that Irish Catholics were 'the people, emphatically the people' and that 'the Catholic people of Ireland are a nation. They should have something in the nature of a national treasury'. O'Connell recognised the support and help received from liberal Protestants but he declared that the real struggle fell upon the Catholics. The *Dublin Evening Mail* highlighted this on 14 July in an editorial entitled 'The Nation!' which stressed the dangers of 'an *imperium in imperio* — a *Roman Catholic nation* subsisting *independently* in the bosom of a *Protestant Empire'*. The *Mail* had already pointed out to 'nominal Protestants' like Stuart, Brownlow, Tuite, Dawson and Westenra, who had carried the liberal Protestant flag victorious in the elections, that were Emancipation to be granted they would be spurned by the Catholics.[89] The answer to Peel's 'old question' appeared to be found in the deeper causes deriving from the history of Catholic and Protestant relations in Ireland. The ground occupied by liberal Protestants could indeed prove treacherous terrain.

A Catholic democracy was emerging with the power to undermine Protestant control in Ireland. In 1826 the Catholic Association, for the first time, provided a national framework for local electoral contests. What was being slowly grasped by the Catholic leaders was the fact that they had created the first mass Irish political party which focused primarily on parliamentary and constitutional objectives. The Waterford leaders, inspired by Wyse, were in the forefront of this development.

The youthful agitators in Waterford had learnt a good deal from their first entry into electoral politics. The debts relating to the 1826 election and the attempt to protect the voters after the campaign remained major issues for a number of years. Wyse, however, had conceived the idea of developing a permanent electoral club in the city and county and a few weeks after the victory he drafted a circular letter to the parishes of Co. Waterford relating to the formation of a County and City Liberal Club.[90] Wyse argued that there was a need to 'mature and consolidate' their conquest and he recognised the importance of Co. Waterford as an example to 'every County and City' in Ireland. The new club would also protect the forty-shilling freeholders. The Association he sketched out was to consist of twenty-one members as founders, and others who would be admitted as members by ballot and who would pay £1. Each parish was to have an association 'composed of the Clergymen, Gentlemen and respectable Farmers in the neighbourhood'. The parish associations were to collect information and funds for the County and City Association which would administer the Relief Fund at weekly meetings. Wyse informed the parishes that the County and City Association was already formed and he asked the parishes to follow this example. Wyse further advocated his plan in a major speech at the Catholic meeting of late July in Waterford. Wyse declared that he wished his associations to be 'as general and as popular as possible . . . neither . . . limited in point of numbers, of rank, of property, or of contribution'. A list of those who wished to join was to be opened at the General News Room.

The first meeting of the Protecting Association was held in Waterford in early August 1826.[91] Wyse wrote to the Parishes recommending 'the immediate formation of a Parish Association'.[92] The immediate need to combat economic reprisals consumed the attention of local activists and Wyse's electoral organisation was not immediately developed.[93] Stuart's popularity began to sink in a matter of weeks and he wrote to Wyse 'that the popular feeling is as Capricious as a Woman's fancies'. Stuart did not attend the Munster provincial meeting in Waterford in late August though Wyse asked him to do so.[94] O'Connell had to prepare the business for this meeting which went off very well. O'Connell drew up the resolutions, one of which pledged never 'to accede to any proposal to limit' the forty-shilling franchise (III, 1334). One local activist told Wyse that he believed parish meetings would be better called after the provincial meeting as the great misery of the people had abated Stuart's popularity.

J. M. Galwey began to fear, in early September, that the priests and forty-shilling voters would never come out 'in the *same way* as *the time past*' because they felt let down by the liberal agitators.[95] By early November Father Sheehan was writing to O'Connell to have money sent to the Protecting Committee:

> The want of it produces the most fatal results amongst our persecuted people. The gentry and the aristocracy here have resolved to wage war *usque ad internecionem* against the Forty-Shilling Freeholders who overturned their power at the last election. The Marquis of Waterford's Trustees have adopted a most harassing system towards them . . . The contest lies then between the Association and the enemies of our liberties . . . If we had a sufficiency of money at the present moment, we would put them down with ease (III, 1349).

The priority was to reorganise the collection of the New Catholic Rent to meet what was in fact a major crisis for the local leadership. A few key activists, such as Thomas Wyse, Father Sheehan, Thomas Meagher and Roger Hayes took on the brunt of the work of the Protecting Association in the troubled wake of the election.

The Catholic leaders had been slow to recognise the possibilities in the general election of 1826. Undoubtedly the enforced disbanding of the Catholic Association in 1825 and the ending of the Rent had enfeebled the Catholic effort in the election. The net gain of pro-Catholic seats was about three (all three anti-Catholic gains were in uncontested boroughs) and taken with the results in Great Britain the new Commons was slightly more anti-Catholic than its predecessor (a net anti-Catholic gain of about thirteen). Popular opinion in Great Britain had a deep 'no-popery' vein which made pro-Catholic views 'an unpleasant disadvantage to many candidates in British elections' (*80*, 86-7). The 'no-popery' cry, while useful and effective in support of various interests in England where the issues were Corn Laws, economic retrenchment, parliamentary reform, and slavery, as well as Emancipation, had not been sufficiently mobilised to remove Emancipation from the realm of immediate practical politics. In Ireland, the significant aspects of 1826 could hardly be ignored: Catholic gains had been won in hotly contested popular victories in a number of counties. The bare results, it is true, could not significantly alter the balance in the new parliament but the successes were of immense potential advantage to the Catholic cause. O'Connell now had to hand an immense new power, which, if exploited to the full at the next general election, was bound to bring on a crisis at Westminster which could not be ignored. Conciliation, on the 1825 model, could now be seen as a lost opportunity for the Protestant Ascendancy.

Henry Hobhouse, a Tory, believed in July the elections in England to

have been decidedly friendly to Ministers, and particularly to the Protestants. The Whigs have been beaten, wherever there have been popular contests, and the radicals have not met with much better success. By better management on the part of the Govt. greater advantage might have been gained. In Ireland the R.C. priests have taken a most formidable lead, and by setting the 40 s. freeholders agt. their landlords have carried several elections, and held out threats to other candidates, who deemed their seats the most firm. Still it is calculated that the Protestant int[erest] has gained in the House of Commons about 32 votes (*2*, 121).

Viscount Palmerston correctly identified the political reality in a letter on 17 July:

In truth the real opposition of the present day sit behind the Treasury Bench; and it is by the stupid old Tory party, who bawl out the memory and praises of Pitt while they are opposing all the measures and principles which he held most important; it is by these that the progress of the Government in every improvement which they are attempting is thwarted and impeded. On the Catholic question; on the principles of commerce; on the corn laws . . .' (*45*, 115).

The battle-lines were more sharply drawn after 1826 between the novel democratic Catholic organisation in Ireland and 'the stupid old Tory party': the more intelligent political leaders, such as Peel, now sought a way to accommodate both realities.

Goulburn lamented to Peel on 26 July 1826 how intangible a force the Catholic movement was:

> The Protestant proceedings are of a nature to render them accessible to the law. They hoist flags, they carry swords, they go in procession to church decorated with ribbons. The Catholics, on the other hand, annoy their Protestant neighbours in a more effectual but less tangible manner. The priest directs them at chapel to abstain from trading with their enemies, and there are many other modes in which the party numerically strongest can easily annoy, irritate and injure their opponents without rendering themselves liable to legal interference.

In this situation the government appeared to Protestants to be partial at best or ineffective at worse: 'We are obliged', wrote Goulburn, 'to prevent an Orange procession because we believe it may tend to riot or to exasperation; we cannot interfere with the Catholic Association, because there is doubt as to the possibility of doing so with effect.' The Irish Orange movement was indeed weak and divided in the summer of 1826; it was without an Irish Grand Lodge. Fragments of the movement remained meeting under warrants issued by the British Grand Lodge or the defunct Irish Grand Lodge. The Unlawful Societies Act had weakened the Protestant movement more than the Catholic because of the Orange propensity for law and order. In July 1826 O'Connell announced a plan for an Order of Liberators, in imitation of a society founded by Simon Bolivar in South America. Qualification for membership would be the performance of acts of distinctive service to Ireland. Liberators would advise against secret societies, would help make peace amongst the violent factions in rural Ireland and would help promote the registry for future elections. O'Connell installed the order in August and appeared in a special green uniform with a new medal for the order. On 27 November 1826 Lady Morgan saw O'Connell walking the streets of Dublin in the 'full dress of a verdant liberator' (*47*, II, 226). While it never became as widespread as O'Connell had hoped it was another worrying development for the Association's opponents.

On 13 September 1826 Goulburn again reported 'exclusive dealing' by Catholics in several towns but he now believed that 'the game of the priests' was 'to keep the country in the highest state of excitement possible short of actual disturbance' (*107*, I, 416-19). Catholic assertiveness had certainly become marked since the election successes. Archbishop Magee told Colchester on 2 October 1826: 'Our Popish demagogues here are going completely mad. No thing or person is now secure from the fury of their attacks at their several meetings.' As Ireland seemed to Magee to be in a 'state of universal inflamation' he could see no issue but rebellion (*20*, III, 448-9).

Colchester was receiving other reports from Ireland of the widespread 'rebellious spirit': a priest named Quin in Roscommon was reported to have declared at a public meeting that 'blood had been shed in Italy, and blood had been shed in France, and why should not Ireland assert her independence?' Ultras like Colchester feared that the Jesuits had laid 'a deep plot' to exterminate Protestants. Roman Catholic chapels were being built 'with cut stone in the most sumptuous manner . . . more like cathedrals, with towers, spires, and minarets; and they no longer call them chapels but *churches*'. Ultras believed that Ireland urgently required a firm law and order Protestant government accompanied by a moral regeneration of the people through scriptural education under Protestant direction (*20*, III, 441-51).

In October Peel was enquiring about the state of military preparedness in Ireland. Goulburn reported that the government had at its disposal 20,000 soldiers though there was the possible danger of Catholic soldiers proving unreliable in a 'crusade'; there were also 4,000 police and 1,500 revenue police and waterguards. If the militia and yeomanry were revived they would release regular troops from the North for deployment elsewhere (*107*, I, 420-22). Later, in December, Goulburn was disturbed by a government decision to remove some of the troops for service abroad.

The new pitch of the Catholic Association was highlighted in Sheil's attack on the Duke of York after a Catholic meeting in Mullingar on 14 September. Pointing to the Duke's 'amalgamation of his passions and his politics, in which his vices and his virtues are fused together' for the purpose of recalling

> the period at which the illustrious person was an object of as much aversion in England, as he is in Ireland at this day. It is for the purpose of branding his protestations about conscience, with all the scorn which they merit . . . to put his morality into comparison with his religion, and to tear off the mask by which the spirit of oppression is sought to be disguised. Conscience, forsooth! It is enough to make one's blood boil to think on't! That he who had publicly, and in the open common day, thrown off every coverlet of shame — who had wallowed in the blackest stye of profligate sensuality, an avowed and ostentatious adulterer, whose harlot had sustained herself by the sale of commissions, and turned footmen into brigadiers! that he — yet hot and reeking from the results of a foul and most disgraceful concubinage — should . . . dedicate himself with an invocation of heaven to the everlasting oppression of my country! This it is that sets me, and every Irish Catholic, on fire. This it is which raises, excites, inflames and exasperates! This it is that applies a torch to our passions. This it is that blows our indignation into flame (*119*, 400)

Legal opinion was taken on this speech in England and it was declared that Sheil was not liable to a public prosecution.[96] Plunket and Joy on 2 November declined to offer any opinion on the expediency of instituting a prosecution as it was clearly a delicate matter for both the Duke of York and the government, given York's character and record. Peel wrote to Wellesley on 14 November declaring that it was not advisable to institute proceedings.

The question of prosecuting the Catholic Association was again raised in December. Wellesley was unwell and not given to any firm advice or opinion. In reality the Catholic movement had become localised and diffused so it could not be readily suppressed by prosecution of the leadership.[97] Between 1822 and 1827, as Peel's biographer has noted, 'the Irish pages of his Home Office administration formed a relatively barren chapter' (*40*, 399).

Michael Staunton later recalled that Sheil was 'in the most exposed position of any man in Ireland, for he went further than all the others to provoke the attacks of the Crown, and was known to have written, or corrected for publication all his speeches' (*71*, I, 322). Durvergier de Hauranne, who toured Ireland after the general election of 1826, recorded his impressions of the Catholic meeting in Ballinasloe and of Sheil:

> An old chapel, without any ornament, white washed, and half in ruins; before the altar a platform, rudely constructed; on the left, a gallery for the men; another for the women on the right; on the platform about two hundred country gentlemen, in a sort of morning dress, which is not without its pretension; and in every other part of the chapel, a peasant population, of a savage aspect, and a picturesque costume.

Duvergier described the impact of Sheil on the meeting: he had never seen 'so absolute a triumph'. As a speaker was deploring the long-continued perfidy of England and recalling the menacing example of America

> thunders of applause burst forth on a sudden from every quarter: every hat was waved over the head; and a piercing cry, the expression of joy amongst the Irish, shook the chapel to its very roof. It was *Mr Sheil*, who had just appeared on the platform . . . Five feet; eyes, quick and piercing; complexion pale; chin, pointed; hair, dark; . . . mouth, middle-sized . . . when you behold that little gascon figure in repose, it is impossible to suspect to what changes passion is capable of converting it . . . His satire is shrewd and biting; his poetry dazzles; his enthusiasm carries you away . . . His voice is meagre, harsh, and shrill; but a profound emotion seems to regulate its vibrations . . . Sheil possesses, in an eminent degree, the surprising

faculty of exerting himself to the very verge of delirium, without once losing his complete self-possession (*132*, II, 1vi-1viii).

Sheil was finally pounced upon by the government after one particular speech in the Catholic Association. He used the publication of the *Life of Theobald Wolfe Tone* to remind the government of the horrors of civil war in a way which might be interpreted as more of a threat than a warning. In the course of his speech he appealed to Canning to go 'with this book in his hand into the cabinet, and plead for the emancipation of Ireland, with the memoirs of Wolfe Tone'. This would avert a civil war in which 'the Cromwellian proprietor' might see 'amidst the shouts of insurgent onslaught his mansion . . . given to the flames' (*119*, 29). The government decided to proceed with a prosecution in January 1827 and Plunket secured a true bill from a Dublin jury in February. Canning always had doubts about the legal aspects of the case and after a postponement of the trial, the prosecution was later withdrawn during Canning's brief administration in 1827.

In early November 1826 Peel speculated to Leslie Foster on the consequences of 'Catholic Emancipation'. He wished to know the 'whole truth' about 'Irish popery' and what safeguards might be necessary to contain it. He told Foster that when he saw Emancipation as 'inevitable' he would, taking due care to free his motives from all suspicion, 'try to make the best terms for the future security of the Protestant' and he asked 'How can this be done if we close our eyes to actual or possible dangers?' He urged Foster to get all the information he could on such 'dangers' through his work on the Parliamentary Education Inquiry. Foster replied on 6 November 1826:

> The most practical safeguard would be a modification of the franchise. If the present election laws were to remain untouched, you would have at least sixty Catholic members. And such Catholics! Sheil for Louth, and O'Connell for any southern county he might choose. Their presence in the House of Commons would be the least part of the mischief, a *bellum servile* would ensue all over Ireland (*107*, I, 422-4).

Meanwhile, Sir George Hill had reported to Peel on 2 November the Ulster opinion that the government had allowed the Catholic Association to develop in order to convince English opinion of the necessity of concession; it was widely felt that in the end there would be 'a bargain' which would 'eventually terminate in Ireland becoming a popish country'; Peel denied this and declared he was as 'unfettered' on the Catholic question as he always had been (*107*, I, 424-6).

Yet he was 'fettered': if the situation continued unchanged the

Catholic Association could capture the county representation of Ireland. The question was now how to grant Emancipation in such a way as to preserve the Protestant interest in Ireland. O'Connell was in no mood to be conciliatory as he told the Knight of Kerry on 31 December 1826:

> I am grown weary of being temperate, moderate and conciliatory to no one useful purpose and without having obtained any one single advantage . . . After all, the Established Church, with her millions of acres and pounds, is our great foe and she may be frightened; but one may as well endeavour to coax a pound of flesh from a hungry wolf as to conciliate the Church.
>
> From our numbers, our combination and the continued expression of our discontent something may be attained . . . there would be no great difficulty in getting the Catholics in every parish in Ireland to meet for the purpose of petition on one and the same day . . . there would appear such a union of physical strength with moral sentiment that Mr Peel would be insane if he continued his opposition. We *never, never, never* got anything by conciliation. Could it be possible to be more conciliatory than we were on the deputation? Yet have we not, in fact, been flung back by our disposition to accede.

O'Connell was now determined to 'speak out boldly' and to 'rouse in Ireland a spirit of action which will bring all our people to show in a legal manner' their detestation of the anti-Catholic policy which made possible 'the worst possible system of government in Ireland' (III, 1354).

5

1827-8: 'Hope Deferred'

'I can easily be *quieted*, but there are the people at large; there
is the Irish nation kept in the miserable state of hope deferred . . .'

O'Connell to the Knight of Kerry,
28 May 1827 (III, 1389).

Eighteen twenty-seven brought much political change: the prostration
by illness of one Prime Minister; the succession and within four months
the death of another; the entrance, to be followed quickly by the exit,
of a third. These rapid changes were heavily influenced by the Catholic
cause and, in turn, affected the Catholic struggle. Events in London and
Ireland interacted so as to restrain the full power of the Catholic movement in Ireland. Pent-up forces could be released if restraint did not
produce results quickly. Eighteen twenty-seven was the lull before the
storm.

The death of the Duke of York early in the year frankly heartened
the Catholic leaders. His intervention had done much to ruin the prospects of the 1825 Relief Bill. Among his last actions in the latter part
of 1826 was unsuccessfully to encourage the formation of an exclusively
anti-Catholic government. Liverpool advised the king 'whether it would
not be as impracticable, at least *now* as in 1812, to form an administration
upon the exclusive Protestant principle, and whether the attempt to do
so must infallibly lead to an administration of an opposite character'
(*80, 88-9*). The Duke failed and died on 5 January. His passing was
noted in the Catholic Association by Sheil, whose fierce attack on the
late Duke for his anti-Catholic actions was still fresh in everybody's
mind. Now Sheil advised the Association in colourful terms that the
Duke would soon be forgotten.

The pomp of death will for a few nights fill the gilded apartments
in which his body will lie in state . . . The bell of St Paul's will toll,
and London − rich, luxurious Babylonic London − will start at the
recollection that even kings must die. The day of his solemn obsequies
will arrive − the gorgeous procession will go forth in its funeral
glory . . . the multitude of the great will gradually disperse; they will
roll back in their gilded chariots, into the din and tumult of the great
metropolis . . . the heir to the three kingdoms will be in a week forgotten. We, too, shall forget; but let us, before we forget, forgive him
(*119*, xxvi-xxvii).

O'Connell declared: 'We war not with the dying or the grave. Our enmities are buried there. They expired with the individual who . . . caused them'.[1] Privately O'Connell asked his friend Richard Newton Bennett to discover whether the Duke of Clarence, who now was heir to George IV, was favourable to the Catholic cause: 'All I want is *"the map of the land"*. I want only the compass, I think I can steer by it . . .'; Bennett was empowered to pledge Catholic attachment to the Duke 'if they shall but get fair play' (III, 1359).

At the beginning of 1827, O'Connell intended to intensify the pressure for Emancipation after the triumphs of the previous year. On 2 January, he sent a letter to all Catholic bishops seeking their support for the Education Census and the New Catholic Rent. He reminded the bishops 'that the persecution of the 40 s. freeholders' had recommenced and that the Association was 'much pressed for relief by persons who suffer persecution for not sending their children to proselytizing schools or who themselves refuse to be perverted'.[2] The Catholic Association in the middle of January held a fourteen day meeting which was characterised by a new and more assertive policy line and by strident speeches by O'Connell. Sheil also tread dangerous waters and his speech on Wolfe Tone's *Life* has been noted as the cause of his prosecution by the government. O'Connell vigorously attacked Peel, Liverpool and Eldon. Wellington was also abused on his appointment as commander-in-chief of the army following the death of the Duke of York. O'Connell declared him a person upon whom 'the people of Ireland look with . . . execration . . . Did he not build his fortunes on the efforts of Irish valour? . . . Was not his first vote, after he had obtained that Dukedom won by Catholic blood, given against the freedom of the Catholics of Ireland?'[3]

At this meeting O'Connell reviewed the 'present posture of Catholic affairs'. He stressed the importance of the political education which had been spread by the Catholic Association, creating a new public opinion. 'That opinion is valuable because it is peaceable – useful because it is constitutional – formidable because it does not fritter away its strength in crime and outrage but reserves it for the exertion of that moral strength exceeding the physical force of any nation . . .' But he posed the threat of Irish disturbance if such constitutional approaches were not heeded: 'who can tell me the period may not arrive when our advice may be rejected – when we may be flung from the surface like small bodies from a wheel when there is too great a rapidity of motion . . .'[4] He used the meeting to attack church rates and other topical grievances such as education and tithes. He raised the question of Irish self-government: 'The Union has been a great curse to us. It has been the bitterest infliction that ever visited this poor country – nothing but its repeal can right us or restore Ireland to what it was . . .' Noting that this was probably the first time the subject of Repeal was brought forward at a Catholic meeting, he warned it would not be the last: '. . . there is nothing like familiarising the public mind and habituating it to the subject. I trust if we are to continue the struggle we shall aim at game of a higher flight and call upon the imperial nation for our Independence'. Lawless supported O'Connell's call for Repeal of the Union; 'all other measures', he declared, 'are miserable half measures'.[5]

Other speakers stressed the importance of the registration of the forty-shilling freeholders and the creation of county organisations to win elections. The example of the Louth Club was much praised in this regard. O'Connell claimed that it was 'the necessity & utility of such a Club as that at Louth' which sparked his plan for the Order of Liberators. The leaders had to be wary of possible legal dangers and Sheil argued that it was unnecessary to have any connection between local political clubs. O'Connell declared he was now convinced 'on the evidence of facts that Catholic Emancipation would not be worth taking qualified by any diminution of the right of election'. The preservation of the forty-shilling franchise had 'become a sacred duty' and they would be 'betrayers of those who stood by us in our worst extremity' if they agreed to disenfranchisement. Sheil agreed strongly, observing that until 'the late Elections we had not rightly appreciated the value of the lower order of the People . . .'[6] O'Connell declared he had 'all the zeal of a convert' and revealed his more radical views '. . . for my own part I have ever been of opinion that every human being arrived at the age of 21 and possessing a certain property was entitled to speak in the House of Commons through his representative'. He lamented and regretted his 1825 stance. Lawless declared that O'Connell had atoned for his error in 1825 and claimed credit for his own role in that crisis.[7] There was a rowdy debate on the question of the payment by the state of the Catholic priests. O'Connell's position was that where government was identified with the people it was proper to provide for the clergy. In Ireland, however, 'No man can think of the English nation without feelings of hatred boiling in his bosom which not even the principles of Christianity can assuage such has been the effect of seven centuries of cruel oppression.'[8] Clearly the tone and temper of the Catholic leaders faced Liverpool's government with an increasingly nationalist and radical policy and an implied threat of popular revolt should they continue to resist concession.

On 17 February Goulburn was closeted with Peel, discussing the Emancipation issue when 'in the middle of our discussion a message was brought to us that Lord Liverpool had been attacked by Apoplexy'. Goulburn told Gregory that as a public man Liverpool 'may be reckoned as dead' and the break up of his government was inevitable:

The embarrassments of the King in making a new Government will
be extreme. He cannot find Protestants enough to make a Protestant Government, he will not like a Catholic one, and I think
that a mixed one can go on no longer . . . It would appear as if
God had determined to punish us by depriving us of those best
calculated to defend the Church in the danger with which it is
threatened (*42*, 225-7).

With Liverpool's sudden removal from the scene British politics entered upon a period of protracted crisis. O'Connell was immediately
appalled at the idea of Wellington being made Prime Minister. He now
changed his tactics dramatically and indicated his preparedness to play
a moderate game on behalf of the Irish Catholics if that would help
form a ministry favourable to Emancipation.

O'Connell was always conscious that his real focus was London and
the play of high politics at Westminster. Hearing rumours of ministerial
changes O'Connell, as early as 15 January 1827, promised to moderate
Irish agitation if the Marquis of Lansdowne 'be about to share power'.
'In fact I think', he told the Knight of Kerry, 'I may venture to say that
the Marquis of Lansdowne would bring with him into office all the
support which the Catholics of Ireland and liberal Protestants could
give any administration.' In his usual exaggerated style he went on
'Such an administration would tranquillize the country in one hour.
One would ask with astonishment, "What has become of the Orange
party?" just as at the Restoration it was asked "Where are they who
dethroned the King?"' (III, 1358). O'Connell's immediate target became
'the Orange Party' who dominated in Ireland and he was prepared to
postpone an Emancipation measure if he got significant changes in the
Irish government and administration from a new ministry. On 22
February he asked the Knight of Kerry: 'Could you suggest any act
of the Catholic body which might facilitate the views of the opposition
at this moment? And, in particular, could we do anything to forward
or support the Marquis of Lansdowne? To him much of our hopes,
almost all, are turned' (III, 1362).

On the following day O'Connell advised Eneas MacDonnell, the
Catholic Association political agent in London, to warn Irish MPs that
they would be deemed '*an actual enemy*' if they did not support
Canning against Peel, Eldon and other 'no-popery' elements. 'If you can
get *at* these gentlemen, assure them that we will organise an immediate
opposition to them in their own counties unless they take a decided
part with Mr Canning in any ministerial struggle now going forward'
(III, 1364). A motion on the Catholic question was awaiting debate in
the Commons and the cabinet persuaded the king to regard Liverpool's
illness as temporary so that the choice of a new premier could be made

after the debate. The choice would be greatly influenced by the size of the pro- or anti-Catholic vote in the Commons as would the composition of the cabinet itself.

The Catholic motion was introduced by Sir Francis Burdett on 5 March. His speech placed Catholic Emancipation in the tradition of Burke, Fox, Pitt, Sheridan and Grattan. Because of such distinguished past advocates the question, he felt, in 1827 'was reduced to one of a plain, simple, common sense, practical nature'. He argued that the Catholics of Ireland, by the Treaty of Limerick, were entitled to participate in all the civil rights of the community: 'The days had passed away when Ireland could be neglected with immunity. The interests of Ireland were now among the most vital interests of the empire.' Burdett stressed the hopes of Catholic Emancipation that had been held out at the Act of Union and when the king had visited Ireland in 1821. He appealed to MPs to overcome their 'nursery recollections of the Pope and the Pretender'. 'The great practical point for the consideration of Parliament was this — "Since we cannot stay where we are, what are we to do?" . . . Either this measure ought to pass, or it ought not. If it ought to pass, then the sooner it did pass, the better . . .' Burdett pleaded with them not to wait for 'the eleventh hour' to concede. Aside from Villiers Stuart's good maiden speech, in which he defended the role of the Catholic priest in politics by declaring that 'he should be glad to know the occasions when the clergy of England had been slack in exerting themselves politically', the debate lacked novelty.

Peel, indeed on 6 March, confessed the problem: 'It was quite painful and nauseating to have to tax one's memory and ingenuity in the devising of novel arguments on a subject which had been already so often discussed and exhausted'. He declared that no claim to Emancipation could be based on the Treaty of Limerick:

> He would own, fairly and candidly, that he entertained a distrust of the Roman Catholic religion . . . Could any man acquainted with the state of the world doubt for a moment that there was engrafted on the Catholic religion something more than a scheme for promoting mere religion? . . . [Catholic] doctrines were maintained for the purpose of establishing the power of man over the minds and hearts of men . . .

He defended the right of 'New Reformation' preachers if their task was 'a fair and honest endeavour to bring others to embrace what was conceived to be a purer system of faith'.[9]

When the division was taken in the early hours of 7 March the Catholic hopes were dashed: Burdett's motion was lost by four votes 276 to 272 and for the first time since 1819 a pro-Catholic vote had failed in the Commons. Thomas Creevey noted perceptively in his diary on 7 March: 'The Catholic question was lost by four last night; but it was, in truth, a fight for power and not for the Catholics . . .' (*85*, II, 108). John Cam Hobhouse declared he had never seen

> such a scene as the Treasury Bench presented . . . Mr Secretary Peel accusing his own Irish Attorney-General of encouraging rebellion, and Mr Secretary Canning tearing to pieces the Master of the Rolls and the Under-Secretary of State. . . . The division took place at a quarter-past four in the morning, amidst vast uproar. . . . We were all in the most feverish state when it was announced that our opponents inside the House were 276. At last we went in and found the rumour to be true. The division was 276 to 272, and was announced amidst the frantic shouts of the anti-Catholics (*15*, III, 175).

O'Connell, in Ennis commencing the electoral organisation of Clare for subsequent elections, was angry at the defeat: 'Another crime has been added to those which England has inflicted on this wretched land; another instance of genuine Reformation bigotry has disgraced the British nation . . . We must rally for a new exertion'. He instructed Edward Dwyer to prepare an address to the king, renew petitions to parliament and to resort to strong measures.

> The more we exhibit our determination to pursue perseveringly constitutional courses and the more frequently we exhibit the bigotry of the boasted British nation to the contempt of all the enlightened people of the civilised world, the better . . . A petition for the Repeal of the Union should be immediately prepared . . . (III, 1370).

O'Connell's strong response upset the moderates such as Sir Thomas Esmonde in the Catholic Association but his letter to Dwyer was received 'with great applause'.[10] O'Connell criticised the 'want of spirit and energy' apparent in those in Dublin who were 'crouching beneath defeat'; he objected to the resolutions passed in Dublin which were 'puling and weeping but suggesting nothing'. He continued 'agitating famously' in Limerick but regretted that no county was 'stirring but those I put in motion' (III, 1374). O'Connell's tendency, after setbacks in London, to raise the issues of Repeal and parliamentary reform scared the more conservative elements in the Catholic Association. He endeavoured to keep up the momentum in Ireland in order to give 'the Eldons, Peels and other bigots no species of rest or relaxation until they are compelled to do us justice'. He sought 'to shame' the English people 'into liberality' and to extend and make permanent the Catholic Rent which the enemies of the Catholic cause 'dreaded' (III, 1376).

In London intrigue, rumour and negotiation were the dominant political activities: Canning remained the leading candidate for Prime Minister and speculation abounded as to what form his government would take. The defeat in the Commons on the Catholic question was a reverse for Canning. It was anticipated that he could do no more than continue the 'open' system under which the Catholics would gain no more than a premier with favourable inclinations. Grey and his Whig followers would only support a government which undertook to adopt Catholic Emancipation. Other Whigs, especially Brougham, wished to form with Canning a liberal Tory-Whig government which would not insist on Emancipation being made a cabinet measure. The Whigs were split on this issue. Ultra-Protestants led by peers such as the Duke of Newcastle hoped to influence the king to form an exclusively Protestant government. On 27 March 1827 the Duke of Newcastle reported to Colchester his interview with George IV on the formation of a Protestant administration; George professed himself 'Protestant heart and soul' and declared that the Prime Minister should be 'for the Protestant side of the question'. He said again and again 'Do you doubt me? But it is not I who fail in my duty. It is you in Parliament. Why do you suffer the d–d Association in Dublin?' (*20*, III, 472-3).

On 10 April the king ended the hiatus by asking Canning to reconstruct the government. George IV probably realised that Canning's past record on the Catholic question was not one which would endanger the Protestant Constitution. Canning had compromised in 1821 while in 1825 he was half-hearted and in effect supported the status quo; in 1826 he had done all he could to suppress discussion on the Catholic question. Canning was immediately faced with the resignation of Bathurst, Eldon, Peel, Wellington and Westmorland, as much from personal dislike or distrust of Canning as from having to countenance his pro-Catholic views. To Eneas MacDonnell Canning was 'a false one' and 'a very slippery gentleman' (III, 1360, 1367). To Tories like Bathurst and Eldon, Canning was an upstart, a *parvenu*, while to Grey and his Whigs he was a 'traitor' to his principles. Croker aptly said it was Canning's misfortune 'that nobody will believe that he can take the most indifferent step without an ulterior object, not take his tea without a stratagem' (*56*, I, 268). Surrounded by such enmity, Canning was in poor health. On 5 April Colchester was riding in Hyde Park when he 'met an elderly-looking gentleman wrapped up in a great coat (*the day very warm*), pale-faced, but with a sparkling eye'. On passing near enough to recognise him Colchester found it was Canning (*20*, III, 476-7). On 17 April 1827 Peel wrote to Canning setting out the official reasons why he declined to serve with him: 'The transfer of the influence of Prime Minister from Lord Liverpool to you is the transfer of that influence from the most powerful opponent to the most powerful advocate of the Roman Catholic claims.' To serve would be lending Peel's name 'to the advancement of a cause which under a different aspect of political affairs I had uniformly and strenuously resisted' (*128*, III, 644-5). There was a real basis in Canning's claim to Wellesley that his success had determined that holding a pro-Catholic opinion did not disqualify *ipso facto* from the first situation in government (*120*, II, 157).

Canning was faced with enormous problems in the formation of a ministry. He could rely on the assistance of the king who was angry with the secession of the Tories and the ultra's attempts to sway his decision. Canning negotiated with Lansdowne and those Whigs willing to enter government on the basis of neutrality on the Catholic question which was the central question in the formation of the government. Lansdowne sought to bargain for a pro-Catholic Irish government but Canning had promised the king that he would make anti-Catholic appointments in Ireland. On 14 April O'Connell pledged Irish Catholic support for Canning in the event of his forming a liberal ministry.[11] He attempted to govern his political actions in Ireland by the party manoeuvres in London so as to produce a favourable government and pro-Catholic Irish appointments. On the same day, the Knight of Kerry appealed to O'Connell for 'a course of the greatest forbearance' to help a liberal ministry emerge (III, 1378). Lansdowne was mainly instrumental in effecting a coalition between a section of the Whigs and the Canningites; O'Connell decided to play a conciliating game even though Eneas MacDonnell warned him not to trust W. C. Plunket, A. R. Blake or any of the overtures stimulated by the crisis. 'You are grossly misled, believe me. Remember 1825', he concluded his letter of 23 April (III, 1381).

Henry Brougham wrote to O'Connell at the end of April seeking to have the Association 'at least for the present' closed to help the new administration. He offered a channel of communication through himself to the new government (III, 1384). At a Catholic meeting in Dublin on 18 April O'Connell carried a resolution favouring the postponement of an aggregate meeting to 1 May, fearing that 'discussions might take place that might be disagreeable to some of their sincere friends': he urged Catholics to wait to test the character of the new administration and to adopt 'a conciliatory tone'. In early May the Association postponed the sending of a petition to parliament and resolved to adjourn for six weeks in order 'to evince the anxiety of the Catholics of Ireland to conciliate their enemies, and to exhibit their confidence in their friends'.[12]

The Whigs who supported Canning did not make government' unity in espousing the Catholic question a condition of taking office. The official minute of the cabinet on the Catholic question of 23 April 1827 stated:

The Catholic question is to remain, as in Lord Liverpool's government, an open question; *upon which each member of the Cabinet is at perfect liberty to exercise his own judgment in supporting that question, if brought forward by others, or in propounding it, in the Cabinet or in Parliament*. But if any member of the Cabinet should deem it an indispensable duty to bring forward individually the Catholic question in Parliament, he is distinctly to state that he does so in his individual capacity' *(27, 92-3)*.

The emphasis is in a copy Lansdowne sent to George Tierney, another Whig who subsequently joined the cabinet. Lansdowne was emphasising the possibility of a cabinet discussion on the Catholic question with the implication that the cabinet was open to persuasion to take it up as a government measure when this was feasible. As the Knight of Kerry told O'Connell on 23 April, to calculate 'on an entirely favourable ministry' was wrong: *'the thing is totally impossible.* Do you think the King is to have no voice on that subject? He cannot disguise what his feelings have been. We must hope that he will gradually come round' (III, 1382). There was in fact little sign of George 'coming round': in March 1827 it became apparent to the diarist Charles Greville 'that the King's opinions on the Catholic question are just the same as those of the Duke of York, and equally strong' *(43, 94)*.

What O'Connell really hoped for was a change of personnel in the Irish government. He wrote confidentially to the Knight of Kerry on 16 May in direct terms:

You may pledge yourself that the Catholic claims can be managed for the proper season if we get in this Cabinet a change of men. If, for example, Gregory be removed from the Castle — his removal is *indispensable* — the Corporation, controlled as it easily can be in the offices of the police, *all held at will*, and if the Law offices be well filled. It will not do to have Joy Attorney-General or either of the Orange serjeants promoted. Indeed, indeed they ought to be dismissed at once. Lefroy is an exceedingly poor creature in point of intellect and Blackburne is excessively overrated . . . I repeat that, if men were changed, it would not be difficult to postpone to the proper season the Emancipation Bill.

On 18 May he re-emphasised his approach by saying that the government of Peel and Lord Manners 'would be more popular and fully as sedative as the new, provided the Trenches continue to rule the Custom House, the Gregorys to *manage* the Castle, the Darleys and Kings to sway the Corporation and the Joys, Lefroys and Blackburnes to top the profession of the Law and *promise* the people a succession of partisan judges' (III, 1387). On 28 May O'Connell told the Knight of

Kerry that Ireland had been governed for the previous twenty years 'by the triumvirate of Lord Manners, Saurin and Gregory' and a change in the system was imperative. 'I can easily be *quieted*, but there are the people at large; there is the Irish nation kept in the miserable state of hope deferred . . . If the system were pursued without a hope of alteration for one year more there never yet was so bitter or so bloody a contest in this country, often as it has been stained with blood' (III, 1389).

Lansdowne was soon under pressure not to make an Irish government on pro-Catholic lines essential to an agreement with Canning; he held out simply for a pro-Catholic Chief Secretary. William Lamb was appointed Chief Secretary as part of the tricky negotiations in the formation of Canning's ministry. Lamb had no particular interest in, or knowledge of, Ireland, 'suspecting', as his biographer observes, 'like most Englishmen, that its people were incomprehensible and its problems insoluble'. Lamb had 'the hauteur of one who had passed his youth in the halls of the Grand Whiggery, played in the nurseries of Devonshire House and sat at the feet of Fox' (*133*, 85, 89). He was disappointed not to have been appointed Home Secretary but at forty-seven years of age, having 'floated irresolutely for more than fifteen years' he was pleased to be in office and to be back in the Commons. He had lost his seat in the general election but Canning now arranged another for him. Canning probably discerned in Lamb's affability a useful attribute for a policy of very gradual change: to prepare the way for an ultimate enactment of justice for all. Lamb would not ostensibly subvert the outworks of Ascendancy but he could ever so gradually mine them from inside. From the beginning Lamb resolved to see and hear everybody. Castle officials, who deplored this openness, recalled 'When Mr Lamb was here the only orders were "Show him in"' (*123*, I, 228-9).

It was always unlikely that Lamb would achieve anything in Ireland. Canning had put together a frail coalition which depended entirely upon his survival and he was a sick man. 'If Canning lasts, the ministry will last', was Lord John Russell's apt comment. Lamb was in favour of Emancipation, a pro-Catholic, but he had also been amongst those who had supported the suppression of the Catholic Association in 1825. It is not surprising therefore that Irish Catholics were suspicious of him and he never felt any real rapport with them: 'As to the Roman Catholics,' he wrote to Brougham in October 1827, 'it is of course better that they should be tranquil and prudent than the contrary, but it is of importance that they should not think that they confer great obligation upon the Government by their tranquillity and forbearance' (*133*, 91). In Dublin his job amounted to keeping the Catholics as happy as possible while not upsetting the Protestants − an impossible task which perhaps only the complacent Lamb could have attempted for a while. The ruling Protestant minority, viewing Lamb as the replacement for Goulburn, felt an even greater suspicion than did the Catholics. Lamb had to work with the rabid Protestant clique which dominated in the Castle – men like William Gregory, the Under-Secretary for the past fifteen years. Gregory was represented as an 'arch-jobber' and 'a man who has the press at his command – a determined intriguer. False as hell. A violent anti-Catholic – a furious Tory – and quite ready to betray the secrets of any one whose confidence he obtains' (*1*, 188). As Wyse points out, Ireland was governed 'by a faction within a faction': 'The petitioner at the Castle did not ask what the Lord Lieutenant thought, but what the Lord Lieutenant's Secretary, or rather what his Secretary's Secretary thought. It was not Lord Wellesley, nor even Mr Goulburn, but it was Mr Gregory who held in his hands the destinies of Ireland' (*132*, I, 356).

In effect, Lamb did little but he was inactive with style and affability and his patent good will, after the ultra-Protestant Goulburn, was enough to endear him to the Catholics. Deep down he recognised that Catholics were 'labouring under a galling exclusion' while Protestants were 'striving to maintain an unjust superiority' as he bluntly told Lansdowne in August 1827 (*133*, 92-5). Lamb had little liking for O'Connell, for whom he had all the usual Establishment contempt, but he was shrewd enough to see that O'Connell's goodwill was essential if Ireland was to be kept tranquil. He passed a message early in June to O'Connell through O'Connell's friend Richard Bennett: *'Tell Mr O'C I must for a time be worse than Peel* but when we can we will do all the good we can. Beg of him to have confidence, though we cannot do much, or worse men will come' (III, 1392). O'Connell wrote to Bennett that he was 'greatly alarmed' at what Lamb had said: 'He has taken up the notion that in order to show his *candour* and *liberality* he will patronise men of the Orange faction . . . It is however idle to expect anything from Mr Lamb. . . . My confidence, I candidly own to you, is worn out or rather trodden to rags' (III, 1394). Before Lamb's message arrived, O'Connell had complained to the Knight of Kerry on 28 May about 'the miserable state of hope deferred' because there was not 'one single movement in Ireland favourable to an alteration in the system, save only the appointment of Mr Doherty [the solicitor-general] . That certainly gave great satisfaction, but then there is the drawback of Joy, an open and avowed Orangeman, who becomes Attorney-General. Can you blame us for impatience?' (III, 1389).

In early June O'Connell received from the Knight of Kerry a letter arguing continued support for Canning's ministry: 'Can you relax your efforts to keep all quiet for the present without incurring a risk, the effects of which we might have to deplore for our lives?' (III, 1390). O'Connell came under pressure for his conciliatory stance from Bishop

Doyle in a letter of 8 June complaining of measures 'having for their object the further aggrandizement of the Irish Protestant Church' being proposed in the Commons. O'Connell was asked by Doyle to make representations because he had taken upon himself the responsibility of giving Canning's government 'the sanction of our general approbation'. Doyle doubted whether it would not have been better for Irish Catholics 'to see Canning and the Grenvilles forced to join the Whigs in opposition, rather than see the Whigs playing second fiddle to Canning, and both truckling to the Court and the Bishops . . .' (III, 1391). In strong language Doyle was putting pressure on O'Connell to insist on the Canning government returning some benefits for the quiescent approach by O'Connell and the Irish Catholics. O'Connell sent Doyle's letter immediately to the Knight of Kerry adding a further protest about the lack of change when what had been hoped for was '*the new order of things*'. O'Connell was in an awkward position. 'You will perceive by this letter the very unpleasant state in which I have placed myself by the very action that I have taken in procuring the suspension of our claims in this session' and he asked plaintively, 'What does Mr Canning mean to do for Ireland or with Ireland? To leave all the old *warriors* in office! There never yet was a game so completely thrown away as this is. Ireland *could* have been, and may still be, brought to perfect unanimity on the subject of our claims and the support of the new Ministry' (III, 1393).

Lamb occupied himself by visiting his new found mistress Lady Branden at her house in Fitzwilliam Square and accompanying her to parties, balls and the theatre, the couple behaving with 'striking indiscretion' (*133*, 102). Lamb charmed the recognition starved Catholics by the simple expedient of keeping an open house, having people like Sheil to dine, allowing access to all, and just simply listening. He also socialised with the liberal Protestant set centred on the Morgans which included Cloncurry, W. H. Curran and Henry Grattan, the Dublin City MP (*47*, II, 241-8). Wellesley, Lord Lieutenant since 1822, was not likely to get Lamb to do much: Wellesley was irresolute, indecisive and by now decidedly nervous.

It was indicated to O'Connell towards the end of June that a patent of precedence would be given him at the Bar as soon as Lord Manners, the Lord Chancellor was changed, 'perhaps sooner' (III, 1395). This would have been of great value to him in his legal practice and he wrote to Bennett that he was 'determined to continue the experiment' of Irish Catholic support for Canning's administration 'but if it does not *result* in Emancipation, all is idle' (III, 1396). It is clear from O'Connell's letter to the Knight of Kerry of 24 June 1827 that he still hoped to 'un-Orange Ireland' as put it:

The Orange faction in Ireland could be made to crumble like a Rope of Sand. It, in fact, *is* a Rope of Sand, but Government patronage has twisted it into a Rope of Steel and then used it to manacle us poor papists. But let the Government force be taken from the twisting machine and a Rope of Sand orangism will be again.

He felt 'the game is in our hands' and he gave examples to Thomas Spring Rice, such as appointments to the Paving Board, where this policy could be made practical (III, 1397, 1398).

Sectarian tensions determined political and social relationships in 1827. This was true both of relationships between Catholics and Protestants and of relationships within denominations, especially within Presbyterianism. In March various Protestant bodies were claiming converts from Catholicism in various parts of Ireland. For example, in early 1827, a meeting of the Protestant clergy in Longford decided to deliver weekly lectures on the 'errors of the Church of Rome'. Soon small numbers of converts were publicised over the whole county.[13] The Protestant gentry supported this 'New Reformation' initiative whilst the Catholic activists helped the priests to counter-attack. On 31 March the *Dublin Evening Post* reported on the 'Counter-Reformation in Longford' where Father Michael O'Beirne of Ballymahon, a noted Catholic Association supporter, was preaching

> two or three times a week to a vast assemblage of Protestants as well as Catholics, and the result is, that within the last four days, four Protestants have embraced the Catholic faith in Ballymahon, and many applications have been made to the Right Rev. Dr Magauran by respectable Protestants who are wavering in their faith.

Eight converts to Catholicism were confirmed at Ballymahon by the bishop on Easter Monday 1827 and there were others confirmed in other parishes — up to forty were claimed.[14]

Proselytes were paraded as local victories in a national, indeed universal, confrontation which encompassed contending political forces in Ireland. The foundations of the Catholic-liberal party and the Protestant-tory party were laid after 1826 in a contest bristling with sectarianism. There was an enormous social and economic gulf between evangelical Protestants and the Catholic masses. Gerald Griffin, in his novel *The Rivals*, published in 1829, makes this explicit in a discussion between Tom Leonard, brother-in-law of the very evangelical Kirwan Damer where Leonard finds an obvious target in the wealth, self-righteousness and piety of the Damer 'Big House':

'Ah! it is an easy matter to be a saint when one has an income of four thousand a-year, with a mansion like this on one's estate . . . It is easy to pray out of a pair of richly-gilt Morocco covers, in a handsome pew, with silk cushions under one's knees, and the thermometer at summer heat. It is not difficult to be punctual at church, in defiance of distance and of weather, when one can go there in a close carriage and four; nor to meet round the fire at evening and read the Bible, and shudder at the poor deluded peasant . . . And he sees our luxury, our self-sufficiency and our presumption. Heaven save us from the sin of the Pharisee! The poor, poor peasant who works from dawn to dusk for eight pence, in cold and heat, in shower and sunshine, to share that eightpence with the whole population of his little cabin, while you and I sit here by our fireside and judge him over our wine!

A great debate was arranged between Father Tom Maguire and the renowned Protestant preacher, the Rev. Richard Pope. It was held in the Dublin Institute in Sackville Street during six days from 19 to 25 April 1827. The hours of debate were from 11 a.m. to 3 p.m. each day. O'Connell acted as one of the Catholic chairman. Great excitement was produced by this confrontation. Pope criticised the Catholic concepts of transubstantiation, purgatory and infallibility while Maguire attacked the Protestant beliefs about justification by faith, the right of private judgment and the divisions caused by the Reformation. Catholics claimed victory for Maguire and O'Connell, in honour of the occasion, gave Maguire silver plate worth £1,000 (*11*, 107).

Both Sheil and O'Connell were closely identified with the Catholic campaign against the evangelical drive of the Established Church. In May 1826 O'Connell had engaged in a public controversy with a Protestant cleric, Rev. Robert Daly. The letters of each were published in a pamphlet.[15] In May 1827 Sheil, as counsel for Eneas MacDonnell, who was prosecuted by Archdeacon Trench for libel, delivered a fierce exposure of the character of the Archdeacon in the Court of King's Bench. Trench was a member of a powerful family 'with an earl and an archbishop at its head', which had devoted great efforts to bring 'scriptural education' to the Irish people (*119*, 113-45). Trench was Archdeacon of Ardagh and the case arose out of a controversy at Ballinasloe over pressure being put on Catholic tenants to send their children to Protestant schools. MacDonnell was sentenced to prison on two charges of libel for eighteen months but he was released in 1828 on grounds of ill-health. Later in December 1827 O'Connell and Sheil were counsel for Father Tom Magure who was charged with seduction but acquitted. O'Connell declared that the charge was fabricated by Maguire enemies.

The Catholic leaders were able to use sectarian episodes to develop the struggle such as those in relation to Catholic burials. In early August 1827 two Catholic priests, neither in canonicals or with prayer books, led the funeral of Thomas Rooney in Howth. When the coffin was lowered in the grave one of the priests proceeded to repeat the *De Profundis* when a Protestant cleric came up and suggested that he desist. 'One of the Howth fishermen . . . immediately cried out "I will say it", and proceeded audibly and distinctly to repeat the *De Profundis*, Lord's Prayer and Hail Mary'. The possibility of a disturbance was avoided but Rooney's son complained to O'Connell (III, 1406). Sheil realised, in his anxiety 'to bring the priests into efficient and *systematic* action', that the burial issue contained 'valuable poison' and in September the Catholic Association appointed a committee to procure free Catholic burial grounds (III, 1414).

During the 1820s there was developing in Ulster Presbyterianism a classic encounter between liberal and conservative forces personified in the conflicts between Henry Cooke and Henry Montgomery. Cooke represented the tradition of the 'Old Light' with its emphasis on strict uncompromising Calvinism while Montgomery represented the tradition of the 'New Light' with its emphasis on individual freedom and toler-ance. Increasingly the Cooke wing became identified with, and associ-ated with, the evangelical societies of the 'New Reformation'. This identification extended to political Protestantism and anti-Catholicism.

From 1813 the Synod of Ulster was officially in favour of Catholic Emancipation, largely due to Montgomery's influence. As Henry Cooke became the dominant personality of Ulster Presbyterianism, there occurred a shift of emphasis so that orthodox or 'Old Light' Presby-terians became identified with the Protestant political interest. From 1827 Cooke's policy was to work for a separation in the Synod of Ulster from those who supported Montgomery's Arianism. This doctrine was heterodox on the Trinity, denying that Christ was consubstantial with God. The form of the conflict centred upon the right to private judgment as opposed to Cooke's insistence that Presbyterian ministers should sign the Westminster Confession of faith.

Cooke, in many respects, was similar to O'Connell: he possessed enormous courage, a striking personality and a sense of mission. He was capable of both eloquence and vulgar repartee. He could sway a crowd without difficulty but often did so by appealing to their worst passions.

To Montgomery Catholic Emancipation was a 'national act of com-mon justice'.[16] Cooke, who had favoured a modified Emancipation which would preserve 'an essential Protestantism in the State' in 1825, was by 1827 very obviously in the camp of evangelical and political Protestantism. Cooke's evidence in 1825 to the Select Committee of the House of Lords had proved controversial, being condemned as 'false and unfounded' by O'Connell. Cooke had stated that there was a growing

Protestant opposition to Emancipation. As Moderator of the Synod that year Cooke had defended his evidence and given 'the first fatal blow' to Arianism in the Synod of Ulster (*111*, 99). Two different concepts of the Presbyterian Church were involved. To Cooke, the Church was the chosen instrument of God for the salvation of mankind with the right to assert authority and impose doctrinal tests and discipline. For Montgomery the Church was simply a mode of ecclesiastical government with no right to impose a test. Montgomery declared he was 'a Presbyterian by education and feeling, and convictions, a Presbyterian because I consider the principles of our Church, essentially favourable to the great cause of civil and religious liberty'.[17] According to Cooke's son-in-law and biographer, Henry Cooke's opposition 'to the revolutionary views and dangerous agitation of O'Connell was scarcely less determined than his opposition to Arianism' (*111*, 104).

The Catholic Emancipation victories in the border counties of Louth, Monaghan and Armagh in 1826 seemed to threaten the traditional position of Protestant dominance in Ulster. The Catholic Association had poor representation from Ulster and had gained little support there. Since the Ulster plantations of the seventeenth century no accommodation had been reached at any stage between the aspirations and prejudices of the Protestant settlers and those of the Catholic natives. The rebellion of 1798 had deepened the sectarian divisions. Cooke himself had childhood memories of the Catholic threat to Protestant families including his own. On the other hand, Montgomery's family had a United Irish connection and he had memories of his home being burned by yeomen. Cooke grew up with a fear of Rome, of the Pope and Popery. From attacking liberalism in theology he moved easily and decisively to attacking liberalism in politics. He correctly pointed out in 1825 that there was not a minister or man in Ulster who had a better means of knowing the state of mind of the common people among orthodox Presbyterians than himself (*111*, 77).

The Presbyterian system of assemblies rising from the congregation to the Synod in which laymen and ministers managed all the affairs of the church was an ecclesiastical democracy in which Cooke's oratory found ready acceptance. At the 1827 Synod, held in Strabane 'No Surrender' and 'Down with the Arians' became synonymous cries: the great debate of 1827 concerned the declaration of the Clerk of the Synod, Rev. William Porter, of his Arianism and of its growing influence in the Synod. Porter had made his declaration before the Parliamentary Commission on Education. Cooke cleverly sought from each minister a declaration of their belief or otherwise in orthodox doctrine. He forced such an oral declaration in the Synod and secured it from the vast majority present.

The decisive crisis in Ulster Presbyterianism could not long be avoided: on 28 June 1828 the Synod of Ulster meeting at Cookstown adopted a resolution for the appointment of a committee for the theological examination of candidates for the ministry aimed at preventing the entry of Arians. Cooke, in the words of his biographer, saw himself as 'contending against a deadly heresy on the one hand, and a powerful and dangerous political movement on the other' (*111*, 86). Both political and theological liberalism in Ulster were under fatal attack. In September 1827 Cooke had a public controversy with the Synod of Munster. He accused it of forming 'a part of a degenerate Presbyterian church' because it disagreed with him; he disavowed connection with it (*111*, 145). Events throughout Ireland in 1827 and 1828 stirred the siege mentality which never lay very far below the surface of Ulster life and by the time of the 1829 Synod of Ulster the Presbyterian Church was split. Cooke and O'Connell had delimited political territory and culture in nineteenth-century Ireland.

During 1827 the work of the New Catholic Association continued in a low key. The progress of the struggle with the 'New Reformation' Protestant societies was watched very carefully and publicity was given to examples of 'Orange persecution'. The New Catholic Rent continued to be collected throughout the year. The total receipts for 1827 were £2,898. This comprised £1,275 from Leinster, £1,203 from Munster, £217 from Connaught and £203 from Ulster.[18] These figures emphasise again how much O'Connell's movement was a Leinster and Munster phenomenon. This money was spent in relieving the forty-shilling freeholders still suffering from the effects of 1826 and in publicising local Catholic meetings.

O'Connell believed strongly in small, regular and permanent contributions to the Rent. In July 1827 Lawless believed that the old system of collecting the Rent was unproductive and too slow. In the New Catholic Association on 21 July he carried a resolution in favour of holding a simultaneous Sunday collection throughout all the Catholic chapels in Ireland so that sufficient funds could be procured to relieve the freeholders. O'Connell profoundly disagreed with this approach both because it would interfere with the voluntary support of the Catholic clergy and the poor and because he believed in the political benefits of continuous small contributions which identified the people with the Association and indicated the degree of public support it had. O'Connell had Lawless's resolution rescinded at, what Lawless claimed, was a packed meeting (III, 1404). In reality the amount of Rent depended upon the level of agitation: in 1827 the amounts were low because O'Connell was keeping a tight rein on the agitation to give the new ministry an opportunity to make Catholic concessions.

One issue O'Connell did highlight was the Sub-Letting Act passed in 1826 to prevent subdivision of Irish land without the head landlord's permission. Moreover, it attempted to have tenants hold directly from the head landlord. Political economists had identified the multiplicity of holdings from middlemen as the great evil of the Irish land system. They sought to consolidate holdings into substantial and commercial farms by clearing estates of vast numbers of small tenants. O'Connell realised that this Act was fatal 'by its influence over the fates and fortunes of the lower orders as they are called but more properly speaking of the poorer classes of society . . .' O'Connell defended the role of the middlemen in the Irish land system and the various gradations in land holding in Ireland. The Act, he said, would destroy 'the middle classes'.[19] Naturally the Act was very unpopular with the people and its repeal became the policy of the Association and was frequently called for at local meetings. In February 1828 O'Connell described the Sub-Letting Act as 'the very worst and vilest piece of legislative folly and injustice that ever was promulgated'; he informed the Knight of Kerry that it ought 'to be called An Act to render it impossible for a labourer to become a farmer, to prevent a farmer from becoming a gentleman, to prevent a gentleman from acquiring property, to purchase an estate. It is the worst of the Penal Code, and a hypocritical Penal Law to boot' (III, 1453).

From the spring of 1827 the Association in Dublin marked time. But important organisational steps were being taken at local level. Since the successes of the 1826 general election the development of local political organisation had proceeded steadily under the stimulation of Thomas Wyse. A new democratic age was dawning in modern politics, according to Wyse and he was concerned to give expression to public opinion through electoral clubs. During 1827 the Liberal or Independent Club was extremely active in Louth, and it became a model for clubs established elsewhere.[20] In Waterford Wyse, while still very much involved in relief of voters after the 1826 victory, made attempts to launch a fully developed electoral club: in April 1827, for example, he had a committee established to draw up the rules and regulations.[21] The relief effort in the county deflected Wyse until 1828 from achieving his fully functioning Liberal Club.

During 1827 a number of other electoral clubs were inaugurated: in Dublin in May 1827 the Dublin Independent Club was formed and a committee of nineteen was established to draw up the rules and regulations.[22] The inaugural meeting was held in Hayes' Tavern, Dawson Street. Further meetings of the Dublin Club took place in June 1827, and members spoke of the necessity of having a club 'upon the same basis as that of Louth and Clare'. The novelty of these clubs is indicated by the views expressed by some conservative speakers who thought 'the very name of a Club was invidious' and that there was 'something Jacobinical in it . . .' Others cited the example of the Louth Club which was 'by no means prone to Jacobinical principles' and argued that the club would instruct its supporters in the exercise of the franchise.[23] The club was established in early June 1827 and O'Connell explained its duties in 'luminous detail'. However, there were some 'secessions' from the Club as it was thought to sound too radical.[24] Other counties such as Roscommon and Kilkenny made less successful efforts in 1827 to establish clubs.[25] In the spring of 1828 moves were afoot to establish an Independent Club in Monaghan.[26]

The genesis and development of the Cork Liberal Club from 1826 illustrates how such local activists organised in response to the national leadership of O'Connell and the Catholic Association. The Cork Club provides an important case history for the growth of local electoral machinery and of the political activists and social groups involved in laying the basis of popular parliamentary politics at local level.

The widespread collection of the Catholic Rent in the rural and urban areas of Cork resulted in the formation of a nucleus of political activists in Cork which remained at the centre of Cork politics. Cork was the pre-eminent Irish county in terms of the amount of Rent subscribed. Activists such as Stephen Coppinger the barrister, Thomas Lyons the woollen manufacturer, and Charles Sugrue the butter merchant were active in Catholic meetings in Cork from 1825.[27]

The 1826 general election in Cork City passed without a contest, the two previous MPs Hutchinson and Colthurst, being returned. However, Hutchinson died shortly after the election and thus another election occurred in December 1826 when John Hely-Hutchinson, a Whig, just managed to defeat Gerard Callaghan, the son of a very successful merchant, who stood as a Tory, by 1,019 votes to 970. Callaghan had turned Protestant and had been MP for Drogheda from 1818 to 1820; he had been well defeated in Cork City in 1820. Catholic distaste for Callaghan is evidenced in the stinging attack on him in the *Dublin Evening Post*, as 'a kiln-dried and medicated mongrel' who had assumed Orangeism for personal gain.[28] The Cork by-election was the first contested election after the electoral 'revolutions' of 1826 and the close result in Cork stirred the local Catholic leaders to consider, as a priority, the electoral prospects of liberals next time around. In contrast to the rest of the country, there were a large number of Catholic meetings — over twenty — in various towns and parishes of Co. Cork in January and early February 1827.[29] In the wake of the election, a meeting was held 'to promote the Registry of freeholds' in which James Cashman, a brewer, who was Chairman of Hutchinson's election committee, was active.[30] In the middle of April 1827 an aggregate meeting in South Parish Chapel was attended by 5,000 people.[31]

The Cork activists established an Association for Promoting the Registration of Freeholds and this body was chaired by James Cashman and had as secretary, Edmund McCarthy, a solicitor in partnership with John Sweeny, South Mall, Cork.[32] This Association, composed of notable commercial and professional men in Cork city, sought to 'rescue' the freeholders of Cork 'from the stigma' which attached to them, by registering all freeholders for future elections. The members of the Cork Chamber of Commerce were a key element in the local leadership; as soon as the health of Hutchinson gave cause for concern after the 1826 general election a meeting was held at the Chamber of Commerce to enquire into the state of the registry and many of those involved in the Registration Association were on the Committee of Management of the Chamber of Commerce.[33]

The members of the Association regretted 'the apathy' of Cork inhabitants towards the state of the franchise and they established a Committee of Solicitation '. . . to wait on, and induce such Gentlemen, as ought, but have not as yet qualified as Electors'. Most of those on this committee had been members and subscribers to the Catholic Association. A number were leading Catholic Association activists and were to become leading local politicians in the 1830s and 1840s — men like Thomas Lyons, the woollen manufacturer and £50 freeholder who became Chairman of the Cork Liberal Club in 1828 and years later Lord Mayor of Cork in the 1840s; Daniel Meagher, wine merchant, subscriber to the Catholic Rent and active in the 1830s in Cork politics, and Charles Sugrue, the butter merchant and Trustee of the Chamber of Commerce (*99*, 424-8). The Chairman of the Association was James Cashman, the brewer who was Hutchinson's election committee chairman; he sought the aid of Cork liberals by way of a printed circular on 8 May 1827 in returning 'free of expense' liberal MPs who would support Emancipation 'as a prelude to other important and beneficial measures'. The Association was 'to guard against the recurrence of such scenes as occurred at the late Election' and to ensure that Emancipation 'which now dawns on this Country' would be translated into benefits, such as municipal reform, ending the *'domineering Ascendancy'* of the Tories: these objects set out in the circular of the Association show that Catholic Emancipation was interpreted by Cork activists as the key to socio-political advance in local affairs.

This 1827 Association evolved quite a sophisticated organisation through district committees: McCarthy, the secretary, wrote to James O'Brien, an accoutrement maker and £50 freeholder of Tuckey Street, to ask him to take charge of District No. 1 which, like all the Districts, was quite small — No. 1 included the east side of South Main Street, west side of Parade, north side of Castle Street, with the streets inside these boundaries.[34] Each district had a small committee: in No. 1 the committee was composed of O'Brien, Thomas Lyons, William Quinlan, a woollen draper, and Michael J. Barry, a grocer. The district committee were to ensure that all freeholders were registered in their areas. The basis was laid for an effective electoral organisation in Cork city well before the formation of Cork Liberal Club in 1828.

Significantly in County Clare a Liberal Club was established in March 1827 with James O'Gorman Mahon in the Chair and Richard Scott, an attorney, as Secretary. At the county meeting which established the Club O'Connell encouraged the establishment of parochial clubs and preparations were made to commence the electoral organisation of the county (III, 1372, 1373). A local meeting in Feakle in August 1827 pledged itself to act 'in unison and accordance with the principles of the Clare Liberal Club'.[35] Members of the Clare Liberal Club attended local meetings and endeavoured to deal with local grievances such as those relating to proselytism. At the quarterly meeting of the Clare Liberal Club in April 1828 money was granted for schools in five or six different parts of the county and between thirty and forty sat down to dinner in Carmody's Hotel, Ennis. This meeting also received a report of a committee which had investigated the accounts of the Club which had some money to credit. Stress was put on the importance of the registry of the freeholders and, significantly, Daniel O'Connell was acclaimed as 'the founder of the Clare Liberal Club'.[36] The existence of the Clare Club for well over a year before the famous by-election of 1828 and the leading role of the Club's activists such as O'Gorman Mahon, Thomas Steele, and Richard Scott in organising the county laid the basis for an historic breakthrough.

During 1828 Thomas Wyse finally got the opportunity to develop his plans for the Liberal Club of Waterford and to spread his views to other counties where local permanent electoral organisations were being founded and developed. Throughout 1827 Wyse had kept pushing for a Waterford Liberal Club, getting a committee appointed to organise such a club in April 1827. He must have been heartened by the establishment of such clubs in Dublin and meetings in places like Kilkenny to form local clubs.[37] Early in 1828 he made a very significant speech to the Catholic Association in favour of a *Political Catechism* for Irish Catholics. The *Political Cathechism* for which Wyse argued was intended to achieve the political education of Irish Catholics for a new emancipated and democratic era. Wyse argued that it was essential 'to enkindle, to enlighten, to direct the popular mind' and the 'scattered and divergent impulses' in the popular movement. Wyse believed it was necessary to compress, concentrate and to direct the force of public opinion; for this a more complete organisation of the Catholics was necessary. He outlined a plan to extend the county clubs through the creation of parochial clubs 'of which the clergy, Church-wardens, and substantial farmers, would form the nucleus'. Wyse's motion was accepted by the Catholic Association and O'Connell spoke in support, stressing that the Irish people should be instructed as to their political conduct and that the *Political Cathechism* 'would join the people of Ireland into one Catholic Association' in the event of an enforced dissolution of the Association.[38] Wyse set to work on the proposed *Cathechism* which he finished and had published in 1829. Wyse envisaged Ireland covered by a network of local electoral clubs using a common political manual; the object he had in view was the political education of the Irish people for the rational and intelligent use of the benefits of the British Constitution.

Local attention continued to be focused on the raising of the New Catholic Rent and the relief of the forty-shilling freeholders; there was considerable dispute over the amount which Co. Waterford received from the Catholic Association and about who should pay the outstanding election debts.[39] Wyse was involved in the attempt to sort out the accounts and to deal with the creditors.[40] A typical case was that of the freeholders of Colonel Greene who, when they returned from the election after voting for Stuart, were refused employment. In their destitution they applied to the priests 'who induced them to vote, contrary to the wishes of their landlord'. The priests secured them meal but there was a bill of £100 still unpaid in 1828.[41] Wyse had to decide whether local subscriptions could be used for the bill or whether money could be supplied by the Catholic Rent Committee.

Despite such pressing local problems Wyse must have been encouraged by the development, albeit slow, of Liberal Clubs in other counties. In June 1828 the *Chronicle* urged that a County and City meeting be held in Waterford 'immediately' to establish a Liberal Club, declaring that Waterford should not 'linger and lag behind'.[42]

'An entirely new scene has opened in the political world': with this phrase Henry Hobhouse noted in his diary the death of Canning on 8 August 1827 (*2*, 140). O'Connell wrote to his wife that it was 'another blow to wretched Ireland'. Mary O'Connell agreed it was a 'dreadful loss' adding 'God forbid that odious Peel or Wellington should again hold any station in the Government' (III, 1407, 1408). Canning was succeeded by the incompetent Goderich.

Officially Goderich's government adhered to the terms of the cabinet minute of 23 April on the Catholic question which had governed Canning's policy. It was, however, added that no member of the Goderich cabinet felt called upon to propound the question in cabinet without having a conviction of the most urgent necessity. This was noted because of a wish to avoid disturbing the king's feeling 'upon a question of so much delicacy and importance' (*3*, III, 276-8). Whatever chance of Catholic gains while the coalition of 1827 existed depended upon Canning: under Goderich no real prospects could be entertained.

O'Connell set out the position clearly in a letter to Richard Newton Bennett on 26 September:

> All the acts of the Administration convince me that they are determined to give us good words as long as these can delude, but their acts, *their acts*, are unequivocal. They have made Joy attorney-general, a more bitter enemy than Saurin because *smoother* but, in fact, a virulent anti-Catholic partisan . . . The Orange faction unchecked. . . . Gregory in full power at the Castle. The Trenches in full pay and patronage at the Custom House as well as in Connaught. Lord Wellesley manifestly treacherous to the new ministry exerting much more power than when he affected to be liberal. The system unbroken in upon in any one branch or department. The Hills and the Blackers and the other [Dublin] *Evening Mail* patrons as strong and influential as ever.

O'Connell himself had not been given a patent of precedence which his career at the Bar amply justified '. . . how impossible it is for me to bargain with an Administration who are to this hour piddling with me as to a mere act of justice' (III, 1413).

A few days later Sheil wrote to O'Connell that 'the public mind is beginning to cool':

> The reason is, I think, this: when Peel and Dawson and our decided antagonists were in office, the Catholics were exposed to perpetual affronts which kept their indignation alive. The priests, especially, were held in constant ferment. But now that Lord Lansdowne is in we say to each other, 'what a pity that our good friends in the Cabinet cannot do us any service!' and, convinced that they cannot, we 'take the will for the deed'. In this view it would be almost better for us to have our open enemies than either our lukewarm and important advocates in power.

Sheil determined to bring 'the priests into efficient and *systematic* action' in a renewed campaign (III, 1414). At a Catholic meeting on 19 December it was resolved that the Catholics of Ireland should meet simultaneously in their respective parishes to petition parliament for unqualified Emancipation and repeal of the Vestry and Sub-Letting Acts of 1826. O'Connell wrote to Bishop Doyle on 29 December of the importance of this major development.

> The combination of national action — all Catholic Ireland acting as one man — must necessarily have a powerful effect on the minds of

the ministry and of the entire British nation. A people who can be thus brought to act together and by one impulse are too powerful to be neglected and too formidable to be long opposed (III, 1448).

Sunday 13 January 1828 was the date fixed for this day of national action.

It was abundantly clear that the 'game' of giving Irish Catholic support to an English ministry in return for practical advances was over. In London the Bishop of Oxford noted on 24 August 1827 to his friend Peel that it was clear that every year 'was thinning the intellectual influence of the Protestant ranks' (*107*, II, 15). This sure but slow erosion had paid little immediate dividends in Ireland to compensate for O'Connell's forbearance in 1827. By October Lamb had discovered, as he told Thomas Spring Rice, that in Ireland 'one party hates the other so cordially that they had rather see a negro promoted than one who is opposed to themselves' (*123*, I, 270-2). The comments of O'Connell in December on the departure of Wellesley, that he 'did nothing for the Catholics . . . he deserves nothing from the Catholics' were re-echoed about Lamb: 'Mr Lamb has done nothing' (III, 1436, 1445). Wellesley's apologist felt that it was 'wonderful that he has been able to effect any good under the difficulties he has had to contend with' (*3*, III, 312). Wellesley left Ireland 'where he had perhaps neither friend nor foe but wished him away' (*42*, 235). During 1827 the Catholic cause had made no tangible advance; if anything it had retreated because the Canning coalition continued the 'open' system with more politicians acquiescing in it, willingly or unwillingly, than ever before. The agitation in Ireland had marked time.

After the relatively inactive year of 1827 the Catholic Association loosened the reins on popular discontent in 1828: as coachman O'Connell needed nerve and judgment to control it. The Association organised on Sunday 13 January 1828, simultaneous parish meetings throughout Ireland. This was a mass mobilisation in about two-thirds of the 2,500 parishes in Ireland. It was a fearsome precedent raising a key question: 'What if the Association at some later period ordered them "to meet *with* arms, for the purpose, not of *petitioning* against, but *resisting* tithes, etc. etc." would they disobey? "The fulcrum and the power were found — the lever could be applied to any thing"' (*132*, I, 303). O'Connell could claim the active backing of the Catholic masses and threatened the government with his ability to evade any law they could devise to suppress Catholic politics:

We will talk of them at dinner, if they prevent us from speaking at our meals, we will proclaim a fast day, and in prayer we shall talk of Catholic politics. We will speak of them, whilst we sip our tea and coffee. I defy them to prevent us — if they prevent us from talking politics, why we will whistle or sing them [*loud cheers*] . We shall implicitly submit to the letter of the law — but that shall be the extent of our obedience.[43]

As Joy, the Attorney-General, noted, the simultaneous meetings provided 'a fatal precedent of a people gathered into a solid and perilous confederacy' (*83*, I, 50).

Eighteen twenty-eight was to prove by far the best single year in terms of Rent subscribed. Organisationally the Association made key innovations: at local level the appointment of churchwardens dramatically improved the collection. Compared with figures such as £7,500 in 1824, £9,200 in 1825, £5,680 in 1826 and £2,900 in 1827, the £22,700 collected in 1828 was a massive indicator of the new level reached by the agitation (*99*, 268-9). Churchwardens, building upon the massive January mobilisation, established a regular communication between the parishes and the Association in Dublin: they had 'the effect of consolidating the Catholic people of Ireland' and they supplied information hitherto often sought in vain from busy or uninterested priests.[44] According to Wyse, tradesmen and intelligent farmers were preferred when the churchwardens were selected (*132*,I,338). Humphrey O'Sullivan, who married into a draper's shop in Callan and who kept an important diary, became a churchwarden in January 1828; as an 'Alms Warden' he organised and collected the Rent and sent it 'to Counsellor O'Connell and to the Catholic Association every month' (*75*, XXX, 221, 227).

The churchwardens were given comprehensive political duties which included the sending of short monthly reports 'after a formula extremely simple and concise' to the Association (*132*, I, 338). The blank report sheets were sent down by the Association and information was sought on the progress of the Rent, the collectors, the number of registered and unregistered freeholds and the state of the parties with a view to the next elections. Evictions, local landlords, education and local greievances were also to be described in the report to the Association. Churchwardens had to supervise the Rent collectors and to publicise the first Sunday of each month as 'Rent Sunday' on which day they were to attend and to receive the Rent. They were also to keep the peace in their parish and prevent secret societies. In September and October 1828, for example, Humphrey O'Sullivan was very active in establishing peace: 'It is on O'Connell's advice this renewal of friendship and this peace is being made among the children of the Gael: but the English do not like it; for they think it easier for them to beat people at variance than people in friendship; and this is true' (*75*, XXXI,

19, 27, 31, 45). The scheme of churchwardens gave the local lay political activists plenty of scope and served to connect local and national politics.

An important part of their duties was to give greater extension to the proceedings of the Association as they were employed 'with great judgment as vehicles for the circulation of the public papers'. A *Weekly Register* was sent down every Saturday and Wyse notes that it was 'quite incredible' to witness the anxiety for political information which this diffusion of newspapers generated in every part of Ireland: the impact was great for people repeated 'for weeks afterwards, passages of speeches gleaned from the press' and the Irish became 'a nation of politicians'. The *Weekly Register*, edited by Michael Staunton, contained a weekly summary of the proceedings at the Corn Exchange and its militant tone was especially popular with provincial Catholics. Shortly before the dissolution of the Association, 6,000 *Weekly Registers* were 'sent to the country' (*132*, I, 339-40).

The churchwardens had an immediate impact on the amount of Rent collected: for the week ending 19 January 1828 the Rent was £199 but for the following week, when thirty-nine parishes had appointed churchwardens, it rose to £604. Peel wrote to Anglesey on 7 April 1828 obviously concerned about the new churchwarden system and the rise in the Catholic Rent (*83*, I, 36-8). The Rent remained at a high weekly level until the early summer months when it fell, as it usually did at that time of year. The Clare election in July, however, shot it out of all comparison with previous weekly amounts to £2,000-£3,000 per week and it ranged between £200-£1,000 from August until February 1829, with most weeks at around £400.

The Goderich government had clearly disintegrated by the end of 1827. On 9 January 1828 the Duke of Wellington was invited to form a government. Peel returned as Home Secretary. Anti-Catholics rejoiced that their parliamentary stalwarts were now at the helm. O'Connell was appalled: on 24 January the Catholic Association declared outright opposition to Wellington's administration with a new policy of opposing any Irish MP who supported the new government whether or not such MPs professed support for the Catholic cause.

Wellington's newly-formed government was initially predominantly pro-Catholic. Wellington and Peel steered well clear of the ultras and included former followers of Canning such as Charles Grant, Lord Dudley, Palmerston and Huskisson. Ultras expressed some concern about Wellington making modified concessions to Catholics. The Duke of Newcastle had hoped for 'a sound, plain-dealing Protestant Administration, divested of all quackery and mysterious nonsense', and on 24 January he expressed his disappointment with the ministry (*20*, III,

534-42). With Ireland the touchstone of politics it was obvious that the composition of the Irish government would reveal the fundamental disposition of Wellington's cabinet.

Henry William Paget, first Marquess of Anglesey, had been selected to replace Wellesley as far back as Canning's government but he had not yet taken up office. Anglesey, a professional soldier of sixty who lost a leg at Waterloo, had held office under Canning and Goderich as Master General of the Ordnance. Wellington decided to support him as Lord Lieutenant. Anglesey had an ambivalent record on Emancipation. While expressing generally favourable sentiments he had declared in the Lords in 1825 that he was prepared to resist Irish Catholic claims in 'a trial of strength' (1, 180). He expressed great distaste for the methods used by the Catholic Association and did not wish to give credence to its techniques of popular politics. Anglesey's interview with the king as he took his departure for Ireland on 21 February 1828 foreshadowed the style of his Lord Lieutenancy: 'God bless you, Anglesey!' said the king, 'I know you are a true Protestant'; to which Anglesey replied, 'Sir, I will not be considered with Protestant or Catholic; I go to Ireland determined to act impartially between them and without the least bias either one way or the other' (1, 184). In fact Anglesey was perceived very quickly as 'Catholic': it became well known 'that at his little dinners a sort of inner cabinet met, Lord Cloncurry, George Villiers, Anthony Blake, W. H. Curran, all of whose names stank in the nostrils of good Protestants, and that many weighty matters were there decided' (42, 238). Sheil indeed was a regular attender at viceregal parties. As O'Connell remarked to Cloncurry in September: in Ireland there was 'no neutral ground' (III, 1483). Whatever did not tend towards Emancipation was regarded as in reality against it. Anglesey's actions were favourable. Anglesey's quickly acquired reputation for lavish hospitality, his encouragement of local trades and proposals for extensive public works were approved by Catholics as was his wearing of a large shamrock in his hat on St Patrick's day. O'Connell declared that 'the tone and temper produced by the Marquis of Anglesea was the best forerunner of an event which must soon occur' (1, 192). Soon Wellington and Peel began to mistrust Anglesey and he in turn found it difficult to regard the ministry as a party to which he himself belonged. Wellington and Peel did not feel able to take Anglesey fully into their confidence.

The immediate question before the government was the Act of 1825 suppressing unlawful societies in Ireland. This had damaged the development of the Association but had been completely ineffectual in its principal aim of putting it down. Now it was due to expire at the end of the 1828 session. On 2 May, on the advice of the Irish government, the 1825 Act was allowed to lapse by the cabinet. As Peel noted, the truth was that without the absolute suppression of all liberty of speech, or at least of the power of holding public meetings of any description, it was no easy matter to frame enactments which should preclude evasion by the able and astute men who directed the proceedings of the Roman Catholic Association . . . (*83*, I, 58).

In April Wellington submitted to the passage of the repeal of the Test and Corporation Acts which removed disabilities from dissenters. Hence, despite the return of Wellington and Peel to power, the Emancipation movement gained enormously in the spring of 1828, through Anglesey's obvious approval of their cause, through the lapse of the 1825 Act and the victory for tolerance in the Repeal of the Test and Corporation Acts.

The principal disability on dissenters had been the requirement of office holders to receive the sacrament according to the rites of the Church of England. Their victory gave a considerable boost to the Catholic cause. In reality, however, equality for dissenters had not the explosive implications latent in Catholic Emancipation. Lady Charleville had clearly expressed to Lady Morgan on 30 December 1827 the typical Protestant fears of Catholicism:

the tendency of Roman Catholic tenets to put down human intellect, to control and guide all human interests to their own profit and to create control even in the heart of every private family . . . Whatever objections philosophical inquiry may incline to make, the Church of England is pure in its precepts, and does not, by oral confession, put us into the hands of creatures as fallible as ourselves . . . I am, and always was, for liberty, for law, and for full exercise of religious opinion; *but* I would have no man a legislator who was bound to follow the direction of his priest, consequently, no Roman Catholic in either house of parliament (*47*, II, 249-53).

Dissenters were in quite a different category. As Peel put it,

The Roman Catholic Church, with its historical associations – its system of complete organisation and discipline – its peculiar tenets and ministrations, calculated and intended to exercise a control not merely spiritual over those who profess its faith, is an institution wholly differing in its political bearings and influence from other forms of religious belief not in accordance with the Established Church' (*83*, I, 5-6).

Dissenters were not linked in the Protestant mind with an extra-national power as were Catholics; they did not subscribe to intolerance as Catholics were supposed to do; and their claims were not linked to a smouldering and dangerous nationalist agitation represented by

O'Connell and the Irish question. Dissenters did not provoke real fears that their emancipation would signal a democratic revolution and almost certainly pave the way for parliamentary reform favoured by the pro-Catholic Whig party. It was known, moreover, that some dissenting sects such as the Methodists, were anti-Catholic and hostile to Catholic Emancipation (*46*, 33-48). Canning had stressed this hostility as an excuse for not considering their relief in 1827. Other dissenters felt it in their interests to make sympathetic noises in support of Catholic Emancipation to influence the pro-Catholic MPs while at the same time others tried to gain anti-Catholic support in order to carry relief.

The principle of breaking in on the Protestant Constitution, represented by the relief of the dissenters, was an important step on the way to Catholic Emancipation even though the privileges of the Established Church were still protected in the Relief measure: 'It is really a gratifying thing', wrote Lord John Russell to Thomas Moore on 31 March 1828, 'to force the enemy to give up his first line, that none but churchmen are worthy to serve the state, & I trust we shall soon make him give up the second, that none but Protestants are' (*80*, 115). Back in February 1821, in a Catholic debate, Peel had maintained that it was not the right of every subject to enjoy access to every office. If this were so it would be necessary to repeal the Test and Corporation Acts which were bulwarks of the Church of England against the perils of non-conformists of all denominations. There was 'a clear distinction between toleration and power', between penal laws and laws which only excluded from civil offices: 'such innovation' as repeal of the Test and Corporation Acts must not occur in the British Constitution.[45] Eldon thought that the Repeal of the Test Acts was 'revolutionary' (*83*, I, 99). Interestingly Lord Ellenborough, a pro-Catholic, believed that the repeal would injure and weaken the Catholic cause (*62*, I, 43). Croker noted in his diary on 18 March 1828 that Peel had given up the Test and Corporation Acts for a Declaration 'which means nothing, and which will never be taken by anyone. This is another step to Catholic Emancipation' (*56*, I, 412). Anglesey thought he saw that the Duke was altering his course a good deal in politics: 'It is time he should', he wrote. 'If he will act by the Catholics as he has done by the Dissenters, all will go well. If he does not, I wish he would come and govern Ireland himself' (*1*, 195). The principle that the State and the Established Church were co-extensive was fundamentally weakened in 1828.

O'Connell identified the Catholic Association and its cause with the struggle of the Protestant dissenters. Both were seeking recognition for the 'sacred principle' of freedom of conscience: on 1 February 1828 O'Connell issued a major *Address of the Catholic Association to the Protestant Dissenters of England*: 'Recollect that we assert two things – FIRST, that the Catholic Religion is friendly to civil liberty – SECONDLY, that the Catholic Religion is favourable to freedom of conscience.' The Address sought to prove these assertions by reference to history.[46] In 1828 about 100,000 Catholics in Ireland signed a petition for the repeal of the Test and Corporation Acts.[47] Wellington's acquiescence in the repeal, in contrast to his previous opposition, was an important clue to his attitude to Catholic Emancipation and to his views on the constitution. Debates in parliament soon revealed to close observers that possibilities had crossed Wellington's mind other than outright opposition.

On 29 April O'Connell wrote to the Knight of Kerry:

> We are in tremulous expectation of the result of the Catholic debate, expecting that the English will give us fresh grounds to hate them . . . Believe me, there is an *under swell* in the Irish people which is much more formidable than any sudden or *showy* exhibition of irritation. I have no doubt that if the present system is persevered in for twenty years, it will end in a separation brought about in blood and confiscation (III, 1457).

The sense of impending crisis struck Anglesey who told Peel in the middle of May that Ireland was 'in a state of balance and a very little bad or a very little good management may turn it either way' (*40*, 511). On 8 May, Sir Francis Burdett had moved a resolution for a committee of the whole House to review the restrictive laws on Catholics and in a division on the night of 12 May obtained a small majority. The debate could only be repetitive of similar debates: Peel repeated his argument that the admission of Catholics to parliament would destroy every link that bound the constitution to the Protestant faith, except the link provided by the crown and that the transfer of power from the Protestant minority to the Catholic majority in Ireland would lead to dissolution of the United Kingdom. The Commons elected in 1826 declared for the first time in favour of Emancipation by producing a majority of six in favour of Burdett's motion, 272 to 266. Peel and Wellington accepted that the ultra battle was lost. Protestant forces had diminished; intellectually the case was on the defensive; the cabinet was divided and Ireland was dominated by agitators. A resolution of the question must be found, preferably by those who could maximise the defences of the Established Church and the Protestant interest generally. Their policy was to secure the king's agreement to an Emancipation which would disturb the status quo as little as possible.

In the interval between the Catholic debates in the lower and upper Houses Peel informed Wellington that he wanted to retire from office as soon as practicable. He urged Wellington not to take a line in the House of Lords on the Catholic question that would preclude him from considering a final settlement in Ireland during the summer recess. Peel's withdrawal from office was not practicable, however, due to the resignation from office of Huskisson and his followers on the East Retford question. (Huskisson had not expected Wellington to accept his resignation over the redistribution of two parliamentary seats — it was a gesture by former Canningites towards parliamentary reform — but Wellington seized the chance to rid his cabinet of these liberals.) This had immediate results in Ireland. William Lamb resigned as Chief Secretary and was replaced by Lord Francis Leveson-Gower, a young man of twenty-eight with mild literary interests. Anglesey did not want Leveson-Gower and the end result of the cabinet reconstruction of May 1828 was a Home Secretary, Peel, in office but anticipating his early retirement; an inexperienced Chief Secretary, Leveson-Gower; and an alienated Lord Lieutenant, Anglesey. The Anglesey/Leveson-Gower combination was not a strong one with which to face a crisis. The cabinet changes also had unforeseen but decisive effects on the struggle for Emancipation when William Vesey Fitzgerald was appointed President of the Board of Trade and was thus obliged to stand for re-election in Co. Clare. The crisis was approaching. Wellington and Peel had lit the final fuse.

The public perception of Wellington and Peel was that they were as resolute against Emancipation as ever. This contrasted with the views of Wellington's intimate contacts such as Dean Philpotts who probed anti-Catholic opinion on possible terms for Emancipation in January 1828 at the Duke's request. On 17 January Palmerston wrote that he found the Duke *'not* a bigot on that Question. He considers it as a political and not at all a religious question, and therefore perfectly open to consideration' according to times and circumstances' (*27*, 99). The balance in the new cabinet was now, if narrowly, anti-Catholic and the ultras were triumphant. Indeed Wellington seemed to court ultra support by attending a dinner of the anti-Catholic Pitt Club where Eldon toasted the 'Protestant Ascendancy'. Wellington's stature was of course enormous. John Cam Hobhouse saw him in May 1828 as 'this extraordinary man, who has changed the destinies of nations more than any other man can be said to have done in our times' (*15*, III, 264). Perhaps his stature might be sufficient to pull off a most difficult manoeuvre. Wellington's strategy was to adopt some form of Catholic relief in such a way as not to shatter the Tory party: 'Now they have cleared the Cabinet of all of us', said Huskisson, 'they will set about settling the question'. Palmerston remarked, 'They may be disposed to do things, when they have the credit of doing them spontaneously, which they refused to do when it would have been supposed that we were urging them to do them' (*80*, 117). Wellington's hopes for ultra neutrality to any form of relief must, in retrospect, seem naive.

Peel and Wellington in discussion in early June accepted that a settlement of Emancipation could no longer be withheld. Peel believed he was bound to give up office because of his long commitment to the anti-Catholic cause; he was in a cruel dilemma in representing the no-popery stronghold of Oxford University but now holding a firm view on the necessity of Emancipation. Peel had progressively moved away from an ultra stance and indeed ultra politics during the 1820s. He wrote to Gregory on the 18 January 1828: 'I care not for the dissatisfaction of ultra-Tories.' A purely Protestant administration was not possible, only one on the Liverpool principle of 'fairness combined with moderation'. Peel had now little time for what Palmerston had described as the 'stupid old Tory party'; as he intimated to Gregory on 1 February, a hard line Protestant government would be

> Supported by very warm friends no doubt, but those warm friends being prosperous country gentlemen, foxhunters, etc. etc. most excellent men, who will attend one night, but who will not leave their favourite pursuits to sit up till two or three o'clock fighting questions of detail, on which, however, a Government must have a majority.

Such a government would 'not have stood creditably a fortnight' but he could not be a party to it even if it could survive (*83*, I, 16-18).

Timing was now going to be of the essence. Some attempt ought to have been made to educate the Tory party to the necessity of Emancipation; the major exercise, however, as it appeared to Wellington and Peel, was to convince the king to concede before cabinet discussions could begin. Only Peel and the Lord Chancellor, Lyndhurst, were fully in Wellington's confidence. Wellington, acting upon a major misunderstanding of what the king had accepted from Canning's and Goderich's cabinets in respect of Emancipation, believed he could not make Emancipation a cabinet question without the king's permission. He understood that the king did not wish the Catholic question to be made a cabinet question when he wrote to Peel concerning the formation of his government on 9 January 1828 (*83*, I, 12-13). Wellington believed that leaving Catholic Emancipation an 'open' question meant that the government as a body could not discuss it or advance it as a measure. In fact the Canning memorandum upon which Wellington acted did allow the question to be raised in cabinet.

Anglesey, having been in Canning's and Goderich's governments, was aware of this and he was bound to be confused and disturbed by the Duke's actions. He was increasingly dissatisfied in Ireland. He was disappointed with his new Chief Secretary. On 20 June he wrote to his brother: 'I demanded to have a safe practical man of business, yet after all, they have given me one who has everything to learn. His scholarship, his taste, his literary acquirements are thrown away upon me.' In Leveson-Gower he had 'a Man whose Manner is so cold, so rebuffing, so distant that it will be impossible to establish free & familiar intercourse, & then His Wife's Connexions are alone sufficient to make his appointment disagreeable, embarrassing & even unsafe for me' (*105*, II, 392). Since the cabinet reshuffle he felt increasingly isolated from his political masters in London and even contemplated retirement. Unwisely he began to consult with friends outside the government as the last remnants of his confidence in Wellington and Peel were destroyed. He laid official correspondence before Lord Holland, the eminent member of the Whig opposition, complaining in August 1828 to him of Wellington and Peel being 'very distant, or rather silent upon the one great question' (*40*, 519). Anglesey believed he was 'in a very cruel position' as he told his brother on 2 June 1828: he was disinclined to embarrass the government by retiring and producing 'much irritation' in Ireland but he had 'a horror of acting with inconsistency & appearing to acquiesce in arrangements which I wholly disapprove'. He would not stand 'an Ultra Tory, Anti-Catholic Cabinet'. He believed that while Ireland was in a deplorable state it was

by no means in a hopeless one. It is capable of great things – of immense improvement. With encouragement, with care, with firmness, with moderation, I am quite persuaded that it would make rapid strides in prosperity from the moment that the great question is satisfactorily adjusted. Even pending the final settlement, much good may be effected, provided a reasonable hope is kept up that the door to emancipation is not finally closed.

Anglesey found even the most violent of the agitators 'are not in *fact* so violent as they would appear. They are amenable & practicable. I find no difficulty anywhere. Even on the other side, that strange man Sir Harcourt Lees & gang are tractable. They will all do anything here with good treatment'. He saw Ireland as 'a strange country' in 'a strange state of society, but with immense capabilities' (*105*, II, 390-1). Croker called on Anglesey on 1 June in Dublin and captured the Lord Lieutenant's unreal grasp of the Irish situation:

The sum of his various statements is this, that he is happy here, and not only well with both parties, but in their confidence; that the Catholics had agreed, out of deference to him, to moderate the Associationists, and to stop the simultaneous meetings; and in the

the other side Sir H. Lees had given up, from the same motive, his Orange meetings in the North (*56*, I, 422).

Wellington had been prepared since at least 1825 to look upon Emancipation as a political question capable of solution rather than as an issue of principle incapable of concession. He had first proposed an accommodation with the Catholics in 1825 to prevent Liverpool's resignation, although publicly he continued to oppose Emancipation. Since the 1826 general election he had become convinced of the necessity for concession. He had not believed in Canning's ability to carry the country and party behind the granting of Emancipation; Wellington believed he could carry the question as he felt he had due regard for the great interests involved. Significantly, on taking office in January 1828 he had probings taken to sound out the terms on which Emancipation could be conceded and accepted by 'Protestant' opinion. However, acting on 'his own distinctly antique notions of constitutional behaviour, notions at least twenty years out of date', he succeeded in exacerbating the public agitation and he failed to bring the Tory party with him even though his great objective was to preserve it as the dominant party in the political life of the country as it had been for so long (*27*, 98). Veiled hints, half confidences, and rumours of his preparedness to consider the question served merely to intensify the divisions. They were no substitute for a clear lead and decisive action, accompanied by the education of public opinion as to the justice of the cause as well as the necessity for concession.

On 10 June, in the Lords debate on Burdett's resolution, Wellington spoke immediately after Wellesley, his pro-Emancipationist brother. He hoped that 'in the end, the views of my noble relation and myself will not be found to differ in reality from each other'. In an extremely vague speech, Wellington did not preclude what Peel called 'taking the whole state of Ireland into consideration during the recess, with a view of adjusting the Catholic question' (*83*, I, 28). The Duke's arguments were grounded entirely on expediency, declaring that if the difficulties of the question were not aggravated by popular agitation, it might prove possible 'to do something'. The motion was lost by forty-four votes but this 'Protestant' victory was overshadowed by the premier's remarks. On 15 June Colchester rode with Lord Enniskillen, who thought that 'the Duke of Wellington had some plan in contemplation about Roman Catholics'. By late June Lord Kenyon was organising ultra opinion against this possibility by raising petitions against Roman Catholics. It was the start of the ultra backlash. As Wellington's biographer remarks, 'Paradox on paradox – into the chamber goes a Prime Minister to speak and vote against a policy which he rather thinks will prove necessary, while over him hangs the resignation of his second-in-command, timed to take place as soon as he has carried out the manoeuvre which his second-in-command considers unavoidable' (*68*, 166). Ellenborough, a pro-Catholic, who was Privy Seal in Wellington's government, noted in his diary on 7 June 1828 that it was his 'firm belief that the general tendency of men's minds' was towards a settlement of the Catholic question. He believed in a settlement with the Pope: 'With the Pope on our side we might laugh at the agitators', he remarked on 10 June. He noted that Wellington had said that he did not yet see 'his way', confessing 'he did not see daylight', as to how to settle the question (*62*, I, 140-3). Greville noted in his diary on 18 June 1828:

> The Duke of Wellington's speech on the Catholic question is considered by many to have been so moderate as to indicate a disposition on his part to concede emancipation and bets have been laid that Catholics will sit in Parliament next year . . . I do not believe he means to do anything until he is compelled to it, which if he remains in office he will be; for the success of the Catholic question depends neither on Whigs nor Tories, the former of whom have not the power and the latter not the inclination to carry it.
>
> The march of time and the state of Ireland will effect it in spite of everything and its slow but continual advance can neither be retarded by its enemies nor accelerated by its friends.

Wellington's speech, as Greville believed, brought to a head the hostility of the Catholic Association: 'The Orange Party is elated with what they call a triumph', wrote Lord Anglesey to his brother on 20 June, and 'the Agitators are furious' (*105*, II, 393). Wellington's speech was so obscure and ambiguous that it was readily assumed to be merely another anti-Catholic method of preserving the *status quo*. On top of the seeming 'ultra' triumph in the cabinet reshuffle it was the last straw. Since Wellington's government had been formed, O'Connell had renewed popular agitation to such an extent that the endemic violence and social disorder in Ireland seemed destined for an explosion into a vast social and religious warfare on a revolutionary scale.

6

1828:
'Ireland Cannot Remain As It Is'

'Be it known to all whom it may concern that I was born on
the 6th August 1775, the very year in which the stupid obstinacy of British oppression, forced the reluctant people of
America to seek for security in arms, and to commence that
bloody struggle for national independence which has been in
its results beneficial to England while it has shed Glory and
conferred Liberty pure and sublime on America'.

Daniel O'Connell,
quoted in *Dublin Evening Post*, 17 July 1828.

On 24 June 1828 O'Connell announced that he was a candidate in the
by-election in Co. Clare. It was the turning point in the Catholic struggle.
It is no exaggeration to state that the Clare election began a new
epoch in Irish politics and in Anglo-Irish relations. This election, the
first in which a Catholic stood as a candidate since the penal era commenced in the 1690s, lit a fuse that led to a bomb. After the election
the government had only two choices, to legislate or to fight. It had
little enough time to decide: Peel and Wellington had to respond with
a workable solution to the Irish crisis before the next session of parliament began in February 1829. They would then be required to
indicate their position openly. It was not at all certain whether the
crisis could be stalled even for six months.

In Peel's words 'the instrument of political power' was 'shivered to
atoms' in Clare (*83*, I, 116-17). The profound shock-waves reverberated
in London, among Protestants, liberal and ultra, in Dublin and throughout Ireland. The election was the decisive event in shaping nineteenth-
century popular politics and in the evolution of political democracy in
Ireland. Out of the eye of the storm after Clare, Irish democratic politics
emerged.

In January 1828 the Catholic Association adopted a resolution to
oppose the return to parliament of every supporter of the Wellington
administration on account of the government's refusal to adopt Emancipation. In early May after the Repeal of the Test and Corporation
Acts, O'Connell, at the instigation of Lord John Russell, moved that

the resolution be rescinded as a gesture to the administration which had taken this important step towards Emancipation. However he was over-ruled in the Association and the policy of outright opposition to every supporter of Wellington, whether pro-Catholic or not, was maintained.

Almost immediately the policy was tested: William Vesey Fitzgerald, one of the members for Clare, was invited by Wellington to join the cabinet as President of the Board of Trade and in accordance with the custom he had to stand for re-election in Clare. Fitzgerald, though a friend of Peel, was in favour of Catholic Emancipation; he was a mem-ber of an old influential family in Clare and his father James Fitzgerald had been a follower of Henry Grattan in the old Irish parliament, where he had opposed the Union. In normal times Fitzgerald would have a walkover in Clare; he had held the seat since 1818 without a contest. The times, however, were far from normal.

The Catholic Association appointed James Patrick O'Gorman Mahon, and Thomas Steele, to go to Clare to invite William Nugent MacNamara, a local Protestant landlord and friend of O'Connell to stand against Fitzgerald. O'Gorman Mahon was a young Catholic graduate of Trinity College, of striking appearance and flamboyant dress. Steel was a Pro-testant graduate of both Trinity College Dublin and Cambridge who had given rein to his adventurous spirit by active service in the Spanish Wars in 1823. Both these Clare men played important roles in the by-election and subsequently in Irish politics. 'Honest Tom Steele' and O'Gorman Mahon, as minor landlords with an eccentric extravagance of gesture and behaviour, lent colour and vigour to the coming struggle.

While attempts were being made in Clare to secure liberal Protestant opposition to the Wellington government, a chance encounter in Nassau Street led to a revolutionary decision. Sir David Roose, a stockbroker and state lottery office keeper who favoured Emancipation, met P. V. Fitzpatrick, son of Hugh Fitzpatrick, the Catholic bookseller of Capel Street on 22 June. Roose suggested that O'Connell himself should stand for Clare. Fitzpatrick remembered old John Keogh's belief that Catholics should return a Catholic to convince parliament to grant Emancipation. Excitedly, he rushed to O'Connell. Then McNamara's refusal of the Association's offer became known; the radical thought became a possi-bility. Yet the refusal underlined the difficulty of opposing Fitzgerald who was a popular Emancipationist MP. Fitzgerald had looked after the interests of the Clare gentry very well since he had obtained access to power: 'the eldest sons of the poorer gentlemen, and the younger branches of the aristocracy had been provided for through his means; and in the army, the navy, the treasury, the Four Courts, and the Custom House, the proofs of his political friendship were everywhere to be found'. He had also laid not only the Catholic proprietors, but the Catholic priesthood, under obligation (*114*, II, 106).

The Association was in a real dilemma: Anglesey told Holland that 'O'Gorman Mahon who had been sent to Ennis & who suddenly came back crestfallen at the defection of MacNamara, actually called upon Wm. Paget [Anglesey's son], before he went to announce the event of the Association, to implore him to stand. William, of course, laughed in his face' (*1*, 372). There was a significant failure here by liberal Protestants to maintain the parliamentary leadership of the Catholic cause. The *Dublin Evening Mail* rejoiced at this exposure of liberal Protestants who had been 'cutting their own throats' in supporting Emancipation: 'Oh! if Emancipation ever pass how we shall triumph over the LIBERALS!'[1]

In June O'Connell, before he had decided on his own candidacy, sent an Address to the members of the Co. Clare Liberal Club urging them to justify his pride in the club on the occasion of the election. On 18 June O'Connell was indicating that Vesey Fitzgerald should be opposed in Clare and that Sheil would go there to help oppose him, as he could not go himself. On 21 June he declared, 'In my judgment the question of Emancipation depends upon the result of the election in Clare'.[2] It is clear that the existence of the club and the groundwork done by its key activists such as O'Gorman Mahon and Steele made it both feasible and imperative to take the radical decision to stand O'Connell: otherwise face would be lost and the Catholic cause would be set back. O'Gorman Mahon's impetuosity carried the waverers. With Steele and John Lawless he had undertaken a whirlwind campaign in Clare even before a candidate had been agreed.

On Tuesday 24 June in the Catholic Association, on the motion of O'Gorman Mahon, O'Connell was adopted as the candidate for Clare. O'Connell went immediately to the office of the *Dublin Evening Post* in Trinity Street, and amid a crowd of excited supporters, wrote his election address:

> You will be told I am not qualified to be elected. The assertion, my friends, is untrue. I am qualified to be elected, and to be your representative. It is true that as a Catholic I cannot, and of course never will, take the oaths at present prescribed to members of Parliament; but the authority which created these oaths in the Parliament — can abrogate them, and I entertain a confident hope that, if you elect me, the most bigoted of our enemies will see the necessity of removing from the chosen representative of the people an obstacle which would prevent him from doing his duty to his King and Country.
>
> The oath at present required by law is: 'That the Sacrifice of the Mass and the invocation of the blessed Virgin Mary and other saints as now practised in the Church of Rome are impious and idolatrous'.

Of course, I will never stain my soul with such an oath. I leave that to my honourable opponent, Mr Vesey Fitzgerald. He has often taken that horrible oath; he is ready to take it again and asks your votes to enable him so to swear. I would rather be torn limb from limb than take it. Electors of the County Clare! choose between me, who abominates that oath, and Mr Vesey Fitzgerald, who has sworn it full twenty times!!!

The historic address concluded: 'Electors of the County Clare, choose one who has devoted his early life to your cause — who has consumed his manhood in a struggle for your liberties, and who is ready to die for the Catholic faith.'[3] This address was widely distributed as a broadside poster. An enterprising Catholic merchant immediately produced a supply of handkerchiefs for the Clare election in green silk with O'Connell's portrait in the centre round which was the motto used repeatedly by O'Connell: 'Hereditary Bondsmen, know you not, who would be free, themselves must strike the blow.' On each corner there was a harp with 'Erin go Bragh' and lots of shamrock. The 'Bondsmen' were now asked to strike an unprecedented 'blow'. O'Connell declared in the Association that he believed, if elected, he was legally entitled to take his seat as no act existed excluding Catholics from the parliament of the United Kingdom. If not allowed, he argued, it would be a violation of the Act of Union and would in effect repeal the Union. This would allow elected representatives in Ireland to hold a parliament in Dublin as before the Union.[4] The future, indeed, seemed filled with novel possibilities.

The Catholic Association voted £5,000 towards the cost of the election as a first instalment and 'as much more as might be required'. Wealthy Catholics of Dublin subscribed £100 each and the flow of money was more than was immediately required. O'Connell was unable to free himself from legal business at short notice but the Clare political machine rolled rapidly into action: Sheil went to Clare as O'Connell's counsel and he has left us a graphic account of the election (*114*, II, 101-56). Steele, he records, 'opened the political campaign by intimating his readiness to fight any landlord who should conceive himself to be aggrieved by an interference with his tenants' and he then proceeded to canvass for votes:

assisted by his intimate friend Mr O'Gorman Mahon, [he] travelled through the county, and, both by day and night, addressed the people from the altars round which they were assembled to hear him. It is no exaggeration to say, that to him, and to his intrepid and indefatigable confederate, the success of Mr O'Connell is greatly to be ascribed.

The press reported O'Gorman Mahon 'travelling at night from chapel to chapel, the people routed from their beds, and half dressed hearing his exhortations from their altars, to act with vigour and promptitude in the cause to which he invited them; the liberation of their country'.[5] Steele and the priest at Ennistymon knelt together at the altar of the chapel 'to mark the spirit in which Catholics and Protestants ought to live together'.

'Honest Jack Lawless' who was very popular because of his outspoken defence of the forty-shilling freeholders, and Father Tom Maguire, the famed disputant who had vindicated the Catholic religion in public debates, were both engaged upon popular tours of the chapels and towns of Clare. Lawless prepared an exhortation against whiskey drinking during the election which received widespread acceptance. He displayed great energy and electoral technique: he traverses the county from end to end, harangues the men, kisses the married women, talks and jokes with the young ones, so that in one way or other he is sure at last to enlist the men under his banner.'[6] Other Association leaders, such as the barrister Dominic Ronayne who spoke both English and Irish, 'wrought with uncommon power upon the passions of the people' as Sheil puts it. On 27 June a letter from Dr Doyle, Bishop of Kildare and Leighlin, was issued in support of O'Connell in Clare: O'Connell declared: 'The approbation of Doctor Doyle will bring in our cause the united voice of Ireland – I trust it will be the vox populi-vox dei'.[7]

On Saturday afternoon, 28 June, O'Connell left Dublin for Clare from the Four Courts amidst a large crowd; attention was paid to visual impact on O'Connell's journey to Clare. Green was the dominant colour – it covered the barouche in which O'Connell travelled and he mounted the box-seat of the carriage dressed in a green coat with white silk lining, and buttons engraved with 'Erin go bragh' enwreathed with shamrocks. The postilions were in O'Connell's liveries of blue and gold. All night the party travelled. At Roscrea on Sunday morning they attended Mass and later were escorted into Nenagh by three thousand horsemen. Reaching Limerick late in the evening, they were received by an imposing procession of the trades. O'Connell's rapid and colourful journey to Clare aroused the usual popular excitement: 'every public house from Nenagh to Limerick was drank dry' according to the *Dublin Evening Post*. Crossing the Shannon at O'Brien's Bridge, they entered Clare and were welcomed by large assemblies of people and bonfires blazing on the surrounding hills. Ennis was reached at two o'clock in the morning of 30 June, the day for nominations to be made.

It was clear from such popular enthusiasm that a historic confrontation was about to occur. On 28 June, in Ennis, Richard Scott, O'Connell's agent issued an Address to the Clare electors. Scott promised the voters protection:

Catholic Electors of Clare — follow the great and glorious example of the 40 s. Freeholders of Waterford, Louth, Westmeath, Monaghan, Cavan, Dublin, and other Counties in Ireland. The Catholic Association have protected such of them as have been persecuted by their landlords for voting in favour of their Religion and their Country. The Catholic Rent and the Catholic Association will also protect the Catholics of Clare if they vote honestly and nobly for DANIEL O'CONNELL.'[8]

The notion had gone abroad in Dublin that the priests 'were luke-warm' but Sheil observes:

With the exception of Dean O'Shaughnessy, who is a relative of Mr Fitzgerald (and for whom there is perhaps much excuse), and a Father Coffey, who has since been deserted by his congregation, and is paid his dues in bad half pence, there was scarcely a clergyman in the County who did not use his utmost influence over the peasantry. On the day on which Mr O'Connell arrived, you met a priest in every street, who assured you that the battle would be won, and pledged himself that 'the man of the people' should be returned.

It was estimated that between 30,000 and 40,000 people crowded an Ennis bedecked in banners: 'processions of freeholders, with their parish priests at their heads, were marching like troops to different quarters' and there was remarkable order. 'There is at Ennis', Anglesey wrote to Peel, 'near 300 Constabulary. At Clare Castle (close at hand) 47 artillery, with two 6-pounders; 120 cavalry; 415 infantry. Within 36 hours, 28 cavalry, 1,367 infantry & two 6-pounders . . . At a further distance, one Regiment of cavalry & above 800 infantry. If this cannot keep one County quiet, we are in a bad way' (*1*, 372).

Baron Tuyll, Anglesey's faithful aide-de-camp, who was in Ennis, ostensibly on a tour of inspection but really to report on developments, described the scene which resulted from instructions at the chapels that the whole adult male population was to gather in Ennis:

Everything is *perfectly quiet*! Thousands and thousands of people were marched into the Town this morning by Priests, and returned to their *bivouacs* this evening in the same good order in which they entered it. No army can be better disciplined than they are. No drunkenness, or any irregularity allowed. O'Connell is called the Irish Washington & Bolivar; and people instead of saying 'God be with you', say 'O'Connell be with you'. The children in the street sing 'Green is my Livery' and 'the Liberty Tree'.

Anglesey directed the sheriff and the magistrates to avoid calling upon the military as long as the public safety would permit. He ordered the commander of the troops 'to avoid collision to the last moment, but on no account to allow the use of *blank* cartridges'.

It was a contest between the Catholic Association leaders, helped enthusiastically by the priests, and the landlords for control of the votes of the forty-shilling freeholders. A classic example of this occurred in the parish of Corofin between Sheil and Sir Edward O'Brien, 'the most opulent resident landlord in the county'. O'Brien had no less than three hundred votes and it was supposed that his freeholders would go with him. 'Determined to assail him in the citadel of his strength' Sheil proceeded on Sunday 29 June to the chapel of Corofin and O'Brien resolved to prevent this 'trespass'. Sheil was met by large crowds, preceded by fifes and pipers, waving green boughs. They passed O'Brien in silence and it was clear that their priest Father Murphy had control. Murphy was an able orator who addressed his people very effectively in Irish to vote for O'Connell in the name of Ireland and the Catholic religion; his appeal proved irresistible.

The hustings were in the old court-house in Market Square, Ennis; it was packed by excited crowds when nominations were to be taken. Vesey Fitzgerald was attended by almost all the gentry of Clare, banded together to resist O'Connell in this revolutionary attack upon their privileges of property and position. Vesey Fitzgerald was proposed by Sir Edward O'Brien of Dromoland in an emotional speech interrupted by cries of 'shameful' and hisses. Proceedings were halted by a clash between the High Sheriff and O'Gorman Mahon who sat conspiciously on the gallery rail suspended above the crowd. The Sheriff demanded that he remove a broad green sash with a medal of 'the order of Liberators' at the end of it. O'Gorman Mahon replied in dramatic terms 'This gentleman [*laying his hand on his breast*] tells that gentleman [*pointing with the other to the Sheriff*], that if that gentleman presumes to touch this gentleman, this gentleman will defend himself against that gentleman, or any other gentleman, while he has got the arm of a gentleman to protect him.' O'Gorman Mahon declared he had round his neck 'the Insignia of his country and *never* shall it be taken from him'. Tremendous shouting greeted this rhodomontade.

Such an extraordinary speech, loudly applauded by the crowd, forced the High Sheriff to back down, as O'Connell exclaimed: 'Green is no party colour; it may, to be sure, be hateful in the eyes of our opponents, but that darling colour shall flourish when the blood stained orange shall fade and be trodden under foot [*cheers*][9] Steele, in a gesture took off his ribbon of the Order of Liberators but O'Gorman Mahon refused and continued to abuse the Sheriff publicly.

Sir Edward O'Brien went on to complain that he had been deserted by his tenants, although he had deserved well at their hands and he exclaimed that the county was not one fit for a gentleman to reside in, when property lost all its influence, and things were brought to such a pass. O'Connell should look to his native Kerry to get elected and Clare should elect a Clare man. Gore, a gentleman of very large estate, speaking in favour of Fitzgerald, quite rightly saw the election as 'a new experiment' which arraigned an MP before 'the bar of public opinion' for his parliamentary conduct. When the Sheriff asked, 'Do the freeholders propose any other candidate?' O'Gorman Mahon, after a long dramatic pause, proposed O'Connell and he was seconded by Thomas Steele. The proceedings were continually interrupted and the pressure of the crowd and the heat were so oppressive that it was almost impossible for the notetakers to maintain their position. Steele's speech encompassed the work of the Clare Liberal Club in resisting 'the Biblicals', memories of 1798 and the brutal suppression of the rebellion of that year: the courthouse and system could only be 'purified and purged with the shout of the freeholders returning Daniel O'Connell — the Catholic Liberator of his Country'.

Vesey Fitzgerald made an extremely effective speech declaring that he did not shrink from scrutiny and admitted the right of electors to examine the conduct of their representative. Fitzgerald, as observed by Sheil, appeared to have 'an air of blended sweetness and assurance, of easy intrepidity and gentle gracefulness' and he was 'a most accomplished speaker' delivering one of the best speeches Sheil had ever heard. He recounted his own and his family's record on the Catholic question and his services to Maynooth College. He genuinely grieved and shed tears over the effect of the contest on his dying father and thus gained both the sympathy and applause of the audience.

O'Connell, to recover from this able speech which had moved the people determined, as Sheil said, to render Fitzgerald 'odious'. In fact it was necessary for O'Connell to make a vicious attack on what he claimed Fitzgerald represented: 'sweet and sugared words and hostile acts'. In the struggle for Emancipation O'Connell could not be fussy over his weapons; as Sheil put it, O'Connell was 'not the man to hesitate in the use of the rhetorical sabre'. O'Connell slashed Fitzgerald mercilessly: he began by awakening the passions of the crowd in an attack on Fitzgerald's landed allies, such as Gore, and then associated him with 'the bloody Perceval': this epithet, wrote Sheil, 'was sent into the hearts of the people with a force of expression, and a furious vehemence of voice, that created a great sensation amongst the crowd, and turned the tide against Mr Fitzgerald'. 'This too is the friend of Peel — the bloody Perceval, and the candid and manly Mr Peel — and he is our friend! and he is everybody's friend! The friend of the Catholic was the friend of the bloody Perceval, and is the friend of the candid and manly Mr Peel.' O'Connell firmly implanted the view that Vesey Fitzgerald profited by up to £20,000 by his place in government.

O'Connell went on to remark that 'the iron never enters deeper into my soul than when I hear of this species of patronage' and he rejected 'silk slippers' on his neck as well as boots. Fitzgerald muttered 'Is this fair?' frequently but O'Connell could not afford to be merciful. 'I never shed tears in public', he mocked, recalling Fitzgerald's references to his father, and he declared: 'I now want to know whether the forty-shilling freeholders of Clare are the slaves of their landlords [*loud cheers*]. Are they, like negroes, to be lashed by their drivers to the slave market, and sold to the highest bidder?' He connected 'the tortures of '98' and the present period of Orange government. He lamented 'the fate that places me and my children at the feet of the Gores and other Protestants in my native land – It is dreadful to be thus branded and degraded . . .' The people swung decisively for 'O'Connell, the Catholic Cause and Old Ireland'. The great mass of freeholders held up their hands for O'Connell and the Sheriff reluctantly declared in his favour in the customary showing of hands after the speeches.

Well might the *Dublin Evening Mail* on 9 July abuse the liberal Protestants noting that the election

> has put an end for ever to the *liberal* Protestants of Ireland. That wretched, degraded lickspittle crew have gone forever. They have done the devil's work, and are laughed at by the fiend . . . Out will go Villiers Stuart – out Henry Grattan – out Spring Rice – out Granny Dawson of Louth – out the sham Knight of Kerry . . . out Judas Brownlow, out all the gang. The Papists whom they served now know their strength; they want these slaves, these poor menials no more. THE LICKSPITTLES ARE DONE.

The *Mail* rejoiced in the demise of 'mock-Protestantism': 'we have now an intelligible distinction between Protestant and papist'.

On Tuesday the polling began; Fitzgerald's committee adopted the expedient of enforcing an oath on every freeholder to delay the election and magistrates had to be found to hear the oath which in other elections was usually dispensed with by agreement of the candidates. By the second day of polling, in very wet weather, the O'Connellites were being sworn *en masse* and it soon became obvious according to Sheil 'that the landlords had lost all their power and that their struggles were utterly hopeless. Still they persevered in dragging the few serfs whom they had under their control to the hustings, and in protracting the election'. The forty-shilling freeholders deserted the landlords in bodies of 400 and 500 according to the *Dublin Evening Post* on 3 July:

> A Mr D'Arcy, who I think, is a Catholic Gentleman . . . brought 400 Freeholders into the town, under a military escort . . . and fed them with beef on their arrival – he was heard to say, that he was

the only Gentleman in Clare who set the priests at defiance. How did his beef-eaters act? They all voted for the MAN OF THE PEOPLE.

Sir Edward O'Brien and the other landlords were mortified to see the priests marching their voters to vote for O'Connell. In reality the Clare campaign assumed the dimensions of a holy crusade. O'Connell set the tone by ostentatiously kneeling in the streets in Ennis for a blessing when he met the Roman Catholic coadjutor bishop, Rev. Dr McMahon.[10] Anti-O'Connellites later lampooned this scene, calling O'Connell the 'Humble Candidate'. His opponents believed that he endeavoured 'by undue influence and corrupt practices . . . to secure a majority of votes . . . by means of riots, violence and terror, intimidate, and procure the intimidation of the electors'. The vast mobs in Ennis carried flags and banners such as 'Vote for Your Religion'. Major Warburton, the officer in charge of the police, confirmed that the priests were 'the best and most active *out* agents' he had ever seen: the appeal was to the religion of the people. Warburton estimated that the crowd numbered from 40,000 to 50,000 in Ennis. 'It was announced from the altars that the male population of each parish from fifteen to eighty years of age should proceed to Ennis . . . in many places the county appeared to be deserted . . .' Yet, Warburton testified to the extraordinary peaceful conduct of the people (*128*, V, 399-400). O'Connell's opponents calculated that there were over 150 priests in Ennis from all over Ireland declaring to the voters that a voter for Fitzgerald was an enemy to his religion. Priests threatened to withdraw the rites of the church and to excommunicate such voters: 'priests . . . marched at the head of several large mobs of people, decorated with badges, through the public streets, and did thereby exercise an absolute government and control over large numbers of freeholders, and thereby terrified them to vote for said O'Connell'. They quoted a parish priest as saying: 'The ball is now up; this is the time for ye, boys, to strike it; and if you do not strike it now, may the Lord strike you in the neck, that we may see the day that there is a race after Protestants as they had after us: do not vote against your religion.' Priests put the sign of the cross on voters going to the booths and actually instructed the voters what to say in the booth. There was also carried

> an empty coffin . . . in procession amidst an immense concourse of people through the town of Ennis, on the fourth day of said election, by the contrivance and with the connivance of said Daniel O'Connell . . . who gave out that the same contained the body of a freeholder who had died suddenly in consequence of having voted against said Daniel O'Connell . . .[11]

Certain priests became immediate oratorical successes. There were three 'remarkable for an extraordinary power of eloquence in the Irish language – the Rev. M. Murphy, Mr Geoghegan, and Mr Duggan . . .' It was Father Geoghegan who told the crowd about the man who died after voting for Fitzgerald when his vote was pledged to O'Connell: all immediately dropped on one knee and prayed to avoid this awful fate.[12]

The threat of eviction hung over many of those voters as small tenants: Baron Tuyll observed: 'Between their landlords and their priests, they are certain to be sufferers in the end, and they seem to feel it. Some were actually seen crying whilst polling' (I, 199). Whatever about their prospects after the election the O'Connellite organisation provided food and sustenance for all the freeholders during the election. The surviving accounts for the Clare election record the 650 separate payments made through priests and many local activists and supporters 'for refreshment and support of freeholders' to the amount of £6,245. One hundred and fourteen of these payments were made through about 100 priests amounting to £1,962. In addition there were 127 agents, poll clerks and tally men paid fees amounting to just under £595.[13]

Sheil paints the lively scene at Mrs Carmody's Hotel, in Ennis where the main organisers dined:

> The whole body of leading patriots, counsellors, attorneys, and agents, with divers interloping partakers of election hospitality, were crammed and piled upon one another, while Mr O'Connell sat at the head of the feast almost overcome with fatigue, but yet sustained by that vitality which success produces. Enormous masses of beef, pork, mutton, turkeys, tongues, and fowl were strewed upon the deal boards . . . A hundred tumblers of punch, with circular slices of lemon, diffused the essence of John Barleycorn in profuse and fragrant streams. Loud cries for hot water, spoons, and materials, were everywhere heard . . .

All the victuallers and taverns in Ennis did very well out of the orders signed by priests for the support of the freeholders. So great, however, was the throng in the town that, although all the stores and warehouses were used for the accommodation of the voters and their friends, they were still many thousand bivouaced in the fields nearby. Huge cauldrons for boiling bacon, cabbage and potatoes were put up in the warehouses, and at stated hours the multitude were fed. The rain fell in torrents but yet there was yelling and music in the streets night and day as peace warders patrolled, having been appointed to control the crowds. O'Connell spread humour and jokes through the crowd: 'Stolen or strayed or otherwise mislaid the Right Honourable President of the Board of Trade'. An O'Connellite verse went:

> Ask your Hearts if Vesey can be true
> At the same time to Wellington and you
> For Ireland's honour nothing can he feel,
> Ally of Eldon, Wellington and Peel.

The polling lasted five days and the final count confirmed what had been obvious: 2,057 votes for O'Connell to 982 votes for Vesey Fitzgerald. O'Connell was deemed elected. Vesey Fitzgerald during the course of the election could not hide his astonishment at the turn of events: 'Where is all this to end?' he asked and found no answer. On the night of the result he wrote to Peel:

> The election, thank God is over, and I do feel happy in its being terminated, notwithstanding the result. I have polled the gentry and all the fifty-pound freeholders – the gentry to a man . . . All the great interests broke down, and the desertion has been universal. Such a scene as we have had! Such a tremendous prospect as opens to us! The organisation exhibited is so complete and so formidable that no man can contemplate without alarm what is to follow in this wretched country.

And Peel noted on the letter 'A prospect tremendous indeed!' (*83*, I, 114-15). Fitzgerald wrote to Anglesey: 'The priests have triumphed!, and through them their brethren, the Catholic parliament will dictate the representatives of every county in the south of Ireland . . . I could not have formed a notion of the extent and power of Catholic organisation!'

A report in the *Times* of 16 July has O'Connell franking his first four letters as MP to Wellington, Lord Eldon, Peel and Goulburn announcing his election. On his return to Dublin he told the Catholic Association: 'What is to be done with Ireland? What is to be done with the Catholics? One of two things. They must either crush us or conciliate us. There is no going on as we are; there is nothing so dangerous as going on as we are.' The Catholic Association could not now be prevented from capturing almost every county seat in Ireland and thus destroying the representative system under the Protestant Constitution. On 6 July Anglesey wrote to Lord Holland: 'Nothing can be more clear than that Ireland cannot remain as it is. The Catholic question must be adjusted, or the Association and the priests must be overruled' (*40*, 525). The widespread religious and political enthusiasm throughout Ireland is exemplified by the entry in Humphrey O'Sullivan's diary on 8 July noting the reaction in Callan, Co. Kilkenny: 'Every window in the town was filled with candles all a-light in honour of Daniel O'Connell who was elected in Clare County to be a member of the London parliament' (*75*, XXX, 299). O'Connell declared that the Clare election was 'in reality, a religious ceremony, where honest men met to support upon the altar of their country, the religion in which they believed. It was a solemn and a religious ceremony . . .'[14] The Clare election was the dramatic flashpoint which finally tipped the balance on the side of the argument of political necessity against the hazards of toleration: 'such is the power of the agitators', wrote Anglesey, 'that I am quite certain they could lead on the people to open rebellion at a moment's notice . . . I believe their success inevitable – that no power under heaven can arrest its progress . . .' (*1*, 201).

Clare opened up a terrifying prospect for the Protestant establishment. Catholics could now be elected but, as they were unable to take their seats, they would form their own unofficial Irish parliament – a natural development of the 'Popish Parliament' as the Catholic Association was nicknamed. The vast potential of the forces displayed in Clare must inevitably have this result if concession were refused. The Union itself was thus vitally threatened by the Catholic electoral revolt.

The immediate worry of the government was the military security of Ireland. O'Connell had publicly hinted at this grave danger: 'Allow me now, Duke of Wellington, to send one whisper to your ear. Three hundred soldiers threw up their caps for me since I left Ennis.'[15] Both Peel and Anglesey worried over the reliability of the Catholic members of the police and the army (*13*, 178-9). Peel was informed that 'implicit reliance could not long be placed on the effect of discipline and the duty of obedience'. These 'delicate matters', as Peel refers to them in his *Memoirs*, could not be openly discussed, but they greatly affected consideration of policy after Clare (*83*, I, 122-6). The agitators might not be able to control the explosive reactions of Catholics and Protestants and insurrection or civil war, or perhaps both, might have to be faced at any moment.

The memories of the widespread agrarian insurrection of the early 1820s and of 1798 were vivid. O'Connell's constitutionalism depended for its real effect on the threat of massive social disorder. Anglesey affected, as he told Peel, to treat the new situation 'lightly' though he did recognise its real character. On 3 July, before the final result in Clare was known, he set out for Leveson-Gower the alternatives:

The present order of things must not, cannot last.
There are three modes of proceeding:–
1st That of trying to go on as we have done
2nd To adjust the question by concession, and such guards as may be deemed indispensable.
3rd To put down the Association, and to crush the power of the priests.

The first I hold to be impossible

The second is practicable and advisable

The third is only possible by supposing that you can reconstruct the
House of Commons; and to suppose that is to suppose that you
can totally alter the feelings of those who send them there. I
believe nothing short of the suspension of the Habeus Corpus
Act, and Martial Law, will effect the third proposition (*83*, I,
138, 148-9).

Anglesey pointed to Wellington's dilemma. The Prime Minister had a
pro-Catholic Commons. He could not dissolve parliament in order to
get a more 'Protestant' Commons as long as the forty-shilling freeholders would vote against every 'Protestant' candidate in Ireland. If
they did it would realise the 'Popish Parliament' nightmare. Before the
Commons would consent to abolish the forty-shilling franchise Wellington would have to pledge himself to Catholic relief. Wellington could
of course resign but the alternative Prime Minister would probably be
Lord Grey and the Whigs would favour a more liberal settlement of
the Catholic question. On 19 July 1828 Leveson-Gower wrote to
Anglesey that he did not believe Wellington meant to respond to the
Irish crisis by the use of force:

Whatever his former opinions may have been, I do not think that, as
a soldier or a politician, he will choose to fight on his *present ground*
a battle for the existence of the Protestant church and the connection
of the two countries. We have, I think, now little security that we
shall not ultimately have to fight this battle, but I am sure Emancipation will give us the best position for doing it.

Peel recognised Clare as 'the turning point' (*83*, I, 106). Wyse has
stated correctly that Clare was 'a new event in the history of the Constitution — it was new in the history of Ireland' because 'a new order
of things had *really* arisen in Ireland': the 'CRISIS HAD COME' (*132*, I,
369, 391-3). Peel's analysis was similar; the forty-shilling franchise, 'the
instrument of defence and supremacy had been converted into a weapon
fatal to the authority of the landlord'. No Protestant candidate was
likely to contest another southern election under more favourable circumstances than Vesey Fitzgerald. It was delusive to believe 'that the
instrument of political power shivered to atoms in the county of Clare
could still be wielded with effect in Cork or Galway'. Peel saw the long-
term threat to the established order:

The Clare election supplied the manifest proof of the abnormal and
unhealthy condition of the public mind in Ireland — the manifest
proof that the sense of a common grievance and the sympathies of
a common interest were beginning to loosen the ties which connect

different classes of men in friendly relations to each other . . . In this case of the Clare election, and of the natural consequences, what was the evil to be apprehended? Not force — not violence — not any act of which law could take cognizance. The real danger was in the peaceable and legitimate exercise of a franchise according to the will and conscience of the holder.

This was 'a revolution in the electoral system of Ireland' which would result in the transfer of political power from one party to another. It was impossible to defeat this revolution and maintain the Protestant Constitution 'at all hazards' as the ultras desired to do: the real difficulty

was in the novel exercise of constitutional franchises — in the application of powers recognised and protected by the law — the power of speech — the power of meeting in public assemblies — the systematic and not unlawful application of all those powers to one definite purpose, namely, the organisation of a force which professed to be a moral force, but had for its objects to encroach step by step on the functions of regular government, to paralyse its authority, and to acquire a strength which might ultimately render irresistible the demand for civil equality (*83*, I, 116-19).

The parliamentary session ended on 28 July without O'Connell appearing at the Commons demanding his rights as a Catholic MP. O'Connell contented himself with public declarations of his belief in 'radical reform' (III, 1467, 1469). He retained more power over the government by remaining in Ireland.

O'Connell sought and was granted a private meeting with Anglesey on 29 July; Peel was aware of this meeting but not of Anglesey's frank conversation with O'Connell. Anglesey made a memorandum of the conversation which records O'Connell's anxiety for the state of Ireland and his defence of the Association's strategy:

the object of the Association was to gain such an influence over the population as to secure the return to parliament of men devoted to their cause and who, by constantly agitating the question and bringing it before the House of Commons, would drive ministers from their station or compel them to grant Emancipation.

Anglesey admitted 'that perseverance and agitation had gained for the Catholics the ground upon which they stood' and his own anxiety for concession. He warned O'Connell about a possible 'no popery' reaction in England and the impossibility of Emancipation if a rebellion occurred. O'Connell revealed his flexibility as to possible obstacles to concession. 'He talked of the facility with which the court of Rome might be engaged to make similar arrangement to those made with the Kings of Prussia and of the Netherlands. He seemed to hold quite cheap any doubt as to the management of the priests.' Anglesey formed the distinct impression that 'the forty-shilling freeholders would *never stand in the way of an adjustment'*. O'Connell hinted that it was the one difficulty and that Catholics could not *'all at once* give them up. We must have time!' Anglesey indicated that, while he had no authority to say it, he believed Wellington meant to set the Catholic question 'at rest by fair concession' but pointed to the Prime Minister's problems with the ultra Protestants and the king.[16]

O'Connell's analysis of the *realpolitik* of the crisis was similar to that of Wellington and of Peel. O'Connell spelled it out for Anglesey on 21 July and later for Pierce Mahony on 17 September:

> We shall never be emancipated but as we were relieved in 1778, 1782 and 1793, that is, when it becomes *necessary* for the English Government to do something for Ireland. I am endeavouring to create that necessity by obtaining a control over the Irish Member of Parliament. If I had fifty county members obliged to attend constantly and to vote against every ministerial measure . . . I do think *the necessity* for Emancipation is nearly created already by the state of Ireland . . . [Clare was] . . . the commencement of practical reform in Parliament (III, 1485).

O'Connell had conjured up the power of the people and channelled it towards a parliamentary objective. At the end of September Prince Pückler Muskau gave an accurate assessment of his approach:

> Daniel O'Connell is indeed no common man – though the man of the commonalty. His power is so great that at this moment it only depends on him to raise the standard of rebellion from one end of the island to the other. He is, however, too sharp-sighted, and much too sure of attaining his end by safer means, to bring on any such violent crisis.[17]

The government, however, could not rely on O'Connell's ability to control the passions of Irish Catholics or the possibly violent reactions of the Protestants.

Wellington penned a startling memorandum to the king on 1 August: 'We have a rebellion impending over us in Ireland, . . . and we have in England a Parliament which we cannot dissolve, the majority of which is of opinion, with many wise and able men, that the remedy is to be found in Roman Catholic emancipation. . .' He sought and obtained the king's permission to consider the question; he offered the king in return secrecy and control of the subject 'till the last moment'. He would consult only Peel and Lyndhurst, the Lord Chancellor. Wellington frankly acknowledged that 'the demagogues of the Roman Catholic Association hold in their hands at the present moment the political power and the fate of Ireland . . .' (*128*, IV, 564-70).

Wellington next dispatched a memorandum to Peel and Lyndhurst advancing plans for Catholic Emancipation accompanied by various securities. Lyndhurst accepted the principle of concession, although he differed with the Duke over possible securities. Peel returned two lengthy documents stating the reasons which had led him to accept the principle of settling the question. However, he pointed out that he would support this only after resignation and when he was out of office. As the leading anti-Catholic in the Commons he could not, he felt, introduce a relief measure without the scorn of his associates and the distrust of the Catholics. Wellington's difficulties were compounded by Peel's great personal crisis on the question as well as by George IV's devious twists and turns. Peel recognised that whatever the ultimate result of concession it would be in British interests to combat any Irish disturbance from the vantage-ground of civil and political equality. But to achieve this he would be exposed to the rage of party, rejection by the University of Oxford which he represented, the shunning of former associates and even 'the interruption of family affections' (*83*, I, 183, 188). Ellenborough on 31 July noted that 'the great difficulty' was Peel's 'position and reputation', as the Duke began to see his way to settle the question (*62*, I, 182). Months elapsed as Wellington grappled with Peel and the king.

On the details of concession there were differences: Wellington had suggested an annual suspension of the oaths excluding Catholics but Peel favoured a permanent repeal and 'equality of civil privilege'. Peel wished only to exclude Catholics from certain high offices or perhaps to place restrictions on the numbers of Catholics in parliament. Both were agreed on the need to raise the franchise in Ireland. Wellington suggested a licensing system for the Catholic clergy but Peel argued against this as it would prove ineffective and give unnecessary state recognition to Catholicism. Peel worried most about the future relation of the Roman Catholic religion to the State.

Wellington's opening manoeuvres were greatly hampered by George Dawson's remarkable speech at Londonderry announcing his conversion to the Catholic cause. Dawson, a Secretary to the Treasury, was the brother-in-law of Peel and hitherto a staunch and vocal anti-Catholic. Now, on 12 August, he secured maximum public attention for his conversion by speaking at the anniversary of the siege of Derry. Dawson praised both Walker and Sarsfield for their valour in the Williamite wars. He pointed out how pervasively the Catholic question marred Irish social and political life: 'The state of Ireland is an anomaly in the history of civilised nations; it has no parallel in ancient or modern history, and, being contrary to the character of all civil institutions, it must terminate in general anarchy and confusion.' Peace depended 'upon the dictation of the Catholic Association' which might decree against the payment of tithes or rents. The Orangemen went into uproar as Dawson spelled out the realities of 'this new phenomena' [*sic*] which was 'all powerful and irresistible' where the Catholic population predominated. They must either crush the Association and go back to the penal laws or settle the question. Dawson declared he personally desired to settle it and was greatly abused by the assembled Orangemen for his unexpected speech which sought, however, belatedly, to reconcile the Williamite and Jacobite traditions (*128*, IV, 605-10).

The speech caused a sensation because it seemed a definite indication of government concession. Greville recorded in his diary on 16 August: 'It is strongly reported that Peel will resign, that the Duke means to concede the Catholic question and to negotiate a *concordat* with the Pope.' Ellenborough wrote on 21 August: 'Dawson's speech at Derry *fait époque* . . . His speech hastens the crisis' and he believed that the violent Orangemen wished to 'bring on a civil contest' to make concession impossible (*62*, I, 199-200). Thomas Creevey noted in his diary on 26 August: 'O'Connell's election and Dawson's speech at Derry are conclusive proofs to me of some great approaching change in the fate of Ireland, and I wish to see that country before and during the operation of this crisis' (*85*, II, 167).

The king regarded his confidence in Wellington's promise of secrecy as shaken and Wellington and Peel were dismayed by this setback. During the succeeding weeks Peel, Wellington and Lyndhurst continued to discuss plans but no real progress could be made until the king gave permission to make Emancipation a cabinet question. George IV was ailing from gout, a bladder complaint and was using knockout doses of laudanum. Wellington saw him infrequently and when he did George ranted about Anglesey, recalling Eldon, and making parliament more 'Protestant'.

Catholics were elated at the turn of events whilst the ultras were furious: Greville on 22 August observed that the Orangemen were 'moving heaven and earth to create disturbances, and their impotent fury shows how far their cause is sunk. The Catholics, on the contrary, are temperate and calm, from confidence in their strength and the progressive advance of their cause.'

To add to Wellington's grave difficulties his relationship with Anglesey came under serious strain. The king proposed the removal of Anglesey, and Wellington while concurring did not wish to comply as it would add to the excitement and danger in Ireland (*128*, IV, 575-7). Anglesey conceived that he had a major role in policy and that he could solve the Catholic question if allowed; Wellington desired him to apply himself to the maintenance of law and order. Anglesey was not privy to Wellington's active consideration of the question and both men completely distrusted each other. Anglesey told Peel on 31 August that 'every hour of delay' would increase 'the difficulty of adjustment' (*83*, I, 205). However capable they were on the battlefield, in politics Anglesey and Wellington lacked the skills required for a most complex crisis. Their combined actions served to increase the agitation in Ireland. The delay in the government response gave time for a serious 'no popery' movement in Ireland and England to emerge.

Protestants were thoroughly alarmed by O'Connell's triumph in Clare; they were also divided. Liberal Protestants continued to believe that Emancipation was necessary but they worried increasingly about the frightening new powers and self-assertion of Irish Catholics. Orange, Tory or ultra Protestants were now determined to organise a new movement to resist Catholic advance by warning the government off concession. Liberal Protestants who actively supported the Catholic Association to the extent of joining were, of course, a minority: Wyse estimates that of 14,000 members enrolled in the Catholic Association 1,400 were Protestants (*132*, II, 83). After Clare, such Protestants found themselves deposed from the leadership of the great parliamentary struggle for Catholic equality and progressively caught between two powerful and extremist political movements. Civil war was regarded as probable.

Many liberal Protestants felt like John Hely-Hutchinson, the Earl of Donoughmore, who told Croker when he visited Knocklofty on 1 October 1828:

> It is only common justice that we should all be on one footing. In this country the Catholics are 50 to 1: in property we are 20 to their 1. Let us start fair as to laws, and I have a *just cause* to embark in and my mind is quite made up to fight them in defence of my property; but I don't like fighting in an unjust cause.

Donoughmore believed that a civil war would be over in a month 'but from that day no Protestant gentleman can live in his country house' (*85*, II, 174-5).

Orangemen believed that their one hope was to make a powerful demonstration of force while the government response was still unclear. The July demonstrations on 'the twelfth' were anticipated with real concern lest they should spark the expected conflagration. Gregory told Peel on 27 June that Orange attitudes had hardened: 'The persons of rank who formerly had influence over them have lost it, and they are in the hands of inferior men, who are as violent as the lowest of the order' (*83*, I, 110). The Catholic Association was worried also; on 5 July it issued an 'Address to the Roman Catholics of the North' calling upon them 'to abstain on 12 July from every act of resistance to the insulting proceedings which are contemplated'. Catholics were asked to avoid the Orange parades and O'Connell addressed a personal message from Ennis: success would attend Catholics 'if we be only *True to Ourselves* and *Obedient to the Laws'.*[18]

The 'twelfth' passed off with comparatively little violence. The *Dublin Evening Mail* on 14 July claimed that 500,000 Orangemen had marched in the North. The Clare election had alarmed Protestants in Ulster but they did not yet feel directly menaced in the frontier counties such as Monaghan where predominantly Catholic areas gave way to Protestant dominated territory. The restraint of the Catholic Association would be the key to their reactions: if that gave way a massive reaction seemed inevitable.

Ultra peers began to reconstruct a major Protestant organisation which would unite all Protestants in Britain and Ireland in defence of the status quo. The *Dublin Evening Mail* on 16 July appealed for Protestant clubs to be established when it reported the steps these peers had taken to form the Brunswick Constitutional Club. The Dukes of Cumberland, Newcastle and Gordon, the Marquess of Chandos, the Earl of Longford, Lord Farnham, Lord Kenyon, Eldon and others were involved. The name 'Brunswick' was selected by Eldon to refer to the dynasty which was particularly committed to Protestant Ascendancy through its accession to the throne following the 'Glorious Revolution' of 1689. Cork Protestants had founded in 1827 the Cork Brunswick Club in reaction to the political stirrings of Cork Catholics.[19]

In Britain Orange Lodges, Pitt Clubs and the new Brunswick Clubs overlapped. Cumberland was both the Brunswick leader and Grand Master of the Orange Institution of Great Britain. His influence continued to stiffen his brother George IV against concession. Ultra peers published calls to the 'Protestants of the empire' to rally behind the Protestant Constitution. The enforced secrecy of the government fed rumours which led ultras to express unalterable opposition to concession. They were aware in early November that the government was preparing some legislative measure to settle the Catholic question. This was noted by Colchester in his diary and he considered publishing his speeches 'to contribute at this crisis'. Dr Philpotts, Wellington's clerical kite-flyer, wrote to Colchester on 16 November setting out how it would be less dangerous to concede now with disenfranchisement of the forty-shilling voters than to consider any other course such as facing a general election in Ireland (*20*, III, 584-6).

Ultras were hindered in raising the 'no popery' tension by their scruples as to the propriety of forming clubs at all. Such clubs had revolutionary connotations and their purpose was clearly to overawe the king's government. Besides many potential supporters could not believe that Wellington and Peel meant to betray the cause. Peel spoke for many conservatives in November when he observed: 'Clubs or combinations of any kind to resist the decisions or influence the deliberations of the legislature are dangerous instruments' (27, 89). Peel was leading a double life now: secretly working for concession, publicly being represented as a Protestant stalwart.

In Ireland the new Brunswick movement was most successful. Protestant Tories were becoming very conscious of the need for leadership, party organisation and policy. They wished to defend their privileges and they sincerely believed that their political and religious liberties were about to be fatally undermined. The Marquess of Chandos contacted Thomas Langlois Lefroy, the well-known anti-Catholic lawyer, on 6 August to stress the need for 'every possible exertion . . . to call forth an expression of Protestant feeling throughout England and Ireland . . . the absolute necessity of taking some steps to check the rapid and alarming strides of Popery'. Chandos told Lefroy that Protestants should establish a club in every village and town to prevent any further concession of political power to Catholics and to prevent a radical alteration of the British Constitution: '. . . the time is arrived when Protestants must do their duty & maintain the laws of their country now threatened . . .' Lefroy was active at the foundation of the Brunswick Constitutional Club of Ireland on 15 August and he proposed the Earl of Longford, Wellington's brother-in-law, as president of the club.[20]

The Brunswick Club was formed 'on the Principle of preserving the Integrity of the Protestant Constitution'. It was dominated by peers: of the thirty vice-presidents only Saurin was not a peer. Many of the Irish Brunswickers such as Lord Lorton, Lord Farnham and, indeed, Lefroy, shared an extremely strong evangelical outlook. A number, like Lefroy, Saurin and the Trench family, were of Huguenot descent and profoundly anti-Catholic; they believed Catholic intolerance had sent them as exiles from France. O'Connell abused Lefroy at a Cork Catholic meeting in late August: 'He is one of those persons who is to be seen on a Sunday walking sanctimoniously through the streets of Dublin to Church with three of his children walking before him, and three following after, everyone carrying an enormous Bible, giving fine materials for an engraving of a religious family'.[21]

The bulk of the Brunswickers were recruited from among former Orangemen and were patronised by such Orange peers as the Earl of Enniskillen. Many were crude sectarians. In September 1828 Prince Pückler Muskau was disgusted to meet an Orangeman who longed for a 'good sound rebellion' in Ireland to settle the Catholic question:

Rebellion! — that's the point at which I want to see them, at which I wait for them, and to which they must be led on, that we make an end of them at once; for there can be no peace in Ireland till the whole race is exterminated, and nothing but an open rebellion, and an English army to put it down can effect this![22]

The local clubs were drawn mostly from the lower classes but were dominated by parliamentarians, lawyers, and the clergy of the Established Church.

The organisation of the Brunswick Clubs was, ironically, modelled on the Liberal Club system developed by the Catholic Association. A collection, known as the 'Protestant rent', was commenced. The movement spread rapidly, especially in Ulster where popular support was widespread. By the time of the first annual meeting of the Club in early November, 108 clubs had been established.[23] By the end of 1828 there were 148 clubs in the towns, twenty-six in the counties throughout Ireland and about forty in England (*113*, 151). An example of such clubs may be found in Co. Longford where the Ballymahon and the Longford Brunswick Clubs were established in October. The clubs represented all the local anti-Catholic feeling in the county — there were a hundred subscribers to the Ballymahon Club and at least 2,000 were reported to have attended at the formation of the Longford club.[24]

Typical of the Ulster clubs was Portadown formed on 25 September 1828: the notice calling the first meeting stated that if the Protestants of the North were unanimous they need not fear: 'Now is the time for a long pull, a strong pull, and a pull together — and let the cry be NO SURRENDER'. There were printed 'Rules for Forming Auxiliary Branches of the Brunswick Club' to guide such local clubs. These rules set out the officers and committee and limited each club's membership to one hundred; each member subscribed between two shillings and one pound annually and was admitted by a membership card to the meetings. Also, no member was to spend more than two pence on liquor at monthly meetings and any member 'who shall wantonly insult, or injure a Roman Catholic' was to be excluded. In the Portadown club any surplus funds was to be sent to the Ulster Brunswick Constitutional Club in Belfast 'to be applied in aid of Protestant Ascendancy'.

The Portadown club was well organised with printed membership forms; it corresponded with the headquarters of the movement in Dublin and with the Ulster Club in Belfast. It received instructions on petitions and notices about the Brunswick newspaper *The Star of Brunswick* to be published in late November and other printed reports of speeches. Significantly, in the light of the emerging split in the Presbyterian Synod of Ulster between Cooke and Montgomery, the club toasted Henry Cooke.[25]

The first annual meeting in the Rotunda of the Brunswick Club on 4 November was a major Protestant demonstration: over 600 sat down to dinner in the Mansion House. Within the movement there were important divisions of opinion.

Among those who wished to pledge the body to 'an eternal hostility to every species of concession' were Rev. Thomas Magee, son of the Archbishop of Dublin, Rev. Charles Boyton, and the two Sheelans, editors of the *Dublin Evening Mail*. Others were more moderate. Great use was made of the press to express Protestant feelings and the cry of 'No Surrender' increasingly embittered the 'New Reformation' evangelical drive.

Leslie Foster told Peel on 14 November that

> almost all the peasantry, the farmers, and mechanics belong, or are on the eve of belonging, to the Brunswickers. The majority of the upper and middle ranks do not belong to them, but wish them all success. None but a few insulated individuals retain any good feeling towards the Catholics. The northern peasantry are scarcely less warlike in their feelings than their ancestors who served in Cromwell's army, but they are manageable by the gentlemen who have placed themselves everywhere at their head.

At this stage Foster thought that if the Catholic Bar was 'silenced' by admitting Catholic lawyers to the bench it would draw the teeth of the Catholic agitation: Sheil and O'Connell would be found in no other profession (*83*, I, 266).

O'Connell reacted to Protestant resurgence in two ways; he attempted to get up liberal Protestant support in public for Emancipation and he determined to expose what he believed to be the weakness of the movement in Ulster. On 4 September he wrote to Cloncurry:

> The Orange faction is endeavouring to beard the Government; that seems quite plain. Their ostentatious display of their peerage strength in the Brunswick Club is manifestly made in order to terrify the Government of Lord Anglesey and to encourage the friends of bigotry in England, where there are many, and some in the highest station. It would be, indeed, quite idle to conceal from ourselves that the great enemy of the people of Ireland is his most sacred Majesty!!

O'Connell appealed to Cloncurry to bestir the liberal Protestants. The Duke of Leinster and others he argued were 'letting slip' a glorious opportunity to do something:

> The assistance of Protestants generates so much good feeling and such a national community of sentiment that I deem it more valuable

than even Emancipation itself . . . I think the Duke of Leinster and every other Protestant peer friendly to the principle of freedom of conscience should avail themselves at once of the formation of the Brunswick Club and come forward and join the Catholic Association. There is in Ireland no neutral ground; whatever is not with us is, in reality, against us. The time is come to take an active part in struggling to preserve the country from bigots (III, 1483).

O'Connell was rightly worried about the strength of the new Brunswick movement. On 1 September Donoughmore had written to Cloncurry spelling out how formidable Brunswick Clubs had become:

> We ought not to conceal from ourselves that there is a great deal of rank and fortune, and even some talent included amongst them. I should despair of getting signatories amongst the Irish liberal Protestants, which could at all compete in number, property, or respectability with that association. The fact is, that the violence of O'Connell and his associates, at least in this part of Ireland, has done the Catholic cause much mischief; and it would be impossible here, [i.e. at Knocklofty] and in the city and county of Cork, to get any considerable number of Protestants to affix their signatories to any document similar to that which you have in contemplation (*109*, 329-30).

On 19 November a public dinner of the Friends of Civil and Religious Liberty was arranged at Lady Morgan's. Prior to this a Protestant Declaration in favour of Catholic Emancipation was drawn up. Local churchwardens, like Humphrey O'Sullivan, were charged with procuring the signatories, as O'Sullivan records in his diary on 11 October 1828:

> I must get the name of every Protestant in the parish signed to it, if I can. Is it not a very lamentable state of affairs that the Children of the Gael should be begging for their liberty as an alms, in their native land? But they themselves are responsible for having this execrable slavery weighing down upon them at the hands of English foreigners, through their own disunion since the days of Brian Boru until O'Connell's recent peace movement' (*75*, XXXI, 37-9).

Eventually two dukes, seven marquesses, twenty-seven earls, eleven viscounts, twenty-two baronets, fifty-two MPs and up to two thousand gentlemen signed the declaration: an impressive enough testimony to liberal Protestantism.

O'Connell supported a 'mission' to Ulster by John Lawless to build Catholic support and expose the weakness of 'the Orange faction' there. On 5 August the Finance Committee of the Catholic Association had instructed Lawless to tour the northern counties to organise the collection of the Catholic Rent. Ulster had always been weak in its support for the Catholic movement and it seemed an ideal area in which to maintain the momentum after the Clare election: fresh fields to be conquered. On 9 August the mission was advertised. O'Connell probably felt that Lawless would conveniently raise the temperature, perhaps even get arrested, while being quite dispensable within the Association. O'Connell failed to appreciate that this 'mission' was very likely to unleash the full force of a popular Protestant backlash to this 'invasion'. Sir George Hill, MP for Londonderry City, told Wellington on 14 August that the 'threat of O'Connell to march 150,000 men from Tipperary into Ulster' had roused 'a spirit amongst the northerners little calculated to make them concede or conciliate' (*128*, IV, 602-10).

The Ulster Protestant community felt uncertain after the Clare election, betrayed by Dawson's speech in Derry, threatened by O'Connell and the Lawless 'mission' and worried by Anglesey's partiality to Catholics and his threats to disband the yeomanry. Advice 'to be moderate and patient' was increasingly likely to fall on deaf ears. O'Connell had little comprehension of popular Orange feeling in Ulster, being acquainted only with the minority 'Orange faction' in the other provinces.

Having hovered for some weeks in the border area of Louth and Meath where he was popularly acclaimed, Lawless was by 23 September making his way through Co. Monaghan from Carrickmacross towards Ballybay. Meanwhile, the Orangemen had been gathering in armed bands under the direction of Sam Grey, the notorious Orange innkeeper of Ballybay. Lawless was accompanied by a huge crowd; he later claimed, rather unreliably, that there were at least 250,000. The military presence in the immediate area, under General Thornton, of about one hundred rank and file, was tiny and quite incapable of preventing a major battle between the Protestant and Catholic forces marshalled around Ballybay.

The Catholic crowd pressed Lawless to enter Ballybay by force but he, wisely, insisted on stopping at the Catholic chapel a mile and a half before the town. Realising that he was on the brink of a tragic and perhaps fatal encounter for the Catholic cause, Lawless fled after a minor skirmish in which two Catholics were killed. Wyse says he missed being shot by a disappointed supporter. Thornton had played a valuable role in negotiating between the forces to prevent an immediate clash. Gradually the respective mobs dissolved. Ballybay, however, might have been the trigger for civil war in Ireland. As Wyse states, the attempt on the North was little less than a 'direct provocative to open combat'. Many Ulster Catholics, including Bishop Crolly of Down and Connor, had advised against such an 'intrusion on the territory of their enemies': Ballybay 'might have been entered, but a rebellion that night would have commenced in Ireland'. Wyse outlines one nightmare scenario:

A defeat of the crowd who accompanied him, would have been followed up by a carnage; the carnage, by a massacre of the Catholics of the North. Their brethren of the South would not have looked on — hundreds and thousands would have marched from Munster — a counter massacre — a Sicilian Vespers, perhaps, would have taken place (*132*, I, 401-18).

On 27 September Leveson-Gower reported on the Ballybay affair and stated that the government should 'consider Ireland as on the eve of rebellion or civil war, or both' (*40*, 538).

Peel reassured the king that all the disposable military forces in Great Britain were situated as far as possible within immediate reach of Ireland (*128*, V, 86-7). An indication of the widespread state of alarm amongst 'the scattered Protestants in the Catholic districts' is given in the letter of Maurice Fitzgerald, Knight of Kerry, to Wellington on 29 September. Fitzgerald referred to an announcement by Sheil that 'if an affray should take place between the Orangemen and the Catholics of the north of Ireland (which is a very probable contingency) it would be followed by a massacre of every Protestant man, woman and child in the south', and urged Wellington to take steps 'against such a catastrophe' by using coastal protection and other measures (*128*, V, 96-7).

Ballybay was regarded as an Orange victory: loud cries of 'Bravo! Ballybay forever' rang out at the large annual meeting of the Brunswick Clubs in Dublin on 4 November.[26] It was, however, a chance missed if the Orange intention was to force Wellington and Peel to fall back on a policy of repression in Ireland. Had Lawless persisted, and violence become widespread in Ireland, the government might have had little alternative but to suppress the Catholic population by force. In the event the 'invasion' of Ulster was abandoned. O'Connell wrote to Dwyer from Derrynane on 1 October, still oblivious of the actual danger in Ulster:

I think Mr Lawless was quite right at Ballybay. If the Chapel had been in the town he should have gone there at all hazards but as it was not he was quite right and the people decidedly wrong. I also think that he ought not to be recalled. He should proceed through the counties of Monaghan and Down and the opposition to him will, I should expect, totally cease. If it were necessary to recall him it would be a great triumph to the *bloodhounds* of all description. I am sorry to see that some members of the Association omit to call the Brunswickers by their appropriate name of 'Bloodhounds' . . . I think Mr Lawless should be left on the subject of his mission to his own discretion, so that if he deemed it right to stop short he should communicate privately with the Association and procure an order to desist (III, 1492).

On 9 October the Catholic Association approved a major *Address to the Roman Catholics of Ulster* which was circulated in large placard posters. The address was to 'our Persecuted Brethren in the North' who suffered under 'a numerous, crafty and well-combined faction' which had 'long usurped all the functions of Government': Orange yeomen 'butcher' Catholics; Orange police 'connive at the crimes of their fraternity'; and Orange magistrates, juries, sheriffs protect the 'murderers' and 'convict of riot the wretched men' who escape assassination. The address went on to refer to Lawless and his mission which it was hoped would have been able to make 'some advances' towards 'the great and glorious end of our Association – the reconciliation of Irishmen of all denominations'. It appealed to Catholics in Ulster to keep the peace, avoid secret societies and 'to join with the Government and the Association' in preserving the peace. If this happened 'the reign of Orangeism will soon cease for ever':

> We call on you to meet – to speak – to resolve for yourselves – to express your sentiments, and take means to protect your Properties and Lives. Let the Counties of Ulster ... assemble to petition the Legislature, and to form Liberal Clubs. And let a Meeting of the Province be held in Belfast ... Let Clubs be multiplied until there is one in every barony and parish in Ulster. They will serve as so many fortresses to which the persecuted may fly for protection. In the meantime, let the Rent be collected without delay throughout Ulster; and a stricter intimacy be kept up between the Catholics of the North and the Association.

The 'Persecuted Priesthood of the North' were asked to lend their 'sacred aid to this holy cause'.[27] In effect, the Catholic Association left the Catholics of Ulster to do what they could for the cause without dramatic outside help such as had been attempted by Lawless. Later, O'Connell proposed a motion of thanks to Lawless for the manner in which he had performed his duty in the North (III, 1494).

Meanwhile the ultras in England were seeking to make explicit the 'no popery' sentiment which they believed was ill represented in the pro-Catholic Commons. They commenced holding large public meetings. The first and most famous of these was held on 24 October on Penenden Heath, near Maidstone, in Kent. It took the form of a public disputation between the Brunswickers, led by Lord Winchelsea, and their opponents. Sheil attended from Ireland. Somewhere between 30,000 and 60,000 attended this meeting with the crowd arranged in pro- and anti-Catholic sections. It was more of a Brunswick triumph on the day but Catholics achieved substantial press coverage for their cause. It proved difficult to get similar meetings organised throughout England but some smaller ones were held. The Brunswick movement in Britain did not reveal the capacity for a national convulsion such as it had in Ireland. But it organised a vast number of anti-Catholic petitions, using in this process a great number of clergy of the Established Church. While such Protestant pressure was being exerted on the government the Catholic Association was engaged in strengthening its grip on Irish electoral politics.

The election of Daniel O'Connell in Clare gave a great boost to the establishment of Liberal Clubs in many counties. Thomas Wyse issued an important letter on the organisation of these clubs on 30 July 1828 in which he pointed that 'the great defect' in the Catholic organisation was 'the want of a good organisation'. Wyse argued that they needed 'a well-digested system of political tactics, enamating from a single point, and extending in circle upon circle, until it shall embrace the entire nation'. The time was past when a mere 'electrical spark here and there from the body' was sufficient. So the county meetings, city meetings, parish meetings and the Association in Dublin should be not simply 'a *series* of *links*, but a *chain*'. Now that the people had risen up it was time to organise the Irish democracy: 'Two or three elections did more in educating them to a proper sense of their wrongs and power, than all the petitioning, and grovelling, and chiding, of the last half century'. Wyse asked '. . . who is he who now dare say to the nation: "Thou shall not advance further?"' Further advance would now come by 'the commonplace, plodding, persevering habit of every day'; through the creation of a national political party, in effect.

Wyse's political party would have the Association as the head club, below which would be the county and city clubs and below them the parish clubs: by this system 'the affairs of the Catholics of Ireland might be conducted with precision, constancy, unanimity, and uniformity'. As a result, every county, in a few months, 'will naturally, and almost of itself, become a Clare or a Waterford'. Wyse was convinced that remedies for Irish ills could not be procured in any other way: 'Political ameliorations in the present state of human knowledge are not to be obtained by physical force' but by 'that great moral power arising from the concert and universality of constitutional exertion' (*132*, II, cxlv-clvi).

After Clare the Catholic Association, at an extraordinary meeting on 4 August, adopted 'pledges' which all candidates for parliament would be asked to take publicly. The first pledge was not to support the administration of Wellington or Peel until Emancipation had been unconditionally granted; the second was to try to repeal the Sub-Letting Act; and the third was to support parliamentary reform, particularly an extension of the franchise and shorter parliaments. The Association would oppose candidates who would not give these three pledges. The Munster Provincial Meeting on 26 August at Clonmel sanctioned the policy of the pledges as well as the recommendation shaped by Wyse on the formation of Liberal Clubs. Other provincial meetings followed suit. Very quickly, therefore, after Clare, the Catholic Association, acting like a national political party, looked to pledge-bound candidates who would be supported in electoral politics by local political machines, called Liberal Clubs. How successful was Wyse's novel scheme of political organisation, which as Peel knew, provided the real long-term challenge to political control in Ireland?

Map 2 illustrates the development of political organisation in Ireland in the years between 1825 and 1830. Starting in Waterford in 1825 and Louth in 1826 it shows the gradual expansion of electoral clubs after 1826: Clare, Cork City, Waterford County, Dublin City and Roscommon were formally organised into Liberal Clubs during 1827. The Clare Liberal Club helped lay the groundwork for O'Connell's dramatic success in 1828. After the Clare election counties Wexford, Galway, Sligo, Limerick, Tipperary, Meath, Kildare, King's County, Queen's County, Longford, Cavan and Monaghan established Liberal Clubs. In addition, many existing clubs such as those in Waterford and Clare, were expanded and re-modelled. A number of towns such as Newry, Athlone and Naas also had Liberal Clubs.

Most of these clubs were exceptionally well organised. In Co. Wexford, from July, preparations were laid which resulted in the organisation of the County Wexford Liberal Club at a meeting in the Commercial News Room, Wexford in early October. The club combined the landed and commercial gentlemen of the county; one pound was fixed as the annual subscription and thirty-one members were elected to the committee as well as four officers. The President was Thomas Boyse, Esq., a Protestant, from Bannow. It was arranged for the Club to meet on the second day of each Assizes and the members of the Club in each barony were to form a baronial committee.

The aims of the Wexford Club were to secure the representation of the county and to collect the Catholic Rent.[28] The establishment of baronial and parish branches of the Wexford Clubs followed upon the formation of the County Club. The baronies of Bantry, Forth and Shelmalier formed Liberal Clubs in December and January. In the parish of Davidstown the parish priest declared that it was the first Wexford parish 'to form themselves into a Branch Independent Club'. Large crowds appear to have attended the formation of these baronial and parochial clubs and one hundred names were read out as members of the Barony of Forth Liberal Club; at the Shelmalier meeting it was stated that these branch clubs would '. . . simplify, and reduce to *effective* operation the complex machinery of our County Club. They will

DEVELOPMENT OF LOCAL ORGANISATION IN IRELAND 1825—1830

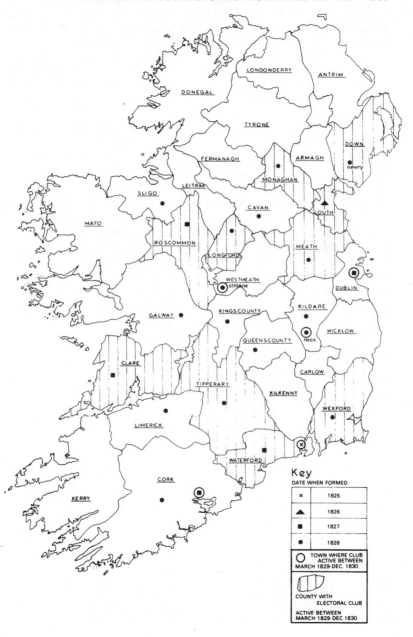

Key

DATE WHEN FORMED.

×	1825
▲	1826
■	1827
●	1828

○ TOWN WHERE CLUB ACTIVE BETWEEN MARCH 1829-DEC. 1830.

COUNTY WITH ELECTORAL CLUB ACTIVE BETWEEN MARCH 1829-DEC. 1830

fan the flame of patriotism though our people . . .' The parish priest acted as chairman of the parochial committee and the baronial secretary of the County Club. Significantly the *Wexford Evening Post* and the *Weekly Waterford Chronicle* were to 'be regularly taken by the several parishes of Shelmalier, at the expense of the Club fund, for the instruction and benefit of the members . . .' Further local meetings took place at New Ross, in the barony of Bargy, in the parishes of St James and The Hook and at the barony of Shelbourne to form units of the County Club.[29] Wexford had therefore developed an advanced political organisation by early 1829.

In the province of Connaught two counties set up Liberal Clubs after the Clare triumph. In Galway, a Liberal Club was established at a meeting in Kilroy's Room, Galway, chaired by Hon. Martin Ffrench. The Galway Club had a small beginning, but there were confident forecasts that it would soon 'rival in number and in power even Louth itself'. This Galway Club had a further meeting in early October.[30] For a while in September it seemed possible that Galway might be the scene of the next dramatic election if the government promoted Peel's friend James Daly to the peerage, thus causing a vacancy. Gregory, however, pleading for 'a little breathing space between the heats' managed to indicate the problems of trying to defeat the Association even with a popular government candidate. Wellington recognised that such a government success would weaken the case for franchise reform while a victory for the Association would further strengthen its hand: 'I confess that what has moved me', wrote Wellington to Peel on 12 September,

> has been the Monaghan, the Louth, the Waterford, and the Clare elections. I see clearly that we shall have to suffer from all the consequences of a practical Democratic Reform in Parliament if we do not do something to remedy the evil; and if I could believe that the Irish nobility and gentry would recover their lost influence, the just influence of property, without making these concessions, I would not stir (*128*, V, 42-3).

O'Connell was instrumental in the formation of the Sligo Liberal Club. He was asked by James Feeny, a baker of Market Street, Sligo, to form such a club when he attended a public dinner at the end of July 1828 (III, 1473). O'Connell's claim to have founded the club was well justified. A 'solemn pledge' was taken to form a club on a plan 'similar to that which has been so successful in the county of Louth'; in October the Sligo Club was functioning on a system of baronial committees similar to the Wexford Club — baronial committees or clubs were established in each of the six baronies in the county; their function was to report quarterly to the general committee on the state of the freeholders in their baronies. The general committee circulated for its quarterly meetings between Sligo, Ballymote and Tobercurry.[31]

Soon after the Clare election the Clare Club was enlarged and re-modelled as the Clare Independent Club and Scott, O'Connell's capable election agent and secretary of the club, set about organising the registry sessions in each barony.[32] In Limerick, Thomas Steele founded the Independent Club at a meeting in the Canal Hotel in August 1828. In late September the new club gave a public dinner for Steele and O'Gorman Mahon. The officers of the Limerick Club included Edmund Ryan, the president, and his brother William Ryan, the treasurer; their father was 'the most extensive and esteemed merchant' in Limerick City. Like many of these Liberal Club activists of the 1820s throughout the country, Edmund Ryan remained active in local and municipal politics, being elected Mayor of Limerick in 1846. The Limerick Club had club rooms in Clare Street, Limerick.[33]

Shortly after the Munster provincial meeting a number of Tipperary gentlemen met to arrange the formation of a county and parish organis-ation. Wyse explained to them the objects of a Liberal Club and he read to them the rules and regulations of the Waterford Club. Officers were elected and Wyse urged the formation of a committee of inquiry to detect municipal abuses in such boroughs as Clonmel and Cashel. He also pressed the formation of parochial clubs.[34] In October Prince Pückler Muskau was invited to join a meeting of the Cashel Liberal Club by its president:

> The Club was instituted with an admirable purpose; it consisted of Catholics and Protestants, who proposed to unite their efforts to reconcile the parties, and to co-operate with all their might to obtain Emancipation. When I entered, I found from eighty to a hundred persons sitting at a long table; they all stood up while the President led me to the top. I thanked them; upon which they drank my health, and I was again forced to reply. Innumerable other toasts followed, all accompanied by speeches. The eloquence of the speakers was not very remarkable, and the same commonplaces were served up over and over again in different words.

Pückler Muskau seized an early opportunity to leave these vocal and enthusiastic democrats.[35]

The Meath Independent Club held its first meeting during September in the parochial schoolhouse near the chapel of Duleek. John Lawless, who was present, was interested in becoming a candidate in the Meath constituency and he attended subsequent meetings of the club. At the first meeting, a member of the Louth Club told the Meath Club that there were 205 members in the Louth Club, and he declared that he expected to see 'an amalgamation of the Liberal Clubs' which would 'purify' the county representation and also reform 'the close and corrupt boroughs'.[36]

In Queen's Co. a county meeting was held to consider the formation of Liberal Clubs. There was a real debate on the question. One speaker declared that 'the Clare election is an event which must be productive of great and momentous consequences ... We shall, for the future, follow the example of Clare, and shall, with the assistance of Liberal Clubs, send honest and patriotic members to Parliament ...' Some priests, however, were opposed to the formation of a club unless a Brunswick Club was formed in the county. They hoped to avoid local animosity. Patrick Lalor, of Tenekill, spoke in favour of the club; another speaker declared that the object of the clubs was 'to teach the people their rights, the value of them, and how they ought to use them'. Lalor wrote a long letter in reply to Father O'Connor, parish priest of Maryborough, who opposed the club on the basis that the Catholics of Queen's Co. were less able to struggle with their landlords than those in other counties; Lalor argued that there was no sign of such a struggle for the tenants and that the resolutions of the provincial meetings in favour should be followed. It was finally agreed to postpone the estab- lishment of the club 'for the present' and this was 'in deference to the opinion of many Liberal and enlightened Protestants'. However, in December, Lalor, Robert Cassidy and other activists were appointed to a committee to consider a club at a meeting of priests, churchwardens and 'other influential Catholics'.[37]

Wyse had pressed Queen's Co. to form a club, though he knew Dr Doyle, the bishop, was opposed to it. Wyse also maintained contact with Robert Cassidy who was a leading activist in Queen's Co. The Queen's Co. Liberal Club was formed and the local organisation sur- vived: Cassidy urged a meeting of vice-presidents of the Liberal Club 'to arrange a plan for future operation and organisation' in April 1829 and the club decided to print 1,000 copies of its regulations, even though zeal was 'much paralysed by the prospect of emancipation'.[38]

To trace these Liberal Clubs is to discover the origins of Irish demo- cratic organisation. They have an importance beyond the immediate struggle for Catholic Emancipation out of which they sprang. Detailed local studies of each club and its context reveal the sophistication reached in democratic development in Ireland which was certainly without comparison in the 1820s in Europe. Counties Waterford and Cork are two examples of the early growth of democratic political con- sciousness.

Waterford city was particularly well organised for the collection of the Catholic rent. A detailed report of a meeting of the Catholic Rent Committee of the city of Waterford was sent to the Catholic Association in early July 1828.[39] This meeting of collectors and contributors quite consciously represented 'the middling and working classes'. All con- tributions from sixpence upwards were noted giving the name, address and occupation of the contributor. O'Connell's candidacy in Clare had filled all 'with astonished delight' and enthusiasm. The list of 436 individual subscriptions of an amount just under £100 includes publicans, coopers, flour factors, shoemakers, clerks, teachers, carpenters, gardeners, painters, cabinet makers, dress makers, huxters, labourers, masons, cooks, corn merchants, servants and maids, grocers, coalmen, stone cutters and slaters, watchmakers, pawnbrokers, chandlers, auctioneers, confectioners, tailors, bookbinders, hairdressers, locksmiths, '4 boys at the *Chronicle* office', 'a dissenting Minister' and seventeen liberal Protestants.

Shortly after this impressive popular display, Waterford Catholics held a meeting with Thomas Wyse in the chair. They formed a Liberal Club for the city and another for the county.[40] Every collector of the Catholic Rent who had acted for six months and who paid sixpence per month would be, *ex officio*, a member of the City of Waterford Liberal Club, though Father Sheehan opposed this because it would endanger the unity and mutual confidence required in the club.[41]

The City of Waterford Liberal Club held regular meetings from July 1828 and it received the full backing of the *Waterford Chronicle* which gave much space to this and other clubs throughout Ireland. The City Club immediately took up local political issues such as the exclusion of Catholics from the City Corporation. This issue was raised even before the rules of the club were finally adopted. One of the two objects of the City Club was to restore to every citizen 'such political and municipal privileges as he may be entitled to of right'. Wyse had a great interest in being allowed to participate in the municipal government of Waterford and he finally achieved his ambition in June 1829. Great care was taken in drawing up the rules of the Liberal Club. Father Sheehan, worried about some features of the proposed rules, wrote for the rules of the Louth Club, and he offered himself as a confidential and loyal secretary.[42] In one address Wyse declared of the club:

We call ourselves *Liberal* — and are what we profess to be — We abhor exclusions, monopolies and oppressions of all kinds, but none more than those created or continued by religious ignorance and intolerance. We are foes to all Ascendancies, whether Catholic or Protestant, which set up the false interests of the few at the expense of the just interests of the many.

To Wyse liberalism involved the participation of all citizens in government and the right 'to worship God according to the dictates of his conscience'; he believed 'that the citizen who contributes to the burdens of a State has a *Right* to the advantages and honours of the State'.

The Liberal Club was to dine at Waterford 'at least once in every two months'; a Committee of Five was to be responsible for organisation and there was to be a Finance Committee responsible for the protection of the tenants 'against the persecution of their landlords'. Wyse saw the clubs as a means of 'fully enlightening the freeholder on the nature of his duties and rights' and in his speech at the first dinner of the County and City of Waterford Liberal Club, attended by Sheil, Wyse foresaw the parish clubs as being '... composed of the Clergy, the resident gentry, and a certain number of the respectable farmers. I say especially the respectable farmers [*cheers*] — they are the bones and sinews of our country and from them and their political education (I mean in proper hands) everything may be justly expected'.[43] At the beginning of August the County of Waterford Liberal Club held its first meeting: the members elected Sir Richard Musgrave as president for six months and Thomas Wyse secretary for six months; Alexander Sherlock was treasurer. The officers were chosen half-yearly as was customary in the Liberal Clubs in Ireland.

Wyse was empowered at this meeting to consult with the principal residents of each parish 'on the feasibility of establishing parochial clubs'. In September he concentrated on the development of the parish associations. He sent a circular to each parish and he received an encouraging response.[44] His contact in Portlaw, J. P. Smith, reported that he had been 'peculiarly successful' in setting up a parish club (right beside the Beresford home of Curraghmore) even though the clergy were not united in support of the Portlaw Liberal Club; one Portlaw priest 'deprecated the introduction of newspapers' into the parish and he recommended his parishioners not to read them. Smith, believing in the educative value of the press, had been circulating two papers throughout the parish three times a week and he told Wyse that there were two regular reading societies in the parish. Smith did not expect any of the local gentry to join the new club but he could afford to be selective in choosing new members as the parish was prosperous due to the employment given in 'Malcomson's extensive factory'. He was prepared to admit members 'known to possess character for regular habits, probity and patriotism'. Smith had also established the New Catholic Rent upon 'a permanent basis' in the parish.[45] Portlaw had rebelled agianst the Beresfords in 1826 upon lay initiative — the priest at first refused the use of the chapel, which was on the Beresford estate, until the bishop ordered it to be opened to the deputation from Stuart's committee (*132*, I, 272-3).

Smith wrote to Wyse to report that over sixty people had joined the club (he sent their names) and that more were about to join; he had acted 'with great circumspection in selecting members — otherwise I might easily double the number'. *Weekly Chronicles* and *Weekly Registers* were to be sent to certain members for circulation and it is clear that these newspapers were an important attraction for parish club members.[46] Wyse notes that the parish clubs were 'formed of the gentry, the clergymen, the reading farmers (for reading was a necessary condition for admission)'; their subscription 'was trifling, sufficient to pay for a weekly paper'. The parish club members elected their own officers, president, secretary, treasurer, and were committed to the control and guidance of the secretary of the County Club (*132*, I, 343-4). Portlaw parish club was a source of satisfaction to Wyse; when he addressed the Friends of Civil and Religious Liberty in Queen's Co. on the subject of county and parochial clubs he gave a prominent place to the Portlaw Liberal Club. Other parish clubs were formed at Ballymacart, near Dungarvan, at Ardmore, at Grange, and in the parish of Aglish.[47]

The development of the City Liberal Club was closely associated with the Catholic Rent collection. The Waterford Catholic Rent Committee appointed eight members from four parishes to the Liberal Club Committee of Inquiry.[48] These Rent collectors were admitted as honorary members of the Committee of Inquiry and, according to Wyse, they were 'employed most efficiently, from their local knowledge, in procuring all materials which might be necessary for the information and guidance of the Committee of Management' (*132*, I, 344). The Committee of Inquiry and the Committee of Management were the two main standing committees of the City of Waterford Liberal Club. The County of Waterford Liberal Club had only one committee, that for management, in charge of the business of the club. In the City Liberal Club, the Committee of Inquiry examined the walks into which the city was divided and prepared schedules for this purpose. This committee also kept a Book of Queries in which various problems were noted.[49] Most of the problems in the surviving Book of Queries relate to establishing the right to become a freeman of the city. The freemen were important in the city electorate and the committee operated a permanent constituency service. Some of the problems were referred to the Committee of Management which established sub-committees to seek elucidation of the tricky legal queries relating to the franchise. From schedules of the various walks the Committee of Management drew up a comprehensive list of the freemen of the city, distinguishing those actually free from the claimants; the claimants in turn were subdivided into claimants by birth, marriage or apprenticeship.[50] A general meeting of the club was convened every month to receive the joint report of both committees and to take any necessary action; these reports were then transmitted to the Catholic Association.

Cork participated in this novel democratic revolution on a scale comparable with Waterford. A very extensive outline of 'what a Liberal Club would do' appeared on 20 August in the *Cork Mercantile Chronicle*: this was essentially Wyse's scheme for a national re-organisation of the Catholic movement. In August, when he visited the Cork activists,

O'Connell proposed the establishment of the County and City of Cork Liberal Club at a meeting 'in the large room of the Chamber of Commerce'.[51] This meeting was chaired by William Thompson, the celebrated political economist from Rosscarbery, many of whose economic theories anticipated Marx.

O'Connell explained the objects of the club which would be similar to those in Clare, Louth, Limerick and Waterford; it would 'attend strictly to the state of representation . . .' and present petitions, obtain the freedom of corporations and open boroughs, such as Youghal, Kinsale and Bandon; it would collect the Catholic Rent and highlight illegal vestries, unjust Grand Jury assessments and oppressive tithes. The new club would be the local reflection of the Catholic Association and it would be significantly wider in political concern and geographic scope than the 1827 Association which was confined to the city parishes. Over 100 enrolled, at this initial meeting in the Chamber of Commerce, for the new club, and a large committee was appointed to make the preliminary arrangements: Thompson was chairman, having received O'Connell's support; James J. Hayes, a druggist, of Grand Parade, was secretary; and Thomas Lyons the woollen manufacturer was treasurer. In late August the rules and regulations of the Cork Club were published when the preliminary organisational work had been done.[52]

Thomas Lyons chaired the meeting of the new club at their room, No. 21 Tuckey Street where a report of the committee on organisation was read on 24 August. The resolutions at this meeting stressed legal and constitutional means of redress and gave a welcome to other Liberal Clubs being established in Bandon, Fermoy, Macroom and other quarters. The business of the club was to be performed by four committees of sixteen members each; there were committees on civil rights and grievances, religious rights and grievances, rent and finance, and parochial organisation. County members were entitled to speak and vote at all meetings of the committees. O'Connell was acclaimed as the founder of the club but Wyse was coupled with O'Connell in the resolution proposed by Thomas Sheehan, a timber merchant:

> The whilst we pay the just tribute of our esteem and gratitude to the distinguished Founder of this Club we cannot pass unnoticed the merits of our statesmanlike, eloquent, and energetic countryman, Thomas Wyse, Esq., at whose call the Liberal Clubs of Ireland have started into existence, and by whose spirit, we trust, they will long continue to be animated.[53]

The rules and regulations of the Cork Liberal Club, like most of the other Liberal clubs, were quite detailed as to the mode of operation in respect of the membership, the officers, committees, meetings and as to future changes in the rules.[54] Every member was to pay five shillings *per annum* on admission and also a monthly subscription of sixpence. A rota was made out for the regular meetings of each of the committees. However, as great importance was attached to parish organisation, the parochial committee could meet 'as often as they deem fit'; in addition, the rules stated that the committees, 'if expedient', were to be composed of two members from each of six parishes. Four from the parishes were to be 'constituted parochial sub-committees for parochial purposes, getting petitions signed, etc. . . .' The Club, as a whole, met on the fourth Monday of each month when each committee was to report.

The social composition of the leadership in Cork Catholic and Liberal politics is quite typical of the urban support evoked by O'Connell. Well-to-do merchants, traders, manufacturers, and shopkeepers were joined by professional men in forming the local nucleus in the city. Represented were barristers, attorneys, apothecaries, general merchants, clothiers, grocers, brewers, boot and shoe makers, butter, timber, and wine merchants. There were a few liberal Protestants such as Richard Dowden, a mineral water manufacturer, and William Thompson. Most significantly, the close involvement of the Chamber of Commerce is apparent in O'Connellite politics: it was in the Chamber that these men first started to organise electorally. When in the autumn of 1828 the Liberal Club had difficulty in procuring suitable rooms, it was decided to use the public rooms of the Chamber of Commerce as 'more than half of the City Members of the Liberal Club are also subscribers to the public room of the Chamber of Commerce, and many of them are also Shareholders of that establishment'.[55] The ethos of the club, while obviously middle class and commercial, was liberal, reformist, constitutional and democratic. It developed as an important centre for political information. Members received London and Dublin newspapers at the club room which was used by 'nearly 500 people'; when the papers failed to arrive it was 'exceedingly unpleasant as it creates considerable discontent and dissatisfaction among our Members who now amount to nearly Five Hundred'.[56]

To induce the formation of parochial clubs a circular letter was sent by James Hayes to all potential local activists in the city and county: this letter is important as it reveals the organisation and mode of operation envisaged in the parishes.[57] Recipients were required to become members of the club and to establish

in your Parish a Parochial Club, on the following principles:
1. The Parochial Club to be composed, as much as possible, of the principal Gentry, Clergy, Churchwardens, and such of the intelligent inhabitants as are able and willing to take part in such proceedings in their parish — These to form the first members — others to be added afterwards by nomination or ballot.

2. The Club, when so formed, to hold Meetings (if possible) once a fortnight; but at all events once a month in such place and time as they may judge expedient.

3. These Clubs and Meetings to have for object keeping every man in constant readiness for further Elections, collecting the Catholic Rent, maintaining the Registers, enquiring into and giving information of any oppression or persecution of Freeholders, or others, and promoting good order, perfect subordination to the laws, political knowledge, and liberal feeling, as much as possible in their parish.

4. A Report of the particulars mentioned in the 3rd article addressed to the Secretary of the County and City of Cork Liberal Club, will be expected once in every three months by the Club and oftener if necessary.

5. To every parochial Club of which 5 members became members of the County and City of Cork Club a Dublin Weekly Newspaper will be sent free of expense.

The response to this circular may be gauged from the surviving correspondence and from press reports.[58] Some areas like Mallow 'dreaded a reaction, or the getting up of Counter Orange or Brunswick Clubs . . .'[59] Some professional men backed off too close an identification with party politics whilst others pleaded time to consider the rules of the club. Some liberal Protestants, such as the Presbyterian minister of Bandon, William Hunter, thought the club's identification with the Catholic Rent made it sectarian.[60]

In most areas, however, the reaction was favourable. A contact in Bandon responded quickly that he had 'no doubt but we shall be enabled to enrol over two hundred members in the course of a few days'.[61] Clubs were established in Rathcormac, Macroom, Fermoy, Bandon, Kanturk and Duhallow. Favourable replies to Hayes' circular were received from Youghal where the contact was John Markham who had been secretary of the Catholic Rent collection since 1824; Dunmanway and Enniskeen and other places. Father Walsh, the curate, who wrote to Hayes from the Enniskeen area, declared that the circular was received 'with a degree of enthusiasm far above anything that I have ever witnessed upon any previous occasion of patriotic excitement . . . we instantly agreed to establish a Parochial Club here which we have accordingly done, and, let me add, which at this moment is well doing its duty . . .'[62]

Thus the Cork Liberal Club began to have direct connections with the local parochial activists who had collected the Catholic Rent since 1824. By November 1828 it had over five hundred members and more advanced plans were made for the collection of the Catholic Rent and for the registration of freeholders. In late November, over three hundred members attended the monthly meeting of the club at which detailed reports were made.[63] Wyse's vision had been realised to an extent which had seemed impossible only a few months before the Clare election.

As time elapsed after Clare the government was faced in Ireland with the dangers of a civil war between increasingly well organised extremist Catholic and Protestant organisations. It was also faced with the possibibity of a mass revolt and campaign of civil disobedience from the Catholic population. The government was also well aware that the Association was organising to control the county representation through the Liberal Clubs. The longer the government delayed the worse the situation became in Ireland.

The language and policy of the Catholic Association had become more extreme after Clare. From the Clare election the weekly Rent returns, ranging from £2,000 to £3,000, gave an accurate barometer of the popular support for the militancy of the Association. It also gave enormous confidence to the leaders in Dublin. Sheil laced his speeches with military metaphors: he talked of 'the excellence of military array', how the Catholic people were united in 'one vast confederacy' and declared that 'the masses had been reduced to an almost military uniformity of movement' (*71*, II, 24-7). And indeed the people had, in certain areas, begun to assemble themselves in 'military' formations. During the large provincial meeting in August, Wyse heard people on the streets of Clonmel ask about O'Connell: '*When will he call us out?*' This was frequently answered with 'the finger on the mouth', a significant smile and wink from the bystanders (*132*, I, 413). O'Connell's language was also radical and extreme — as certain Protestants indicated the necessity for a second 1798 O'Connell countered: 'Oh! would to God our excellent Viceroy Lord Anglesey would but only give me a commission, and *if* those men of blood should attempt to attack the property and persons of His Majesty's loyal subjects, with a hundred thousand of my brave Tipperary boys, I would soon drive them into the sea before me' (*132*, I, 415). The 'brave Tipperary boys' increasingly looked as if they would not await Anglesey's commission, or O'Connell's either, before attacking their enemies. Fears of an agrarian revolt worse than the early 1820s revived as the people themselves mobilised in September in the southern counties, especially in Tipperary. O'Connell was the only figure who could hope to control the explosive situation. Anglesey admitted to Wellington on 24 September that there was 'a revolutionary spirit abroad' and he also told Sheil that the outbreak of rebellion would inevitably delay Emancipation (*71*, II, 24). Sheil and

O'Connell undertook to halt the large processions through a 'general pacification' plan.

Humphrey O'Sullivan gives an account of his own rôle, as church-warden, in establishing peace amongst the crowds dressed in green with green flags, and between different factions in sashes of various colours. He notes on 28 September: 'It is on O'Connell's advice this renewal of friendship and this peace is being made among the children of the Gael but the English do not like it; for they think it easier for them to beat people at variance than people in friendship; and this is true.' O'Sullivan feared that the 'green flags with the image of O'Connell' would 'arouse the Williamite faction, the Orangemen' against the Catholics. On 4 October he records:

> I have been extremely busy for the past week persuading O'Connell's followers that they ought not to walk in green clothes, nor with O'Connell's image and music. The Catholics of Callan promised that they would not [so] walk any more. The Protestants pretend that they are very much afraid, but it would delight their hearts to be spilling the Catholics' blood.

He noted that a police barracks had been burned down near Nenagh, and that a 'Liberator' had been committed to Clonmel jail; this was 'bad work' if the Catholics 'do not call a halt in time' (75, XXXI, 19-31).

Both the government and O'Connell *had* called a halt. On 26 September the Association passed a series of resolutions calling for a cessation of the meetings and the disturbances which threatened to get out of control in Tipperary. On 30 September O'Connell issued a major 'Address to the Honest and Worthy People of the County Tipperary' from Derrynane, after the Catholic Association had requested him to address them:

> You have obeyed my advice; you have made PEACE amongst your-selves; you have prevented the recurrence of Whiteboy Crimes and Nocturnal Outrages . . . In making Peace, you have held large Meet-ings. My opinion is, that you were right at first in holding such Meet-ings, because you held them, as I advised, in perfect obedience to the Law . . . You were so kind as to call yourselves my Police . . . But the time is come to discontinue these public Meetings.

The Address praised Anglesey, Sir Anthony Hart, the Lord Chancellor, and Leveson-Gower, 'the friendly part of the government, and it appealed to the people to allow the Catholic Association 'to conduct the great CATHOLIC CAUSE to final success'. O'Connell outlined his plan for 'general pacification' which would involve each one hundred and twenty people electing a 'pacificator' and the appointment of two assis-tant 'regulators' to keep the peace, suppress illegal societies, collect the Rent and generally support the Association. He concluded with his vision:

> We will plant in our Native Land the Constitutional Tree of Liberty. That noble tree will prosper and flourish in our Green and Fertile Country. It will extend its protecting branches all over this lovely island. Beneath its sweet and sacred shade, the universal People of Ireland, Catholics and Protestants, and Presbyterians, and Dissenters of every Class, will sit in peace and unison, and tranquillity. Commerce and Trade will flourish; Industry will be rewarded; and the People, contented and happy, will see Old Ireland what she ought to be,
>
> Great, Glorious and FREE.
First flower of the Earth, first gem of the Sea.

Anglesey's proclamation forbidding meetings was published on 1 October. The cabinet had decided on this on 26 September. Ellenborough noted that day: 'it is a fearful step and may precipitate the crisis'. Conscious of Ballybay, he observed that it was only 'by a lucky accident' that collision had been prevented between Catholics and Protestants (*62*, I, 226-30). Reinforcements were summoned from Liverpool and Bristol. Lawless was arrested on 10 October; he was held for a short time, released and never brought to trial. The combination of government and O'Connell was sufficient to control what was a most threatening situation. On 28 October Humphrey O'Sullivan noticed four cannons going through Callan and he thanked God southern Ireland was 'never as peaceful as it is now: accordingly there is no need for the great guns against the Southern Children of the Gael. But the Protestants of Ulster and of England, that is, the Brunswickers are mad, just like bloodhounds, to devour the Catholics' (*75*, XXXI, 45).

Within the Catholic Association a more radical wing had emerged: Wyse speaks of an 'internal revolution' as many were beginning to consider 'even Catholic Emancipation but a very partial remedy for the political and moral evils of Ireland':

> They laughed at any thing less than self-government in its amplest sense; — separation, and republicanism were the two head articles of their political creed. Such a party . . . [had] been rapidly increasing in Ireland; far more formidable than the French party which haunted the imagination of Mr Grattan . . . it based its projects, not on the fanciful theories of the French revolutionists, but on the practical model which it saw in America . . .

Wyse found the 'American' influence 'in the frankness and fervour of familiar conversation' in the large commercial towns, amongst the younger members of the Bar and even in the Catholic Church. The

Established Church, the aristocracy, the unreformed parliament and the land question were attacked and 'as often as an opportunity admitted, under the question of the repeal of the Union, they went so far, as to attack the connexion with England itself'. Wyse discerned that this 'violent party' would ultimately triumph over the moderates, as delay had created 'a spirit of *republicanism*'. O'Connell was obliged 'to moderate and to allay' frequently the proposals of this group within the Association (*132*, I, 315-23).

American support had become significant for the Catholic struggle. American newspapers endorsed Catholic Emancipation and fully covered the issue. The pro-Andrew Jackson press, responding to Irish-American allegiance to the Democratic Party, vigorously advocated the removal of the disabilities of Irish Catholics in the name of basic American principles of civil and religious liberty. There was also a widespread development of chapters of the Friends of Ireland – there were twenty-four in the United States and the New York branch had more than 1,000 members (*88*, 362-70). American influence helped to shape the views of the more radical members of the Catholic Association; this was more important than the dollars sent to Ireland from the United States to help the struggle.

On 6 November the question of 'exclusive dealing' was raised in the Association: it was proposed to avoid all intercourse between Catholics and Orangemen. It was proposed by the Catholic solicitor William Forde. Wellington had feared such a development and had pointed out the dangers to the king in a letter on 14 October asking what if Catholics refused to pay rents and tithes:

> The clergy and the landlords might have recourse to the law. But how is the law to be enforced? How can they distrain for rent or tithes millions of tenants? . . . there is no remedy for this state of things excepting by means of a consideration of the whole state of Ireland. On no other ground will Parliament adopt what is necessary to be done (*128*, V, 133-6).

Wellington and Peel realised that a national combination to resist payment of rent, tithes and other charges would prove much more formidable than isolated murders or outrages; already there were local signs of such combinations (*128*, V, 176-7). Wellington frankly told the king on 16 November in a long memorandum on Ireland: 'Nobody can answer for the consequences of delay.' Reluctantly the king allowed Wellington to consult with the bishops of the Church of England about Emancipation (*128*, V, 252-68).

O'Connell managed to get Forde's proposal referred to a Committee of the Association which would investigate and report on the operation of 'exclusive dealing', especially as Orangemen operated it in relation to their servants. O'Connell reported on behalf of this committee on 13 November saying that it was intended to advertise for persons who had been persecuted to come forward. About this time Prince Pückler Muskau visited the Catholic Association, 'the present Irish Parliament':

> The Room is not very large, and as dirty as the English House of Commons. Here too every man keeps his hat on, except while he is speaking; here too are good and bad orators; but certainly less dignified manners than there. The heat was suffocating, and I had to sit out five hours; but the debate was so interesting that I scarcely remarked the annoyances. O'Connell was undoubtedly the best speaker. Although idolized by the greater number, he was severely attacked by several, and defended himself with equal address and moderation . . . It was easy to perceive that much intrigue and several firmly united parties, whose minds were made up before hand, were to be found here, as in other bodies of the like kind . . .

Pückler Muskau noted that Forde spoke well 'with great dignity of manner'.

In December a major debate took place in the Association on the extent of anti-Catholic persecution: threats of organised runs on banks were made, particularly on the Protestant-controlled Bank of Ireland. A limited run on local banks in Wexford and the south-east had already occurred. O'Connell had this policy of social warfare defeated in the Association (*132*, I, 423-35). A general system of exclusive dealing would have played havoc in Ireland and would have been difficult for O'Connell to control once commenced.

Meanwhile the relationship between Wellington and Anglesey continued to deteriorate: Anglesey was most unhappy about implementing a repressive policy without obvious concrete steps towards Emancipation. Wellington was of course asking the right questions but in secret. He wrote to Peel on 12 September 1828:

> The questions are these: Are we not in a new position in respect to Irish affairs? Can we any longer delay to do something? Must not that *something* be either restraints in Ireland unknown in the ordinary practice of the Constitution, or concession in some form or other? Can we hope to prevail upon Parliament to impose such restraints? Have we any resource but concession in the existing state of men's opinions in as well as out of doors? If we have I would willingly adopt it (*128*, V, 44-5).

Wellington was attempting to convince Peel to remain at his post and help carry concession. On 18 September Peel wrote to Wellington that he had informed Anglesey

> that previously to the meeting of Parliament the King's advisers will

take the present state of Ireland into consideration . . . What more can I say to him? Under any circumstances I should doubt the policy of communicating now to Lord Anglesey the resolution of the Government – supposing a resolution to have been formed (*128*, V, 61-3).

Peel was deeply unhappy with Anglesey and sought a special cabinet to discuss Anglesey's administration in Ireland on 23 September. On 28 September Wellington clearly told Anglesey that 'the first step' to a consideration by the government of Emancipation was to reconcile the king's mind to an arrangement. Yet Anglesey was reluctant to accept this approach and continued to incur the wrath of Wellington and Peel for his approach to law and order in Ireland.

Wellington believed that the Irish gentry had lost their influence. If he dissolved parliament the Association 'would return sixty out of the hundred members for Ireland' and these sixty 'in addition to the Radicals already in the House of Commons, would be too much for any government'. There was no use in a cry in favour of the Protestant religion: 'The difficulties of the times', he told the Earl of Westmorland, on the 16 October, 'have been accumulating for nearly forty years; and I must find a way out of them!!! It is not by means of Brunswick Clubs' (*128*, V, 142). He felt he was attempting to extricate Ireland from a civil war and he believed that his own personal authority with the Tory majority in the Lords, and indeed with the king, would be necessary to get a measure of Emancipation through into law.

During November Anglesey's friendly relations with Lord Cloncurry – they attended the Curragh races together – and his refusal to dismiss Steele and O'Gorman Mahon from the magistracy, led Wellington to exclaim to Bathurst on 24 November that Anglesey 'is gone mad. He is bit by a mad Papist, or instigated by the love of popularity'. To add to these indiscretions Anglesey's aide-de-camp, Baron Tuyll, and his son Lord William Paget, had attended Catholic Association meetings. For all the hints Anglesey was apparently unable to assess Wellington's intentions. Thomas Creevey dined with Anglesey and was convinced that the Viceroy was unaware of the Prime Minister's real opinions and intentions on the Catholic question (*85*, II, 189-90). Anglesey's removal was, in effect, agreed by the king and Wellington as soon as the opportunity arose or he offered to resign (*128*, V, 275-81).

The aged Archbishop Curtis wrote to Wellington on 4 December suggesting a possible method of government control over the appointment of Catholic bishops as a means out of the impasse. Curtis suggested that after the usual mode of election of a bishop, but before he entered his diocese, the new bishop should be presented to a government commissioner or commission where he could be vetted and investigated: if there were any specific charges which he could not 'clear up to the satisfaction of the commission or of government' he then could not take possession of the diocese. Curtis said this would give a 'real veto' to the government and it was exactly what had been done in his own case in 1819 when Wellington had taken part in his appointment. Curtis said the pope and the bishops would cheerfully acquiesce in this suggested arrangement (*128*, V, 308-9).

On 11 December Wellington replied to Curtis stating that he was sincerely anxious to witness a settlement of the Catholic question: 'I confess that I see no prospect of such a settlement . . . If we could bury it in oblivion for a short time, and employ that time diligently in the consideration of its difficulties on all sides (for they are very great), I should not despair of seeing a satisfactory remedy.' Wellington's letter to Curtis was apparently opened en route to Armagh and became public knowledge: on 23 December it was published in the *Dublin Evening Post*. Anglesey, after seeing Wellington's letter which Curtis sent to him, wrote to Curtis saying that he had now learnt of Wellington's intentions for the first time. He pointed out the difficulties of the Duke's situation but disagreed with Wellington that the question could be buried in oblivion for a short time: 'Let the Catholic trust to the justice of his cause, to the growing liberality of mankind' and he advised only the use of constitutional means to forward the question (*1*, 214-15). He allowed his own letter to be published in the *Dublin Evening Post*. On 24 December the cabinet decided to recall Anglesey, which news was softened by the hint of hope in the Wellington letter of 11 December. Croker noted on 26 December that Wellington's letter contained the same position as he had outlined in parliament in June but that it was 'on the whole' favourable to the Catholic cause 'because it admits the *principle*': the difficulties alluded to were only of a temporary nature (*56*, I, 434).

Ireland faced the new year, 1829, apparently on the brink either of Catholic Emancipation and a new political era or of civil war and repression on a scale comparable to 1798. Time for decisions was clearly short, for parliament was due to meet on 5 February: what would be in the King's Speech?

7

1829: 'O'Connell's Victory'

'If everything that is written about Eire be true,
It (takes) long to bring the demand to a head:
Emancipation to come under seal,
Leave for the Gael to be as high as the Gall.

Guns and firing and bonfires
Shall we have tomorrow, and it is time,
Since O'Connell has gained victory over the enemy
Blossoms shall ripen and there shall be fruit on the trees.'

Anthony Raftery, 'O'Connell's Victory',
translated by Douglas Hyde (*52*, 267-71).

The new year began with the Catholic question quite unanswered: it was clear that the margin of time was slim before the government must respond. Parliament was summoned to meet on 5 February, and O'Connell had announced his intention of going to London to take his seat on the first day of the new session. Whatever was going to be done – concession or repression – would have to be indicated in the King's Speech.

In the search for a settlement of the Catholic question the members of Wellington's government faced the declared opposition of the king, the House of Lords and the Established Church. Their hopes could be completely dashed if the king were to make a public formal declaration of his resolve to oppose Emancipation. Wellington, according to Peel, began 'to despair of success' (*83*, I, 278-9). His objective was to adopt a form of Catholic relief which would not destroy Tory unity. However, his enforced secrecy and delay between July 1828 and January 1829 had given time for a widespread anti-Catholic movement to develop and he had also allowed the Catholic Association to strengthen its democratic grip on the vulnerable county constituencies.

As he surveyed his political options, the Prime Minister realised that the same considerations were uppermost now in January that had been foremost in July 1828. The neutrality which had been practised by successive cabinets since 1812 must be abandoned: the choice lay between unalterable resistance to Catholic claims accompanied by a prolonged Irish crisis or conceding on the best terms possible for the Protestant interest. In the parliamentary situation an ultra government could not survive nor even find sufficient able men to hold office. A 'Protestant' government would find it necessary to raise the franchise in Ireland to forestall the impending electoral revolution, and it was clear this would fail in the Commons if unaccompanied by concession. If parliament was dissolved on a 'no popery' issue no overwhelming Protestant strength in a new Commons could be predicted and the Irish O'Connellite influx, under the Catholic Association's pledges, would more than offset any gains in England. Worse still, they might remain in 'the popish Parliament', challenging the Union itself. Hence the Wellingtonian solution: a cabinet led by the great war hero with the Protestant interest uppermost in view should concede with the necessary securities. If the Whigs were allowed in to settle the question they might not regulate the franchise. The extra-parliamentary power of the Irish Catholics would be tamed and the political power Catholics would gain would be so hedged around as to be the least hazardous to the Protestant interest.

Meanwhile in Ireland liberal Protestants were making public gestures to strengthen the Catholic cause. On 12 January Wellington coldly acknowledged an Emancipationist address from Irish Protestants sent by the Duke of Leinster, in his celebrated 'tin case' letter: 'I have had the honour of receiving this morning', wrote the Duke, 'your Grace's letter of 7th inst., and a tin case containing the declaration of certain Protestants in Ireland respecting what is called Roman Catholic Emancipation . . .' This brusque note further alienated liberal Protestants from Wellington.

On 19 January Anglesey departed from Dublin amidst a public display of mourning by an O'Connellite crowd. Lord Ellenborough, the pro-Catholic Privy Seal in Wellington's government, has left a most valuable political diary which reveals a great deal about the crisis; he believed Anglesey's answer to Curtis justified his removal in December. On 9 January the cabinet decided on his peremptory recall from Dublin. Anglesey was escorted to Kingstown by a large crowd bearing banners of white silk bound with mourning black. It was a sentimental farewell to a land which had wrecked the careers of more able British politicians than Anglesey. Ultras took comfort in his departure, feeling that it indicated Wellington's intention to stand firm. The crowd, led by O'Connell, was dismissed even by the pro-Catholic Ellenborough as 'a rabble' which mercifully had not rioted (*62*, I, 287, 292, 310).

Next day a great meeting of the Friends of Civil and Religious Liberty was held at the Rotunda, Dublin, under the chairmanship of the Duke of Leinster. Lady Morgan felt that this gathering of Irish liberal Protestants recalled 'the public spirit of 1782'. Among those present were Lords Cloncurry, Milltown, Forbes, Glengall, Clanmorris, Bective, Killeen, Riversdale, Rossmore, and Dunally. It was resolved to petition the king in favour of Emancipation and that the Duke of Leinster would present the petition accompanied by a large number of noblemen and MPs.[1] Thomas Wyse and the 'élite of the élite', in Lady Morgan's phrase, who attended the meeting dined with the Morgans (*47*, II, 275-6).

At a Catholic meeting in St Patrick's chapel, Donegall Street, Belfast, on 27 January presided over by William Crolly, Catholic Bishop of Down and Connor, the Rev. Henry Montgomery, champion of the liberal Presbyterians, appeared and endorsed the Catholic cause. In October 1828 Montgomery and his minority of supporters in the Presbyterian communion had adopted a 'Remonstrance' which was to lead shortly to their final separation from the Synod of Ulster and the establishment of a Remonstrant Synod. The issue that brought Presbyterian divisions to a head was the question of subscribing to the Westminster Confession of Faith. The liberal Montgomery opposed subscription, finding among other objections the Confession's description of the pope as anti-Christ highly repugnant. Henry Cooke demanded that all Presbyterian ministers subscribe to his definition of orthodoxy. Montgomery's courageous stand with Belfast's minority of Catholics was noble given the uneasy degree of sectarian excitement which prevailed.

In early January Wellington tried to get the Archbishop of Canterbury and the Bishops of London and Durham to consent to a settlement of the Catholic question. If these bishops consented he might be able to outflank the king's resistance by pointing to the Church's readiness to concede. He failed. Ellenborough thought that the bishops were scared off by the abuse they had suffered in 1828 because of their obvious vacillation on the Test and Corporation Acts. If the government got as far as concession in the King's Speech he believed the bishops would again support the government's resolve (*62*, I, 297, 301). Getting the king to that point had so far eluded the Prime Minister. As yet he had not managed very adroitly.

The king was in poor health and was proving most difficult. On 12 January Charles Greville recorded his views on George IV: 'a more contemptible, cowardly, selfish, unfeeling dog does not exist than this king, on whom such flattery is constantly lavished'. Greville noted the king's strong anti-Catholic feelings. 'He says that "his father would have laid his head on the block rather than yield, and that he is equally ready to lay his head there in the same cause."'

The government's position was worse than ever. Robert Peel now made one of the major critical decisions in his political career. Perhaps he relished the role of the 'daring pilot in extremity' (*83*, I, 366). On 12 January, immediately after the discussions with the bishops, he wrote to Wellington that if his resignation was 'an insuperable obstacle' to Emancipation he would be prepared to stay in office (*83*, I, 283). With this letter he sent a long memorandum of his views on the Catholic question which might be laid before the king. The Duke delivered Peel's memorandum to George IV on 14 January. Wellington was now able to unite his cabinet behind a request to the king that the government be permitted to take the Catholic question into consideration.

On 15 January the king gave separate interviews to the six cabinet ministers who had been anti-Catholic — Wellington, Lyndhurst, Bathurst, Peel, Goulburn and Herries — and each confronted him with what amounted to a unanimous demand. The king consented to the cabinet considering the Catholic question but he pointed out he was still not pledged to accept any advice from the government on the question. The final royal engagement lay ahead. Peel's role was central and decisive: George himself had demanded of Peel why, if he supported the measure, would he not make the same sacrifice of consistency which he asked of the king and remain in office to carry out the policy he advised. The cabinet considered the Catholic question on 17 January: to a pro-Catholic, like Ellenborough, it was 'like a dream' to have the government take up the question during the lifetime of George IV (*62*, I, 304-5).

The cabinet had just eighteen days to prepare the presentation of the question to parliament in the King's Speech. Peel's work over the previous months now paid off and upon him rested the main responsibility for the principles and the details of the various measures. In over a week of intensive preparation between 21 and 26 January, during which there were daily meetings, the basic decisions were made. It was decided that Roman Catholics should have civil equality with the exception of certain offices, that the Irish forty-shilling freeholders should be disenfranchised and the Catholic Association suppressed. Ellenborough thought that 'the great difficulty will be the 40s freeholders'. Many of the Whigs were against the measure: if the opponents of Emancipation joined the Whigs in endeavouring to defeat the whole bill by attacking the government on the forty-shilling measure they might succeed. Peel, on 21 January, stated to the cabinet that he believed that Catholic influence would not be much diminished by the measure 'that the only thing done would be the placing a landlord-ridden man in the place of the priest-ridden tenant' (*62*, I, 300-8).

The mode of relief was largely decided by the form in which the disabilities were imposed on Catholics: admission to parliament and to high civil offices was barred by the oath which, though it contained no declaration of the sovereign's spiritual supremacy, had continued to be called the Oath of Supremacy. The oath was objectionable to Catholics because it contained a condemnation of the doctrine of transubstantiation, the invocation of saints and the sacrifice of the mass. The initial decision was what reference to make to the question in the King's Speech. Peel correctly spoke 'of the thunderclap of the announcement': the cabinet was, as Ellenborough realised 'treading on very dangerous ground'. Few knew of the government's intentions and there could well be 'a violent reaction' which would make 'it almost impossible to carry the measure'. Ellenborough obviously hoped the political realities would impinge not only on the king but also on the Tory party. He thought Peel should speak boldly and early and 'put the Protestants down by a single speech' (*62*, I, 309-13).

The king was obviously reluctant on 28 January when he heard the cabinet's plans. When Wellington said that Catholics were to be excluded from judicial office connected with the Church, the king said, 'What, do you mean a Catholic to hold any judicial office? To be a Judge of the King's Bench?' Again, when the Duke mentioned parliamentary seats, he said: 'Damn it ... you mean to let them into Parliament?' On 2 February the complete version was read at a council meeting before the king. After lamenting the existence of the Catholic Association, 'dangerous to the public peace, and inconsistent with the spirit of the Constitution' and declaring that it was to be suppressed, it read:

> when this essential object shall have been accomplished, you should take into your deliberate consideration the whole condition of Ireland; and that you should review the laws which impose civil disabilities on His Majesty's Roman Catholic subjects. You will consider whether the removal of those disabilities can be effected consistently with the full and permanent security of our establishments in Church and State, with the maintenance of the Reformed Religion established by law and of the rights and privileges of the Bishops and of the Clergy of this realm, and of the Churches committed to their charge.
>
> These are institutions which must ever be held sacred in this Protestant kingdom and which it is the duty and the determination of His Majesty to preserve inviolate.[2]

The king agreed to the words proposed but he attempted to drop the phrase about 'reviewing the laws which impose civil disabilities on His Majesty's Roman Catholic subjects':

> The king said: 'The whole condition of Ireland includes the Catholic question, and I see no reason why that part of the paragraph should not be omitted'. The Duke said: 'Your Majesty has Roman Catholic subjects in other parts of your dominions besides Ireland'. The King acquiesced, and at the end of the speech he expressed himself quite satisfied with it (*62*, I, 332).

The easiest part of the programme was the suppression of the Catholic Association: it was decided to frame a relatively simple bill giving power to the Lord Lieutenant to suppress any association or meeting which he thought dangerous to the public peace or incompatible with the proper administration of the law. It was an arbitrary power to bestow on the Lord Lieutenant and it was therefore proposed to limit the Act to one year. The Disfranchisement Bill was more difficult: Leslie Foster, who knew from his bitter Louth experience the power of the forty-shilling voters, was secretly brought in to cabinet 'by the Park into the Foreign Office, and thence into the Cabinet-Room', to give advice. The irony of the situation struck Ellenborough: 'Leslie Foster consulting with the cabinet how Catholic Emancipation may best be brought about!' (62, I, 321).

Peel was anxious for the cabinet to be guided by Irish Tory Protestants and Leslie Foster, Vesey Fitzgerald and George Dawson formed a small committee to consider the issues. The purpose here was clear: limit the democratic Catholic influence. After much discussion it was finally agreed to fix the new qualification at £10 in the counties subject to previous investigation by an assistant barrister at registry sessions. Cities and towns, despite the great abuses in the franchise, were left alone. Ellenborough noted on 17 February: 'we are afraid to touch Corporate rights . . . yet the Corporation of Dublin lately elected as members the President, Vice-President, Treasurers, and all the officers of all the Brunswick Clubs in Ireland – about 1,200 persons' (62, I, 351).

The central measure was the proposed Catholic Relief Bill. Peel proposed a measure of full civil equality, with a new civil oath. Catholics were to be ineligible for offices in the Established Church, the universities, the offices of Lord Chancellor in England and Ireland, and Lord Lieutenant of Ireland. The Duke was anxious to control the Catholic clergy by state payment and by a system of clerical licensing. The problem of how a fundamentally Protestant State was to relate to the Roman Catholic Church was complex. There could be no formal concordat in view of the statutory legislation prohibiting intercourse with Rome and of the special relationship between the king and the Established Church. After much debate in cabinet both state payment and registration were abandoned because of the degree of formal recognition for the Catholic Church involved as well as the political or technical problems encountered. Ellenborough feared that 'we may have run the securities too close, and that there may not be enough to satisfy the King and the Protestants' (62, I, 322).

Rumours soon spread that some major government initiative was imminent. The *Dublin Evening Mail* on 2 February carried the sensational news that Emancipation was in the King's Speech linked to the suppression of the Association. On 3 February in the Catholic Association Sheil urged a dampening down of agitation in view of the disposition of the Ministry to meet Catholic claims. On 4 February O'Connell added a private note on a circular letter to Bishop Doyle: 'The reports about an Emancipation Bill are true. I believe the Clare contest has greatly contibuted to this result' (IV, 1513). The first open intimation of government policy was given to government supporters in the House of Commons at a dinner on 4 February, the eve of the new session. Until this many were entirely ignorant of the 'thunderclap'. On the same day Greville noted in his Journal:

> All the details that I have yet learnt confirm my opinion that the spirit in which the Duke and his colleagues approach this great measure is not that of calm and deliberate political reasoning, but a fearful sense of necessity and danger, to which they submit with extreme repugnance and with the most miserable feelings of pique and mortification at being compelled to adopt it.

When parliament opened the next day a shocked atmosphere prevailed. Peel spoke of having made 'the severest sacrifices of a public man', that of separating from friends on this issue:

> He pretended to no new lights on the subject of the Catholic claims. He retained the same opinion which he ever entertained in reference to that question. He saw as clearly as ever the dangers . . . but he had no hesitation in saying, that the pressure of present evils was so great and overwhelming, that he was willing to encounter the risk of those contingent dangers . . .

Peel argued that any alternative seemed better than the 'present evils': the cabinet divisions since 1804, the divisions in the Irish government, the divisions between the Lords and the Commons on the question, the impossibility of an anti-Catholic government and the fact that cabinet neutrality was out of the question.[3] He was applauded mainly by the opposition who had been quite ignorant of the government's intentions: the Whig members, wrote John Cam Hobhouse, 'could not help smiling to hear from his mouth arguments which he had so often opposed' (*15*, III, 302).

Leslie Foster argued for 'the necessity of making what he would call a Protestant settlement of this question': Ireland was 'nearly as possible ripe for civil war', and 'it was difficult to tell how soon the first flames of it might burst out'. In a 'Protestant settlement' Catholics should be required 'to shut their religion up within their own hearts — to leave the tenets of their church at the door of parliament, and shut the door upon it . . . all past experience showed that the discipline and doctrine of the Roman Catholic Church were incompatible with the principles of the British Constitution'. George Dawson hailed Emancipation as 'the happiest event, that could be found recorded in the page of Irish history for a long period. He looked upon it as the dawn of the prosperity of Ireland, after a long night of misery and wretchedness'.[4]

In the Lords, Winchelsea attacked Wellington and Peel for 'a gross violation of political rectitude and consistency'. Eldon declared '. . . if ever a Roman Catholic was permitted to form part of the legislature of this country, or to hold any of the great executive offices of the government, from that moment the sun of Great Britain would set [*a laugh*] . . .'[5] It was clear that Wellington and Peel would have to bear the full brunt of Protestant anger for their 'conversion': cartoonists were soon showing Wellington and Peel with rosaries in their hands, kissing the pope's toe. It remained to be seen how strong ultra and Brunswick pressure would be on king and country and how skilful the government would be in defusing the reaction.

On 6 February the *Dublin Evening Mail* railed against the apostasy of Wellington:

> We tell him there is a power in the Empire, a power even in Ireland superior to him and to his policy — one that will not brook his measures, nor submit to his encroachments — a power that will never prostrate itself before Popish domination. He may drive the Protestants into rebellion — he may banish them from their native land — and if he persevere he will; but we tell him that he can never coerce them into passive submission to a measure, which places their lives and their liberties, their institutions and their religion at the mercy of a faction who thirst for their blood.

Later the *Mail* realised that Peel and Wellington had 'betrayed' the Protestant cause since August 1828 in a 'counter-revolution of 1688': had it been 1700 rather than 1829 Peel, it declared, would have been impeached.[6] Eldon, more thoughtful than the *Mail*, felt on 7 February that 'the best course now for the Protestants in Parliament was to obtain as soon as possible a full statement of the intended measures of relief, etc., and then to obtain as long an interval of delay as possible for and during the discussion.' This would give time for the shock and dismay of the ultras to give way to concerted action to rouse the people behind the king (*20*, III, 566-7). One opponent of Emancipation can speak for all outraged anti-Catholics:

> And here is Robert Peel — the staunch Tory and anti-Catholic whose judgement was so unerring, whose integrity was so unquestionable, who knew popery well enough to declare that papists could give no security to a government who might be so liberal and silly as to trust them — Peel the chosen of the University of Oxford — whose very name was the rallying word for good true strong unaltering constitutional British feeling — he is convinced too that emancipation must be granted — the apostate (*46*, 44).

The key people for Wellington and Peel as regards reactions to their 'thunderclap' were the less rabid anti-Catholic Tories. Sufficient conversions would be required to pass the measures and to retain broad Tory support for the government. E. J. Littleton, a Whig opponent, described the dilemma of such Tories in his diary on 6 February:

> All the High Church Tories, Peers, Bishops, & MPs in a quandary – some facing about at the Duke's Command and without hesitation, though with evident shame – others pretending to be squeamish . . . only waiting for time to come round decently, others more bigoted & therefore more honest. We liberals are dying with Laughter at the just confusion & shame, to which . . . Selfishness & Intolerance are at length put (*80*, 165).

Significantly, on 11 February Creevey noted that it was 'such a new and important feature in this Tory Revolution to have no blackguarding or calling names of any one' (*85*, II, 195). Ellenborough felt in late February that 'some time must be allowed to enable our people to come round. It has been a great shock to them. Most, however, begin to confess the Government could not have acted otherwise' (*62*, I, 340).

The reactions amongst the Whigs were important also. According to Thomas Creevey, they were as sore as the Brunswickers on 5 February as the Duke's turnabout had scuttled their plans for opposition (*85*, II, 195). Ellenborough found the Whigs 'very sulky' as Emancipation carried by the Tories might destroy the Whig party 'by leaving it no bond of union' (*62*, I, 337).

'In all these proceedings there has been so little of reason, principle or consistency; so much of prejudice, subserviency, passion, and interest, that it is impossible not to feel a disgust to parties in general'; so Greville mused in his Journal on 6 February. Greville felt that the Duke would get credit for eventually making up his mind, for firmness, prudence and dexterity

> but to O'Connell and the Association, and those who have fought the battle on both sides of the water, the success of the measure is due . . . If the Irish Catholics had not brought matters to this pass by agitation and association, things might have remained as they were forever, and all these Tories would have voted on till the day of their death against them.

O'Connell left Dublin for London on 6 February. His absence from Dublin was to have an important bearing on the Irish response to the government's proposals. He had intended to assert his right to take his seat in the Commons until the moment it became clear that a new situation had developed after the King's Speech.[7]

Immediately a debate arose as to the policy of the Catholic Association. Only in January had the Association revamped the Catholic Rent collection system by introducing a system of Catholic Rent Inspectors for each county.[8] On 3 February in the Catholic Association O'Connell had a resolution, which was seconded by Sheil, passed to declare 'that when the Catholics of Ireland petitioned for unconditional Emancipation they meant what they said — namely Emancipation without any conditions'. At this meeting O'Connell had approved a motion breaking off all relations with the English Catholic Association until it clearly proclaimed 'unconditional Emancipation'. O'Connell favoured the Association remaining in existence until Emancipation should become law. He wrote to the Association advising this, from Shrewsbury, on his way to London on 8 February:

> My earnest advice (which I offer with the most respectful deference) is to pause before any one act is done on our part to recognise the guilt with which we are so unjustly charged. The Association should not, in my humble judgement, be dissolved by any act of ours before Emancipation, complete and unconditional. If the Constitution is to be trampled under first, let it be the act of our enemies ... every attempt to interfere with the elective franchise should be met by a petition from every parish in Ireland to reject any bill of Emancipation, no matter how extensive, if accompanied by any such interference ... *Ireland never yet confided but she was betrayed.*

Maurice O'Connell read this public letter to the Association and it was inserted in the minutes (*132*, II, ccxciii-ccxciv).

On 10 February Sheil delivered a 'long and powerful speech' in which he declared he had the opinion of twenty-two Catholic bishops that the Association should be immediately dissolved. On this day also Peel rose in the Commons for leave to bring in a Bill 'for the suppression of dangerous associations or assemblies in Ireland'. Notice was given by Sheil of a motion for a dissolution of the Association within a week. Rather worriedly Edward Dwyer wrote to O'Connell on 11 February: 'God send there is no snake in the grass. It would be presumption in me to offer advice but were I to do so it would be in three words, Caution, Caution, Caution.' Dwyer pointed out that in respect of immediate dissolution of the Association

> All the bishops now here recommend it. Indeed they even go so far as to say that they will withdraw their names and countenance from it should we not comply. The opinions of our Protestant as well as Catholic friends here is that we should dissolve and not await the fiat of Parliament for putting us down' (IV, 1519).

Maurice O'Connell attempted to postpone Sheil's motion to dissolve but Sheil carried his motion on 12 February.[9] Lady Morgan attended this final meeting:

> *The great question* — the dissolution of the Catholic Association was the subject of debate; and every ardent mind came worked up for the contest. All the best feelings, cool judgment, and tact, was evidently for the prompt and voluntary extinction of this great engine of popular opinion' (*47*, II, 275).

This precipitate dissolution of the Association considerably weakened O'Connell's room for manoeuvre on the forty-shilling freeholders question. The resolutions dissolving the Association declared that in so doing the Association rejected any law abridging the rights of the subject or which interfered with the discipline of the Catholic Church; official policy remained complete and unqualified Emancipation. This hurried dissolution, however, revealed the conservative, and perhaps cynical, nature of the Association's leadership in relation to their poorer and more exposed supporters.

Peel's Suppression Bill faced little opposition. On 10 February in the Commons he declared that his 'great object was, to maintain the Protestant interest inviolable — to consult the safety of the Protestant Establishment — and, at the same time, to ensure the peace and tranquillity of Ireland. He had not abandoned his opinions; but he had changed his course.' He made much of the September 1828 military style assemblies of the people, citing detailed evidence to show how 'a mere spark might have kindled one of the most fearful conflagrations'. On 12 February he said 'it was with the utmost reluctance that he had at length consented to break in upon the constitutional settlement of 1688'.[10] The ultras could not vote against the measure and most Emancipationists accepted it as a necessary preliminary to the main measure of Catholic relief. It passed into law on 5 March.

Meanwhile on 15 February the chief hope of the ultras, the Duke of Cumberland, appeared in London from Germany. Could he take the place of the late Duke of York as the real anti-Catholic power behind the throne? Certainly Wellington had tried to keep him away from George IV but now that he was back the best face was put forward. Ellenborough noted on 15 February that Peel and Wellington were now rather glad Cumberland had come: 'They say his arrival will frighten the Whigs, and make them quiet about the 40s freeholders Disfranchisement Bill' (*62*, I, 347). Cumberland was personally unpopular because of great scandals which attached to his name and this hindered his leadership of the ultra cause.

Cumberland's sudden appearance put the king in a panic. George immediately protested that he did not know 'that Wellington's plans included Catholic Emancipation and said that he could never consent to such a measure'. Lyndhurst, when tackled by Cumberland about his anti-Catholic speeches of 1827 and 1828 and his volte-face on concession in 1829 was more frank: 'A political man must learn to forget today what he said yesterday.' Cumberland saw the king again on 17 February: 'When I told him that the Duke of Wellington had made no secret of his intention of granting the Catholic Emancipation, he flew out in the greatest *rage* and said that he *never* would consent to it; that if the Duke pretended to say that such was the meaning of the Speech he had *deceived* him most grossly' (*131*, 177).

On 23 February, in the Lords, Cumberland attacked concession and became embroiled in an undignified quarrel with his pro-Catholic brothers, Clarence and Sussex. Cumberland exercised on George a powerful influence and the king became quite inconsistent and irrational. The cabinet had to confront him again.

Before this final crisis between crown and cabinet Peel lost his Oxford University seat to Sir Robert Inglis by 755 votes to 609. Peel had resigned because of his dramatic change of course. On 28 February Ellenborough noted of the Oxford election: 'The violence of the parsons was beyond belief and far beyond decency ... Now 700 parsons, flushed with triumph, will return to their parishes like firebrands and excite the whole country' (*62*, I, 366). Peel after his humiliating setback found another seat in a hurried and undignified manner in the pocket borough of Westbury. The episode underlined the dangers of the sectarian backlash on the career of a man like Peel who was regarded as having 'ratted' on the Protestant cause. He was no sooner back in the Commons than it appeared as if the government would fall because of the king's obstinacy.

During the first week of March the world of 'high politics' was filled with drama. It became apparent that the king was not going to see Emancipation through: the cabinet told him that the suppression of the Association was only one of a series of related measures. Ministers could not advise him to give his assent to the Suppression Bill unless he continued to approve the general course of policy they were following with regard to Ireland. They also needed the royal influence and authority, to which they felt entitled as ministers of the crown, to have such a major measure as Catholic Emancipation passed. At last the king desired to see the Duke, Lyndhurst and Peel at noon on 4 March. Peel was due to introduce the Roman Catholic Relief Bill, the central measure of Emancipation, next day in the Commons.

When the ministers arrived they found the king, not only suffering, as they knew, from obvious mental and physical ailments but indulging liberally in brandy and water. Peel explained the main heads of the Relief Bill: 'What is this? you surely do not mean to alter the ancient

Oath of Supremacy!' exclaimed George to each minister. George refused to sanction any change in this oath. He then asked each what course they proposed to take now, knowing his feelings: 'Now, Mr Peel, tell me what course you propose to take tomorrow.' Peel and the others declared they would resign and inform the Commons of this next day (*83*, I, 344). The five-hour interview ended with the three ministers resigning and the king, giving them the customary kiss on each cheek, accepted their resignations.

The three ministers returned to London and went to a cabinet dinner at Lord Bathurst's where they told their colleagues they were out. The Duke said he had never witnessed a more painful scene. The king was so evidently insane and drunk with brandy (*62*, I, 376-7). It appeared to the cabinet that there was no alternative ministry and the Duke expected to be called for again in a few days as soon as George realised the predicament in which he had placed himself. Perhaps George was cleverly signalling to the ultras that he was forced to concede Emancipation which he personally abhorred: if so, his theatrical performances might contribute to the longer term unity of the Tory party, as all shades of Tories might agree to keep out the Whigs and support the government which the king desired as the best and most Protestant available. Bathurst believed the king quite capable of pretending to be mad in order to thwart the Duke (*62*, I, 381). It was not easy to follow the king's strategy, if indeed he had one at all.

However, as soon as the ministers had left, George was advised by Sir William Knighton and Lady Conyngham that no other ministry could be found. He was also told that if he based his resistance on the issue of the oath it would be impossible for him to retreat with any honour. At once the king wrote to Wellington accepting the inevitable:

> As I find the country would be left without an administration, I have decided to yield my opinion to *that* which is considered by the Cabinet to be for the immediate interests of the country. Under these circumstances you have my consent to proceed as you propose with the measure. God knows what pain it causes to write these words.

Bitterly the king remarked that Wellington was now 'King Arthur', O'Connell was 'King of Ireland' and he was merely 'Dean of Windsor' (*20*, III, 62). Wellington and Peel now made sure in the exchange of letters that George finally and fully accepted their proposals. Wellington got the king's clear agreement in a letter from Windsor Castle dated 'Thursday morning, quarter past 7, from my bed' which said: 'You have put the right construction upon the meaning of my letter of last evening' (*128*, V, 515-19). At a quarter past midday Ellenborough was asked to go to Wellington. He went thinking that the Prime Minister had to announce the king's insane refusal to co-operate. The Duke, however had to announce 'a complete victory' (*62*, I, 378-9).

Meanwhile great crowds had gathered from 10 o'clock in the morning outside the House of Commons. The public gallery was opened just after six o'clock in the evening: 'the rush was tremendous; in two minutes not a seat was unoccupied, and the doors and lobby were crowded with people anxious to avail themselves of any resignations that heat, pressure, and fatigue might occasion'.[11] The people were unaware of the last minute crisis with the king but they were conscious of a great historic parliamentary occasion as Peel stood up in the House of Commons to move for a committee of the whole House to consider the laws imposing disabilities on Roman Catholics.

Peel delivered an outstanding speech lasting over four hours which totally captured his audience. 'At times the cheers were so loud as to be heard in Westminster Hall and the passages leading to the lobby', according to the parliamentary notetaker. He first pointedly declared that he rose 'as a minister of the king'. He went on to refer to his own previous struggle to maintain the exclusion of Catholics from parliament and high office, to the inevitability of concession, and the necessity for it at this stage:

> I do not think it was an unnatural or unreasonable struggle. I resign it, in consequence of the conviction that it can be no longer advantageously maintained; from believing that there are not adequate materials or sufficient instruments for its effectual and permanent continuance. I yield, therefore, to a moral necessity which I cannot control, unwilling to push resistance to a point which might endanger the Establishments that I wish to defend.

He traced the record of division in British governments since 1794: in every ministry there had been division on the Catholic question; two had fallen on the issue; four of the five Houses of Commons elected since 1807 had pronounced, in some form or other, in favour of a settlement and the fifth only voted against by a margin of two votes. This reflected the divisions in the country. What, he asked, was to be the end of these interminable and fruitless contests? He rejected the idea of another general election rousing the people with the cry of 'No Popery' and he pointed out that the rising political talent in the House was overwhelmingly pro-Catholic.

Having demonstrated the domestic political reason why resistance could no longer be maintained, Peel analysed the conditions in Ireland which made concession necessary. He pointed out that the Union had failed to bring about normal administrative conditions: indeed for scarcely a single year since the Union had Ireland been governed by the ordinary process of law. He catalogued the emergencies, through the legislation withheld such as habeas corpus, or introduced such as the Insurrection Act of 1807, in most of the years since the Union. Ireland needed a firm policy but this could not be based upon resistance to Emancipation. He recognised that Irish agitation could not be suppressed by legal means: 'there exists a spirit too subtle for compression, a bond of union which penal statutes cannot dissolve'. This was Peel's phrase to acknowledge the invincibility of O'Connellism.

Peel pointed out that over twenty Irish counties would follow the example of Clare and it would not be possible to have the House of Commons disenfranchise the Irish freeholders without extending the rights of Catholics as well. To hold another Irish general election would sever the last links between landlord and tenant and would make effective government in Ireland impossible:

> We have removed, with our hands, the seal from the vessel, in which a mighty spirit was inclosed – but it will not, like the genius in the fable, return within its narrow confines to gratify our curiosity, and to enable us to cast it back into the obscurity from which we evoked it.

To govern Ireland in the face of opposition from five out of the seven million of its inhabitants – and the two million minority largely concentrated in Ulster and itself divided on the expediency of concession – would be impossible in time of peace except by military means and in time of war would provoke foreign intervention and civil war. Peel's arguments were based on expediency, not upon a discussion of rights; it was not what was desirable but only what was possible and practical for the government:

> No doubt there are difficulties; but what great measure, which has stamped its name upon the era of its adoption, has been carried through without objections and obstacles, insuperable if they had been abstractedly considered? What was the Revolution itself, but a violation of principles which would have been respected in ordinary times and under ordinary circumstances?

The rest of his speech was mainly devoted to an exposition of the details of the plan drawn up by the ministry: the admission of Roman Catholics to parliament without conditions or restriction. He did not wish to leave behind 'A Catholic Question'. Catholics would still be debarred from the office of Regent, Lord Chancellor in England and Ireland, Lord Lieutenant of Ireland and offices connected with the Church of England or Ireland. What was envisaged, he emphasised, was political and not religious concession: the proposals did not sanction, still less encourage, any religion other than that established by law. There would be no compact with Roman Catholicism, and parliament would be free to exact any securities in future as deemed necessary. The only real security in future would be the alteration of the county franchise from forty-shillings to £10 and the registration of such freeholds by judicial machinery.

He ended with an expression of hope that the expectations of those who had argued so long for emancipation would be fulfilled:

> Sir, I will hope for the best ... But if these expectations are to be disappointed, if unhappily civil strife and contention shall survive the restoration of political privilege; if there be something inherent in the spirit of the Roman Catholic religion which disdains equality and will be satisfied with nothing but ascendancy; still I am content to run the hazard of the change. The contest, if inevitable, will be fought for other objects and with other arms. The struggle will be, not for the abolition of civil distinctions, but for the predominance of an intolerant religion.[12]

Peel's speech was a triumph and gained the initiative in the long debates which followed. The motion was carried by a majority of 188 and this in turn helped settle the feeling of the country. It is perhaps difficult to assess, at this remove, the 'state of great political excitement' evoked by the Catholic question during these debates. On 11 March, John Stuart Mill sent this account to his friend Gustave d'Eichthal:

> The excitement does not reach the labouring classes but it pervades all the rest of the community to such a degree that, as I am creditably informed, it has to a great degree put a stop to buying and selling, at least on a large scale, as no one can think of any thing except the Catholic question. Since the debate in the House of Commons, and the majority of 188 in favour of the question, nobody doubts the success of the bill; and it is very gratifying and most creditable to our ministers, that they have not clogged the measure with any objectionable or ungracious provisions or restrictions (86, XII, 26).

It was a most exceptional parliamentary success by the man who only a month before had been publicly regarded as the most able anti-Catholic politician and the Protestant champion in the Commons.

While the cabinet were involved in the final royal confrontation O'Connell was negotiating with the Whigs on the proposals, especially their attitude to the freehold measure. He certainly demonstrated real commitment to the cause of the forty-shilling freeholders but he found the ground cut away from under him by both the Whigs and the Catholics in Ireland. On 3 March O'Connell wrote to his wife:

> Mr Brougham was with me this morning for an hour. Let this fact
> not get into the papers. He spoke to me a great deal on the freehold
> wing. He wanted to get some countenance from me for the Whigs
> supporting that wing. I need not tell you that he totally failed. They
> *trapped* me before. They cannot possibly succeed in that way a
> second time. Besides, darling, I really am too much indebted to the
> 40s freeholders. You do not think I could ever turn my back on the
> poor fellows in Clare. I argued with Brougham in the strongest terms
> on the subject and showed him how useless it would be to call it a
> measure of concession if they were at the same time to destroy the
> rights of the people at large.

On the same day he reported to Edward Dwyer on the meeting and on
the freehold wing:

> I declared my perpetual and unconquerable hostility to it; I showed
> that emancipation accompanied by that wing, would rather irritate
> than assuage; I showed him that the people would get into worse
> hands than ours. In short, he left me convinced that it was the duty
> of the Whigs to take as decisive a part as possible in preventing the
> Ministry from bringing in such a wing (IV, 1525, 1526).

O'Connell suspected Brougham of exerting a subtle pressure on him
as the morning he called upon O'Connell was the day on which a Committee of the House of Commons was to be appointed to try a petition
against O'Connell's return for Clare in 1828. O'Connell was naturally
anxious to have a favourable Committee and the Whigs could help if
he would let them off the hook on the franchise question. If that was
the intention it failed and O'Connell, on 6 March, was declared duly
elected by the Commons Committee.

On 5 March O'Connell, though aware that the king had played 'all
manner of tricks', expressed to his wife his only anxiety: the freehold
wing. Next day he wrote:

> The bills are announced. Great and glorious triumph as far as the
> Emancipation bill goes — no Veto — no payment of the clergy — no
> ecclesiastical arrangements. So far the bill is excellent. If it passed
> alone it would be the greatest of triumphs ... Next comes the mis-
> chief — bill to raise the freehold qualification to ten pounds. This is
> bad, very bad, and we must prevent it if we can. I will publish on
> Tuesday a letter on this subject, but everything else is admirable.
> Whoever thought we could get such a bill from Peel and Wellington.
> Catholics may be judges, mayors, sheriffs, aldermen, common counsel-
> men, peers of parliament, members of parliament, everything, in
> short, everything.

O'Connell went on to say that the £10 franchise would 'really give more power to the Catholics. I must however support the freeholders ... Oh, if I could support the 40s freeholders! *That that* is the only blot' (IV, 1528, 1529). On the same day he wrote to O'Conor Don that the 'only drawback' to Emancipation was the freehold wing and he asked that petitions be poured in against it: 'There is no time to be lost. My opinion is that the liberal clubs ought not to dissolve themselves'. It is clear that while O'Connell 'treaded on air' because of his 'bloodless revolution' he sought to resist the franchise measure. On 6 March, writing privately to Edward Dwyer, he commenced by quoting

> And we will plant a laurel tree,
> And we will call it liberty

but he streessed that the freehold wing '*must be opposed in every shape and form*' (IV, 1532).

On 6 March a Whig meeting at Burdett's revealed a strong and general hostility to a measure of disenfranchisement, but when it was realised that opposition might endanger Emancipation only a handful were prepared to reject it (*87*, 215). On 6 March Brougham informed the Commons that he would accept disenfranchisement as the price of Emancipation. O'Connell wrote next day an Address to the People of Ireland which exulted at the victory over Emancipation but which sought 'decided, determined, energetic, but constitutional opposition' to the freehold wing.[14] On 7 March, at a meeting at the Thatched House Tavern, O'Connell found considerable opposition to the *prudence* of petitioning in favour of forty-shilling freeholders but he carried the point in spite of 'some curious trimming' by Pierce Mahony, Lord Killeen, N. P. O'Gorman, and Eneas MacDonnell. O'Connell was supported by O'Gorman Mahon, Tom Steele and Jack Lawless (IV, 1533).

O'Connell found, in fact, little inclination in either England or Ireland to fight for the forty-shilling freeholders. There was not very much time to mount a huge campaign: Peel moved the following week to bring in both the Relief and Disfranchisement Bills on 10 March and the debate proper began on 17 March. However there was little support for such a campaign as O'Connell desired, even had time been on his side.

Thomas Wyse, for example, attempted to agitate on behalf of the forty-shilling voters but he was told by his brother George that even the Catholic Rent collectors did not favour such an agitation:

> I do assure you they are all heartily sick of the forty-shillingers — the specimen òf the last election is the best cure of their patriotism — besides the peasantry are even in favour of the change ... in fact I say with confidence that every rational man approves of

Peel's plan — You may depend upon it that O'Connell will fail in this country at least in raising the opposition to the Bill — I do not anticipate a *single* meeting on the subject . . .[15]

Wyse felt that the Disfranchisement Bill was partial and a bad precedent; it was, he felt, contrary to the very principle of the Relief Bill which was 'an Equalization Bill'. Wyse noted George's letter and also similar accounts from other parts of Ireland, in his diary and he concluded that 'the country at large' was 'perfectly indifferent' to the question.[16]

In Cork the majority wished to dissolve the Liberal Club but as Stephen Coppinger, who was opposed to dissolution, told Wyse, 'the precedent set by the Catholic Association' was 'triumphantly urged against us'.[17] Richard Dowden, while supporting the dissolution of the Liberal Club, admitted that he had 'mixed motives'; he argued that the prospect of Emancipation and the law against 'dangerous assemblies' made it desirable to have a 'short repose after a brave and victorious struggle' but he pointed out that issues such as tithes, church rates, and corporate reform were still to be resolved and he also looked forward to parliamentary reform. Dowden recommended that the members of the club hand over to a committee which would run the News Room. This 'would allow every one who was a member of the Liberal Club, and who has paid or may pay up his subscription due to the Club, to enjoy the privileges and be considered a subscriber to the Reading Room'.[18] The News Room was established and, in effect, carried on the functions of the Liberal Club as the rallying point of liberals and as a centre for political information.[19]

The Cork activists were anxious for the benefits of Emancipation to materialise in the form of local advance for Catholics but Coppinger failed to interest them in a protest against the removal of the forty-shilling freehold franchise which he believed was 'the right arm of Catholic Ireland' threatened 'with immediate amputation'. He complained to Wyse that many of 'the leading Catholics' in Cork were '. . . not only decidedly opposed to any meeting having for its object to stand by the poor Freeholders in their day of need, but actually delighted and quite in raptures with the proposed "Relief Bill"'. The Chamber of Commerce, though originally founded upon popular principles in 1819, had become, according to Coppinger, 'an aristocracy too, the *aristocracy of wealth*'. He was

> literally *disgusted* with the total want of principle, evinced by the leading Catholics of Cork many of whom in their eagerness to come in for a share of the loaves and fishes of corruption, I verily believe, would not hesitate to throw not alone Jesuits, Monks and Friars overboard, but *Priests* and *Bishops* after them, rather than be delayed

from entering into the haven of what they call *emancipation*. In the County and City of Cork News Room, late the Liberal Club, I found Sheehan of the *Chronicle* and a few others disposed for the most part to agree in my views but at the same time they considered that with the members of the Chamber of Commerce who form what may be called the *elite* of our public meetings, not merely neutral, but *directly opposed* to us, all chance of getting up a meeting was out of the question.

In fact an influential member of the Chamber of Commerce threatened a counter petition if the News Room petitioned in support of the forty-shilling freeholders.[20]

Now that Emancipation appeared certain, O'Connell, whose radical views had become more public, found he had little influence with the conservative Catholic leadership in Ireland. He remarked to Dwyer on 11 March:

> How mistaken men are who suppose that the history of the world will be over as soon as we are emancipated! Oh! *that* will be the time *to commence* the struggle for popular rights.

All he could manage in Dublin was a holding operation, as in Cork, whereby the Catholics would have a Reading Room to serve 'as a nucleus for talking over Catholic and Irish affairs'. He found, in England, that he could get no support for the forty-shilling freeholders:

> You know already that we sent a Resolution to the Whigs calling upon them to resist the Disfranchisement Bill at all hazards. It was I who drew it up, and Purcell O'Gorman took it to Sir Francis Burdett's where they were all assembled. Yet Brougham and all the party gave in. The Opposition, to a man, will vote for it; it almost drives me to despair on this subject.

Hunt and the Radicals O'Connell also found to be ineffective and without any real following. Next day, 12 March, he reported glumly to Dwyer:

> The Irish forty-shilling freeholders have no friends amongst the English members; the Whigs and all are against them. Even Lord Grey declares he will not oppose the Disfranchisement Bill. This is cruel — very cruel . . . We must put on record our decided hostility to it in every shape and form so as to enable us hereafter, *and soon*, to do battle in favour of a restoration of this right' (IV, 1536, 1537).

The debate on the Relief Bill began on 17 March. It involved rancour and innuendo especially directed towards Peel for 'miserable, contempt-ible apostasy' as Wetherell, the Attorney-General, put it. Peel once more had to defend his decision on the basis of expediency and to counter the charge that the ministers who had left Canning in 1827 and had joined in hunting him down to his death had been moved by anything but principle. The bill passed by 180 votes after the two-day debate.

The Disfranchisement Bill had promised to be one of the most vulnerable parts of the government's programme, because many Whigs disliked it. Approached by Althorp and Spring Rice, Peel refused to compromise. He told them that he could not give up the disenfranchisement of the forty-shilling freeholders for without it he could not hope to carry the bill and for the same reason he refused to alter the main bill so as to allow O'Connell to take his seat for Co. Clare. The Whig leaders and their followers finally agreed that the settlement as a whole was so fair and satisfactory that they ought not to endanger it by opposing any part of it (*15*, III, 309). By this time it was also known that O'Connell could offer no effective resistance to disenfranchisement. He told Pierce Mahony in a letter intended to reach the eyes of the government on 28 March that he had 'an insurmountable repugnance to give the Ministry any species of trouble *as connected with the Catholic question*'. At this stage O'Connell was aware he could not eliminate the Disfranchisement Bill and he was now concerned about the ultimate success of the Catholic Relief Bill about to enter the Lords. He was also concerned about the effect of an attempt to take his seat which might impede the Relief Bill; he sought government gestures to Ireland to accompany Catholic Relief such as impartial administration and public works grants (IV, 1544). P. V. Fitzpatrick, Sheil and Conway also wrote to Mahony at this time to indicate that Irish reaction to disenfranchisement need give the government no cause for concern (*113*, 169). The Catholic leadership were understandably wary of the fate of their Bill in the Lords. The government obtained a majority of over 200 in a small House on the freehold measure.

The succeeding week, 23-27 March, was largely taken up by a detailed consideration of the Relief Bill in committee. All substantial opposition amendments were defeated and on 30 March on the third reading there was a 178 majority. On the same night the Disfranchisement Bill was read a third time and passed by an even greater majority. To the end the Protestant party fought desperately and bitterly for their lost cause: passionate denunciations in the Commons reflected violent feelings outside. They felt that Peel and Wellington had ratted and betrayed them; that they had surrendered completely and had provided no security or guarantees to protect the Protestant Constitution. At one point Wellington fought a duel with Winchelsea who accused the Prime Minister of having an insidious design to establish popery. Peel was criticised for refusing to challenge Wetherell, the dismissed Attorney-General.

The first two weeks of April saw the passage of Catholic Emancipation through the House of Lords. The Protestant forces had been outgunned in the Commons and deserted by the king. Some, like Cumberland, who 'looked upon this measure as one of the most outrageous ever proposed to Parliament, and one which fundamentally shook the Constitution of the country' were, of course, irreconcilable.[21] Others, like the Bishop of Winchester, Dr C. R. Sumner, took a more pragmatic approach. Sumner wrote on 9 March to the king to outline why he would support Catholic Emancipation: he believed it was both a matter of *political expediency* and *religious expediency*. Without it he argued 'the Irish branch of the united Church of Great Britain and Ireland cannot long stand'. As proposed the measures did not tend to injure the Protestant or strengthen the Roman Catholic religion. He would have opposed vetos, concordats, or state payment to Catholic clergy or 'any other mode of national recognition' which 'would have incurred the guilt of countenancing and supporting a corrupt Church'. However, Peel's measure would give 'fair play to the Protestant religion in Ireland' and in fact give a greater opportunity for the conversion of the Irish people. In this way, he felt, the king could reconcile his support of Emancipation with his Coronation Oath 'to maintain the Protestant religion' (*3*, III, 455-6).

Wellington's speech in the Lords on 2 April on the second reading of the Relief Bill was well calculated to appeal to men susceptible to Sumner's arguments. He pointed to the state of Ireland and the possibility of civil war and argued that 'neither the law nor the means in the possession of government enable government to put an end to these things'. He underlined the 'horribleness of civil war' from his personal memories of 1798. He then pointed to the considerable numbers of Irish Protestants who were in favour of Emancipation and he instanced the recent Protestant Declaration in favour of civil and religious liberty. The permanent achievements of 1688 would not be affected: the liberties of the people and the Protestant monarchy. He declared that they should limit exclusion from the benefits of the Constitution as far as possible.[22]

For the opposition Archbishop Beresford from Armagh asked the key question: 'Are you prepared to sacrifice the Irish Church Establishment and the Protestant institutions connected with it – to efface the Protestant character of the Irish portion of the Empire – to transfer from Protestants to Roman Catholics the ascendancy in Ireland?' Beresford reflected ultra beliefs when he declared that the practical effects of Catholic doctrine and tenets upon the human mind were irreconcilable with 'purity of faith and morals'.[23] On 4 April the majority in the Lords on the second reading was 105.

On 10 April Colchester recorded in his diary:

House of Lords. The Roman Catholic Relief Bill read a third time and passed by 213 to 109. The Roman Catholic Relief Bill, so called! which puts an end to the Protestant monarchy of Great Britain in so far as it permits all the duties of the kingly office to be executed by Roman Catholic Ministers' (*20*, III, 611).

Certain Church of Ireland bishops in early April addressed the king in a last ditch attempt to persuade him to withhold his royal sanction. Public protests in London to influence the king petered out. The Roman Catholic Relief Act (10 George IV, c.7) received the royal assent on 13 April 1829.

Ellenborough could hardly believe what had happened: 'Really it seems like a dream! That I should, if I lived, live to see this I did expect; but that I should see it so soon, and that I should happen to be a member of the government that carried it, I did not expect. I must say with what delight I view the prospect of having Catholics in Parliament' (*62*, II, 6). Next day O'Connell wrote to Dwyer, dating his letter 'The first day of freedom! 14 April 1829':

> It is one of the greatest triumphs recorded in history – a bloodless revolution more extensive in its operation than any other political change that could take place. I say *political* to contrast it with *social* changes which might break to pieces the framework of society. This is a good beginning and now, if I can get Catholics and Protestant to join, something solid and substantial may be done for all (IV, 1551).

O'Connell advised the Catholics to refrain from illuminating Dublin in celebration of Emancipation lest such a demonstration of triumph should lead to disturbance.[24] Eighteen twenty-nine decisively altered the Anglican settlement made at the 1688 Revolution. If the liberals regarded Emancipation as the long-delayed remedy for an outstanding social injustice, the Protestants saw in it the overthrow of the principle on which the Constitution stood. It was the ultimate humiliation for them that it should be engineered by their own leaders: their sense of betrayal and resentment destroyed the Tory party and opened the way to the reform era under the Whigs.

In May O'Connell presented himself at the Commons to be allowed take his seat and spoke at the bar of the House. On 18 May it was decided by 190 to 116 votes that O'Connell should not be allowed to take his seat without subscribing to the old Oath of Supremacy as he had been elected before the Relief Act. As he put it to Charles Sugrue 'between Tory falsehood and hypocrisy and Whiggish *uncertainty*, the question was lost' (IV, 1569). The government penalised him by forcing him to be re-elected in Clare. On 25 May he issued his famous 'Address of the Hundred Promises' pledging restoration of the forty-shilling freehold franchise as well as a radical programme for reform in Ireland. On 30 July he was re-elected in Clare without a contest. It was an inauspicious start to the post-Emancipation era.

Epilogue:
'The Struggle for Popular Rights'

'How mistaken men are who suppose that the history of the world will be over as soon as we are emancipated! Oh! *that* will be the time *to commence* the struggle for popular rights'.

O'Connell to Edward Dwyer,
11 March 1829, (IV, 1536)

The Protestant Establishment was profoundly shocked by Catholic Emancipation: 'The World seems altered in every way, it seems that seasons, people, & principles, are so altered that I can hardly believe that I am still in poor old England', wrote Lord Kenyon's aunt in early May 1829 (*80*, 180). Immediate horror was to be expected but it was the delayed shock, especially in Ireland, which proved more traumatic. Elizabeth Bowen in *Bowen's Court* graphically describes the Earl of Kingston's plunge into insanity after his tenants rebelled and voted against his candidate in a by-election in Co. Limerick in 1830. Kingston, known as 'Big George', ruled extensive estates in Cork, Tipperary and Limerick as a benevolent despot. He had dazzled the south of Ireland with his new castle built at Mitchelstown in the early 1820s. Tenant revolt was the beginning of the end of the *ancien regime* in Ireland.

Elizabeth Bowen captures the essence of the new post-Emancipation era:

> The sense of dislocation was everywhere. Property was still there, but power was going. It was democracy ... that sent Big George mad. In other cases, the line between sanity and insanity was less perceptibly crossed ... Society — which can only exist when people are sure of themselves and immune from fears — was no longer, in the Anglo-Ireland I speak of, in what I called the magnetic and growing stage; it was on the decline; it was breaking up. It could exist in detail — comings-and-goings, entertainments, marriages — but the main healthy abstract was gone (*12*, 258-9).

O'Connell's achievement was indeed primarily psychological: a new mentality came in the course of the 1820s to life outside the Big House. Inside some of the occupants physically or mentally withdrew from this Ireland. Lord Sligo, 'disgusted with what he considered the ingratitude of the people of Westport and its neighbourhood', withdrew his countenance and favour from the town and its inhabitants before he left Ireland for Jamaica (*55*, 257). Maria Edgeworth abandoned Irish themes in her fiction in a conscious decision, as she observed in 1834:

> It is impossible to draw Ireland as she now is in the book of fiction – realities are too strong, party passions too violent, to bear to see, or care to look at their faces in a looking glass. The people would only break the glass, and curse the fool who held the mirror up to nature – distorted nature, in a fever. We are in too perilous a case to laugh, humour would be out of season, worse than bad taste (*31*, III, 85).

Maria Edgeworth's first reaction was that Wellington had certainly prevented a civil war in Ireland but her initial optimism about the effects of Emancipation soon evaporated.

Liberal Protestants, such as the Edgeworths, quickly realised that they had no hope of a successful modification of the Protestant Ascendancy in the face of a triumphant O'Connellism. Their efforts, like those of all Protestants, Liberal or Tory, concentrated upon saving the Union from a massive national assault in the decades after 1829. By January 1839 we find Maria echoing the Protestant hardliners: 'Really though I wrote a story called *The Absentee* I begin to think that it is but reasonable that a country should be rendered fit to live in before we complain more of Absentees' (*18*, 453).

The Anglo-Irish Protestant Ascendancy found, from the 1820s, the current flowing strongly against them for the rest of the nineteenth century as the long-term implications of Emancipation became evident: the attack on the Established Church and the 'tithe war', disestablishment, municipal reform, the struggle over tenant-right and the downfall of the landlords, the long struggle for repeal of the Union, home rule and finally separation from Britain. All were based upon the restoration of Catholic power and influence. Most Protestants resisted the new forces in Irish politics while a minority, like Sir Samuel Ferguson, sought 'an ascendancy of the heart'.

Ferguson's 'A Dialogue between the Head and the Heart of an Irish Protestant' published in the *Dublin University Magazine* in November 1833 is the classic beginning of the literary and political encounter between the Catholic and Protestant traditions in the new era. Ferguson fears the Catholic Church and for 'our estates, our liberties of conscience; our personal liberties; our lives; ... for if Catholic Emancipation produce repeal, so surely will repeal produce ultimate separation; and so sure as we have a separation, so surely will there be war levied, estates confiscated, and the Popish church established'. The only recourse for Protestants in Ireland, he felt, was to assert their Irish identity, learn the 'arts of agitation' practised by Catholics and attempt to reconcile the two religious communities that constitute the Irish people through a mutual exploration of history and literature.

Towards the end of the century, the great Protestant historian Lecky was to discover 'in the long popular agitation for Catholic Emancipation' the foundation for 'the political anarchy' of his own day: for it was in the end granted in a manner 'likely to produce most evil and to do least good'. 'It was the result of an agitation which, having fatally impaired the influence of property, loyalty and respectability in Catholic Ireland, had brought the country to the verge of civil war, and it was carried avowedly through fear of that catastrophe, and by a ministry which was, on principle, strongly opposed to it' (*63*, 254-5, 480).

The period between 1829 and 1832 was an exceptionally important time in which the political forces in Ireland adjusted to the new era. The air was filled with reform and revolution: the final struggle for parliamentary reform; the fall of Wellington's government and the coming to power of the Whigs; the French and Belgian revolution in 1830; the 'Swing' riots in Britain and the beginnings of the 'tithe war' in Ireland, all contributed to an atmosphere of expectation, tension, hope and repression. What was the policy of Peel and Wellington towards an emancipated Ireland?

Soon after Emancipation we find Peel writing to Lord Francis Leveson-Gower on 30 July 1829 that they 'must seriously consider some extensive and decisive system of measures for the permanent civilisation of Ireland'. Peel said they had 'got rid of the Catholic question' but that was of little value unless it enabled them to induce parliament to pass measures 'calculated not merely to repress casual outrages and insurrectionary movements, but to habituate the people to a vigorous unsparing enforcement and administration of the law, criminal and civil'. Peel postponed consideration of extensive schemes for employment, education and the improvement of the condition of the people. He addressed himself to two measures which he believed must be preliminary and indispensable to the success of all such schemes: the constitution of a thoroughly efficient police and the punishment of crime under central government direction:

> Ten years' experience of the advantage of obedience will induce a country to be obedient without much extraordinary compulsion . . . The time is come when it is unnecessary any longer to pet Ireland. We only spoil her by very undeserved flattery, and by treating her to everything for which she ought herself to pay (*107*, II, 122-4).

Peel believed that many Irish ills were outside the control of the government; his quest was a permanent means of executing the ordinary laws in Ireland. On 19 November 1829 Peel told Leveson-Gower that the 'great object' was to establish some permanent protection for life and property that would outlive one or two sessions of parliament and 'lay the foundations of a better state of society hereafter'. He compared Irish society in its primitive state with society in the remote period of Saxon times in English history (*107*, II, 133-7).

Wellington wrote to the Duke of Northumberland, the new Lord Lieutenant, on 16 July 1829 that there must be tranquillity in Ireland to justify the concession of Emancipation: 'We can make no further concessions. We have nothing to concede excepting the property of the Church or of individuals'. Northumberland replied by stating of Emancipation: 'Great and efficacious as it is, it could not be expected at once to civilise an ignorant population, and miraculously to assuage those religious animosities which have existed for centuries' (*128*, VI, 19-22). Wellington, at least, recognised O'Connell's potency. He disagreed with the Duke of Buckingham who thought in December 1829 that O'Connell was about 'to share the fate of an extinguishing tallow candle, and die in his own stink'. Wellington wrote of O'Connell on 30 December: '... he is a very diligent and a very able lawyer, and a good debater, and if he should be only moderate in his language and he behaves at all like a gentleman he will be listened to and his influence will be greater than ever'. Peel and Wellington had a policy of detaching 'Sheil and his friends' from O'Connell: the old 'divide and rule' recourse of an imperial power in difficulty (*128*, VI, 253, 346, 355).

The Irish government felt in 1830 that Emancipation had averted an Irish revolution prompted by the French and Belgian examples. On 21 October 1830, Northumberland warned Wellington of the effect of the Belgian Revolution, and credited a great deal to Emancipation:

> The argument is short and stimulating: *'That which the youth of Bruxelles has effected the boys of Dublin can surely perform'* . . . in this singular crisis we have more and more reason to be thankful that the 'Relief Bill' has removed all reasonable grounds of complaint and has enlisted on our side many most powerful and influential allies, who, in other circumstances, would have taken a decidedly hostile part.
>
> It is my clear conviction, if that law had not passed, that Ireland would have been at this moment in arms, with a divided Cabinet in England, a distracted Government in Dublin, and a grievance resented by all Catholics, and acknowledged by half the Protestants in the country. We have now good and tenable ground (*128*, VII, 311-14).

Thomas Lefroy, engaged upon the work of reconstructing a Tory party in face of the powerful surge in favour of Repeal, feared in December 1830 'a second Edition of the Belgian drama' as he put it to

Lord Farnham.[1] An Irish revolution did not occur in 1830. Wellington's Irish policy had defused a potentially revolutionary situation but at the cost of 'estranging' his own party to such a degree that the Whigs gained office. Wellington and Peel had no constructive Irish policy for the new era of political equality. Emancipation led to the end of the long Tory dominance in British and Irish politics.

The reaction to Catholic Emancipation amongst Irish Catholics was initially optimistic. This was true both of the upper classes and of the people at large. Soon, however, a grievous sense of disappointment set in. Thomas Moore wrote on 17 April 1829 that the victory brought the 'end of my politics', declaring to John Murray that 'the Duke has had the merit of exorcising the devil of rebellion out of me . . . In this feeling, too, I rather think I am the representative of the great mass (or rather mass-goers) of my countrymen. All we wanted was fair treatment . . .' He wrote in a similar vein to Lord John Russell on 22 April: 'I consider my politics entirely at an end – nothing in the world can ever again conjure up a spirit in me like that which the Duke has now laid, and for anything of a secondary class – anything short of seven millions of people – it is beneath my notice' (*30*, II, 633-5). In late March O'Connell had written to Pierce Mahony of the government's opportunity for reconciliation by 'fair treatment' and expenditure on public works:

> The people will be taken out of *our* hands by Emancipation as we took them from Capt. Rock by *our* agitation. They may fall back into Rock's hands unless the Government have the common sense to take them into their own. This can easily be done by giving them present employment and taking the simple precaution of not making a hatred of the people one of the qualifications for office according to the hitherto approved practice (IV, 1544).

What was the popular understanding of Emancipation? Clearly at one level it was understood as a general act of liberation by 'the Liberator', O'Connell. One peasant's reported reaction is in this general sense of delivery from injustice:

> We may have a light if we please now; and we walk about without being stopped by the soldiers; and it'll not be long before we get law and justice, and Catholic magistrates that will believe the truth from a Catholic. Oh! the devil fly away with Protestant magistrates that find all Catholics guilty (*16*, 438).

An old farmer told Lady Gregory:

> When the bill passed, there were bonfires lit all about the village, and
> on top of the hill, and the greatest excitement that ever was. The
> people didn't know exactly what it was about. They thought
> O'Connell and Sheil would stream gold into their pockets, and I
> know some that wouldn't sow a crop in those years because they
> had been told the millenium was coming (*42*, 267).

W. R. Le Fanu remembered 'the exaggerated notions' of the peasantry
of the benefits of Emancipation: 'Wages were at once to be doubled,
and constant, well-paid employment was to be given to every man'. On
the day Emancipation became law, bonfires blazed on the tops of the
mountains and hills of Co. Limerick (*51*, 51-2). O'Connell was seen by
many as a second Moses in popular songs such as one celebrating 'the
Catholic Victory':

> The bondage of the Israelites our Saviour he did see,
> He then commanded Moses for to go and set them free,
> And in the same we did remain suffering from our own
> Till God he sent O'Connell, for to free the Church of Rome.
> (*134*, 34).

Peasants had little enough understanding of the play of 'high politics'.
For many Emancipation was about the inauguration of a just order and
a defeat for Protestant oppressors. This is evident in the popular
reception of Pastorini's prophecy that Protestantism would be completely destroyed in 1825 and in the popular ballads and songs of the
1820s. There was also, however, a great expectation of practical benefits
at local level. It was very much a question of 'the law' being 'once
again' in 'our hands' with the 'coming of Emancipation' to use the
words of a contemporary Gaelic poet. Humphrey O'Sullivan, the hedge
school teacher who married into a draper's shop in Callan, Co. Kilkenny
and a local activist in the Emancipation campaign, spelled out in a
speech what Emancipation meant in popular terms:

> But perhaps you do not know what help or advantage Emancipation
> is to the poor man. I will tell you at once. Catholic Emancipation
> means this, that all power and honours now enjoyed by Protestants,
> should be within the reach of Catholics, on equal terms. For instance,
> if there were a Catholic sheriff, there would, of course, be no Orange
> juries trying Catholics and hanging and torturing them as in Ulster.
> If there were a Catholic judge, no Grand Jury could fasten a 'straddle
> of misery' on your backs twice every year, putting on you a county
> cess as high as are rents elsewhere, and imposing a county cess on
> the houses in Callan . . . these and a hundred other rates and dues
> that I cannot at the moment recall to mind. Were it not a great

incentive to the Catholic soldier to be able to entertain the hope of rising one day to the rank of general or other higher officer . . .

O'Sullivan pointed out that if there were Catholic lords and 'other noblemen' in parliament, 'the present swaddlers could not be calumniating us before Parliament without anyone there to stand forth in our defence' (*75*, XXXIII, 108-15).

As far as middle- and upper-class Catholics were concerned Emancipation had allowed them to escape from their alliance with the peasantry. In December 1829 Sheil wrote a detailed article on the 'Effects of Emancipation' in which he maintained that Ireland had been saved from civil war: 'the revolutionary tendencies are entirely gone by'. He adopted the metaphor of a ship to describe Ireland — a ship which has escaped being wrecked:

> although the vessel is in her moorings, yet she requires to be refitted; there is no risk of her going down, but her rigging must be repaired; full many a rotten plank, which had well nigh let in destruction, must be struck boldly out; and although a great part of her framework must remain, yet, when she is put on the stocks, she must be newly timbered.

He looked forward to a 'great moral and political change' in every walk of Irish life — the spirit of Emancipation

> must be diffused and dispersed into every department of state . . . it must be worked into the essence and being of the Government. It must be found everywhere — at the desks of office; on the bench of justice; at the green tables in the courts in the boxes of the jury, and of the sheriff; in the treasury, the custom-house, and the Castle; nay, it must appear in the village school room and in the policeman's barrack.

Sheil foresaw the 'continuance of a modified Protestant ascendancy' as being compatible with Catholic claims, for Protestant property would insure Protestant predominance. He argued for an 'alliance of the Catholic clergy with the State' and the indirect payment of the clergy 'by circuitous conductors' in education subsidies and grants to Maynooth. The police force should be predominantly Catholic and the priests should have a rôle in selecting officers and men for the force. 'Let not the members of the Establishment', Sheil declared, 'take alarm, their millions of acres will outweigh the school-houses of the Catholic clergy and the barracks of a Catholic police' (*114*, II, 219-56).

In July 1828 Sheil had sought to demonstrate that the 'crimes' associated with the land system were connected with the 'radical imperfection in the general system' by which the country was governed:

'the Whiteboyism of 1760' corresponded 'with that of 1828':

> It may be asked, with a great appearance of plausibility (and indeed
> it is often inquired) what possible effect the exclusion of a few
> Roman Catholic gentlemen from Parliament, and of still fewer
> Roman Catholic barristers from the bench, can produce in deterior-
> ating the moral habits of the people? . . . The just mode of presenting
> the question would be this: 'What effect does the penal code pro-
> duce by separating the higher and the lower orders from each other?'

Sheil argued that the system of religious separation nurtured the passions
of the peasantry:

> They are not permitted to forget that Protestantism is stamped upon
> every institution in the country, and their own sunderance from the
> privileged class is perpetually brought to their minds. Judges,
> sheriffs, magistrates, crown counsel, law officers – all are Protestant
> . . . It is not, therefore, wonderful that they should have a conscious-
> ness that they belong to a debased and inferior community . . .

The people as a result evolved their own primitive and barbarous
legislation. A change of system, with Emancipation, would not produce
immediate results or effects but 'the experiment' would be 'worth the
trial' (*114*, I, 317-28).

Both the upper and the lower classes were disappointed with the
results of Emancipation. As early as June 1829 O'Connell noted in a
postscript to Pierce Mahony: 'The old system of government is in full
force here – not the least change in the government – all as bitterly
Orange as ever' (IV, 1581). By September he was complaining to the
Knight of Kerry 'that the decided countenance given to the Orange
faction prevents Emancipation from coming into play. There is more
of unjust and unnatural virulence towards the Catholics in the present
administration than existed even before the passing of the Emancipation
Bill' (IV, 1608). In April 1830 he explained to the Knight:

> The working of the system here is as completely Orange as if the
> Relief Bill had not passed. Can any thing in nature be more paltry
> than the *refusing* silk gowns to Catholic barristers? I do not of course
> allude to myself but twelve months are now elapsed and the Catholic
> Bar is as excluded as ever. The truth is we have an Orange Attorney-
> General, many Orange Judges, Gregory – the very demon of Orange-
> ism at the Castle, Darley who insulted the King is still at the head of
> the police. In fact Peel wedded the Orange Party while he was in
> Ireland and he has not the least idea of the rest of the country being
> of any value or estimation (IV, 1662a).

Catholics could now aspire to the highest positions but they were to find the mesh of privilege and procedures which surrounded the Establishment very difficult to penetrate. Formal exclusion was hardly more galling than 'virtual' exclusion. In 1841 a Protestant barrister wrote '. . . the heads of the post office, the poor law, and the police are all Englishmen or Scotchmen, and the native Indian is hardly more carefully excluded from offices of the first rank in Calcutta than is the native Irishman . . .'[2] In December 1844 Peel was able to observe that the Protestants

> have had pretty nearly a complete monopoly of every good thing that this Government have had . . . to dispose of. Take political office, ordinary civil service, representative peerage, honorary distinctions, legal appointments . . . notwithstanding the nominal equality of civil privileges by statute, the practical result is that the Roman Catholics gain little by it (*61*, 74-7).

The Catholic and O'Connellite sense of grievance was justified: this consciousness of exclusion explains much of the force behind O'Connellite politics after 1829 and the negative Catholic attitudes to the Union.

Popular Catholic disappointment had set in almost immediately: a local priest who had spoken to a leader of the Whitefeet, who were behind a wave of rural outrages in the early 1830s, reported his views as follows:

> The law does nothing for us. We must save ourselves. We have a little land which we need for ourselves and our families to live on, and they drive us out of it. To whom should we address ourselves? We ask for work at eightpence a day and we are refused. To whom should we address ourselves? Emancipation has done nothing for us. Mr. O'Connell and the rich Catholics go to Parliament. We die of starvation just the same (*29*, 132).

Another priest who said that he often heard the conversation of the Whitefeet reported them as saying: 'What good did Emancipation do us? Are we better clothed and fed? Are we not as naked as we were, and eating dry potatoes when we can get them? Let us notice the farmers to give us better food and better wages, and not give so much to the landlord and more to the workmen' (*66*, 109-10).

As a result Macaulay was able to describe Irish disturbance in the House of Commons on 6 February 1833 as worse than civil war:

> Recollect that, in one county alone, there have been within a few weeks sixty murders or assaults with intent to murder and six hundred burglaries. Since we parted last summer the slaughter in Ireland has exceeded the slaughter of a pitched battle: the destruction of

property has been as great as would have been caused by the storm-ing of three or four towns. Civil war, indeed! I would rather live in the midst of any civil war that we have had in England during the last two hundred years than in some parts of Ireland at the present moment.

Gerald Griffin's novel *Tracy's Ambition*, published in 1829, portrays a turbulent and disordered society bitterly divided into two sectarian camps — even the horses at the local races had 'Catholic' or 'Orange' identities. But the most shocking aspect of that society was the malign attitude of authority to the Irish people. The magistrate Dalton hated the people though he could not avoid seeing what would make them better: '. . . They are a disgusting horde, from first to last. I enquire not into causes and effects; I weigh not the common cant of misrule and ignorance; I look not into historical influences; I speak of the men as I find them, and act by them as such . . . I hate the people'.

The passage of Emancipation did not answer the immediate and prac-tical demands of Irish Catholics for 'fair treatment' in law, politics, land or administration. It failed to do this or to inaugurate a period of recon-ciliation because of the context in which it was passed and because it did not address the fundamental divisions within Ireland or between Ireland and Britain. When Macaulay set out his purpose for his *History of England* in 1848, he saw 'the history of our country during the last hundred and sixty years' as 'eminently the history of physical, of moral, and of intellectual improvement' but to this Ireland was an ex-ception and he must record 'how Ireland, cursed by the domination of race over race, and of religion over religion, remained indeed a member of the empire, but a withered and distorted member, adding no strength to the body politic, and reproachfully pointed at by all who feared or envied the greatness of England' (77, 52). On 19 February 1844, in a debate on the state of Ireland in the House of Commons, he put his finger on the reasons why Emancipation had failed as a solution to the Irish question:

> In 1829, at length, concessions were made, were made largely, were made without the conditions which Mr. Pitt would undoubtedly have demanded, and to which, if demanded by Mr. Pitt, the whole body of Roman Catholics would have eagerly assented. But these concessions were made reluctantly, made ungraciously, made under duress, made from the mere dread of civil war. How then was it possible that they should produce contentment and repose? What could be the effect of that sudden and profuse liberality following that long and obstinate resistance to the most reasonable demands, except

to teach the Irishman that he could obtain redress only by turbulence?

We can identify the reasons for the government's evasion of the Catholic question in the thirty years after the Union – the power of the crown, the looseness of the cabinet system, the ideological panic after the French Revolution which postponed essential reforms for thirty years, the independence of the legislature and the fear of the 'no popery' prejudice of the English – but whatever the reasons the consequences were fatal to the Union itself. By the end of the 1820s the government had faced the grim possibility of another rising or civil war merely thirty years after 1798; moreover, it had faced the electoral revolt in the counties which would have given control of the popular representation to Catholics even without concession. It had faced a paralysis of legal and civil administration through non-payment of tithes and rents and exclusive dealing in the towns. As Wyse observed: 'Had things gone on in the state in which they were, it is quite certain the great mass of the Catholics, at no distant period, would scarcely have thought it worth their while to have continued asking any longer, for what had been so long and so punctiliously refused them' (*132*, I, 323).

William Lamb, surveying the persistent Irish discontents of the 1830s, commented sceptically on the prognostications of the eager reformers:

> 'Our ablest men', he used to say, 'or at least our ablest in debate, seem to be the most stinted by nature in the quality of foresight. Look at what has occurred with respect to the Catholic question: What all the clever men, Whigs and Tories, foretold as the consequences of Emancipation has been falsified, and religious rancour influences party politics nearly as much as did before (*123*, II, 315).

Lamb recognised that the good effects which were hoped for from Emancipation had been baffled by the long delay in its passage. 'As a political measure, it has hitherto been a signal failure', said Bishop C. R. Sumner about Emancipation in 1845:

> It has not restored tranquillity to the country – it has not lightened the difficulty in the councils of the state – it has not contributed to the safety of the branch of our church in Ireland – it has not opened up the way to converts from Popery . . . if I could have read that measure by the light of the fifteen years which have elapsed since its enactment, I could not have given, in 1845, the vote I gave in 1829 (*80*, 192-3).

The effects of Emancipation outlined by its opponents were by and large more accurate than those of its proponents. The ultra Protestant fears were well grounded. The prescription of such Protestants, however, for Irish ills — moral reformation of the Irish character — was to say the least unrealistic given their public opposition to everything the people regarded as measures of justice and liberation. These Protestants were singularly ill-fitted to play the rôle of moral leaders of the people.

Catholic Emancipation disappointed every important section of society in its immediate aftermath. The hopes for the measure were divergent and often simplistic. However Catholic Emancipation, because of this sense of failure, should not be seen to have only secondary significance. It was of fundamental importance in British and Irish history. It marks the transformation of the politics of the old order into the politics of the new.

In May 1828 Gustave d'Eichthal saw that it was generally recognised that Catholic Emancipation was 'only the prelude to more important changes in the Constitution' and that it indicated the declining importance of the Established Church in the face of the rise of liberalism: 'The liberal reforming party is to be found here as it was in France on the eve of the Revolution, and so is the system of privilege which extends from the aristocracy right down to the village. The struggle is between these two parties' (*112*, 25, 32).

Peel, who as Bagehot remarked had 'the powers of a first-rate man and the creed of a second-rate man', recognised the liberal trend in public opinion quite early. On 23 March 1820 he wrote to John Wilson Croker: 'Do not you think that the tone of England — of that great compound of folly, weakness, prejudice, wrong feeling, obstinacy, and newspaper paragraphs, which is called public opinion — is more liberal — to use an odious but intelligible phrase — than the policy of the Government?' He detected a feeling becoming more general 'in favour of some undefined change in the mode of governing the country'. By 1827 the break-up of the parties in the Commons had begun: Henry Brougham in the *Edinburgh Review* in 1827 prophesied that party distinctions would be resolved into two great divisions of 'Liberal' and 'Illiberal'.

Eighteen twenty-seven began a constitutional revolution which culminated in the passage of the great Reform Act of 1832. Sidney Smith later remarked that the period from 1800 to the death of Liverpool 'was an awful period for those who had the misfortune to entertain liberal opinions' (*121*, I, viii). Catholic Emancipation was central both to the great liberal awakening and to the constitutional revolution of 1827-32.

On 11 March 1829 John Stuart Mill wrote to Gustave d'Eichthal that Catholic Emancipation 'has given a shake to men's minds which

has loosened all old prejudices, and will render them far more accessible to new ideas and to rational innovations on all other parts of our
institutions'. For this reason Mill believed that the probable effect of
the measure in Ireland would 'be a trifle compared to its effect in
England':

> It forms an era in civilisation. It is one of those great events, which
> periodically occur, by which the institutions of a country are brought
> into harmony with the better part of the mind of that country . . .
> this measure will bring forward the rear-guard of civilisation: it will
> give a new direction to the opinions of those who never think for
> themselves, & who on that account can never be changed unless you
> change their masters & guides.

He thought, correctly as it transpired, that the Tory party was broken:

> It is entirely gone. It placed all on this stake, & it has lost it . . . the
> clergy have opposed this with all their might, & as they have failed,
> the influence of the church, its moral influence at least, is gone . . .
> All its influence rested upon the opinion of its power (*86*, XII, 26-8).

Curiously Mill's analysis was very similar to that of thoughtful
Orange opponents of Emancipation. William Saurin in a major speech
on 19 February 1829 to the Second General Meeting of the Brunswick
Constitutional Club of Ireland described Catholic Emancipation as a
'revolution in the Government': 'It was, with its concomitant measure
called Parliamentary Reform, the offspring of that spirit, and those
principles of democracy and revolution, which, for the last forty years,
have been assailing, and shaking to its centre, the British Constitution'.
Saurin declared that models of government, such as in the United States
of America, where equality of political rights, the absence of an established church, the openness of every office and the wide franchise were
leading features, were quite unsuited to the British Empire. There was
'no natural right to office':

> The measure now proposed, professing to settle a question, suffer
> me to say, will, in my opinion, settle nothing. It may, and will reverse
> a policy which we have adhered to for 260 years; it will unsettle
> men's minds; it will unsettle the Constitutional settlement of 1688:
> it will destroy all standard of Constitutional sentiment and opinion;
> but it will settle nothing. It must be considered as a compromise
> with that spirit of radicalism and democracy, supported by the spirit
> of party, which has long been encroaching upon our Constitution,
> and threatening it in all its parts and proportions'.[3]

Major events which 'unsettle' or 'shake men's minds' tend to have varied
and unexpected effects. Catholic Emancipation was of seminal impor-

tance: it facilitated the Reform Act of 1832; it altered fundamentally church-state relations; it was the fruit of the rise of democracy in Ireland; and it decisively swung the long-term balance of power in Ireland as between Catholics and Protestants.

Horace Twiss wrote, 'The Catholic Emancipation had riven the conservative body asunder and through the chasm the Reform Bill forced its way'. The crisis over Emancipation ended the conservative alliance which had ruled Britain since the 1790s. The ultras could never forgive Wellington and Peel for their abandonment of the Protestant basis on which the Constitution had stood since the Anglican settlement made at the 1688 Revolution. 'Breaking in upon the Constitution', to use Peel's phrase, rang in their ears as a great betrayal and the start of a continuous encroachment not only on the Constitution but on the Church and on the privileges of the landed classes. They were right: under Peel there followed a progressive liberalisation of the Tory party during the 1830s and 1840s. Wellington's ineptitude as a politician was of course a contributory factor in the decline of his government and the accession to power of Grey's reform ministry. The death of George IV in June 1830 led to a general election which weakened Wellington; Grey came to office in November. But of more fundamental significance than the individual skills of political leaders was the fact that the Catholic struggle had set the pattern for the 'struggle for popular rights'. The period 1827-32, in retrospect, may be seen as a time of constitutional revolution, a revolution which in Macaulay's phrase 'brought Parliament into harmony with the nation'. Emancipation was a victory for the Commons against the Lords, the cabinet against the crown, and of extra-parliamentary organisation against the closed circle at Westminster. Directly the model of the Catholic Association became the prototype for the alliance between the middle and the lower classes essential for the success of extra-parliamentary campaigns which now became extensive. It is perhaps now difficult to realise the full novelty for politicians in the 1830s who had to accept that a body like the Catholic Association had a right to co-exist with parliament and indeed to influence parliament's deliberations. The Chartists and the Anti-Corn Law League, as well as O'Connell's own associations, depended on the struggle of the 1820s for inspiration.

In October 1829, in a comment to Jeremy Bentham, O'Connell identified the nature of the new democratic movement: 'The *History of the Catholic Association*', wrote O'Connell, referring to Wyse's instant *Historical Sketch*, 'omits that part of the struggle which is most interesting, and is most instructive, I mean the working up of small means into mighty engines. The progress from political infancy, through political infantile squabbles, into something of youthful strength, and then into great manhood and vigour' (VIII, 3416). When Thomas

Attwood, the radical Birmingham banker, formed the Birmingham Political Union he was directly modelling his organisation on the Catholic Association as he acknowledged in a speech in May 1829:

> By union, by organisation, by general contribution, by patriotic exertion, and by discretion, keeping always within the law and the constitution. These are the elements of Reform. By the peaceful combination of means like these the Irish people have lately obtained a glorious and bloodless victory . . .' (*113*, 174).

Attwood consulted O'Connell in early 1830 about the legality of the Birmingham Union which O'Connell, as a radical Reformer, joined giving advice which summarised the techniques of the Catholic Association:

> There are two principal means of attaining our constitutional objects which will never be lost sight of. The first is the perpetual determin-ation to avoid anything like physical force or violence and by keep-ing in all respects within the letter as well as the spirit of the law, to continue peaceable, rational, but energetic measures so as to com-bine the wise and the good of all classes, stations and persuasions in one determination to abolish abuse and renovate the tone and strength of the representative system. The other is to obtain funds by the extension of a plan of collection which shall *accept* from no man more than he can with the utmost facility spare even in these times of universal distress. The multiplication of small sums, of very small sums, should be the proper as it would be the efficacious popular treasury. Its guardian should be the publication of every item of receipt and expenditure. I offer my experience to assist in arranging a plan for this purpose. The people should incessantly call for reform until their cry is heard and *felt* within the walls of West-minster' (IV, 1640).

In the spring of 1830 O'Connell was much in demand in reform politics: he chaired the meeting which formed the Metropolitian Poli-tical Union in London modelled on the Birmingham Union and spoke in favour of universal suffrage, shorter parliaments, the ballot and law reform. In tribute to his standing he was regularly invited to such places as Coventry and Wolverhampton as guest of their Political Unions. He played a large part in the passage of the Reform Act of 1832, in the abolition of slavery and in the whole course of liberal legislation which transformed social, political and administrative structures in the United Kingdom during the 1830s. He had already in the 1820s bequeathed to popular politics his major contribution: the modern political party. The Catholic Association foreshadowed in almost every single feature modern democratic political parties and gave new hope for peaceful change. Thomas Wyse wrote in 1829:

Every day, the chance of regenerating a nation by the coarse expedient of physical force is, thank God! becoming less and less.
There is every day a greater confidence in the power and efficacy of
mere mind; there is every day a more firm assurance in the strength
and sufficiency of unassisted reason. France and England are now
the great scenes for the fullest development of this important problem. From those two countries must flow henceforth the political
education of Europe (*132*, I, 7-8).

In 1830 'the exhilarating events' that were daily springing up seemed
to O'Connellites like P. V. Fitzpatrick 'an almost miraculous illustration'
of O'Connellite 'principles and doctrines' (IV, 1713). O'Connell himself
believed that 'the aspect of the times' was 'exceedingly favourable'.
He got up 'a most numerous meeting in honour of the French and
Belgic revolutions in the court house of Tralee and passed many honest
resolves' (IV, 1714, 1716). For O'Connell the struggle for popular
rights was universal and the issues transcended race and nation. John
Stuart Mill attempted to capture 'The Spirit of the Age' in an essay in
the *Examiner* in early 1831: 'The first of the leading peculiarities of
the present age is that it is an age of transition. Mankind have out-
grown old institutions and old doctrines, and have not yet acquired new
ones.' Mill noted the spread of discussion: 'Men may not reason better,
concerning the great questions in which human nature is interested, but
they reason more.' Ultimately he foresaw that

> Worldly power must pass from the hands of the stationary part of
> mankind into those of the progressive part. There must be a moral
> and social evolution, which shall, indeed, take away no men's lives
> or property, but which shall leave to no man one fraction of unearned
> importance.

Catholic Emancipation inaugurated the liberal democratic era.

Beginning with the electoral 'revolts' of the 1826 general election local
political machines developed in Ireland and very soon became an essential part of what might be called, in Professor Gash's phrase, 'the ordinary working world of the politician' (*41*, ix). If MPs' electoral influence
was being overthrown — as between 1826 and 1828 it clearly was —
their general local influence was also being directly undermined and
thus their utility as local agents of law and order. MPs were central to
local administration as governors, deputy governors, magistrates, grand
jurors and landlords. They were key contacts in the distribution of local
places and patronage from the position of sheriff down. By the end of
1828 many areas were electorally organised to defeat MPs who sup-

ported the government and it took five-sixths of the infantry force of the United Kingdom to maintain law and order in Ireland. Catholic Emancipation relieved the immediate threat in Ireland but 'the strong democratic feeling' described by Sheil as having been engendered by the Catholic struggle was bound to find expression after the great victory had been won (*114*, II, 254).

Despite the narrow franchise of the years between Emancipation and Reform, 1829 to 1832, popular success was still possible in the counties as 'Big George' had discovered to his cost in Limerick in 1830. The key elements of the democratic revolution of the 1820s, the drilled, disciplined electorate, the pledge-bound party, the nation-wide communications network, the alliances between town and countryside, between the middle class leadership and the Catholic Church, survived intact. T. L. Lefroy asked at the Second General Meeting of the Brunswick Constitutional Club in February 1829: 'Can we doubt that the union between Popery and Liberalism and the enormous party which will grow out of such a union must be dangerous to our Established Church and its reformed faith?' Out of the panic created by Emancipation grew a new Irish Tory party to defend 'the old Orange Principle' as Lefroy put it to Lord Farnham in December 1830.[4] When in August and September 1832 O'Connell called for 'a parochial committee in each parish [and] a County Independent Club in each county' to fight the coming general election and to collect the National Rent he was, in effect, seeking the reactivation of the 1820s system of local and county clubs which had marked time but not ceased to exist since 1829.[5] The prospect of a reformed franchise and the system of registration secured a widespread reactivation; in 1832, at least twenty-four constituencies possessed clubs in the Repeal interest and eleven had Whig-Liberal organisations. The Tories were similarly organised in nine constituencies (*81*, 89-94).

The details of the Liberal Clubs given by Wyse are essentially accurate but as Wyse wrote his *Sketch* in 1829 it has been assumed that there was little direct continuity from the 1820s to the club system of the 1830s. O'Connell's opinion in March 1829 was that 'the Liberal Clubs ought not to dissolve themselves' as he believed that they did not come within the act designed to suppress the Catholic Association. O'Connell advised that the Catholic Association should be changed into the Catholic Reading Rooms and he was conscious of the need for 'a rallying point', believing 'a reading-room is just the very best you can have'. A new registry of voters was held following the alteration of the franchise in 1829 and O'Connell was anxious that this be acted upon in Clare and other places and that Staunton be allowed 'to continue his weekly papers to the churchwardens' either at O'Connell's expense or through the Finance Committee of the Catholic Association which continued to meet until December 1829 to deal with claims outstanding on the Catholic Association and to wind up the accounts (IV, 1566). Many of the local clubs, such as Waterford and Cork, dissolved in the spring of 1829 but, in effect, they continued as News Rooms or were quickly re-established as Independent Clubs.

The Louth Club met in May 1829 for their usual quarterly meeting. Some members favoured dissolution but this was opposed by Sheil who wanted to stand for Louth at the next election. The Louth Club, with 'the aid of their professional agents', were reported as very active at the registry sessions in June 1829. At the next quarterly meeting the motion to dissolve was 'negatived by an immense majority'; at this period the contest between Sheil and R. M. Bellew for the popular nomination ensured a lively club attendance and indeed new members were admitted. Also in Louth, the Drogheda Independent Club met in September 1829 and was addressed by Sheil. In January 1830, O'Connell presided at the anniversary dinner of the club when Repeal and 'radical reform' were the toasts. In 1830 John Henry North defeated Maurice O'Connell, the Liberator's eldest son, for the seat in Drogheda and O'Connell was informed that the registry was 'most defective' because of lack of attention by the Liberal Club (IV, 1701). In January 1830 the Louth Independent Club held their annual meeting and dinner. It continued to hold regular quarterly meetings.[6] The popular activists, Sheil, Bellew and of course, the MP, Dawson, paid close attention to the club which was essential for their success at the polls. All three stood in 1830 though only Dawson was elected; Sheil and Dawson were elected in 1831 and R. M. Bellew was elected in 1832 when Sheil was returned for Tipperary. Significantly in 1832 when Sheil was seeking election in Tipperary he re-established with the local activists a Liberal Club in Clonmel (IV, 1927).

In other counties the Liberal Clubs remained active; the Monaghan Club met, after a couple of postponements, in September 1829 at Clones.[7] The Roscommon Independent Club held a quarterly meeting at Castlerea when fifty gentlemen dined together in July 1829. In August this club was remodelled as the 'Roscommon Independent Election Club' and a number of large subscriptions were paid to defend the county from a Tory challenge. The Roscommon Club met in March and August 1830.[8] In October 1829 plans were made in Wexford to call together the County Wexford Independent Club. In Clare O'Gorman Mahon studiously worked the constituency through meetings and a canvass; both he and W. N. MacNamara were elected in 1830.[9] Letters in O'Connell's correspondence between April and July 1830 provide revealing glimpses of local electoral activity in Clare showing that local opinions and issues were important considerations for the candidates and how O'Connell's local machinery of 1828 responded. In Co. Down, a liberal Independent Freeholders Club supported Matthew Forde, though unsuccessfully, in 1830.[10]

O'Connell believed in the value of local organisation. The firm basis for powerful political clubs existed in Cork, Waterford, Louth, Monaghan, Roscommon, Wexford, Clare and Down. In other counties tentative moves were made in 1830 to reactivate local electoral organisations. In Meath, for example, an Independent Club functioned and had local branches such as the Ratoath Independent Club. In the 1831 election O'Connell feared for Grattan's success because 'the Club' was divided; however according to *The Pilot* Grattan's election was due largely to the work of the Club in Meath (IV, 1834). In Tipperary a freeholders meeting, led by Wyse, at Thurles resolved to form a committee to forward the registry.[11] In Carlow in 1830 an O'Connellite Club met (IV, 1681). In Westmeath the Athlone Liberal Club functioned in 1830.[12] In Co. Longford the Liberal Club was active in the elections of 1830 and 1831 (*99*, 571-83).

From 1830 O'Connell was concerned to provide a central political organisation in Dublin which would co-ordinate the local political clubs. In July 1830 he took the chair at a large meeting of the Metropolitan Political Union which had been formed to support radical reform in March 1830.[13] The Dublin Trades Political Union was originated in 1830 and later became the National Trades Political Union in 1831. O'Connell's letter to John O'Brien, a Dublin merchant, in September 1830 on the organisation of the Dublin Trades Political Union parallels that which he wrote to Thomas Attwood on the Birmingham Political Union (IV, 1710). During the early 1830s O'Connell's political movement was subject to measures adopted by the government to curb his agitation and thus he was forced to float a number of bodies in quick succession but, in essence, their purpose was the same. O'Connell managed to maintain and develop in Dublin a central party organisation which was vital, as Dublin and its politics exercised a powerful influence on the whole electoral system. This organisation was always modelled on the great movement of the 1820s led by the Catholic Association. For example, in August 1834, O'Connell, when wishing to revitalise the tithe agitation, told P. V. Fitzpatrick that 'the impulse should be given to the establishment of County Liberal Clubs and Liberal Clubs in every town' (V, 2105).

In the period between 1829 and 1832 local political organisations continued to meet and function, though because of the narrow franchise their effect was limited in terms of parliamentary seats. However, given the expectation of reform of the franchise and the Reform Act of 1832 O'Connell was able to sustain the new politics at local level which involved popular 'control' of the MP through local clubs. In Co. Waterford the political organisation, which had its roots in the Catholic

Rent and the 1826 general election, survived the dissolution of the Catholic Association and the disenfranchisement of the forty-shilling freeholders in 1829. Quickly the Rent collection system was followed by the collection of the O'Connell Tribute. Leading activists such as Wyse, Galwey, H. W. Barron, Hayes and P. G. Barron, became parliamentary candidates or MPs for the county or city, and Waterford remained a Liberal or Repeal stronghold after 1832.

The basis of Cork popular politics was laid in the 1820s and the leading activists of that decade continued in local politics until the 1850s. The city and county of Cork sent eight MPs to parliament; in terms of parliamentary politics Cork was a Liberal/Repeal preserve from 1832 as a result of the politicisation of the 1820s. Cork, like the other counties with active local political organisations, responded for the first time to a national leader and a national programme.

Ireland caught the attention in the 1830s of Alexis de Tocqueville and his friend Gustave de Beaumont because of O'Connell's novel democratic politics. In imitation of Tocqueville's masterpiece, *Democracy in America*, first published in 1835, Beaumont published his *Ireland: Social, Political, and Religious* in 1839. Given Tocqueville's and Beaumont's absorbing interest in the rise of democracy it was understandable that they should turn from the United States where they studied 'the image of democracy itself' to Ireland where O'Connell's popular democracy had emerged.

March 1829 had seen the passage of Catholic Emancipation in London and also the triumphant popular inauguration of Andrew Jackson as President in Washington. Jacksonian democracy, like O'Connellism, spelled the end of the easy ascendancy of the elite ruling classes: the day of the multitude had dawned. In the new democratic era, with the creation of the broadly-based national organisation, power was not imparted from above but was built up from the ground. Tocqueville and Beaumont believed that the future of European society lay with democracy; people were 'beginning to get the idea that they, too, could take part in government' (*29*, 14). Beaumont examined with great clarity the causes by which Ireland tended 'to become a democratic country': amongst the main causes was the political organisation which developed from the Catholic struggle, Daniel O'Connell's leadership, as well as the development of the Irish middle class.

Both Tocqueville and Beaumont reflected on the 'democratic' tendency of the Catholic clergy in Ireland. In July 1835 Tocqueville dined with some Irish bishops and priests and he noted his impressions:

The feelings expressed were extremely democratic. Distrust and hatred of the great landlords; love of the people and confidence in them. Bitter memories of past oppression. An air of exaltation at present or approaching victory. A profound hatred of the Protestants and above all of their clergy. Little impartiality apparent. Clearly as much the leaders of a party as the representatives of the Church' (*29*, 130).

In the 1820s O'Connell, Doyle and MacHale had given the Catholic Church a new vital sense of its potential influence in political affairs. The priests had been essential lieutenants assisting the local organisation of the Catholic Association. Given the Association's policy of exerting the maximum moral force in favour of Emancipation the personnel of the Catholic Church were an obvious mainspring for O'Connellite organisation: O'Connellites had cultivated a coincidence of purpose with the Catholic Church (*97*, 317).

Beaumont identified the Ulster Presbyterians as another possible democratic influence in Ireland; he noted that the democratic nature of their organisation could be compared with the Constitution of the United States. While Catholicism proceded from a principle of authority Presbyterianism proceded from a principle of liberty yet, according to Beaumont, in Ireland both had a common democratic effect which was a 'remarkable phenomenon'. He observed the division of Irish Presbyterians into those who saw some political interests in common with Catholics and those who saw only religious barriers between themselves and Catholics. Both liberal Presbyterians and Catholics were opposed to the aristocracy – the first because they saw an Anglican Establishment and the Catholics because it was Protestant and anti-national. The tendency towards democracy in Ireland could derive immense power from the union between these interests but Beaumont realistically posed the question: 'Is not this alliance between the Presbyterians and Catholics factitious and transitory?' He certainly believed that it was – the gap between 'the Scotch Puritan of the North' and the Catholic was too great. Beaumont had visited Ulster in July 1837 and was a witness to 'hateful passions'. He concluded that Ulster '. . . might be supposed constantly on the eve of a civil war'.

Beaumont realised the political significance of the emergence of an urban, educated Catholic middle class which had made a dramatic entrance into the political stage: '. . . to be suddenly summoned to the direction of public affairs, the middle class of Ireland seems almost dazzled by its own splendour. It scarcely believes in so magnificent an elevation succeeding so rapidly to so great degradation'. This merchant class was naturally opposed to revolution; indeed the middle class would have 'to sustain a struggle in order to remain democratic'. The class aspiring to power was bound to be influenced by the aristocracy which was the only pattern of political power and privilege then known.

Beaumont feared this 'feudal contagion'. It was fortunate, he believed, that the Irish middle class was not put at once into possession of its full powers: 'Before it can govern well, it must learn the science of government. It is in this respect that the labours of the national association are still of such immense importance: it is a school of government where instruction is every day afforded to the class that is destined to govern.'

Wyse saw his plan for a national political organisation in the context of the growth of the idea of self-government and the development of political democracy. He wished to prepare post-Emancipation Ireland for the new democratic age. In this he was at one with O'Connell who also sought 'to bring the great principles of democratic liberty and self-government into practical operation' (IV, 1703). Wyse, like de Tocqueville, believed that there was a great transition in every part of Europe from an aristocratic to a democratic era and in an unpublished 'Essay on Irish Politics' Wyse explored this 'work of a deep and gradual preparation' in 'the national mind'.

Wyse argued for a Board to be established for the self-government of the country which would bring all classes of which the nation was composed into the administration of its affairs.[14] In a published letter Wyse described how the Catholic cause in Ireland was 'a universal and unequivocal manifestation of the will and energies of the nation. The cause is the greatest now fighting in the world — or rather it is a part only of that great combat of the new age against the old, which occupies everything that is thought, intellect, or spirit in every country in Europe'.[15] Thus in 1828 Wyse foreshadows the Tocqueville thesis and expresses his belief in the coming of democracy in a similar vein to that which Tocqueville was to explore in *Democracy in America*. In this remarkable letter Wyse explains the utility of his *Political Catechism*, which he was preparing under the auspices of the Association.

Wyse's *The Political Catechism, Explanatory of the Constitutional Rights and Civil Disabilities of the Catholics of Ireland*, published early in 1829, was intended to be a popular manual of liberal Catholicism. He outlined the practical rôle of the Liberal Clubs, which were 'very nearly general in Ireland', in mobilising public opinion. Wyse also called for Irish Catholics to meet 'in a special annual session' immediately before the meeting of parliament; this was a device to be used by O'Connell when he called a National Council meeting in 1833. Wyse wished to crown his national political organisation with this annual session which would replace the Catholic Association at the apex of the national system of county and city clubs, baronial clubs and parochial clubs. This, he urged, would complete the democratic organisation of the people of Ireland.

The European significance of the Irish political party organisation can hardly be over-estimated. As late as 1902 Ostrogorski in his pioneer-work *Democracy and the Organisation of Political Parties* remarked: 'In almost every country of the European continent the organisation of parties working regularly outside parliament is still but little developed' (*103*, I, liii). One of Ostrogorski's chief worries about political parties was that they did not provide political education, being more 'electioneering machines' and that they tended to create a 'stereotyped opinion' (*103*, I, 584-6).

The Catholic Association marked the early political mobilisation of a largely rural electorate. It secured in 1829 the first great legislative measure forced on parliament through the pressure of a political organisation outside parliament. What pattern of popular politics did it establish in Ireland? The key aspect of the politicisation of the 1820s was that it was based upon Catholic grievances. There was given to Irish democracy and nationalism a sectarian base which has severely handicapped subsequent attempts to define and gain acceptance for a more comprehensive Irish nationalism. It is surely significant that Macaulay was able to point out in the House of Commons on 6 February 1833 that

> every argument which has been urged for the purpose of showing that Great Britain and Ireland ought to have two distinct parliaments may be urged with far greater force for the purpose of showing that the north of Ireland and the south of Ireland ought to have two distinct parliaments. The House of Commons of the United Kingdom, it has been said, is chiefly elected by Protestants, and therefore cannot be trusted to legislate for Catholic Ireland. If this be so, how can an Irish House of Commons, chiefly elected by Catholics, be trusted to legislate for Protestant Ulster? . . . It is indeed certain that, in blood, religion, language, habits, character, the population of some of the northern counties of Ireland has much more in common with the population of England and Scotland than with the population of Munster and Connaught.

The *Northern Whig* on 2 April 1829 had noted that 'an inveterate and determined hostility exists among the ignorant mass of the Presbyterian body against the Catholic claims'.

The two peoples on the island of Ireland grew further apart during the 1820s. Indeed, both Cooke and O'Connell had created 'stereotyped opinion' north and south. A distinction must be made between the personal tenets held by a great charismatic leader and popular folk hero like O'Connell and the impact of O'Connellism upon the mentality of the masses. O'Connell's personal principles were liberal, indeed radical and democratic: no man should be discriminated against on the grounds of religion or race; a people had the right to self-government because it would be the best government for them; politics was not the preserve of an oligarchy but the province of the people. Popular political communication could not, however, be a rational business. Followers of O'Connell were induced by appeals to their emotions, by social and religious pressures, and the sense of participation gained through political ritual such as parades, songs and emblems. The 'crowd' was excluded from real political participation by the leadership as far as 'high politics' was concerned, yet in a deeper sense collectively the people began to arbitrate on their own destiny as never before. It is apparent from their songs and folklore that a profound psychological satisfaction attached to the popular overthrow of the traditional holders of authority, as in Ennis in July 1828. In the context in which O'Connell worked he inevitably became 'the Great Catholic leader'. His campaign was rooted in the 'practical' grievances of the Catholic people which were derived from the Protestant Ascendancy.

In O'Connellite politics, then, social and and economic issues were secondary. The leadership of the local organisations was primarily from the urban and rural middle and upper classes: the impressive network of local branches was formed and led by a large discontented segment of the urban population drawn from the professions, trade, manufacturing and the shopkeepers, supported by the Catholic country gentry and tenant-farmers. This leadership was motivated by an aspiration for social and political influence, by a wish to end religious discrimination, by a powerful drive to advance Catholics in general in public life. The era of middle-class predominance in society was dawning. Economic grievances abounded but they were kept firmly in second place as O'Connell overcame the inherent incompatibility of interests between the social groups he led, by a broad campaign for 'Catholic' rights and justice. Local Catholic politicians and the Catholic Association dealt with specific grievances of their 'clients' but they did not propose to their followers a social or economic policy to transform their situation. Clientalism as the mark of Irish popular politics originated in the 1820s. The grievances of the poor and the less well off peasants were joined to the aspirations articulated by the more politically conscious middle and upper classes.

The ideology of Irish liberal Catholicism was propagated by a relatively small and closely knit group. Sheil and Wyse were schoolfellows and friends who represented the small professional group who emerged through Stonyhurst and Trinity College in the early years of the century. Thomas Moore was closely associated with the Catholic leadership and with O'Connell. Bishop Doyle corresponded frequently with the Catholic leaders. John MacHale was to translate Moore into Irish and both he and Doyle were the most dynamic leaders of the Catholic Church. Essentially this small group with their allies, especially the newspapers editors F. W. Conway and Michael Staunton, consciously shaped the political ideology of the first mass movement in modern

Irish history: the Irish Catholic would be advanced through reconciliation with Protestants (J.K.L. even proposed a union of the Churches)
and with England under the British Constitution. This Constitution was
given a very liberal interpretation which necessitated reform and a
change in the way it was generally understood in the early nineteenth
century: liberal Catholics had to argue for the enlargement of the scope
of the Constitution, to include all subjects. In practical terms they enlarged the Constitution by developing in it a place for political parties.
It was an achievement of seminal importance.

Irish liberals like Doyle, Moore and O'Connell showed a deep interest
in the cause of liberty in other countries. Doyle himself had taken part
in Portugal's struggle against the French; Moore celebrated Greek independence in his writings; and O'Connell's commitment to South
American liberty and universally accepted liberal causes was well
known. These Irishmen looked forward to the universal success of
liberty, tempered by constitutional government. It was no accident,
then, that continental interest in Ireland was at a peak during the
O'Connellite era. O'Connell, by showing how the people could participate in politics, helped to quell liberal fears of the tyranny of the
majority over the minority — fears of mob rule grounded in the excesses
of Jacobinism.

The Irish crisis became central to the great reforming debates in British
politics. The Irish Catholic leaders would not have disagreed with
Macaulay when he wrote in the *Edinburgh Review* in October 1829:

> Our fervent wish . . . is that we may see such a reform of the House
> of Commons as may render its votes the express image of the opinion
> of the middle orders of Britain . . . We should wish to see an end put
> to all the advantages which particular forms of property possess over
> other forms, and particular portions of property over other equal
> portions. And this would content us.

Liberals were not always fully democratic: they did not wish to see
all power reside in the people. They did believe that progress was to be
achieved by means of free institutions: a freely elected parliament, a
ministry dependent on parliament, an independent judiciary, freedom
of speech and assembly and all offices to be open to talent. They were
prepared to ally with the masses to achieve these constitutional advances
but they would always try to stop their 'revolutions' in the initial stages:
memories of the French Revolution were still powerful. This new creed
in Europe found unusual expression in Ireland, where it was associated
with Catholicism.

The Emancipation debate affected the whole question of the relationship between church and state within the British Constitution and during the 1830s the great church reform discussions occurred in the context of working out the implications of a mixed legislature in its future dealings with the Established Church. Publications such as H. Froude's *Remarks on the Interference of the State in Matters Spiritual* and Gladstone's *The State in its Relations with the Church* attempted to define the relationship in the wake of Emancipation. Gladstone's book, published in 1838, declaimed against the 'proud, ungodly spirit, which brands the forehead of the age' and argued that there was a central link between the Established Church and the state, that religious liberalism was wrong and that there was more to church-state relationships than a marriage of convenience: both had moral functions and the state had a duty to distinguish between truth and error and to support the true religion of the Established Church. How far circumstances since 1829 had made Gladstone's views unrealistic is revealed by Peel's brutal reaction. Richard Monckton Milnes, who was a guest of Peel when the book arrived, observed that

> Peel turned over the pages of the book with somewhat scornful curiosity, and, after a hasty survey of its contents, threw the volume on the floor, exclaiming as he did so: 'That young man will ruin his fine political career, if he persists in writing trash like this'.

Macaulay's brilliantly hostile review of the book in the *Edinburgh Review*, April 1839, in which he characterised Gladstone as 'the rising hope' of those 'stern and unbending Tories', revealed how the fate of the Irish Established Church as a testing ground was quite ill-suited for a defence of the Anglican Establishment in the United Kingdom. The Irish Church was, in Macaulay's words, 'a national church regarded as heretical by four-fifths of the nation committed to its care, a church established and maintained by the sword, a church producing twice as many riots as conversions'; a church which 'though possessing great wealth and power, and though long backed by persecuting laws, had in the course of many generations, been found unable to propagate its doctrines, and barely able to maintain its ground'; a church 'whose ministers were preaching to desolate walls, and with difficulty obtaining their lawful subsistence by the help of bayonets'. Such a church could not be defended. The state should not ally itself with such a church. There could be no turning back the clock. Macaulay's views gave assurance that British society and politics were developing on lines that regarded the 1829 settlement as irreversible.

Macaulay considered 'the primary end of government as a purely temporal end, the protection of the persons and property of men . . . Government is not an institution for the propagation of religion . . . all civil disabilities on account of religious opinions are indefensible . . .' A revolution in constitutional thought is represented by the gap between Gladstone and Macaulay. The Protestant Constitutionalists believed that there existed an indissoluble link between church and state. After Emancipation the secular concept of the state became dominant.

The meaning, then, of 1829, was profound. It was central to the growing official commitment to impartiality between the claims of the different religious groups. This impartiality, most dramatically seen in Peel's career as he moved from the leading church and state advocate to his major conciliatory measures for the Irish Catholic Church in the 1840s, was a powerful solvent of the traditional order, especially in Ireland. It demolished the basis for the Protestant Ascendancy: now such an Ascendancy was to be justified in terms of political expediency, not on religious grounds. Inequality could not be long defended on grounds of expediency. The state now implied that religion, rather than forming the underlying basis for the entire structure of government and society, was increasingly a private matter – a question of individual morals and ethics.

In the European context, where Catholicism after 1815 supported absolutism – the alliance between throne and altar – Irish liberal Catholicism was indeed exceptional. In this era of Papal conservatism and Metternichian reaction only in Ireland did the Catholic Church become committed to a great popular political struggle. In the first half of the nineteenth century, and indeed much later, liberalism was a novel, even a revolutionary force, and the Catholic Church was its leading opponent. Irish liberal Catholics predated the efforts of European liberal Catholics by reconciling the cause of library with religion: in Europe the chief field of action was in France where Lamennais and his disciples Gerbet and Lacordaire and, later, Montalembert attempted to modernise Catholicism through the adoption of liberal principles. Lamennais's *Paroles d'un Croyant* (1834) created uproar among governments, who scarcely expected to be stabbed in the back with so reliable a weapon for the defence of the status quo as Catholicism. He was soon condemned. As late as 1864 the Catholic Church denounced liberalism as one of the errors of the age. Hence Ireland was an important exception in Europe in that liberalism and Catholicism were linked together in a Catholic country and it became an inspiration to continental liberals; hence also Montalembert's famous address to O'Connell, on his last journey to Rome, extolling his work for liberalism and his universal significance.

The stance taken by Irish Catholics from the time of the Veto controversy was unusual. There was no novelty in Europe in Protestant as well as Catholic princes being accorded the *ius patronatus*, the patron's privilege of nomination to bishoprics. Indeed the attitude of the Roman Catholic Church can be briefly stated: in practical terms the Church taught that a Catholic government must assist and protect the Church and its teaching and such a government must not allow, except for reasons of prudence, the propagation of contrary doctrines. This teaching was confirmed by Gregory XVI's encyclicals *Mirari Vos*, 1832, *Singulari Nos*, 1834, Pius IX's *Syllabus Errorum*, 1864, and Leo XIII's *Immortale Dei*, 1885, which condemned the principle, though not necessarily the practice, of religious freedom. Such freedom remained condemned in official teaching until the Second Vatican Council: in the *Declaration of Religious Freedom*, 1965, the Vatican Council stated that every man has the right to worship God publicly according to his conscience and to propagate his religious beliefs.

O'Connell stood for no state interference or temporal rewards or penalties for religious belief. Whilst in practice the identification of Catholic and Irish politics resulted from the struggle of the 1820s it was O'Connell's ardent desire to achieve a 'complete severance of the Church from the State': he hailed this separation in the wake of the French Revolution in a public letter to the *Dublin Morning Post* in September 1830. The Catholic clergy, O'Connell felt, were placed in a 'false position' because of the excesses of the first French Revolution, and they associated

the safety of religion with the security of the throne . . . religion was wedded to loyalty . . . Catholicity in France was situated somewhat as Protestantism has been, and to a certain extent still is, in Ireland. It was considered to be the enemy of the people and of liberty . . . I do therefore most sincerely rejoice at the severance of the Church from the State in France. It is an example of great and most useful import. Why should such an incubus as our unwieldy Protestant Church temporalities oppress the Catholics and various Dissenters in Ireland? France has set the great and glorious example and it only remains for every other country, where rational liberty and common sense are respected, to imitate the precedent and protect the people from the oppressive absurdity of supporting clergymen from whom they do not derive any benefit whatsoever.

A great virtue of Emancipation, from O'Connell's point of view, was that it was passed without the British state attempting to enter into an organic relationship with the Catholic Church in the form of Protestant supervision of Catholic spiritual organisation. Had this been done, and Wellington desired it, it would surely have produced a bitter *Kulturkampf* in Victorian Britain.

Catholic Emancipation had a formative influence on Anglo-Irish re-lations. The manner of its achievement — the calculated brinkmanship of O'Connell's constitutional struggle which depended for its force on the threat of massive social disorder and violence — moulded the political reflexes of Irish politicians faced with an ill-informed and often callous Westminster. Robert Peel himself was very much aware of 'House of Commons' arguments': he pointed out to the Bishop of Oxford on 19 February 1828 that one had to convince 'People who know very little of the matter — care not much about it — half of whom have dined or are going to dine — and are only forcibly struck by that which they instantly comprehend without trouble' (*83*, I, 66-7).

Shortly before he died in 1836 Lord Fingall is reported to have recognised the need for O'Connell's forceful strategy, admitting the 'criminal cowardice' of the Catholic aristocrats and gentry:

> We never understood that we had a nation behind us — O'Connell alone comprehended that properly, and he used his knowledge fitly. It was by him the gates of the Constitution were broken open for us; we owe everything to his rough work, and to effect further services for Ireland, there must be more of it (*33*, I, 161-2).

O'Connell, and other Irishmen such as Plunket, faced English antipathy as they entered the closed circle in London. English Catholics in May 1829 'black-beaned' O'Connell in their Cis-Alpine Club (IV, 1566). In November 1830 Ellenborough notes: 'O'Connell has not been spoken to in the clubs he has entered. At Brooks's they turned their backs upon him' (*62*, II, 409). In 1827 Plunket was forced to give up an appointment as Master of the Rolls in England because the English Bar objected to him as an Irishman. He was appointed Chief Justice of the Common Pleas in Ireland as a compensation and raised to the peerage. Such anti-Irish feeling in Britain powerfully influenced the evolution of Irish nationalism.

Key British politicians, such as Peel and Lamb, had direct and formative experience in Irish politics in the 1820s where the struggle encompassed the religious, constitutional and economic issues which were to form the substance of Anglo-Irish relations for the rest of the nineteenth century. Peel's role in the struggle was decisive both in helping to prolong the issue and in the manner of resolving it.

The charge may be brought against Peel that he led the Protestant party against the rising genius of the Commons and by his personal efforts prolonged a hopeless contest by refusing a just demand: by reason of this prolongation he brought Ireland to the brink of civil war even though he was for a number of years conscious that he was fighting a losing battle. Peel was, of course, clear that for him it was a choice of evils in which he had to balance conflicting political necessities. As Bagehot noted of his career

Of almost all the great measures with which his name is associated, he attained great eminence as an opponent before he attained even greater eminence as their advocate . . . He did not bear the burden and heat of the day, other men laboured, and he entered into their labours . . . He was converted at the conversion of the average man (*5*, 6-7).

As Plunket told the House of Commons on 28 February 1825 in a famous passage: 'It is the province of human wisdom to wait upon the wings of time – not with the vain hope of arresting his progress, but to watch his course – to adopt institutions to new circumstances as they arise, and to make their form reflect the varying aspect of events.' Peel had a good deal more of this 'human wisdom' than most Tories. He had none the less built his career on the case for Catholic disabilities. The case was a powerful one, based upon the historical evolution of the British Constitution, the character of the Roman Catholic Church, and the nature of the Irish threat to the unity and security of the United Kingdom. If it is recollected that only in 1960 did a Catholic become President of the United States and that he had to offer repeated reassurances that there would be no papal interference in his presidency, some idea of the strength of Protestant fears about Roman domination may be gained. Peel's ultimate fears for the Church of Ireland, the Anglo-Irish landlord class, and the safety of the Union were successively realised over time after 1829. O'Connell had shattered the Anglo-Irish world.

Thus Peel's volte-face of 1828-9, the first of a series taken by him and others in the nineteenth century, was only possible when the balance of political necessity had been tipped sufficiently in favour of Emancipation. As Gladstone wrote in 1868:

If we have witnessed in the last forty years beginning with the epoch of Roman Catholic Emancipation, a great increase in the changes of party, or of opinion, among prominent men, we are not at once to leap to the conclusion that public character, as a rule, has been either less upright, or even less vigorous. The explanation is rather to be found in this, that the movement of the public mind has been of a nature entirely transcending former experience; and that it has likewise been more promptly and more effectively represented, than at any earlier period, in the action of the Government and the Legislature (*45*, 234).

Catholic Emancipation was a symbolic victory for the Catholic people of Ireland: the first token of national rehabilitation and self-respect obtained by the efforts of the people themselves. In 1839 Sydney Smith declared that he did not retract 'one syllable (or *one iota*)' of

what he had said or written upon the Catholic Question: 'What was
wanted for Ireland was Emancipation, time and justice, abolition of
present wrongs; time for forgetting past wrongs . . . It is now only
difficult to tranquillise Ireland, before Emancipation it was impossible'
(*121*, I, 84). Time and justice were in short supply. Ultimately Ireland
remained a chessboard upon which two powerful external authorities
– the British government and the Roman Catholic Church in different
manifestations – competed for control of the people's destiny in terms
of their own wider interests. The poet William Allingham observed in
1852: 'In Ireland, the mass of the people recognise but two great
parties, the one, composed of Catholics, patriots, would-be-rebels –
these being interchangeable ideas; the other, of Protestants, Orangemen,
wrongful holders of estates, and oppressors in general – these also being
interchangeable ideas' (*134*, 45).

> They're gone, they're gone, those penal days
> All creeds are equal in our isle;
> Then grant, O Lord, thy plenteous grace,
> Our ancient feuds to reconcile.
> Let all atone
> For blood and groan,
> For dark revenge and open wrong;
> Let all unite
> For Ireland's right,
> And drown our griefs in freedom's song;
> Till time shall veil in twilight haze,
> The memory of those penal days.

Thomas Davis, who wrote those lines, had more reason than most,
having clashed dramatically with O'Connell, to be aware of the grosser
aspect of both the Catholic and the Protestant mind in Ireland. Like
Peel in his famous speech introducing Catholic Emancipation in 1829,
Davis must have wondered if there was something 'inherent in the spirit
of Roman Catholicism which disdains equality'. He feared a new
Catholic ascendancy. He had difficulty in coming to terms with the
logical outcome of the rise of democracy in Ireland: Catholics, as the
majority, must in the last analysis, prevail and exercise power. But given
the gulf between the mental worlds of the Protestant and the Catholic
and their widely different historical perceptions of the same events in
Irish history, could they ever trust each other?

Davis, at least, knew that if the attempt was not made Protestants
had no common future with their Catholic fellow Irishmen. Most
Protestants, however, clung to the Union with Britain and were unpre-
pared to countenance their welfare being connected with what they
saw as the ultramontane authoritarian Catholic Church. As late as the

1930s David Thomson described the likeable and benevolent Ivy Kirkwood, the Anglo-Irish mistress of Woodbrook, Co. Roscommon, who

> because of the religion of the people who loved her . . . could not wholly return their love. She could not trust them. Doubt spoils love. She said to me more than once that Roman Catholic teaching was founded on deceit; for example that the high-ups of that Church thought of transubstantiation as symbolically true, but taught it as though it were literally true. She believed that anyone brought up in an atmosphere of deceit must acquire a deceitful nature. It was impossible to trust a Roman Catholic (*122*, 70).

Could Catholics, in their turn, build upon O'Connell's distinction between church and state or, in Davis's phrase, would their 'step betray, the freedman born in penal days'? Could Catholics really consider Protestants as Irish instead of as an English garrison? The liberal Catholicism espoused by O'Connell and compromised by clerical dominance in the Repeal movement of the 1840s, was of course insufficient to attract the confidence of most Protestants to the ideal of a self-governing Ireland. It does, however, provide a necessary, if not sufficient condition, for a comprehensive Irish nationalism that would comprehend the pluralist origins of the Irish people. The fact that it was so clearly and courageously enunciated in the rampantly sectarian 1820s, and in a constitutional and democratic manner, leads one to hope that its rediscovery might aid the process of reconciliation which would make it possible that the prayer of Davis might indeed be answered.

Note on Sources

The primary sources relating to the Catholic struggle within the United Kingdom of Great Britain and Ireland during the 1820s are plentiful, rich and varied. For this book I have drawn upon manuscript sources selectively, and in particular at those points where it seemed to me advisable to re-examine the accepted accounts. This is particularly evident in my treatment of the emergence and working of the local political organisations, the Liberal Clubs. For a fuller description of the primary sources the reader is referred to R. F. B. O'Ferrall, 'The Growth of Political Consciousness in Ireland 1823-1847: A Study of O'Connellite Politics and Political Education', Ph.D. thesis, Trinity College, Dublin 1978.

The records of the Catholic Association, which survive in the Dublin Diocesan Archives, in the collection known as 'Catholic Proceedings', provide the essential source for the workings of the Association, the methods used by the Association and their effects throughout Ireland. This major collection has been sorted only very recently. Reference should be made to Rev. Fergus O'Higgins, P.C., 'Catholic Association Papers in the Dublin Diocesan Archives', *Archivium Hibernicum*, Vol. XXIX, 1984, pp. 58-61. The Wyse Papers, now sorted in the National Library of Ireland, are the prime manuscript collection for the evolution of political organisations at local level. Other manuscript sources throw important light on local politics: these include the Day Papers in the Cork Archive Council; the Lefroy Papers, in Carrigglas Manor, Co. Longford; the Brunswick Club material in the National Library of Ireland. For specialised local studies of the struggle a combination of estate papers, the sources in the Irish State Paper Office, and in the national collections, with the printed sources, such as newspapers and parliamentary papers will, with persistence, yield the basis for a detailed reconstruction.

The detailed reports of Catholic Association meetings, set down generally verbatim by reporters employed by the government or by secretaries in the Association, survive in the Catholic Association Papers, Irish State Paper Office; the 'Catholic Proceedings' records in Archbishop's House, Dublin; in the National Library of Ireland (Mss 3289-90); and the Public Record Office, London (Home Office, 100/211-224). Taken together they provide an almost complete 'Hansard' of the

Catholic Association. These may be supplemented by the detailed reports found in newspapers such as the *Dublin Evening Post*. The Wellesley Papers are valuable and duplicates of Wellesley's official correspondence and his correspondence with Sir Robert Peel are in the National Library of Ireland. The originals are in the British Library.

The printed material ranges from contemporary newspapers, parliamentary papers, contemporary publications and collections of letters, speeches, memoirs and journals. There are also valuable contemporary works of reference. The following newspapers have been used either for the whole decade 1820-30 or selectively because complete runs do not survive or because particular local episodes were being examined:

Cork Mercantile Chronicle
Dublin Evening Post
Dublin Evening Mail
Freeman's Journal
Midland Chronicle and Westmeath Independent
Northern Whig
Ramsay's Waterford Chronicle
The Times
Waterford Chronicle
Waterford Mirror
Westmeath Journal
Westmeath Guardian and Longford News-Letter

The parliamentary debates and the various reports in parliamentary papers are of obvious importance. The principal contemporary publications such as Bishop Doyle's *A Vindication of the Religious and Civil Principles of the Irish Catholics* (Dublin 1823) will be found cited in the text and references. Pride of place amongst the edited letters must be taken by Professor M. R. O'Connell's multi-volume *The Correspondence of Daniel O'Connell* (Dublin 1972-80). This edition has finally placed O'Connell studies on the requisite basis of scholarship. The remaining printed contemporary material is listed in the Bibliography. The prime sources to be noted include A. Aspinall (ed.) *The Letters of King George IV 1812-30*; Lord Colchester (ed.) *The Diary and Correspondence of Charles Abbot, Lord Colchester*; Lady Gregory (ed.) *Mr. Gregory's Letter Box 1813-1830*; W. Hepworth Dixon (ed.) *Lady Morgan's Memoirs*; Lord Ellenborough, *A Political Diary 1828-1830*; W. T. McCullagh, *Memoirs of the Right Honourable Richard Lalor Sheil*; Peel's own apologia in volume one of his *Memoirs* published in 1856 by Lord Mahon and Edward Cardwell; D. Plunket, *The Life, Letters and Speeches of Lord Plunket*; M. W. Savage (ed.) *Sketches Legal and Political of the Late Right Honourable Richard Lalor Sheil*; and the Duke of Wellington (ed.) *Despatches, Correspondence, and Memoranda of*

Field Marshal Arthur Duke of Wellington. Thomas Wyse's *Historical Sketch of the Late Catholic Association of Ireland* published in two volumes in 1829 is most valuable as a record by a key participant of the struggle; the material in volume two is of particular value.

Reference should be made to quite recent scholarship relating to certain aspects of the story of Catholic Emancipation. Dr Jacqueline E. Hill's 'National festivals, the State and "Protestant Ascendancy" in Ireland, 1790-1829' published in *Irish Historical Studies*, Vol. XXIV, No. 93, May 1984, pp. 30-51 explains why such incidents as the 1822 clashes over the dressing of King William's statue were crucial in the evolution of Irish political culture. Norman Vance in his article 'Celts, Carthaginians and Constitutions: Anglo-Irish literary relations, 1780-1820' published in *Irish Historical Studies*, Vol. XXII, No. 87, March 1981, pp. 216-38 examines hitherto neglected cultural developments before the critical decade of the 1820s. Professor Norman Gash has written two important books relevant to the whole period: *Aristocracy and People: Britain 1815-1865*, London 1979, and *Lord Liverpool: The Life and Political Career of Robert Banks Jenkinson, Second Earl of Liverpool, 1770-1828*, London 1984. Dr K. T. Hoppen has produced a major study on post-Emancipation Irish politics, *Elections, Politics and Society in Ireland 1832-1885*, Oxford 1984, which explores the relationship between local political realities and national politics.

I have examined the involvement of Catholic priests in Irish politics during the struggle of the 1820s and, in particular, the question of whether Maynooth education was the critical factor in that involvement in an article, '"The Only Lever . . .?" The Catholic Priest in Irish politics 1823-29' in *Studies*, Vol. LXX, No. 280, Winter 1981, pp. 308-24. Those particularly interested in this aspect of the struggle are referred to the sources cited in that article.

A valuable contemporary work of reference is *Pigott's Directory, 1824* which lists for local towns and for major cities the principal merchants, traders, shopkeepers as well as some of the local gentry and landholders. Other important works of reference include E. Wakefield, *An Account of Ireland Statistical and Political*, 2 vols (London 1812) and S. Lewis, *A Topographical Dictionary of Ireland*, 2 vols (London 1837).

Considerable insight into the struggle in Ireland during the 1820s may be obtained by reading the contemporary novelists such as Maria Edgeworth, Gerald Griffin, William Carleton, John Banim, Lady Morgan and from such minor writers as Harriet Martin whose novel, *Canvassing*, gives something of the atmosphere of a contested election. Social and political comment of value may also be gleaned from the diaries and works of travellers and from the contemporary Irish sources such as Anthony Raftery and Humphrey O'Sullivan.

References

PREFACE
(p. xiii-xv)
1. Rev. Ian Paisley in interview with Padraig O'Malley, 30 December 1981 quoted in P. O'Malley, *The Uncivil Wars: Ireland Today*, Belfast 1983, p. 17.
2. *New Ireland Forum, Report*, 2 May 1984, paras. 4.8, 4.9.2.
3. Thomas Moore, *Memoirs of Captain Rock*, London 1824, p. 368.
4. *The Economist*, Vol. 291, No. 7344, 2 June 1984, p. 14.

Prologue:
'THE STATE OF THINGS IN IRELAND'
(pp. 1-29)
1. *The Royal Visit*, Dublin, 1821, pp. 136-9.
2. [John Banim], *The Anglo-Irish of the Nineteenth Century*, 3 Vols., London, 1828, Vol. 2, pp. 153-4.
3. Parl. Deb. N.S., Vol. IV, 28 February 1821, cols. 960-1004.
4. [John Banim], *The Anglo-Irish of the Nineteenth Century*, Vol. 2, p. 154.
5. Parl. Deb. N.S., Vol. IV, 17 April 1821, cols. 291-317.
6. *F. J.*, 8 January 1822.
7. *F. J.*, 15, 16 January 1822.
8. Rev. Sydney Smith, *A Letter To the Electors Upon the Catholic Question*, York 1826, p. 18.
9. ibid, p. 30.
10. *First Report From the Select Committee on Districts of Ireland Under the Insurrection Act*, 1824, (372), VIII, 4.
11. *Report From the Select Committee on the Employment of the Poor in Ireland*, 1823, (561), VI, 334-5.
12. ibid, 461.
13. Wellesley to Peel, 3 February, 1822, Add. Mss 40, 324.
14. Parl. Deb. N.S., Vol. VI, 22 April 1822, col. 1504.
15. T. Crofton Croker, *Researches in the South of Ireland*, London, 1824, pp. 1-2.
16. ibid, p. 329.

Chapter 1
1823-1824: 'BEGINNING A GENERAL RALLY'
(pp. 30-55)

1. *F. J.*, 3 February 1823.
2. *F. J.*, 26 April 1823; *DEP*, 26 April, 1 May 1823.
3. [John Banim], *The Anglo-Irish of the Nineteenth Century*, 3 vols, London 1828, Vol. 2, p. 155.
4. *F. J.*, 1 May 1823.
5. *F. J.*, 6 May 1823.
6. *F. J.*, 10 May 1823.
7. *F. J.*, 13 May 1823; *DEP*, 13 May 1823.
8. Wellesley to Peel, 12 May 1823 and Peel to Wellesley, 16 May 1823, Add. Mss 40, 324.
9. *DEM*, 26 May, 9 June 1823.
10. [John Banim], *The Anglo-Irish of the Nineteenth Century*, Vol. 2, p. 161.
11. I.C.F., *An Impartial Review of the Proceedings of the Catholic Association; comprehending remarks on the various political projects of that Institution*, Dublin 1825, pp. 21-2.
12. *F. J.*, 21 May 1823.
13. *DEP*, 17, 20 May 1823.
14. *F. J.*, 7, 9 June 1823.
15. *DEP*, 8 July 1823.
16. *DEP*, 15 July 1823.
17. *DEP*, 10 June 1823.
18. *F. J.*, 30 June 1823; *DEP*, 1 July 1823.
19. *F. J.*, 7 June 1823.
20. *F. J.*, 17 June 1823.
21. *F. J.*, 14, 15, 16 October 1823.
22. *F. J.*, 3 November 1823.
23. Wellesley to Peel, 23 January 1822, Add. Mss 40, 324.
24. Peel to Wellesley, 22 February, 10 March 1822, Add. Mss 40, 324.
25. Wellesley to Peel, 22 June 1823, Add. Mss 40, 324.
26. Henry Goulburn to Wellesley, 5 May 1823, Add. Mss 37, 301.
27. *F. J.*, 20 June 1823.
28. See, for example, *DEP*, 12 July, 26 August, 28 August 1823 and *F. J.*, 16 July 1823.
29. *DEP*, 25 November 1823.
30. Report of Meeting, 27 December 1823, ISPO CAP.
31. Report of Meeting, 1 November 1823, ISPO CAP.
32. Report of Meeting, 20 December 1823, ISPO CAP.
33. Report of Meeting, 3 January 1824, ISPO CAP.
34. *DEP*, 10 January 1824 and Report of Meeting, 17 January 1824, ISPO CAP.

35. *DEP*, 22 January 1824.
36. *DEP*, 27 January 1824.
37. Report of Meeting, 24 January 1824, ISPO CAP and *DEP*, 27 January 1824.
38. Report of Meeting, 4 February 1824, ISPO CAP.
39. Copies of the Report are in DDA, CP 60/2/2; it was published in *DEP*, 19 February 1824.
40. Conway in the Association, 19 June 1824, PRO HO 100/213.
41. *DEP*, 4 March 1824.
42. Report of meeting, 7 February 1824, ISPO CAP.
43. Report of meeting, 14 February 1824, ISPO CAP.
44. *DEP*, 19 February 1824.
45. *DEP*, 24 February 1824.
46. Report of Meeting, 21 February 1824, ISPO CAP.
47. Report of Meeting, 27 February 1824, ISPO CAP.

Chapter 2
1824: 'THE GRAND, THE WISE, THE NOBLE PLAN'
(pp. 56-85)

1. Report of Meeting, 18 February 1824, ISPO CAP
2. The audited accounts for 1824, as published in *DEP*, 17 February 1825, set out the sums received from each county every month.
3. The General Account of the Catholic Rent to March 1825, when the Association was suppressed, was published in *DEP*, 27 April 1826.
4. Report of Meeting, 25 February 1824, ISPO CAP; since the foundation of the Association 213 members had paid in £242 5s 9d and expenses of about £70 had been incurred.
5. Reports of Meetings, 12, 19 June 1824, ISPO CAP, PRO HO 100/213.
6. Report of Meeting, 6 March 1824, ISPO CAP.
7. Report of Meeting, 20 March 1824, ISPO CAP.
8. Reports of Meetings, 8 May, 7, 14 August 1824, PRO HO 100/213.
9. Report of Meeting, 13 November 1824, ISPO CAP.
10. Report of Meeting, 9 December 1824, ISPO CAP.
11. Report of Meeting, 6 March 1824, ISPO CAP; *DEP*, 16 March 1824.
12. *DEP*, 3 April 1824.
13. *DEP*, 3, 15 April, 18 May, 6, 29 July, 14 August, 14, 25, 30 September 1824.
14. Parl. Deb. N.S., X, 1479-84, 29 March 1824.
15. Report of Meeting, 5 April 1824, PRO HO 100/213.
16. Report of Meeting, 10 April 1824, PRO HO 100/213; *DEP*, 15, 17 April 1824.

17. *DEP*, 27 April, 4, 11 May 1824.
18. Report of Meeting, 1 May 1824, ISPO CAP.
19. Report of Meeting, 8 May 1824, PRO HO 100/213; *DEP*, 11 May 1824.
20. *DEP*, 18 May 1824; Reports of Meetings, 12, 15, 26 May 1824, PRO HO 100/213.
21. Report of Meeting, 26 June, 9 July 1824, PRO HO 100/213.
22. Reports of Meetings, 23 November, 3 December 1825, and Edward Dwyer to James Sugrue, 8 November 1825, DDA, CP 56/2/IV (No. 12, No. 15); 60/2/X (14). O'Connell later paid Dwyer £300 each year from 1829 to his death in 1837 (III, 1186).
23. Reports of Meetings, 29 May, 9, 12, 18, 19, 26 June 1824, PRO HO 100/213, ISPO CAP.
24. *DEP*, 13, 20 July 1824.
25. Reports of Meetings, 14 August, 25 September, 9 October 1824, PRO HO 100/213; *DEP*, 3 August, 21 September 1824.
26. *DEP*, 13 July 1824.
27. *DEP*, 17, 24 April, 1, 15 May, 10 July, 25 September, 30 November 1824.
28. The development of the Catholic organisation in Cork can be traced in the newspapers; see, for example, *DEP*, April – July 1824.
29. A society called 'The St Patrick's Constitutional Society' was to collect the Rent. See Reports of Meetings, 27 March, 3 April 1824, PRO HO 100/213 and 20 March 1824, ISPO CAP; Report of Meeting, 14 August 1824, PRO HO 100/213.
30. *DEP*, 31 July 1824.
31. Report of Meeting of parishes of St Mary and St Peter, 3 September 1824, PRO HO 100/213.
32. *DEP*, 2 September 1824.
33. See unsigned draft, 14 October 1824, O'Connell Papers, UCD, P. 12/3/149.
34. See Report of Meeting of Finance Committee, 18 September 1824, PRO HO 100/213.
35. Report of Meetings on 'Rent in Dublin', 4, 8 March 1825, ISPO CAP; *DEP*, 5 March 1825.
36. *DEP*, 7 September 1824; *Pigott's Directory 1824*, pp. 166-7; *A List of all The Freeholders... County Longford to January 1830*, G.O. 444.
37. *The Westmeath Journal*, 9 September 1824.
38. *DEP*, 14 September 1824; *Pigott's Directory 1824*, pp. 166-7; TAB 19/8; *A List of all The Freeholders... County Longford to January 1830*, G.O. 444.
39. *DEP*, 2 November 1824; *A List of All The Freeholders... County Longford to January 1830*, G.O. 444; TABs 19/21, 19/16, 30/29.

40. A small, but probably representative sample of these 'grievance letters' survives as 'Appeals for Legal and Financial Aid 1824-8' in DDA, CP 55/3/111 (1-24).
41. *DEP*, 17 February 1825.
42. *DEP*, 2 September 1824.
43. Rev. P. Sheehy, P.P., Clonrush, Scarriff to M. Staunton, 6 January 1825, DDA, CP 55/3/111 (5).
44. The inhabitants of the parish of Clonalvey, Co. Meath to the Catholic Association, 9 January 1825, DDA, CP 55/3/111 (6).
45. O'Connell's phrase, quoted *DEP*, 17 August 1824.
46. Goulburn to Peel, 16 November 1824, PRO HO 100/213.
47. *DEP*, 15 June, 1 July, 5 October 1824; Warburton to Goulburn, 11 November 1824 (copy), PRO HO 100/211; Goulburn to Peel, 16 November 1824, PRO HO 100/211.
48. Report of Richard Willcocks, 29 December 1824, PRO HO 100/211.
49. *DEP*, 3, 13 July 1824.
50. Geo M. Drought to Henry Goulburn, 11 November 1824, Goulburn to Peel, 16 November 1824, enclosing extract, PRO HO 100/211.
51. *DEP*, 28 October 1824.
52. Reports of Meetings, 2 December 1824, 15 February 1825, ISPO CAP.
53. Wellesley to Peel, 2 December 1824, PRO HO 100/211.
54. Report of Meeting of Finance Committee, 17 November 1824, DDA, CP 60/2/XI (13).
55. *DEP*, 18 November 1824.
56. *DEM*, 3 January 1825.
57. Report of Meeting of Finance Committee, 2, 9 February 1825, DDA, CP 60/2/XI (23).
58. Journals of the House of Commons, Vol. 79, 1824, indexed under 'Roman Catholics, Petition in favour'.
59. *DEP*, 10 August 1824.
60. Report of Finance Committee Meeting, 10 December 1824, DDA, CP 60/2/XI (15).
61. Report of Finance Meeting, 13 January 1825, DDA CP 56/2 and Report of Meeting of Catholic Association, 9 March 1825, ISPO CAP.
62. *DEP*, 1 January 1825.

Chapter 3
1825: 'EVENTS ARE NOT YET RIPE'
(pp. 86-113)

1. Parl. Deb. N.S., Vol. XII, 10 February 1825, Cols. 170-185.
2. Parl. Deb. N.S., Vol. XII, 10 February 1825, Cols. 207-232.
3. Parl. Deb. N.S., Vol. XII, 10 February 1825, Col. 248.

4. Parl. Deb. N.S., Vol. XII, 11 February 1825, Cols. 314-315, 15 February 1825, Cols. 463-490.
5. Parl. Deb. N.S., Vol. XII, 15 February 1825, Col. 453.
6. Parl. Deb. N.S., Vol. XII, 15 February 1825, Col. 498.
7. Parl. Deb. N.S., Vol. XII, 14 February 1825, Cols. 362-375.
8. *Political Register*, LV, 13 August 1825.
9. *F. J.*, 10 March 1825.
10. *F. J.*, 19 March 1825.
11. *Political Register*, LIII, 19 March 1825.
12. Parl. Deb. N.S., Vol. XIII, 19 April 1825, Cols. 23-34.
13. *Review of the Evidence Taken Before the Irish Committees of Both Houses of Parliament*, Dublin 1825, p. 2.
14. *Report From the Select Committee on the State of Ireland*, H.C., (129), VIII, 1825, 210.
15. ibid, 85-107.
16. *Report From the Select Committee on the State of Ireland*, H. L., (181), IX, 1825, 123-171.
17. *Report From the Select Committee on the State of Ireland*, H. L., (129), VIII, 1825, 48-85.
18. Parl. Deb. N.S., Vol. XIII, 25 April 1825, Cols. 138-142.
19. Parl. Deb. N.S., Vol. XIII, 17 May 1825, Cols. 665-752.
20. *DEP*, 2 June 1825.
21. *DEP*, 9 June 1825.
22. *DEP*, 25 June 1825.
23. Report of Aggregate Meeting, 13 July 1825, ISPO CAP, and also 'Rules and Regulations of New Catholic Association', 21, 23 July 1825, DDA, CP 60/2/xiv.
24. *F. J.*, 25 July 1825.
25. *DEP*, 21, 25 June 1825.
26. *DEP*, 17 September 1825.
27. *DEP*, 27 September 1825.
28. *DEP*, 27 September 1825.
29. *DEP*, 25, 28 June 1825.
30. *DEP*, 30 June 1825.
31. *DEP*, 12 July 1825.
32. *DEM*, 10 June 1825.
33. *DEP*, 4 August 1825; Report of Meeting, 20 August 1825, DDA, CP 60/2/X (11).
34. Speech by O'Gorman to Catholic Association, 9 November 1825 recommending 'this plan' for the other provinces, DDA, CP 56/2/11 (No. 6).
35. *DEP*, 3 November 1825.
36. Report of Meeting, 23 November 1825, DDA, CP 56/2/IV (No. 12).
37. *F. J.*, 11, 20 July 1825; *DEP*, 12 July 1825.
38. *M. R.*, 16 December 1825.

Chapter 4
1826: 'THE WHOLE NATION IN ONE CRY'
(pp. 114-152)

1. *DEP*, 31 January 1826.
2. Thomas Wyse to Catholic Association, 28 January 1826, ISPO CAP.
3. E. A. Kendall, *Letters to a Friend on the State of Ireland*, 3 vols, (London 1826), Vol. 3, Appendix IV, pp. xiv-xvi.
4. *M. R.*, 24 November 1825.
5. *DEP*, 4 February 1826.
6. [Thomas Spring Rice], *Catholic Emancipation considered on Protestant Principles in a Letter to the Earl of Liverpool*, London 1827, pp. 8-14.
7. For complete electoral details see *Parliamentary Election Results in Ireland 1801-1922*, ed. B. M. Walker, Dublin 1978.
8. *DEM*, 12 June 1826.
9. *DEP*, 10 August, 21 September 1824.
10. *DEP*, 3 June 1826.
11. *DEP*, 2 December 1825.
12. *DEP*, 3 June 1826.
13. *Pigott's Directory 1824*, p. 265; *Waterford Mirror*, 24 March 1824.
14. See notice to the 'Independent Interest' to register their freeholders for the county election, *Waterford Mirror*, 10 July 1824.
15. *Waterford Mirror*, 27 July, 11, 25 August 1824.
16. *Ramsay's Waterford Chronicle*, 1 February 1823.
17. *Waterford Mirror*, 8 December 1824.
18. *Waterford Chronicle*, 8 July 1826.
19. *Waterford Mirror*, 27 March, 30 October, 27 November, 4 December 1824; *Pigott's Directory 1824*, p. 318.
20. *Waterford Mirror*, 23, 27 October 1824.
21. *DEP*, 10 February 1825.
22. *DEP*, 18, 21 June 1825.
23. *DEP*, 2 August 1825.
24. *DEP*, 20 August 1825.
25. *DEP*, 20, 22 September 1825.
26. *DEP*, 25 October 1825.
27. See Wm. Barron to Thomas Wyse, 5 October 1825 and Duke of Devonshire (to the Catholics of Waterford), 9 September 1825, Wyse Papers, N.L.I., Ms 15,023 (1).
28. *DEP*, 27, 29 October, 8 November 1825.
29. *DEP*, 7 January 1826.
30. Details on prominent Waterford families are given in the collection of newscuttings 'Glimpses of Waterford', N.L.I., Ms 5,697 and in *Pigott's Directory 1824*.
31. *DEP*, 21 February 1826.

32. *DEP*, 5 January, 4 March 1826.
33. George Wyse to Thomas Wyse, 19 February 1826, Wyse Papers, N.L.I., Ms 15,020 (1).
34. See John Musgrave, Youghal, to Thomas Wyse, 9 June 1826, Wyse Papers, N.L.I., Ms 15,024 (4); Musgrave was asked to join such an Association and he agreed to join.
35. John Burke to the Committee for Conducting the Waterford Election, 30 May 1826, Wyse Papers, N.L.I., Ms 15,023 (2).
36. R. Curtis to R. Duckett, 3 June 1826, Wyse Papers, N.L.I., Ms 15,023 (3).
37. See Pat Hayden, Carrick-on-Suir, to Philip Barron (or Counsellor Hayes), 1 June 1826, Wyse Papers, N.L.I., Ms 15,023 (2) and Pat Hayden to T. Wyse, Thursday (29 June 1826), Wyse Papers, N.L.I., Ms 15,023 (3).
38. See John Magin, Ballybricken, local agent, to Thomas Wyse, 2 September 1826, Wyse Papers, N.L.I., Ms 15,023 (2); Magin claimed he was engaged as agent since the arrival of Stuart in early August 1825.
39. See Dominick Tallon, Dungarvan, to Thomas Wyse, 15 May 1826; Pat Hayden, Carrick-on-Suir, to Philip Barron (or Counsellor Hayes), 1 June 1826, Wyse Papers, N.L.I., Ms 15,023 (2).
40. See R. Greene, Dungarvan, to T. Wyse, 3 June 1826, Wyse Papers, N.L.I., Ms 15,023 (2); *Pigott's Directory 1824*, p. 265; large printed sheets for use by agents with 13 columns in which to record details about each voter survive in Wyse Papers, N.L.I., Ms 15,028 (1).
41. Charles Bianconi to Thomas Wyse, 14 April 1826, Wyse Papers, N.L.I., Ms 15,023 (2).
42. R. J. O'Brien, Dungarvan, to Thomas Wyse, 22 June 1826, Wyse Papers, N.L.I., Ms 15,023 (3), see *DEP*, 15 June, 22 June 1826 for the widespread use of horse transport.
43. See detailed proposal of Mr. J. Allen, May 1826, Wyse Papers, N.L.I., Ms 15,028 (1).
44. James Sullivan to T. Wyse, 24 May 1826, Wyse Papers, N.L.I., Ms 15,023 (4).
45. See R. Russell to T. Wyse, 31 May 1826 and P. Hayden to T. Wyse, 18 August 1826, Wyse Papers, N.L.I., Ms 15,023 (4); Hayden later complained that poll-agents had not been paid and some were in distress; see also P. Hayden to T. Wyse, 4 August 1826, Wyse Papers, N.L.I., Ms 15,023 (3).
46. H. Winston Barron to T. Wyse, 22 May 1826; marked 'Private and Confidential', Wyse Papers, N.L.I., Ms 15,023 (4).
47. See Beresford petition in *Journals of House of Commons*, Vol. 82, 1826-28, pp. 22-3.
48. *DEP*, 4 March 1826; ms draft Address by Tenants to Lord Viscount

Hayes Doneraile, Wyse Papers, N.L.I., Ms 15,028 (1).
49. George Wyse to Thomas Wyse, 19 February 1826, Wyse Papers, N.L.I., Ms 15,020 (1).
50. See Patrick Power to Thomas Wyse, 17 May 1826, Wyse Papers, N.L.I., Ms 15,023 (3), R. Power, Georgetown, to Rev. John Sheehan, 22 March 1826, Wyse Papers, N.L.I., Ms 15,023 (2) and John Power, publican, Crook, to T. Wyse, 18 April 1826, Wyse Papers, N.L.I., Ms 15,023 (2).
51. Rev. R. Murphy to W. Barron, 31 May 1826, Wyse Papers, N.L.I., Ms 15,023 (4) (emphasis in original).
52. P. G. Barron to T. Wyse (May 1826), Wyse Papers, N.L.I., Ms 15,023 (2).
53. R. J. O'Brien, Dungarvan, to Thomas Wyse, 22 June 1826, Wyse Papers, N.L.I., Ms 15,023 (3); see Rev. Fogarty to T. Wyse, 20 June 1826, Wyse Papers, N.L.I., Ms 15,023 (4).
54. J. M. Galwey to Thomas Wyse, 4 June 1826, Wyse Papers, N.L.I., Ms 15,023 (3).
55. R. J. O'Brien to Thomas Wyse, 7 June 1826, Wyse Papers, N.L.I., Ms 15,023 (3).
56. J. M. Galwey to T. Wyse, 7 June 1826, Wyse Papers, N.L.I., Ms 15,023 (3).
57. *DEP*, 28 March, 15, 27 April, 13 May 1826.
58. SPO CSO RP – (Outrage)/Report, 18 May 1826/Carton 1157/C.7.
59. Much of the Wyse Papers are concerned with election claims after 1826, see especially Ms 15,028.
60. *Waterford Chronicle*, 29 August, 10 October 1826, 10 November, 22 December 1827.
61. SPO CSO RP – (Outrage)/Reports, 19 October 1826/C.54/and 31 October 1826/Carton 1157.
62. See *An Account of the Number of Stamps issued to each Newspaper*, H.C. 1826, (235), XXIII, 385; this return has figures for 1822-26 inclusive; see also return of newspapers stamps, H.C. 1831-2 (242), XXXIV, 124-5; H.C. 1836, (146), XIV, 359-60; H.C. 1843 (282), XXX, 555-6.
63. In 1827 Coppinger moved that the Catholic Association take the *Chronicle* as a mark of esteem for the part it had played, see *Waterford Chronicle*, 12 July, 14 July 1827; O'Connell paid tribute to the provincial press and cited the *Chronicle* amongst others as examples of the new 'patriotic spirit existing in Ireland', *Waterford Chronicle*, 5 February 1828.
64. *DEP*, 10 June 1826.
65. *DEM*, 19 June 1826.
66. *DEP*, 1 July 1826.
67. *Waterford Chronicle*, 8 July 1826.

68. *Journals of the House of Commons*, Vol. 82, 1826-28; pp. 22-3; *DEP*, 7 September 1826.
69. Wyse Papers, N.L.I., Ms 15,028 (1).
70. *DEM*, 23 June 1826.
71. *DEP*, 8 July 1826.
72. Reports from Major Carter in SPO CSO RP — (Outrage)/19 August 1826/C.32; 19 October 1826/C.54 Carton 1157.
73. *DEM*, 16 June 1826.
74. *Report From the Select Committee on the Galway Election*, H.C., IV, 1826-27, 955-1002.
75. [Harriet Martin], *Canvassing*, (London 1838), pp. 164-239.
76. *F. J.*, 28 June 1826.
77. *DEP*, 29 June 1826.
78. *DEM*, 30 June 1826.
79. *F. J.*, 14 June 1826, *DEM*, 12 June 1826.
80. *M. R.*, 17 June 1826.
81. *DEP*, 29 June 1826 has account of Cavan election.
82. See *A Report of the Meeting of the Roman Catholics, of the County of Monaghan, held on Tuesday January 10th 1826*, (Monaghan 1826), p. 9.
83. *DEM*, 16 June 1826; *Monaghan Election 1826* (election scrapbook); N.L.I., IR. 32341 m 52.
84. *Monaghan Election 1826* (election scrapbook), N.L.I., IR. 32341 m 52.
85. *DEP*, 6 July 1826.
86. *DEP*, 10 August 1826.
87. *DEP*, 6 July 1826.
88. See O'Connell's 'Letter to the Catholics of Ireland', 10 July 1826 in *DEP*, 11 July 1826.
89. *DEM*, 3 July 1826.
90. Wyse Papers, N.L.I., Ms 15,030 (1) draft letter dated 20 July 1826.
91. *Waterford Chronicle*, 29 July, 5 August 1826.
92. See, for example, T. Wyse to J. P. Smith, Portlaw, 11 August 1826, Wyse Papers, N.L.I., Ms 15,023 (3).
93. *Waterford Chronicle*, 22 August, 28 September 1826; *DEP*, 4 January 1827.
94. H. Villiers Stuart to T. Wyse, 19 August 1826, Wyse Papers, N.L.I., Ms 15,023 (1); *DEP*, 31 August 1826.
95. Pat Hayden, Carrick-on-Suir, to T. Wyse, 23 August 1826; J. M. Galwey to T. Wyse, 7 September 1826, Wyse Papers, N.L.I., Ms 15,023 (2).
96. See legal opinion of English law officers, 26 October 1826, Add. Mss No. 37304 (ii).
97. See legal opinion of Irish law officers, 2 December 1826, Add. Mss No. 37304 (ii).

Chapter 5
1827-28: 'HOPE DEFERRED'
(pp. 153-187)

1. *DEP*, 11 January 1827.
2. See circular letter from O'Connell to Catholic bishops, 2 January 1827, DDA, CP 59/1/XXI (1) and letter 1356 in Vol. III of O'Connell Correspondence.
3. *DEP*, 18 January 1827.
4. O'Connell to Catholic Association, 16 January 1827, 'Proceedings of the Fourteen Days Meeting', DDA, CP 59/1/I.
5. See Report of Catholic Association meeting, 18 January 1827, DDA, CP 59/1/III.
6. Report of Catholic Association meeting, 22 January 1827, DDA, CP 59/1/V.
7. Report of Catholic Association meeting, 24 January 1827, DDA, CP 59/1/VII.
8. Report of Catholic Association meeting, 27 January 1827, DDA, CP 59/1/X.
9. Parl. Deb. N.S. Vol. XVI, 5, 6, March 1827, Cols. 826-966.
10. *DEP*, 13 March 1827.
11. *DEP*, 17 April 1827.
12. *DEP*, 19 April, 3, 12 May 1827.
13. *DEP*, 6 February, 6, 27, 29 March 1827.
14. *Midland Chronicle and Westmeath Independent*, 2 May, 13 June 1827; *DEP*, 31 March 1827.
15. *Letters of Rev. Robert Daly to Daniel O'Connell with the reply of Mr O'Connell*, Dublin 1826.
16. *Northern Whig*, 19 May 1825.
17. *Northern Whig*, 26 July 1827.
18. *DEP*, 28 February 1828.
19. O'Connell's speech to Separate Meeting of Catholics, 7 February 1827, DDA, CP 59/1/XV.
20. See *DEP*, 13 January, 6, 8 March, 21 April, 30 June, 5 July, 18 September, 8 December, 1827 for activities of Louth Club.
21. *DEP*, 19 April 1827; *Waterford Chronicle*, 26 April 1827.
22. *DEP*, 29 May 1827.
23. *DEP*, 2 June 1827.
24. *DEP*, 9 June 1827.
25. *Waterford Chronicle*, 19, 21 July 1827, *DEP*, 3 November 1827.
26. *DEP*, 17 April 1828.
27. *C. M. C.*, 14 February, 4, 9 March 1825.
28. *DEP*, 19 December 1826, 2 January 1827.
29. *DEP*, 25 January, 6 February 1827.
30. *C. M. C.*, 3 January 1827; see *Lists of the Freemen and Freeholders*

. . . *who voted at the Cork Election December 1826*, Cork 1827.

31. *DEP*, 17 April 1827.

32. See printed circular of Association for Promoting the Registration of Freeholds, dated 8 May 1827, in Day Papers, Cork Archive Council (hereafter Day Papers, C.A.C.); the Day Papers are a valuable source for Cork politics in this period; McCarthy was member of Catholic Association, *C. M. C.*, 9 March 1825.

33. *C. M. C.*, 24 July 1826.

34. See E. McCarthy to James O'Brien, Tuckey St, 12 June 1827, (letter written on copy of printed circular), Day Papers, C.A.C.

35. *DEP*, 1 September 1827.

36. *DEP*, 15 November 1827, 19 April 1828; *Waterford Chronicle*, 24 April 1828.

37. *Waterford Chronicle*, 26 April, 29 May, 19 July 1827.

38. *Waterford Chronicle*, 5 February 1828.

39. *Waterford Chronicle*, 7, 12 February, 4 March 1828, see P. Power to T. Wyse, 11 February 1828, Wyse Papers, N.L.I., Ms 15,023 (7) suggesting Stuart, Power and the county gentlemen should subscribe £4,000 'to liquidate all just demands'.

40. See report and resolutions from meeting of creditors at John Power's, Ballybricken, 7 February 1828, Wyse Papers, N.L.I., Ms 15,028 (8).

41. Rev. Thomas Flannery P.P., Clonmel, to T. Wyse, May 1828, Wyse Papers, N.L.I., Ms 15,028 (8).

42. *Waterford Chronicle*, 17, 19 June 1828.

43. *DEP*, 19 February 1828.

44. *DEP*, 14 February 1828.

45. Parl. Deb. N.S. Vol. IV, 28 February 1821, Cols. 991-2.

46. Printed *Address of the Catholic Association to the Protestant Dissenters of England*, 1 February 1828, DDA, CP 60/1/II (1).

47. A copy of the printed model for the petition for Repeal of the Test and Corporation Acts survives in DDA, CP 60/1/II (1).

Chapter 6
1828: 'IRELAND CANNOT REMAIN AS IT IS'
(pp. 188-233)

1. *DEM*, 30 June 1828.

2. *DEP*, 19 June, *DEM*, 20 June, *Waterford Chronicle*, 21 June 1828; *County of Clare Election* (printed by J. Connor, 14 Tuckey Street, Cork) [1828], p. 6.

3. *DEP*, 24 June 1828.

4. *County of Clare Election* (printed by J. Connor, 14 Tuckey Street, Cork) [1828], pp. 29-30.

5. *DEP*, 1 July 1828.
6. *DEP*, 1, 3 July 1828.
7. *County of Clare Election* (printed by J. Connor, 14 Tuckey Street, Cork) [1828], p. 27.
8. Address 'To the Independent Electors of Clare', 28 June 1828, Ennis, by Richard Scott, DDA, CP 60/1/II (3).
9. *DEP*, 3 July 1828; see detailed 'Proceedings at the Court House at Ennis, Co. Clare for the Election of a Knight of the Shire to serve in Parliament commencing 30th June 1828', State of the Country Papers, Ser II, 1828, ISPO.
10. *DEP*, 3 July 1828.
11. See copy of Clare petition against the return of Daniel O'Connell, *DEP*, 9 August 1828.
12. *DEP*, 5 July 1828.
13. Detailed account books for the 1828 Clare Election survive in DDA, CP 390/2/X; they provide a most valuable listing of the O'Connell-ite organisation in Clare and itemise the Clare election finances in detail.
14. *DEP*, 10 July 1828.
15. *DEP*, 12 July 1828.
16. Memorandum of conversation between O'Connell and Anglesey, 29 July 1828, Public Record Office, Northern Ireland, Anglesey Mss 619/1/2.
17. [Prince Pückler Muskau], A German Prince, *Tour in England, Ireland and France in the Years 1828 and 1829*, 2 Vols, London 1832, Vol. I, p. 333.
18. See placard poster 'Address to the Roman Catholics of the North', 5 July 1828, DDA, CP 60/1/II (6).
19. *C. M. C.*, 21 February 1827.
20. Chandos to T. L. Lefroy, 6 August [1828] ; Minutes of the First Meeting of the Brunswick Club, 15 August 1828, Lefroy Papers.
21. *DEP*, 26 August 1828.
22. [Prince *puckler Muskau*], A German Prince, *Tour in England, Ireland and France in the Years 1828 and 1829*, 2 Vols, London 1832, Vol. 1, p. 257.
23. See *A Full and Authentic Report of the Proceedings of the First Annual Meeting of the Brunswick Constitutional Club of Ireland held in the Rotunda on Tuesday November 4th 1828*, Dublin, 1828, p. 7.
24. *The Westmeath Journal*, 9 October, 6 November 1828, 15 January 1829.
25. See Brunswick Club Mss, N.L.I., 5017 for records of the Portadown Club.
26. See *A Full and Authentic Report of the Proceedings of the First*

Annual Meeting of the Brunswick Constitutional Club of Ireland held in the Rotunda on Tuesday November 4th 1828, Dublin, 1828, p. 8.

27. See 'Address to the Roman Catholics of Ulster', 9 October 1828, DDA, CP 60/1/II (8).

28. See *Waterford Chronicle*, 22, 26, 29 July, 4, 7 October 1828; *DEP*, 31 July, 2 August 1828, 16 October 1828.

29. *Waterford Chronicle*, 1, 6, 15, 31 January, 19 February 1829.

30. *DEP*, 19 August, 4 October 1828; *Waterford Chronicle*, 21 August 1828.

31. *DEP*, 5 August, 13, 18 November 1828.

32. *DEP*, 26 July 1828.

33. *DEP*, 23, 30 August, 4, 9, 11 October 1828; see also P. J. Lynch, 'Tom Steele, a Sketch', *Journal of the North Munster Archaeological Society*, Vol. 1, No. 4, 1911, 247-252, which reproduces the Rules of the Limerick Independent Club.

34. *DEP*, 2 September, 14 October 1828; for a meeting of the Clonmel Liberal Club see *Waterford Chronicle*, 15 January 1829.

35. [Prince Pückler Muskau], A German Prince, *Tour in England, Ireland and France in the Years 1828 and 1829*, 2 Vols, London 1832, Vol. 2, pp. 32-3.

36. *DEP*, 18 September, 4, 9, 11 October 1828.

37. *DEP*, 21 October, 1, 11 November, 11 December 1828; see entry in Wyse's Diary, 1 January 1829, Wyse Papers, N.L.I., P. 5078.

38. See R. Cassidy, Jamestown, Monastereven, to T. Wyse, 2 April 1829, 4 June 1829, 12 September 1829, Wyse Papers, N.L.I., Ms 15,023 (9).

39. See Report of Meeting of Catholic Rent Committee, City of Waterford, 5, 7 July [1828], DDA, CP 56/1/II.

40. *DEP*, 10 July 1828; *Waterford Chronicle*, 8 July 1828.

41. Rev. J. Sheehan to T. Wyse, 10 July 1828, Wyse Papers, N.L.I., Ms 15,030 (1).

42. *DEP*, 2 August 1828; the Rules and Regulations of the City Club were published in *Waterford Chronicle*, 26 July 1828 and see also the printed 'Rules and Regulations of Waterford Liberal Club', Wyse Papers, N.L.I., Ms 15,030 (1).

43. *Waterford Chronicle*, 2 August 1828.

44. See circular, 30 August 1828; R. Sausse, Carrick, to T. Wyse, 13 September 1828 and G. Connolly, Dungarvan, to T. Wyse, 11 September 1828, Wyse Papers, N.L.I., Ms 15,030 (1).

45. J. P. Smith, Milfert, Portlaw, to T. Wyse, 12 September 1828, Wyse Papers, N.L.I., Ms 15,030.

46. J. P. Smith, Portlaw, to T. Wyse (September 1828); there were five secretaries in the Portlaw district who received newspapers, see List

of Parish Clubs, dated 1829, Wyse Papers, N.L.I., Ms 15,030; see also bills to be paid by Liberal Club, mostly relating to circulation of the press, 1828, Wyse Papers, N.L.I., Ms 15,030 (1).

47. See J. P. Smith, to T. Wyse, 21 November 1828, Wyse Papers, N.L.I., Ms 15,023 (8); M. Tobin, Dungarvan, to T. Wyse, 17 November 1828, Wyse Papers, N.L.I., Ms 15,023 (7); List of Parish Clubs, dated 1829, Wyse Papers, N.L.I., Ms 15,030; *Waterford Chronicle*, 18 September 1828.

48. *Waterford Chronicle*, 31 August 1828.

49. See Book of Queries of Committee of Inquiry of Liberal Club, Wyse Papers, N.L.I., Ms 15,030 (1).

50. Second Report of the City of Waterford Liberal Club, 3 November 1828, Wyse Papers, N.L.I., Ms 15,030.

51. *DEP*, 26 August 1828; *C. M. C.*, 25 August 1828.

52. *C. M. C.*, 29 August 1828; see printed notices and circulars of Liberal Club in the Day Papers, Cork Archive Council.

53. See report of meeting 24 August 1828 in newspaper cutting in the large volume of newspaper cuttings 1827-1856, in Day Papers, Cork Archive Council.

54. See printed 'Rules and Regulations of County and City of Cork Liberal Club', Day Papers, Cork Archive Council.

55. *C. M. C.*, 1, 6, 13 October 1828.

56. F. A. Walsh, pro-Secretary, Liberal Club, to Michael Staunton, Dublin, 9 November 1828; J. K. Warren, pro-Secretary, Liberal Club to *Morning Herald* office, London, 9 November 1828, copies No. 1 and No. 2, Day Papers, Cork Archive Council.

57. See printed circular from J. J. Hayes, Secretary, County and City of Cork Liberal Club, [August 1828], Day Papers, Cork Archive Council.

58. See 'County and City of Cork Liberal Club Correspondence C1 – 32', Day Papers, Cork Archive Council.

59. See Rev. Wm. Jones, Mallow, to J. J. Hayes, 27 September 1828, ibid, C. 15.

60. See William Hunter, to William Thompson, 9 October 1828, ibid, C. 22.

61. Cornelius Hurley, Bandon, to J. J. Hayes, 25 August 1828, ibid, C.1.

62. John Markham, Youghal, 19 September 1828, Cornelius O'Leary, Kanturk, 19 September 1828, Arthur O'Brien, Dunmanway, 28 September 1828, Rev. William Walsh, Secretary, Parochial Club, Enniskeen, to J. J. Hayes, ibid, C.12, C.11, C.17, C.19; *C. M. C.*, 8, 13, 31 October, 26 November, 5 December 1828.

63. *C. M. C.*, 5, 19, 26 November 1828.

Chapter 7
1829: 'O'CONNELL'S VICTORY'
(pp. 234-257)

1. *DEP*, 20, 22, 24 January 1829.
2. Parl. Deb. N.S. Vol. XX, 5 February 1829, Cols. 3-5.
3. ibid, Cols. 72-87.
4. ibid, Cols. 106-110.
5. ibid, Cols. 14-17.
6. *DEM*, 9, 11 February 1829.
7. See O'Connell to the Members of the House of Commons of the United Kingdom of Great Britain and Ireland, 2 February 1829, *DEP*, 7 February 1829.
8. See the printed 'Catholic Rent Inspectors — Report agreed to by the Catholic Association, on the 13th January 1829', DDA, CP 55/3/I (25) and also 60/1/III (2).
9. The Minutes of the Catholic Association meetings on 3 February and 12 February 1829 are in DDA, CP 60/1/III (6, 10); see also *DEP*, 10, 12, 14 February 1829.
10. Parl. Deb. N.S. Vol. XX, 10, 12 February 1829, Cols. 181-9, 276.
11. ibid, 5 March 1829, Cols. 726-7.
12. ibid, Cols. 728-80.
13. ibid, 6 March 1829, Cols. 835-6.
14. O'Connell to the People of Ireland, 7 March 1829, *DEP*, 12 March 1829.
15. George Wyse to Thomas Wyse, 14 March 1829, Wyse Papers, N.L.I., Ms 15,020 (2).
16. See Diary of T. Wyse, 5, 17 March 1829, N.L.I., P. 5078; also S. Coppinger to T. Wyse, 9, 20 March 1829, Wyse Papers, N.L.I., Ms 15,023 (9).
17. S. Coppinger to T. Wyse, 7 March 1829, Wyse Papers, N.L.I., Ms 15,023 (9).
18. Dowden's speech in newspaper cutting in Newspaper Cuttings 1827-1856, Day Papers, C.A.C.
19. By April 1829 John Reynolds, an attorney and £50 freeholder of South Mall, Cork, who was Secretary of the News Room was issuing a printed circular announcing the 'permanent basis' upon which the News Room had been placed and pointed out the local issues to which the Committee were to give attention, see Liberal Club Correspondence, C. 29, Day Papers, C.A.C. Reynolds was active in the Liberal Club and politics since 1826, see for example, his letter in *C. M. C.*, 5 January 1827.
20. S. Coppinger to T. Wyse, 23 March 1829, Wyse Papers, N.L.I., Ms 15,023 (9).
21. Parl. Deb., N.S., Vol. XX, 18 March 1829, Col. 1294.

22. Parl. Deb., N.S., Vol. XXI, 2 April 1829, Cols. 42-9.
23. ibid, Col. 74.
24. *DEP*, 14 April 1829.

Epilogue:
'THE STRUGGLE FOR POPULAR RIGHTS'
(pp. 258-289)
 1. T. L. Lefroy to Lord Farnham, 7 December 1830, marked 'private and confidential', Farnham Papers, N.L.I., Ms 18,611 (1); the Farnham Papers are an important source for the evolution of Irish conservatism.
 2. Hercules Ellis to Sir James Graham, 19 September 1841, PRO HO 100/257.
 3. *Speech of the Right Honourable William Saurin, delivered at the Rotunda, in the City of Dublin on Thursday, the 19th February 1829 being the Second General Meeting of the Brunswick Constitutional Club of Ireland* (Dublin, printed by order of the Club, 1829), pp. 3-17.
 4. T. L. Lefroy to Lord Farnham, 2 December 1830, Farnham Papers, N.L.I., Ms 18,611 (1).
 5. See Daniel O'Connell, *Seven Letters on the Reform Bill and the Law of Elections in Ireland*, Dublin 1835, which reprints O'Connell's public letters to the *Pilot* in 1832.
 6. *DEP*, 2, 5, 26 May, 2, 9 June, 16 August, 19 September 1829; 14, 16, 21, 26 January, 29 April, 10 July, 2 October 1830.
 7. *DEP*, 11 April, 25 July, 24 September 1829.
 8. *DEP*, 7 July, 15 August 1829; 4, 11 March, 19 August 1830.
 9. *DEP*, 8 August, 10 September, 20, 29 October 1829; 12 January 1830.
10. *DEP*, 31 August, 10, 14, 25, 28 September 1830.
11. *DEP*, 25 September, 1830.
12. *DEP*, 29 July 1830.
13. *DEP*, 15 July 1830; O'Connell had previously established a Parliamentary Intelligence Office in Dublin, see *DEP*, 12 January, 8 April, 20 July 1830.
14. See notebook containing an undated 'Essay on Irish Politics' in Wyse Papers, N.L.I., P. 5078.
15. Letter of Thomas Wyse to Mr. O'Gorman, 14 December 1828, *Waterford Chronicle*, 10 January 1829.

Bibliography

The works listed here are those which are cited in the text. This is not intended to be a complete bibliography of the Catholic Emancipation struggle in the 1820s. Useful bibliographies may be found in two valuable modern studies: G. I. T. Machin, *The Catholic Question in English Politics 1820 to 1830* (Clarendon Press, Oxford, 1964), J. A. Reynolds, *The Catholic Emancipation Crisis in Ireland, 1823-1829* (Yale University Press, New Haven 1954).

1. Anglesey, The Marquess of, *One Leg: the Life and Letters of Henry William Paget, First Marquess of Anglesey, 1768-1854*, London 1961
2. Aspinall, A., ed., *The Diary of Henry Hobhouse 1820-1827*, London 1947
3. Aspinall, A., ed., *The Letters of King George IV 1812-30*, 3 vols, Cambridge 1938
4. Auchmuty, J. J., *Sir Thomas Wyse 1791-1862*, London 1939
5. Bagehot, W., *Biographical Studies*, ed. R. H. Hutton, London 1881
6. Barker, R. and Howard-Johnston, X., 'The Politics and Political Ideas of Moisei Ostrogorski', *Political Studies*, Vol. XXIII, No. 4, December 1975
7. Beames, M., *Peasants and Power: the Whiteboy Movements and Their Control in Pre-Famine Ireland*, Brighton 1983
8. Best, G. F. A., 'The Protestant Constitution and its Supporters, 1800-1829', *Transactions of the Royal Historical Society*, Fifth Series, Vol. 8, 1958
9. Best, G. F. A., 'The Whigs and the Church Establishment in the Age of Grey and Holland', *History*, Vol. XLV, 1960
10. Bowen, D., *Paul Cardinal Cullen and the Shaping of Modern Irish Catholicism*, Dublin 1983
11. Bowen, D., *The Protestant Crusade in Ireland 1800-70*, Dublin 1978.
12. Bowen, E., *Bowen's Court*, 2nd edition, London 1964
13. Broeker, G., *Rural Disorder and Police Reform in Ireland 1812-36*, London 1970
14. Brougham, W., ed., *The Life and Times of Henry Brougham*, 3 vols., Edinburgh 1871
15. Broughton, Lord, *Recollections of a Long Life*, ed., Lady Dorchester, 6 vols, London, 1909-11

16. Brown, T. N., 'Nationalism and the Irish Peasant 1800-1848', *The Review of Politics*, Vol. 15, No. 4, October 1953.
17. Butler, Iris, *The Eldest Brother: the Marquess Wellesley, the Duke of Wellington's Eldest Brother*, London 1973
18. Butler, M., *Maria Edgeworth: a Literary Biography*, Oxford 1972.
19. Cahill, M., 'The 1826 General Election in County Monaghan', *Clogher Record*, Vol. V, No. 2, 1964
20. Colchester, Lord Charles, ed., *The Diary and Correspondence of Charles Abbot, Lord Colchester*, 3 Vols, London 1861
21. Collison Black, R.D.C., *Economic Thought and the Irish Question 1817-1870*, Cambridge 1960
22. Connolly, S. J., *Priests and People in Pre-Famine Ireland 1780-1845*, Dublin 1982
23. Crotty, R. D., *Irish Agricultural Production: its Volume and Structure*, Cork 1966
24. Cunningham, T. P., 'Catholic Rent Lists, Cavan 1824', *Breifne*, Vol. II, No. 6, 1966
25. Cunningham, T. P., 'The 1826 General Election in County Cavan', *Breifne*, Vol. 2, No. 5, 1962
26. d'Alton, I., *Protestant Society and Politics in Cork 1812-1844*, Cork 1980
27. Davis, R. W., 'The Tories, the Whigs, and Catholic Emancipation, 1827-1829', *The English Historical Review*, Vol. XCVII, No. 382, January 1982
28. de Beaumont, G., *Ireland, Social, Political and Religious*, trans. W. Cooke Taylor, London 1839
29. de Tocqueville, A., *Journey to England and Ireland*, ed. J. P. Mayer, London 1958
30. Dowden, W., ed., *The Letters of Thomas Moore*, 2 Vols, Oxford 1964
31. Edgeworth, R. L. Mrs, *A Memoir of Maria Edgeworth*, 4 Vols, printed privately 1867
32. Elliott, M., *Partners in Revolution: the United Irishmen and France*, New Haven 1982
33. Fagan, W., *The Life and Times of Daniel O'Connell*, 2 Vols, Cork 1847-8
34. Fitzpatrick, W. J., *History of the Dublin Catholic Cemeteries*, Dublin 1900
35. Fitzpatrick, W. J., *Lady Morgan: Her Career, Literary and Personal*, London 1860
36. Fitzpatrick, W. J., *The Life, Times and Correspondence of Dr Doyle*, 2 Vols, Dublin 1880
37. Fogarty, M. P., *Christian Democracy in Western Europe 1820-1953*, London 1957

38. Garvin, T., 'Defenders, Ribbonmen and others: Underground Political Networks in Pre-Famine Ireland', *Past and Present*, No. 96, August 1982
39. Garvin, T., *The Evolution of Irish Nationalist Politics*, Dublin 1981
40. Gash, N., *Mr Secretary Peel: the Life of Sir Robert Peel to 1830*, London 1961
41. Gash, N., *Politics in the Age of Peel: a Study in the Technique of Parliamentary Representation 1830-1850*, London 1953
42. Gregory, Lady, ed., *Mr Gregory's Letter Box, 1813-1830*, London 1898
43. Greville, C. C. F., *The Greville Memoirs*, ed. Henry Reeve, London 1894
44. Gwynn, D., *The O'Gorman Mahon: Duellist, Adventurer and Politician*, London 1934
45. Hanham, H. J., ed., *The Nineteenth-Century Constitution, 1815-1914: Documents and Commentary*, Cambridge 1969
46. Hempton, D. N., 'The Methodist Crusade in Ireland 1795-1845', *Irish Historical Studies*, Vol. XXII, No. 85, 1980
47. Hepworth Dixon, W., ed., *Lady Morgan's Memoirs: Autobiography, Diaries and Correspondence*, 2nd edition revised, 2 Vols, London 1863
48. Hill, J., 'The Politics of Privilege: Dublin Corporation and the Catholic Question, 1792-1823', *The Maynooth Review*, Vol. 7, December 1982
49. Hinde, W., *George Canning*, London 1973
50. Holmes, F., *Henry Cooke*, Belfast 1981
51. Hurst, M., *Maria Edgeworth and the Public Scene*, London 1969
52. Hyde, D., *Songs Ascribed to Raftery*, Shannon 1973
53. Ilchester, Sixth Earl of, ed., *Journal of Henry Fox*, London 1923
54. Inglis, B., *The Freedom of the Press in Ireland 1784-1841*, London 1954
55. Inglis, H. D., *A Journey Throughout Ireland During the Spring, Summer and Autumn of 1834*, 5th edition, London 1838
56. Jennings, L. J., ed., *The Croker Papers: the Correspondence and Diaries of Rt Hon. John Wilson Croker*, 2nd Edition revised, 3 Vols, London 1885
57. Jephson, H., *The Platform: its Rise and Progress*, 2 Vols, London 1892
58. Jordan, H. H., *Bolt Upright: The Life of Thomas Moore*, 2 Vols, Salzburg, Austria 1975
59. Jupp, P. J., 'County Down Elections 1793-1831', *Irish Historical Studies*, XVIII, 1972
60. *Karl Marx and Frederick Engels on Ireland*, London 1971

61. Kerr, D. A., *Peel, Priests and Politics: Sir Robert Peel's Administration and the Roman Catholic Church in Ireland 1841-1846*, Oxford 1982
62. Law, Edward, Lord Ellenborough, *A Political Diary, 1828-1830*, ed. Lord Colchester, 2 Vols, London 1881
63. Lecky, W. E. H., *A History of Ireland in the Eighteenth Century*, abridged with introduction by L. P. Curtis jr, London 1972
64. Lecky, W. E. H., *The Leaders of Public Opinion in Ireland*, 2 Vols, new edition, London 1903
65. Lefroy, T., *Memoir of Chief Justice Lefroy*, Dublin 1871
66. Lewis, G. C., *Local Disturbances in Ireland*, London 1836
67. Linker, R. W., 'The English Roman Catholics and Emancipation: the Politics of Persuasion', *Journal of Ecclesiastical History*, Vol. 27, No. 2, April 1976
68. Longford, E., *Wellington: Pillar of State*, London 1972
69. Lynch, P. J., 'Tom Steele, a Sketch', *Journal of the North Munster Archaeological Society*, 1911
70. MacCartney, D., 'The Writing of History in Ireland 1800-30', *Irish Historical Studies*, Vol. X, No. 40, 1957
71. McCullagh, W. T., *Memoirs of the Right Honourable Richard Lalor Sheil*, 2 Vols, London 1855
72. MacDonagh, O., 'The Politicization of the Irish Catholic Bishops 1800-50', *The Historical Journal*, XVIII, 1975
73. MacDonagh, O., *States of Mind: a Study of Anglo-Irish Conflict 1780-1980*, London 1983
74. McDowell, R. B., *Public Opinion and Government Policy in Ireland 1801-1846*, London 1952
75. McGrath, M., ed., *Cinnlae Amhlaoibh Uí Shuileabháin*, Irish Texts Society, Vols. XXX-XXXIII, London 1936
76. MacHale, J., *The Letters of Most Rev. John MacHale, D.D., 1820-34*, Dublin 1893
77. Macaulay, Lord, *The History of England*, abridged by H. Trevor-Roper, Penguin 1979
78. Machin, G. I. T., 'Resistance to Repeal of the Test and Corporation Acts, 1828', *The Historical Journal*, Vol. 22, No. 1, 1979
79. Machin, G. I. T., 'The Catholic Emancipation Crisis of 1825', *English Historical Review*, Vol. LXXVIII, 1963
80. Machin, G. I. T., *The Catholic Question in English Politics, 1820 to 1830*, Oxford 1964
81. MacIntyre, A., *The Liberator: Daniel O'Connell and the Irish Party 1830-1847*, London 1965
82. Madden, D. O., *Ireland and its Rulers Since 1829*, 2 Vols, London 1843-44.
83. Mahon, Lord (now Earl Stanhope), and Edward Cardwell, *Memoirs*

by Rt Hon. Sir Robert Peel, 2 Vols, London 1856-57

84. Malcomson, A. P. W., *John Foster: the Politics of the Anglo-Irish Ascendancy*, Oxford 1978
85. Maxwell, Sir H., *The Creevey Papers*, 2 Vols, London 1903
86. Mineka, F. E. ed., *The Earlier Letters of John Stuart Mill 1812-1848* (Vols. XII and XIII of *Collected Works of John Stuart Mill*), London 1963
87. Mitchell, A. *The Whigs in Opposition 1815-1830*, Oxford 1967
88. Moriarty, T. F., 'The Irish American Response to Catholic Emancipation', *The Catholic Historical Review*, Vol. LXVI, 1980
89. Norman, E. R., *Anti-Catholicism in Victorian England*, London 1968
90. O'Brien, J. B., *The Catholic Middle Classes in Pre-Famine Cork*, O'Donnell Lecture, National University of Ireland 1979
91. Ó Casaide, S., *A Guide to Old Waterford Newspapers*, Waterford 1917
92. O'Connell, J., ed., *The Select Speeches of Daniel O'Connell*, 2 Vols, Dublin 1854
93. O'Driscoll, R., *An Ascendancy of the Heart: Ferguson and the Beginnings of Modern Irish Literature in English*, Dublin 1976
94. O'Faolain, S., *King of the Beggars: a Life of Daniel O'Connell, the Irish Liberator, in a study of the rise of the Modern Irish Democracy*, new edition, Dublin 1970
95. O'Ferrall, F., *Daniel O'Connell*, Dublin 1981
96. O'Ferrall, F., 'The Growth of Political Consciousness in Ireland 1824-1848', *Irish Economic and Social History*, VI, 1979
97. O'Ferrall, F., 'The Only Lever . . .?The Catholic Priest in Irish Politics, 1823-29', *Studies*, Vol. LXX, No. 280, Winter 1981
98. O'Ferrall, F., 'The Struggle for Catholic Emancipation in County Longford, 1824-29', *Teathbha* (Journal of the Longford Historical Society), No. 4, 1978
99. O'Ferrall, F., 'The Growth of Political Consciousness in Ireland 1823-1847: a Study of O'Connellite Politics and Political Education', unpublished Ph.D. thesis, Trinity College, Dublin 1978
100. O'Neill, J. W., 'A Look at Captain Rock: Agrarian Rebellion in Ireland, 1815-1845', *Eire-Ireland*, XVII, 3, 1982
101. O'Neill, T. P., 'Clare and Irish Poverty 1815-1851', *Studia Hibernica*, No. 14, 1974
102. Osborne, J. W., 'William Cobbett's Rôle in the Catholic Emancipation Crisis, 1823-1829', *The Catholic Historical Review*, 1963
103. Ostrogorski, M., *Democracy and the Organisation of Political Parties*, 2 Vols, London 1902
104. Ó Tuathaigh, G., 'Gaelic Ireland, Popular Politics and Daniel O'Connell', *The Journal of the Galway Archaeological and Historical Society*, XXXV, 1975

105. Paget, Sir A., *The Paget Papers*, 2 Vols, London 1896
106. Pankhurst, R. K. P., *William Thompson 1775-1833*, London 1954
107. Parker, C. S., *Sir Robert Peel From His Private Correspondence*, 3 Vols, London 1891-99
108. Pearce, R. R., *Memoirs and Correspondence of the Most Noble Richard Marquess Wellesley*, 3 Vols, London 1846
109. *Personal Recollections of the Life and Times with extracts from the Correspondence of Valentine Lord Cloncurry*, Dublin 1849
110. Plunket, D., *The Life, Letters, and Speeches of Lord Plunket*, 2 Vols, London 1867
111. Porter, J. L., *The Life and Times of Henry Cooke, D.D., LL.D.*, London 1871
112. Ratcliffe, B. M., and W. H. Challoner, ed., *A French Sociologist Looks at Britain: Gustave d'Eichthal and British Society in 1828*, Manchester 1977
113. Reynolds, J. A., *The Catholic Emancipation Crisis in Ireland, 1823-1829*, New Haven 1954
114. Savage, M. W., ed., *Sketches Legal and Political by the Late Right Honourable Richard Lalor Sheil*, 2 Vols, London 1855
115. Senior, H., *Orangeism in Ireland and Britain 1795-1836*, London 1966
116. Shaw Lefevre, G., *Peel and O'Connell*, London 1887
117. Spater, G., *William Cobbett: The Poor Man's Friend*, 2 Vols, London 1982
118. Strauss, E., *Irish Nationalism and British Democracy*, London 1951
119. *The Speeches of The Right Honourable Richard Lalor Sheil*, with memoir by Thomas MacNevin, Dublin, n.d.
120. *The Wellesley Papers*, by the editor of 'The Windham Papers', 2 Vols, London 1914
121. *The Works of the Rev. Sydney Smith*, 4 Vols, London 1839-40
122. Thomson, D., *Woodbrook*, Harmondsworth 1976
123. Torrens, W. M., *Memoirs of the Right Honourable William, Second Viscount Melbourne*, 2 Vols, London 1878
124. Twiss, H., *The Public and Private Life of Lord Chancellor Eldon*, 3 Vols, London 1844
125. Wakefield, E., *An Account of Ireland, Statistical and Political*, 2 Vols, 1812
126. Walker, B. M., ed., *Parliamentary Election Results in Ireland 1801-1922*, Dublin 1978
127. Wall, T., *The Sign of Doctor Hay's Head*, Dublin 1958
128. Wellington, The Duke of, ed., *Despatches, Correspondence, and Memoranda of Field Marshal Arthur Duke of Wellington K.G.*, 8 Vols, London 1867-80

129. Whyte, J. H., *Catholics in Western Democracies: a Study in Political Behaviour*, Dublin 1981
130. Williams, G. L., ed., *John Stuart Mill on Politics and Society*, London 1976
131. Willis, G. M., *Ernest Augustus, Duke of Cumberland and King of Hanover*, London 1954
132. Wyse, T., *Historical Sketch of the Late Catholic Association of Ireland*, 2 Vols, London 1829
133. Ziegler, P., *Melbourne*, London 1978
134. Zimmermann, G-D., *Songs of Irish Rebellion: Political Street Ballads and Rebel Songs 1780-1900*, Dublin 1967

Appendix 1

TOTAL CATHOLIC RENT SUBSCRIBED IN IRELAND

These figures exclude (as far as it is possible) subscriptions of members, interest earned and money subscribed abroad. Accurate figures are given in accounts for 1824, 1825, 1826 and 1827 published in the *Dublin Evening Post*, 17 February 1825, 27 April 1826, 29 March 1827, 28 February 1828. The figures for 1828 and 1829 are based on the published weekly returns in the newspapers. Audited accounts for these years were not published. The figures are given in a different but somewhat incorrect form in T. Wyse, *Historical Sketch of the Late Catholic Association*, Vol. 2, Appendix No. XXXIII, where Wyse gives wrong dates for the 1825 totals, pp. cclxx-cclxxiii; J. A. Reynolds, *The Catholic Emancipation Crisis in Ireland, 1823-1829*, New Haven 1954, p. 62 provides estimates, which include money such as members' subscriptions and subscriptions from abroad, and therefore somewhat higher figures than cited here.

Old Catholic Rent	£	£
May 1824 – December 1824	7,573	
January 1825 – March 1825	9,263	
Total first phase		16,836
New Catholic Rent		
July 1826 – December 1826	5,680	
January 1827 – December 1827	2,900	
January 1828 – December 1828	22,700	
January 1829 – February 1829	3,712	
Total second phase		34,992
TOTAL		51,828

Appendix 2

THE LEGAL AND CONSTITUTIONAL POSITION OF ROMAN CATHOLICS AFTER 1829

In order to appreciate the legal implications of the Roman Catholic Relief Act, 1829 (10 George IV, c.7), commonly referred to as 'Catholic Emancipation', some understanding of the means by which Roman Catholics were progressively relieved of their disabilities since the middle of the eighteenth century is necessary. The legal and constitutional position of Roman Catholics after 1829 remained complicated, uncertain, and often obscure for many decades after 'Emancipation'.

The great range of penal laws against Roman Catholics were passed between the reigns of Elizabeth I (1558-1603) and George II (1727-1760). In the oft quoted remark, an Irish judge in 1759 told a Catholic gentleman that 'a Catholic could not breathe without the command of government' and that the law did not 'suppose any such person to exist as an Irish Roman Catholic except for repression and punishment'.[1] Between 1759 and 1829 a succession of Relief Acts in Great Britain and Ireland (notably those of 1778, 1782, 1791, 1792 and 1793) relieved Roman Catholics of their most pressing disabilities under the penal laws.

These Relief Acts, including that of 1829 ('Catholic Emancipation'), did not simply repeal penal statutes as a method of relief. In most cases the old penal laws were left untouched. What the Relief Acts did was to make exceptions for Roman Catholics, subject to certain conditions. Hence legal disabilities, in practice mostly inoperative or obsolete, remained on the statute book after 1829. When Roman Catholics fulfilled the specified conditions, such as taking a special oath, relief became operative. Those who refused to abide by such terms were still, legally, subject to all disabilities as in the past.[2]

1. See W.J. Amherst, *The History of Catholic Emancipation and the Progress of the Catholic Church in the British Isles from 1771 to 1820*, (London 1886), Vol. 1, pp. 59-63; and P. Hughes, *The Catholic Question 1688-1829: a Study in Political History*, (London 1929), p.114; the best brief outline of the Penal Laws in Ireland is M. Wall, *The Penal Laws 1691-1760*, 2nd edition (Dundalk 1967).
2. B. Ward, *The Sequel to Catholic Emancipation: the Story of the English Catholics continued down to the re-establishment of their Hierarchy in 1850*, (London 1915), vol. 2, p. 72. The laws affecting Roman Catholics and the disabilities which remained throughout the nineteenth century are outlined in detail in T. C. Anstey, *A Guide To the Laws of England Affecting Roman Catholics*, (London 1842); and in W. S. Lilly and J. E. P. Wallis, *A Manual of the Law Specially Affecting Catholics*, (London 1893).

Throughout the period after 1829, and right up to the present day, the legal and constitutional position of Roman Catholics within the United Kingdom and Ireland has evolved against the complex inheritance of the struggle for Catholic Emancipation. In the words of a modern historian, there existed at law 'a maze of inconsistent legislation' and 'a mass of disputable legal points'.[3] One of Robert Peel's principles in 1829, when bringing forward the Catholic Relief Bill, was to maintain intact and inviolate the integrity of the Protestant Established Church, its discipline and government, and also to maintain the essential Protestant character of the Constitution. He achieved this at the same time as making accessible to Roman Catholics civil and political rights by means of a new oath. This special oath for Catholics, while offensive to Catholic susceptibilities (in that it reflected Protestant fears and myths concerning the Pope's temporal and spiritual power and it enforced a sworn support for the Protestant Established Church), was, in conscience, acceptable to Catholics in order to qualify for the franchise or for office.

The oath prescribed for Catholics in 1829 obligated Catholics to 'abjure any intention to subvert the present church establishment as settled by law . . . or weaken the Protestant religion or Protestant government in the United Kingdom'. This oath remained until the Parliamentary Oaths Act, 1868 (31 and 32 Victoria c. 72) which abolished all existing oaths for parliament and substituted an oath of allegiance to the crown and the Protestant succession to be taken by all members. The Promissary Oaths Act, 1871 (34 and 35 Victoria c. 48) formally repealed the 1829 Roman Catholic oath. (An oath of faithfulness to 'King George V, his heirs and successors by law' was, of course, a very divisive issue consequent upon the Treaty between Great Britain and Ireland, December 1921). The legislation on oaths in 1868 facilitated Catholics in campaigning for the disestablishment of the Church of Ireland which was achieved in the Irish Church Act, 1869. Within Ireland, this latter Act marked a further advance towards the achievement of a neutral State by breaking absolutely the legal connection between Church and State.

After 1829 there remained many disabilities affecting Catholics relating to worship, church buildings, tithes, use of offices, religious orders, marriage, bequests and charities and exclusion from certain offices. Catholics were to conduct worship only in their churches or in private and the wearing of Catholic vestments or habits in public was forbidden. The registration of Catholic churches was possible only if they were without a steeple or bell. The use of ecclesiastical tithes similar

---

3. K. Roche, 'The Relations of the Catholic Church and the State in England and Ireland, 1800-52', *Historical Studies*, Vol. III, 1961, p. 14.

to those used by Anglicans was forbidden. Public office holders were not allowed to wear ceremonial dress at Catholic places of worship. Fresh restrictions were placed on religious orders in 1829: Jesuits and male religious orders had to register, and the clear legal intention was to suppress such orders. Any member of such an order who came to the United Kingdom after 1829 was to be banished for life (though short-term licences were possible from Protestant Secretaries of State and British subjects abroad could return home). The administration of vows was made an indictable offence.

The 1829 Act did not affect marriage law. Under the Marriage Act, 1752 (26 George II c. 33) no marriage was valid in civil law except one contracted before a clergyman of the Established Church. Catholic charities had no legal recognition and legacies and bequests for the celebration of Masses remained void after 1829. Property bequeathed for what the law continued to regard as 'superstitious uses' was liable to confiscation. Religious orders were placed at a grave disadvantage in establishing title to bequests, as the law did not presume their existence: the penal clauses of the 1829 Act resulted in the loss to such orders of many bequests. The 1829 Act reserved for Protestants the crown, the Regency, the Viceroyalty of Ireland, the Lord Chancellorship of Great Britain or Ireland, and offices or places in universities or schools. Restrictions were placed in 1829 on Catholic office holders in government as to their power to advise the crown in relation to Established Church offices or preferments or to grant licences to Catholic religious orders. Catholics were, of course, specifically excluded from both the Established Church and the Ecclesiastical Courts (or any court of appeal from or review of the sentences of such courts). After 1829 the Established Church continued to have the right to exact tithes from the entire population and whenever a matter had to be referred to an ecclesiastical court, as for example in the probate of wills, it was referred to the courts of the Established Church. The Roman Catholic Church was kept at a legal distance from the State and no formal diplomatic relations existed with the Pope. (Legally, official communication with the See of Rome could be construed as high treason; in practice the government engaged in diplomacy through a minister at Florence and in other ways.)

Many of the surviving disabilities affecting Catholics were addressed in legislation passed between 1829 and the present day. Formal repeal of many of the penal laws occurred in Acts such as Anstey's Act of 1844 and the relatively recent Catholic Relief Act of 1926 (16 and 17 George V c. 55). Also the various Statute Law Revision Acts repealed penal laws or sections of them. The Roman Catholic Relief Act, 1829, itself, was wholly repealed as obsolete in the Republic of Ireland by the Statute Law Revision Act, 1983.

Lifting 'the shadow of the penal laws' from Catholic life after 1829 proved a long drawn out process.[4] There were periodic anti-Catholic movements (notably over Maynooth in 1845, the 'Papal Aggression', 1850 and Papal Infallibility in the early 1870s). The restoration of the Roman Catholic hierarchy in England (that is, government by bishops-in-ordinary replacing vicars-apostolic in districts) led to the restatement of the prohibition of the use of ecclesiastical titles in the Ecclesiastical Titles Act, 1851 (14 and 15 Victoria c. 50). Otherwise legislation was, for the most part, favourable to Catholics in its effects.

The Marriage Act, 1836 (6 and 7 William IV c. 85) established the validity in civil law of Catholic marriages. Conflicts between the canons of the Roman Catholic Church and the law of the land in relation to marriages (and the survival of penal statutes such as the one making void a marriage between a Catholic and a Protestant if celebrated by a Catholic priest) can be traced with the passage of a number of statutes, especially the Marriages (Ireland) Act, 1844, the Marriage Law (Ireland) Amendment Act, 1863, the Registration of Marriages (Ireland) Act, 1863 and the Matrimonial Causes and Marriage Law (Ireland) Amendment Acts 1870, 1871. Conflicts remain between civil law and Roman Catholic canon law in respect of nullity in the Republic of Ireland. The 1937 Constitution of Ireland prohibits the introduction of divorce legislation.

The Roman Catholic Charities Act, 1832 (2 and 3 William IV c. 115) put Catholic charities on the same footing as those of Protestant dissenters. It was followed by the more famous and controversial Charitable Bequests Act, 1844.[5] The years between 1830 and 1838 saw a long campaign of resistance in Ireland to the payment of tithes. Various Acts were passed in these years to address the problem but with little success until that of 1838 (1 and 2 Victoria c. 109). This Act imposed a rent charge, payable by landlords, in place of tithes; landlords added the cost to the rents paid by tenants.

In 1848 an Act was passed enabling diplomatic relations to be established with the Vatican ('the Sovereign of the Roman States') for the first time (11 and 12 Victoria c. 108). However, all ordinary diplomatic agents of the Holy See (i.e. those in holy orders) were excluded from London under the Act and no regular diplomatic relations were established under this statute. Only in 1982, prior to the visit of Pope John Paul II to Britain, were full diplomatic relations developed between the United Kingdom and the Vatican.

4. See Edward Norman, *The English Catholic Church in the Nineteenth Century*, (Oxford 1984), p. 16; this book has a valuable account of post-Emancipation English Catholicism.
5. For a detailed account of the controversy, see D. A. Kerr, *Peel, Priests and Politics: Sir Robert Peel's Administration and the Roman Catholic Church in Ireland 1841-1846*, (Oxford 1982).

The Religious Disabilities Removals Act, 1867 lifted restrictions on Catholics in public life and also repealed the 1829 clause which prohibited civic dignitaries from appearing in Catholic places of worship wearing their insignia of office. In 1867 also, the office of Lord Chancellor of Ireland was opened to Catholics. The Government of Ireland Act, 1920 removed the disqualification on Catholics becoming Lord Lieutenant of Ireland, at a time when the course of history was decreeing the imminent redundancy of the office itself. The Irish Church Act, 1869, besides its symbolic importance for Catholics in disestablishing the Church of Ireland, had the effect of removing the ecclesiastical law of the Church of Ireland from the law of the land; from 1871 it merely had contractual force and its courts ceased to exercise coercive jurisdiction.

In Great Britain parliament has remained the supreme legislature governing the Established Church. In 1919 an Enabling Act gave the Church of England the power to pass its own legislation (as 'measures' of the General Synod) subject to the approval of parliament. This gives the decrees of the Church of England legal authority throughout England. In July 1984 the House of Commons refused to approve a Church of England Synod 'measure' and the Archbishop of Canterbury, Dr Runcie, publicly sought for parliament to honour Church freedom.[6] While it is clear that the 'Protestant Constitution' has substantially crumbled it has not yet completely collapsed in Britain. The Church of England and the Church of Scotland, as 'established' churches, are in more privileged positions than other churches; the monarch must be in communion with the Church of England and the archbishops and bishops of the Church of England sit in the House of Lords.

Within the Republic of Ireland there is no established church and constitutionally there exists a separation of Church and State. However, the Constitution of Ireland (enacted in 1937) and certain aspects of modern legislation reflect a Catholic ethos. Professor Basil Chubb states that the 1937 Constitution 'marked the overt recognition of Roman Catholic principles in the country's political life and institutions'.[7] The *New Ireland Forum Report* (May 1984) stated: 'It is clear that a new Ireland will require a new constitution which will ensure that the needs of all traditions are fully met. Society in Ireland as a whole comprises a wider diversity of cultural and political traditions than exist in the South, and the constitution and laws of a new Ireland must accommodate these social and political realities' (4.14). The tragic odyssey of Catholics living in Northern Ireland since 1920 still continues though

6. See report in *Irish Times*, 14 November 1984.
7. See B. Chubb, *The Government and Politics of Ireland*, (London 1971), p. 67.

their legal position has been improved since 1969.[8]

It is relevant to note that the Coronation Oath, long held to be an obstacle to Catholic Emancipation, remained the same after 1829 as it had been in 1689 (with some verbal corrections and amendments). The interpretation first put upon the words by George III, to the effect that he was sworn to resist Catholic Emancipation, was held not to bind the king in his legislative capacity but only in his executive capacity.[9]

The British Constitution is the system of laws, customs and conventions which defines the composition and powers of the organs of the State, and which regulates the relations of the various State organs to one another and to the private citizen. It has evolved over centuries. In the context of legal and constitutional developments since the middle of the eighteenth century the Catholic Relief Act of 1829 may be seen as the major milestone on the road leading to complete legal and constitutional equality between Catholics and Protestants. Despite the subsequent legal enactments, the 'Protestant' character of the British State survives at the expense of the full and final achievement of comparable treatment of all subjects.

8. For a balanced account of religious discrimination in Northern Ireland since 1920 and a history of Northern Ireland, see F. S. L. Lyons, *Ireland Since the Famine*, (revised edition, London 1973), pp. 695-78. For legal measures to insure equality of opportunity and prevention of discrimination since 1969, see C. K. Boyle, D. S. Greer, *The Legal Systems, North and South* (New Ireland Forum, published by Stationery Office n.d. [1984], pp. 34-6, 42.
9. See *Select Statutes Cases and Documents*, ed. C. Grant Robertson (5th edition, London 1928), pp. 117-19.

Index